A People's Army

Fred Anderson

A People's Army

Massachusetts Soldiers and Society in

the Seven Years' War

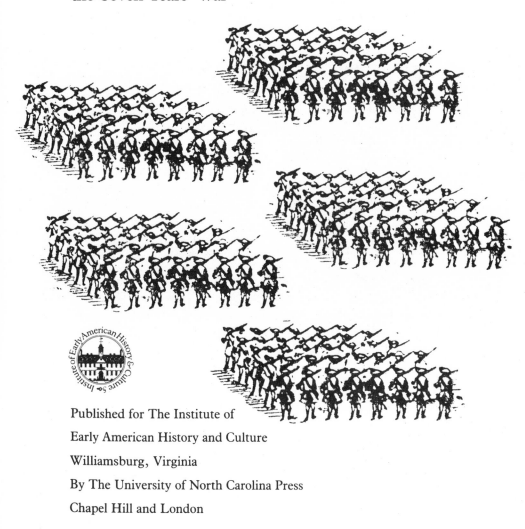

Published for The Institute of

Early American History and Culture

Williamsburg, Virginia

By The University of North Carolina Press

Chapel Hill and London

The Institute of Early American History and Culture
is sponsored jointly by The College of William and Mary and
The Colonial Williamsburg Foundation.

This book was the winner of the
Jamestown Manuscript Prize for 1982.

Library of Congress Cataloging in Publication Data

Anderson, Fred, 1949–
    A people's army.

    Includes index.
    1. Massachusetts—History—French and Indian War, 1755–
1763.   2. Massachusetts—Militia—History—18th century.
3. Soldiers—Massachusetts—History—18th century.
I. Institute of Early American History and Culture
(Williamsburg, Va.)   II. Title.
EI99.A58   1984   973.2'6   84-2344
ISBN 0-8078-1611-6 (cloth : alk. paper)
ISBN 0-8078-4576-0 (pbk. : alk. paper)

Portions of chapters 2 and 6 appeared in the
William and Mary Quarterly, 3d Ser., XXXVIII (1981), 395–417,
and XL (1983), 499–527.

99 98 97 96   6 5 4 3 2

To my mother

and to the memory of my father

Preface

This book examines the experiences of New England provincial soldiers in the last and greatest of America's colonial wars. It thus partakes of two historical genres, one of which is comparatively new, while the other is the oldest of all. But even as it shares certain characteristics with both, it differs from each in important ways.

Because I have chosen to investigate the lives of large numbers of ordinary men engaged in a commonplace pursuit, and because in some measure I have approached the task through quantification, this book can be considered a work of social history. It differs from much recent social history, however, in that it concerns not the *longue durée*, but the impact of an event, the Seven Years' War, in the lives of the people it affected most directly. Given a sufficiently olympian approach to social history, it would be possible to interpret the war as a brief perturbation in the long run of colonial New England's agrarian stability. To treat it thus, however, would be to misconstrue the war as a social phenomenon. Understood in terms of personal experience and taken as a proportion of the lifetimes of the people it touched, the Seven Years' War was anything but a deviation from business as usual. It was instead a world-shaping event, an occurrence with the power to unify the experiences of those across whose lives it cut. The Seven Years' War, like World War I, was capable of creating a generation of men with a "common frame of reference" that set them apart from those who had preceded them in time, and which would "later distinguish the members of the generation from those who follow[ed] them," as Robert Wohl has written in *The Generation of 1914* ([Cambridge, Mass., 1979], 210).

The men of the "generation of 1914" whom Wohl examined, of course, were members of a comparatively tiny, highly self-conscious, highly literate elite, and thus quite unlike the farmers, laborers, and artisans who made up the provincial armies of New England in the Seven Years' War. Yet Wohl's insight into what makes a generation may be applied as fittingly to the eighteenth century as to the twentieth:

> A historical generation is not defined by its chronological limits or its borders. It is not a zone of dates; nor is it an army of contemporaries making its way across a territory of time. It is more like a magnetic field at the center of which lies an experience or a series of experiences. It is a system of references and identifications that gives pri-

ority to some kinds of experiences and devalues others—hence it is relatively independent of age. The chronological center of this experiential field need not be stable; it may shift with time. What is essential to the formation of a generational consciousness is some common frame of reference. . . . This frame of reference is always derived from great historical events like wars, revolutions, plagues, famines, and economic crises, because it is great historical events like these that supply the markers and signposts with which people impose order on their past and link their individual fates with those of the communities in which they live. [P. 210]

Because the story I have chosen to tell centers on war and military service, this book is also a work of military history. I have, however, avoided the classic approaches of military historians: the narration of campaigns and the analysis of generalship. Anyone who is looking here for a traditional military account should look instead to the works of its masters—especially to Francis Parkman's incomparable *Montcalm and Wolfe* and to the life's work of Lawrence Henry Gipson, *The British Empire before the American Revolution*. Instead of concentrating on campaigns and battles, I have focused on the mundane aspects of soldiering—daily life, discipline, common attitudes to war, and so on—in order to gauge the effects of military service on the provincial troops themselves. This approach, in turn, has led me to conceive an objection to traditional military history, which I will now register.

Wars are waged to be won, and too many writers of military history have taken it as their main task to isolate the elements that have made for success or failure, trying (for example) to explain how General A could fight a battle brilliantly against great odds while General B could manage to dissipate his advantages and butcher his own men. This attention to winning and losing is understandable, but it has led military historians to judge past armies and soldiers by professional standards of discipline, efficiency, and cohesion. The dangers of ahistoricism in such judgments are clear enough, but have been too often overlooked. Professional military ideals have not always and everywhere been determining factors, or even significant ones, in motivating the men who made up the army or fought the war in question. In the pages that follow, I will argue that the New England provincials of the Seven Years' War subscribed to notions about military service and warfare that were wholly incompatible with the professional ideals and assumptions of their British regular army allies. Judged by timeless standards of military professionalism, the provincials seem merely to be what the British said they were: bad soldiers. Examined in light of their own ideas about what it meant to serve in an army or to fight a war, however, the provincials' apparently unsoldierly conduct can be seen to have been highly consistent, and indeed highly principled. To judge the provincials only as deficient versions of professional troops, without reference to the provincials' shared values and their beliefs concerning war and military service, would be to misunderstand the actions and motivations of eighteenth-century New Englanders at war. And war, as much as peace, typified New England life in the eighteenth century.

This, then, is the soldiers' story. It is divided into three parts. The first section concerns the contexts of military service. Chapter 1 sketches the chronology of the struggle for the North American continent as viewed from Massachusetts and then frames the argument of the book as a whole. Chapter 2 addresses the social context of military service in New England and investigates the composition of provincial armies. Among other things, this section suggests that the way in which provincial armed forces were recruited strongly influenced their performance in the field, and that while the structure of provincial armies was superficially similar to the model of a professional army, their functioning depended on factors entirely uncomprehended in their formal organization.

The second section describes the physical realities of military life, examining the nature and effects of diet, shelter, disease, discipline, work, and combat. It traces the outlines of a harsh experience, radically unlike anything in the civilian lives of the soldiers—an experience capable of creating a unique frame of reference for the men who shared it.

The third section explicates the terms in which the provincials understood military service and warfare. As I have suggested, their understanding of these concepts was virtually incomprehensible to their superiors, the British regular officers; yet it was an understanding deeply rooted in the New England provincial culture in which the soldiers, enlisted men and officers alike, were raised.

This book is based in large part on the writings of the provincial soldiers themselves, which survive in a surprisingly large body of diaries, letters, orderly books, memoirs, and miscellaneous documents. These sources communicate the experiences of the soldiers with great vividness, but also with considerable inexactitude in grammar, punctuation, and spelling. The following excerpt from an orderly book and journal kept by Sergeant Samuel Merriman of Deerfield in 1759 demonstrates the difficulties of interpretation introduced by the informality of punctuation and phonetic spelling:

> General orders—it is vary Nitoriously tru that profane cosing & swaring praules in ye campt; it is vary far from ye cristian solgers Deuty; it is not only vary Displasing to God armeyes, but dishonorable before men. it is theire fore Required & it will be expected that

for ye futer ye odus sound of cosing & swaring is to be turned in to a prefoun silence. ifter ye publish of these orders if any is found gilty of Bracking after these orders, theay may expect to suffer punishment, & all former orders to be observed. [4 July 1759; quoted in George Sheldon, *A History of Deerfield, Massachusetts* (Deerfield, Mass., 1895–1896; reprint, Somersworth, N.H., 1972), I, 663]

While such passages, particularly in small doses, have considerable charm, they can also become stumbling blocks for the reader. Accordingly, I have modernized all quotations from soldiers' writings, following the method outlined by Samuel Eliot Morison in *The Harvard Guide to American History* ([Cambridge, Mass., 1974], 31–33). In doing so I have followed modern orthography and spelling, expanded abbreviations, and repunctuated to bring out the sense of the passage. I have not altered the words themselves, except where necessary to convey the sense of a garbled text, and in such cases I have enclosed my insertions in editorial brackets. Thus the order quoted above, if it were to appear in the text, would read as follows:

General orders. It is very notoriously true that profane cursing and swearing prevails in the camp. It is very far from the Christian soldier's duty; it is not only very displeasing to [the] God [of] armies, but dishonorable before men. It is therefore required, and it will be expected, that for the future the odious sound of cursing and swearing will be turned into a profound silence. After the publish[ing] of these orders if any is found guilty of breaking . . . these orders, they may expect to suffer punishment. And all former orders to be observed.

Clearly, such modernized transcriptions contain judgments that in the best of all possible worlds would be left up to the reader. In this passage, for example, I have intentionally rendered "cosing" as "cursing," even though Sergeant Merriman undoubtedly pronounced the word as "cussing." By transcribing the word in its formally accepted spelling rather than its dialect form, I have inevitably deprived the reader of experiencing something of Merriman's pungent New England speech. But the modernized version preserves his meaning without introducing notions of quaintness, and all the condescension that quaintness implies. In making such decisions I have been guided by the presumption that the lack of articulate writing in no way indicates the absence of coherent thought; and since provincial troops were indeed shrewd observers of their world, it has seemed to me only just that their observations should be presented in a form that does credit to their shrewdness.

Sergeant Merriman's orderly book points up another issue, as well: the nature of the texts on which I have drawn. So far as I have been able to learn, Merriman's journal is no longer accessible in manuscript, and I perforce have relied on George Sheldon's scrupulosity as a copyist, even though I have only a general sense of the editorial methods he employed. As a rule, I have consulted the manuscript versions of printed diaries and orderly books insofar as possible, and have checked quoted passages in detail when I was in doubt about the reliability of a printed version. Unfortunately, the manuscripts have not always been available; thus in cases where passages of doubtful accuracy could not be verified, I have refrained from direct quotation.

Finally, this book is based on a doctoral thesis with extensive annotation. I have occasionally made reference to much lengthier notes in that dissertation, "War and the Bay Colony: Soldiers and Society in Provincial Massachusetts during the Seven Years' War, 1754–1763" (1981), which may be consulted in the Harvard University Archives, Pusey Library, Cambridge, Massachusetts.

A number of institutions and more than a score of people have had a hand in this project, either as a dissertation or as a book. The United States Army Center of Military History provided a yearlong fellowship that allowed me to make my first sustained push toward the completion of the thesis. Harvard University offered support in the form of a summer grant, funds for computer use, and the Artemas Ward Dissertation Fellowship. The staffs of several archives and libraries were of assistance, but those of the William L. Clements Library, in Ann Arbor, Michigan; the Henry E. Huntington Library, in San Marino, California; the Massachusetts Historical Society, in Boston; and the American Antiquarian Society, in Worcester, Massachusetts, were especially helpful.

Scholars and friends at a variety of schools have offered encouragement, advice, and criticism. Steven Botein of Michigan State University, Nathan Hatch of the University of Notre Dame, Sung Bok Kim of the State University of New York at Albany, John Murrin of Princeton University, and John and Arlene Shy of the University of Michigan have all helped me to define, sharpen, and develop the project. Fellow graduate students and other friends contributed greatly to the progress of the thesis; in particular I must recognize Kent Coit, Eugenia Delamotte, Barbara DeWolfe, Walter Jackson, William Kelly, Patricia Denault, Kenneth Sokoloff, Helena Wall, and Jonathan Zorn for their help and support. During the writing of the dissertation and after its completion, David Jaffee offered particularly helpful commentary and energetic encouragement. I must also single out two special friends: both Randy Fertel, now of Le Moyne College, and Jon Roberts, of Harvard University, gave freely of their time and critical energy when they were heavily taxed by academic obligations and the demands of new fatherhood. And although both would disclaim it, William Griswold and Arthur Worrall must be recognized as my oldest and, in many ways, my greatest intellectual creditors. Without the stimulation of their teaching at Colorado State University in the late 1960s I would never have tried to become a historian; thanks largely to their continued encouragement and to the examples of their personal integrity and professional dedication, I am still trying.

More even than most colonialists, I am indebted to the Institute of Early American History and Culture. The Jamestown Prize Committee has, of course, a special place in my long list of benefactors. The portions of this book that first appeared in the *William and Mary Quarterly* are much the better for the scrupulous attention they received from Michael McGiffert. Douglas Edward Leach and Pauline Maier took time out from busy schedules to read a draft with care and to make perceptive, helpful suggestions for revision. Norman Fiering, Gil Kelly, and Daniel Vickers provided commentary and useful advice. Most of all, the Acting Editor of Publications for the Institute in 1982–1983, Thomas Doerflinger, deserves thanks: he was the book's faithful and sharp-eyed shepherd, and for his care and intelligence I am deeply grateful.

Finally, my three advisors remain to be recognized: one appointed by Harvard to the task, one by friendship, and one by marriage. Without Bernard Bailyn's acute criticism and steady support, the dissertation would never have assumed the form it did; without the strenuous example that his own scholarship has set, I know that I would have tried less hard to do my best. To Christopher Jedrey I owe more than I can easily say, for a decade and more of intellectual companionship, discerning criticism, and friendship. While I cannot hope to repay that debt, I take special pleasure in being able to acknowledge it publicly, at last. But of all my many creditors, Virginia DeJohn Anderson has given the most to this project as its principal critic, helper, and dauntless supporter; and the most to me, as my life's partner. I have dedicated this book to my mother and to the memory of my father; but my mother well knows (as my father would have understood) that it is no derogation of their place to conclude that, like its author, this work is also Virginia's—more than she knows.

Contents

Illustrations

Tables

Part One ❖ The Contexts of War

Chapter 1 ❖ War and the Bay Colony
An Overview

In 1754 the people of Massachusetts Bay embarked on what would prove to be the final stage of their epic struggle with the French and Indians of Canada. Armed conflict with the papists had been going on longer than most Bay colonists could remember. Four successive spasms of violence, named in honor of three monarchs and a royal governor, had dominated public affairs in the province since the late seventeenth century. First in King William's War (1689–1697), then in Queen Anne's (1702–1713), Governor Dummer's (1722–1725), and King George's wars (1744–1748), the Bay Colony had contributed its share and more of blood and treasure to Great Britain's worldwide contest with France.[1] None of the previous conflicts, however, had foreshadowed the toll that this climactic confrontation, the Seven Years' War, would exact from Massachusetts.[2] Before the Seven Years' War was over, it would draw a third or more of the colony's service-eligible men into provincial armies and employ additional thousands in tasks directly related to the military effort. It would drive taxes to the highest levels in the history of the province, create a massive public debt, and bring the government on one occasion to the brink of bankruptcy. The war would also cause a massive influx of British specie and credit, temporarily expanding Massachusetts' hard-money economy. It

1. With the exception of Governor Dummer's War, these were all American phases of European conflicts: the War of the League of Augsburg (1689–1697), the War of the Spanish Succession (1702–1713), and the War of Jenkins' Ear / the War of the Austrian Succession (1739–1748).

2. "The Seven Years' War," alas, is a convenient rather than an accurate appellation for a war that has never had a consistent name. The war lasted nine years, not seven, in the New World, although in fact Massachusetts forces actually pressed campaigns against the French in seven of the war years. To call it "the French and Indian War" fails to distinguish it from its predecessors, all of which were fought against the French and Indians; "the Fourth Intercolonial War," Herbert Levi Osgood's clinical-sounding contribution to its fund of names, is inaccurate in that Massachusetts fought the French five times, not four, during the colonial period. With considerable justification Lawrence Henry Gipson called it "the Great War for the Empire," and if any scholar ever earned the right to give the conflict a name, he did; yet his label shifts the focus to the empire, while this book concerns only the Bay Colony. The colonists called it "the French War," and later "the Old French War," but these are scarcely remembered in our own day and are no more distinctive than "the French and Indian War." Rather than compound the confusion by adding yet another name, I will refer to the conflict by what is at least the most common of its many misnomers, "the Seven Years' War."

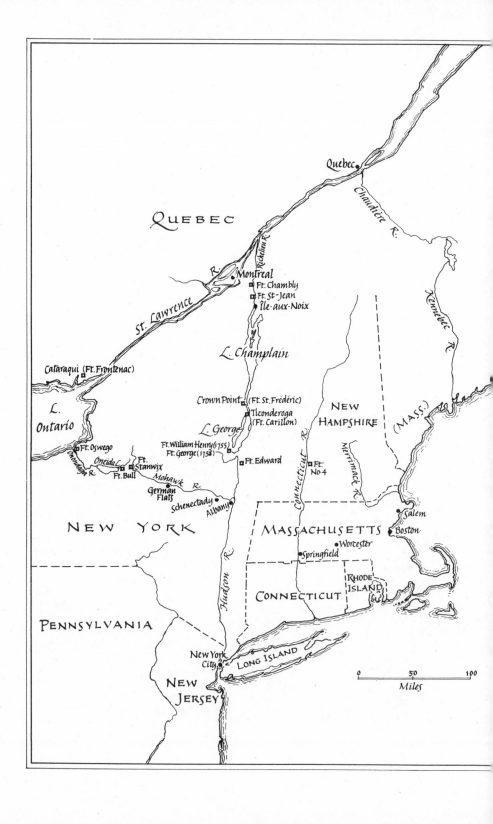

QUEBEC

Quebec

Chaudière R.

Richelieu R.

St. Lawrence R.

Montreal
□ Ft. Chambly
□ Ft. St-Jean
● Île-aux-Noix

Kennebec R.

L. Champlain

Cataraqui (Ft. Frontenac)

L.
Ontario

Crown Point □ (Ft. St. Frédéric)
□ Ticonderoga
(Ft. Carillon)

NEW
HAMPSHIRE

(MASS.)

L. George

□ Ft. Oswego
Onondaga R.
Oneida L.
Ft. Stanwix
Ft. Bull
Mohawk R.
German Flats
Schenectady
Albany

Ft. William Henry (1755)
Ft. George (1758)
□ Ft. Edward

Connecticut R.

□ Ft.
No. 4

Merrimack R.

NEW   YORK

MASSACHUSETTS

● Salem
● Boston

● Worcester
● Springfield

Hudson R.

PENNSYLVANIA

CONNECTICUT

RHODE
ISLAND

New York
City

LONG ISLAND

NEW
JERSEY

0   50   100
Miles

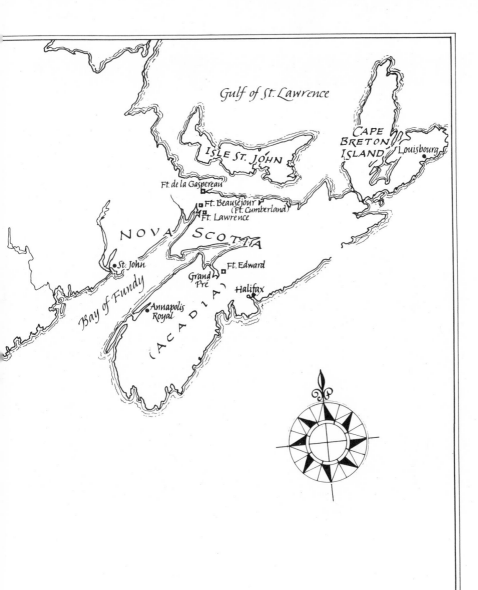

Massachusetts and Its Principal Theaters of Military Activity in the Seven Years' War.
After Lester J. Cappon *et al.*, *Atlas of Early American History: The Revolutionary Era, 1760–1790* (Princeton, N.J., 1976), 2–4. Drawn by Richard Stinely

would transform the scale and nature of provincial politics and create a
new sense among Bay colonists of their importance and participation in
the British Empire.[3]

Most significantly, the Seven Years' War would decisively terminate the
imperial presence of France in North America. The war can thus be said to
have decided the cultural and institutional future of the vast area between
the Appalachian crest and the Mississippi River, stretching from the Gulf
of Mexico to Hudson's Bay. Since the late eighteenth century it has been
argued that the removal of France made possible, or even inevitable,
America's movement for independence.[4] On a less elevated historical plane,
the war was a vivid episode in the lives of thousands of men who served in
Massachusetts' provincial armies. The provincials were, however, merely
the humblest participants in a single theater of a world war. This was an
enormous conflict that pitted the forces of Britain and Prussia against the
combined might of France, Austria, and Spain all around the globe—
in Europe, the Mediterranean, West Africa, India, the Philippines, and
the Caribbean, as well as the wilderness of North America. Viewed from
the provincial perspective, the war looked quite different than it did to the
politicians and bureaucrats at Whitehall. Events in which the Bay colonists took part were seldom the result of their own province's initiatives: in
general the colony responded less to local challenges and conditions than it
did to policies instituted in Europe and altered to suit European concerns.

So great indeed is the discrepancy between the war understood as a
global conflict and the war as experienced by Massachusetts soldiers that
the first order of business in interpreting the conflict from the provincial
standpoint must be to establish a consistent perspective on the events of
the struggle. Broadly speaking, the years of the war can be divided into
four phases.[5] The first period began in 1754, when French adventuring in
the trans-Allegheny West triggered military responses from Virginia and

3. For the most complete account of the war's larger effects on Massachusetts political life,
see William Pencak, *War, Politics and Revolution in Provincial Massachusetts* (Boston, 1981).

4. See John M. Murrin, "The French and Indian War, the American Revolution, and the
Counterfactual Hypothesis: Reflections on Lawrence Henry Gipson and John Shy," *Reviews
in American History*, I (1973), 307–318.

5. This version of the war's events has been distilled from several standard accounts. The
sources consulted were: Lawrence H. Gipson, *The Great War for the Empire: The Years of
Defeat, 1754–1757, The Victorious Years, 1758–1760*, and *The Culmination, 1760–1763*, in
Gipson, *The British Empire before the American Revolution* (New York, 1936–1969), VI–VIII,
passim; Thomas Hutchinson, *The History of the Colony and Province of Massachusetts-Bay*, ed.
Lawrence Shaw Mayo (Cambridge, Mass., 1936 [orig. publ. London, 1828]), III, 13–73;
Benjamin W. Labaree, *Colonial Massachusetts: A History* (Millwood, N.Y., 1979); Douglas
Edward Leach, *Arms for Empire: A Military History of the British Colonies in North America,
1607–1763* (New York, 1973), 351–485; Stanley McCrory Pargellis, *Lord Loudoun in North
America* (New Haven, Conn., 1933), *passim*; Francis Parkman, *Montcalm and Wolfe* (Boston,
1901 [orig. publ. Toronto (1884)]), *passim*; Howard H. Peckham, *The Colonial Wars,*

Massachusetts. Fighting proceeded with little interference or direction from Europe for two years. During this time Great Britain formulated no coherent war aims. Militarily, the beginnings of the conflict brought mixed results: the Anglo-Americans made halting advances in maritime Canada and stymied a French probe in northern New York, but suffered great setbacks in the Pennsylvania-Virginia backcountry.

The second major phase of hostilities began with the declaration of war in Europe in 1756 and lasted until early 1758. This was a time of near-catastrophe for British arms and of high tension between the colonies and the mother country. The British commander in chief in North America sought to bring colonial governments under his central control, and their resistance nearly scuttled the war effort in the New World. The third phase began in 1758 when William Pitt, who in effect had become prime minister in the previous year, assumed personal control of the British military program. Thereafter, the domineering Pitt directed the war with ferocious energy. ("Nobody ever entered his closet," wrote one political colleague, "who did not come out of it a braver man.")[6] Pitt's openhanded fiscal policies and his willingness to seek accommodation with the colonies quickly won over the provincial governments, and harmonious relations were the rule for the rest of the war. The third phase was marked by great English victories in America, culminating in the conquest of Canada in 1760.

The final stage of the war, 1761–1763, saw military emphases shift away from North America as the English pressed on to conquer French possessions in India, Africa, and the Caribbean. The nature of the conflict altered markedly late in the autumn of 1761. The new king, George III, earnestly desired peace, whereas Pitt wanted nothing more than to expand the war even further. By a secret compact with France, Spain had promised to begin hostilities against Britain if peace were not concluded before 1 May 1762. Pitt had proof of the treaty and resolved to attack Spain in Europe and the Americas before she could prepare for war. George III and his supporters in the ministry would have none of it, and Pitt resigned. Spain entered the war anyway and effectively prolonged the war for another year, but Britain's victory was never in doubt. Hostilities ended with the Treaty of Paris, 10 February 1763.

1689–1762 (Chicago, 1964), 120–221; Pencak, *War, Politics and Revolution*, 115–184; George A. Plimpton, "French and Indian Wars (1741–1763)," in Albert Bushnell Hart, ed., *Commonwealth History of Massachusetts* (New York, 1928), II, 419–454; John A. Schutz, *William Shirley: King's Governor of Massachusetts* (Chapel Hill, N.C., 1961), 80–250; and John A. Schutz, *Thomas Pownall, British Defender of American Liberty: A Study of Anglo-American Relations in the Eighteenth Century* (Glendale, Calif., 1951), 105–180. Footnotes will be used in the following narrative section only in identifying direct quotations or in citing works not included in this note.

6. Isaac Barré, quoted in Parkman, *Montcalm and Wolfe*, II, 49.

With this overview in mind, the more specific developments in Massachusetts and the North American theater can be seen in perspective, during the four phases of the war.

Phase I: Governor Shirley's War, 1754–1755

If ever a conflict could be identified with one man, the Seven Years' War, at least in its early years, was William Shirley's war. Over the sixteen years (1741–1757) that he served as royal governor of Massachusetts, Shirley's political fortunes rose highest in wartime and ebbed lowest during periods of peace. While Shirley, like all royal governors, enjoyed enormous formal powers within the province he administered, his real power to govern depended instead on his ability to distribute patronage among his followers in the provincial legislature.[7] In times of peace his patronage resources were simply too slender to ensure him anything like a majority in the Massachusetts General Court. War, however, brought a rich harvest of military commissions, supply and clothing contracts, credit, and hard cash. With these assets and the sense of common purpose war engendered, Shirley could create a truly effective network of supporters in the political and commercial elites of the province. Thus it was in his own interest as much as the king's that the governor became the most accomplished projector of military schemes in eighteenth-century North America. Although he had been trained as a lawyer and possessed no formal military background, Shirley proved to be as adept and resourceful a strategist as he was a politician.

The governor's military career had begun auspiciously in King George's War when he promoted a New England expedition against the fortress of Louisbourg, on Cape Breton Island. Under the leadership of a merchant-turned-general, William Pepperell, four thousand New England volunteers succeeded in capturing "the Gibraltar of the New World" on 17 June 1745. The siege lasted only six weeks, and the New Englanders were supported in it only by a British naval squadron and by—everyone agreed—the hand of God. Although the reduction of Louisbourg was virtually the only American victory of King George's War and the fortress was promptly handed back to the French at the conclusion of hostilities, the exploit had two abiding consequences. First, it inflated the military reputation of the New Englanders, particularly among themselves. Second, the home government reimbursed Massachusetts for the entire cost of the expedition, £183,649 sterling—the largest reimbursement in the history of the province. The sum was paid in coin, which in 1750 was used to provide a specie base for a reformed provincial currency, the Lawful Money

7. Bernard Bailyn, *The Origins of American Politics* (New York, 1968), 72–80, 116–117.

that supplanted Massachusetts' grotesquely depreciated Old Tenor paper money. This measure halted the inflation that had plagued the colony for most of the century, and secured lasting support for the governor among the mercantile interest of the province.

Thus in 1754 when Shirley began to hear of French intrigues in the Pennsylvania backcountry and of French forts being constructed along the Nova Scotia frontier, he lost no time in nudging the General Court toward belligerency. The expedition that he managed to promote that first year was tactically insignificant—a bloodless foray by eight hundred men, whom John Winslow of Marshfield led up the Kennebec River in search of a rumored French settlement. That the expedition found no settlement and slew no papists, and indeed had no military consequence whatever, did not faze the governor. The scent of patronage burned in his nostrils, and he bounded ahead with bigger plans for the following year.

By the winter of 1754, however, Shirley found that he no longer had to act purely on his own initiative, since orders arrived at that point from England to begin taking more vigorous action against the French. After a good deal of fluster and confusion, the Newcastle ministry had decided to remove the French "encroachments" from the colonies' frontiers in 1755. Two understrength Irish regiments under Major General Edward Braddock were accordingly dispatched to Virginia. Braddock was named commander in chief of his majesty's forces in North America. Shirley, with the rank of major general, was made his second in command and ordered to cooperate with the regular military authorities in Nova Scotia to limit the influence of the French in the area. The governor thus approached the Massachusetts Assembly with a plan to raise two colonial battalions, to be paid from the royal exchequer but otherwise to serve as provincials, for a limited term. The legislators responded enthusiastically because, as a discerning contemporary observed, Shirley enjoyed "one peculiar advantage for promoting his military schemes in the assembly. Many of the field officers and other officers who were at Louisbourg [in 1745] . . . were now members of the assembly, and the more readily fell in with his proposals." [8] Again, John Winslow was to be the chief officer from Massachusetts.

The General Court voted two thousand soldiers, who were soon recruited and dispatched to Nova Scotia. Together with a small contingent of British regulars, they succeeded in ejecting the "encroaching" French garrisons from Forts Beauséjour and Gaspereau. The New Englanders spent the rest of the summer in rounding up and deporting the indigenous Acadians. These so-called French neutrals, an inoffensive peasant population of about six thousand, had been living quietly under British control since

8. Hutchinson, *Mass.-Bay*, III, 20–21.

their homeland had been added to the empire during Queen Anne's War. Now they were expelled because most refused to take oaths of allegiance to the crown and were therefore deemed a security risk. The Acadians were dispersed throughout the thirteen mainland colonies, and their confiscated lands were colonized by migrants from New England.[9]

Even as Shirley was planning to send provincials to Nova Scotia, he was also trying to persuade the Massachusetts assembly to appropriate funds for a second force, to be used in operations to the west of the province. Everyone knew that the French had fortified Crown Point, on Lake Champlain, in 1731; Shirley now advocated a large expedition to neutralize that post, Fort Saint Frédéric. Massachusetts, he proposed, would contribute twelve hundred men, Connecticut one thousand, New Hampshire six hundred, Rhode Island four hundred, and New York eight hundred men to an expeditionary army that would be commanded by William Johnson, New York's powerful commissioner of Indian affairs. Some of the Massachusetts representatives balked at the plan, since in this case the colony, not the crown, would have to pay the soldiers' salaries. Shirley argued in response that reimbursements would be voted by Parliament, just as they had been for the 1745 expedition against Louisbourg. Reassured, the legislators appropriated funds for the mission.

Problems of coordination delayed the departure of the force until late summer 1755, but about thirty-five hundred provincials and four hundred Indians eventually assembled at the head of Lake George, the principal tributary of Lake Champlain. The impending change of season was lessening the likelihood that Johnson's expedition would ever get beyond its camp, when fourteen hundred French and Indians under the Baron Dieskau arrived on 8 September, spoiling for a fight. In the melee that followed, Dieskau's troops inflicted heavy damage on the colonials before Dieskau himself was wounded and captured, and the raiders withdrew in confusion. This violent, muddled encounter, with casualties of about 230 for the French and 262 for the provincials, was soon dignified as the Battle of Lake George and greeted in New England as a signal victory. The soldiers on the spot were too weak and disorganized to pursue the enemy back to Fort Saint Frédéric, however. Johnson, shaken by a slight wound to what was diplomatically called "the thigh," elected to go on the defensive and build a fort near the site of the battle. This post, Fort William Henry, would mark the limit of the Anglo-American advance in New York for the next three years.

Meanwhile, other events had altered the course of the war. On 9 July

9. See Gipson, *Years of Defeat*, 243–344, for the most complete account of the fortunes of the Acadian population in exile.

the North American commander in chief, Edward Braddock, was killed in the wilderness of Pennsylvania when a French and Indian force attacked his sixteen-hundred-man expedition at the Monongahela River. This halted the British effort to expel the French from their outpost on the Ohio, Fort Duquesne, and it caused the supreme command in North America to devolve upon William Shirley. Shirley canceled the expedition he had been leading against the French military and fur-trading post at Fort Niagara, set his troops to work constructing a complex of forts near the eastern end of Lake Ontario, at Oswego, and returned to New York City to assume his new position. Thus at the end of 1755, the first year of serious fighting, the British had made modest gains in maritime Canada while suffering a serious defeat that cost them the only experienced senior commander in the North American theater. The French, stung but not seriously discomfited by the loss of two small Acadian posts and the capture of Dieskau at Lake George, moved to reinforce Canada and appointed a new commanding general, the brilliant Louis Joseph, marquis de Montcalm. The British command remained for the time being in the hands of William Shirley, who with characteristic vigor began to plan a war of conquest.

Because the Newcastle ministry as yet limited its official policy to the removal of French encroachments, Shirley conceived his program primarily in terms of provincial efforts. Assuring the northern colonial assemblies that parliamentary reimbursements would be forthcoming, he obtained authorizations to raise eighty-eight hundred soldiers (seven thousand of whom eventually reached the field) from New England and New York to use in expelling the French from Crown Point. Massachusetts led the way once again. Spurred by the promise that John Winslow would command the expedition and further strengthened in resolve by Shirley's promise of a thirty-thousand-pound-sterling loan, the General Court approved the enlistment of three thousand men for the coming year.

Shirley as commander in chief, like Shirley as governor of Massachusetts, used military contracts and commissions as patronage to create a network of personal supporters. The policy was undeniably effective in the short run, since it lined influential pockets and allowed the colonial assemblies to exercise considerable control over the war in return for their financial support. It was, however, a most unorthodox way to run a war, and it soon proved to be Shirley's downfall.

Almost from the moment Shirley had assumed command, the ambitious and egocentric lieutenant governor of New Jersey, Thomas Pownall, had been scheming against him. Pownall found natural allies in the powerful De Lancey faction in New York, competitors of the Livingston-Morris party, to whom Shirley had awarded immense supply contracts. By January 1756, Pownall and the De Lanceys had made enough headway with the members of Newcastle's administration to seal Shirley's fate. The ministers dithered, however, and decided on no replacement until March. Shirley himself did not know that he had been dismissed until June. His successor was John Campbell, fourth earl of Loudoun, a Scots professional officer who had served in the suppression of the 1745 Highland rebellion and who was esteemed a proficient administrator. Shirley's successor as governor of Massachusetts was none other than Thomas Pownall. Supply contracts were diverted to the De Lanceys. Shirley, his career in ruins, was recalled to England under suspicion of malfeasance. His tangled accounts with the Livingstons were audited by the Treasury, a process that was not complete until 1763.

Phase II: Centralization and Defeat, 1756–1757

The change in command profoundly affected military operations in 1756. Lord Loudoun fervently wished to exercise direct control over provincial troops, a measure that the provincials resisted with equal fervor. Weeks were lost in apparently trivial squabbling over rank and precedence while Loudoun and his American subordinates (who preferred to think of themselves as his allies) took each other's measure. The marquis de Montcalm, meanwhile, had assumed command of the French forces in Canada and now wasted no time in launching an expedition against the British outpost at Fort Oswego. The garrison, weakened by disease and lack of provisions, surrendered after a brief defense and was carried en masse to Canada. This setback threw the Anglo-American forces in New York into a panicky defense and precluded all further thought of marching on Crown Point. It also bought the French enough time to complete an advanced post at the south end of Lake Champlain, between Crown Point and the British position at the head of Lake George. The new strongpoint, Fort Carillon (known among the Anglo-Americans by its geographical name, Ticonderoga) would pose the principal obstacle to a British advance on Canada for the next three years. The 1756 campaign ended with scarcely a shot fired by Winslow's provincials, who had come thoroughly to detest their new commander in chief, Lord Loudoun.

The feeling was mutual. Unlike Shirley, Loudoun was a professional soldier who believed that he deserved the unquestioning obedience of the provinces, particularly in helping to pay for the war. He had brought several regular regiments with him and proposed to do the fighting mainly with them. Loudoun wanted provincial troops for work mainly as auxiliaries, and he wanted provincial monies on his own terms. Never disposed to dicker with the colonial assemblies, he flatly refused to follow Shirley's policy of promising reimbursements. Lord Loudoun's instructions conferred great authority, in effect making him England's North American viceroy. He expected to create a centralized military effort but had no knowledge of American political realities. This ignorance of American ways would soon thwart his attempts to wage war efficiently.

Loudoun's imperial policy and imperious personality practically extinguished colonial cooperation. Massachusetts, enthusiastic in 1755 and 1756, only grudgingly complied with the new commander's directives in 1757. Only eighteen hundred Massachusetts provincials were raised, under a single colonel. They served mainly on the New York frontier, under the command of regular officers at Fort William Henry and Fort Edward (an older post about thirteen miles to the south of Lake George, on the upper Hudson River). For the first time, provincials were under redcoat discipline and provisioning, as they would be for the rest of the war. Provincials remained summer soldiers, however, who served for a year or less and were paid by their colonies rather than the crown. This made them inefficient and expensive and increased Loudoun's reluctance to employ them in large numbers.

In England, William Pitt's star was rising rapidly, and he was gaining more and more control over the war effort. In 1757 he directed Loudoun to put the New York sector on the defensive and to concentrate on mounting a siege of Louisbourg. If that great fortress could be captured, Pitt reasoned, the Saint Lawrence would be closed to French shipping, and Canada's defenders would eventually be strangled by lack of supplies and reinforcements. Loudoun's effort to seize the stronghold first was stalled by unfavorable weather, then was blocked at the last moment by the arrival of a French naval squadron. On 4 August he called off the attempt. One day earlier, far to the west, a powerful French army under Montcalm had laid siege to Fort William Henry at the head of Lake George. The garrision, which included eight hundred Massachusetts troops and the province's highest ranking officer, held out for only six days. News of the defeat, arriving in Massachusetts on the heels of reports that the Louisbourg venture had been abandoned, dealt a heavy blow to the morale of the Bay colonists and greatly diminished their legislature's willingness to cooperate further with the supreme commander.

Through the winter of 1757–1758, Loudoun continued to press the increasingly resistant colonial assemblies for troops and money. His haughty manner infuriated provincial politicians, whose sensibilities he had already offended by his refusal to grant them any say in the disposition of the troops and funds he demanded. The supreme commander responded to their opposition by trying to force colonial governors to compel the assemblies to obey orders.

What Loudoun required of the governors was politically costly, if not impossible. His policies were especially at odds with Thomas Pownall's plans. From the time Pownall had succeeded Shirley as governor of Massachusetts, he had allied himself with country-party elements in the General Court, the very politicians who were most averse to administrative centralization. The climax of their defiance came in early March 1758: with Thomas Pownall standing idly by, the Massachusetts House of Representatives refused to vote any troops whatever for the coming campaign.

Phase III: Pitt, Reimbursement, and Victory, 1758–1760

The legislators of the Bay Colony had never been known for sweet temper or tractability, but the General Court was in a particularly stubborn, ugly mood on the morning of 10 March 1758 when a surprising packet of letters arrived from William Pitt. The letters informed the members of the assembly that Lord Loudoun was being recalled and went on to ask that they authorize the recruitment of an unprecedented number of soldiers for the coming campaign. By the end of that afternoon, the House of Representatives had unanimously voted to raise seven thousand troops and to place them at the disposal of the new commander in chief.

Pitt achieved this remarkable reversal in colonial attitude by jettisoning, along with Loudoun, everything Loudoun had stood for. In his request for troops, Pitt had promised reimbursement, in specie or credit, from the Treasury. In appealing directly to the assembly, moreover, he had signaled the demotion of the commander in chief from viceroy to mere military leader. This at once freed all future supreme commanders from the necessity of browbeating reluctant governors and recalcitrant assemblies, and it reassured the assemblymen that the demands of the war would not be used to deprive them of control over their colonies' finances. Pitt's new "requisition system" worked smoothly from the beginning. In 1758 and every year thereafter, "Pitt wrote . . . to the governors asking for men and promising financial assistance; the assembly voted them, and then notified the commander in chief that they were on the march; [he] sent warrants for victualling them on the road at the usual fourpence a day, and named the rendezvous; the assembly then collected from parliament its reimbursement for the expenses of the campaign. There was no pleading, no cajoling, and few threats."[10] Lord Loudoun's niggling insistence on control and compliance had been sand in the gears of colonial cooperation. Pitt's appreciation of the matchless lubricating qualities of money and autonomy, on the other hand, guaranteed an enthusiastic American response to his imperial enterprise.

10. Pargellis, *Loudoun*, 351–352.

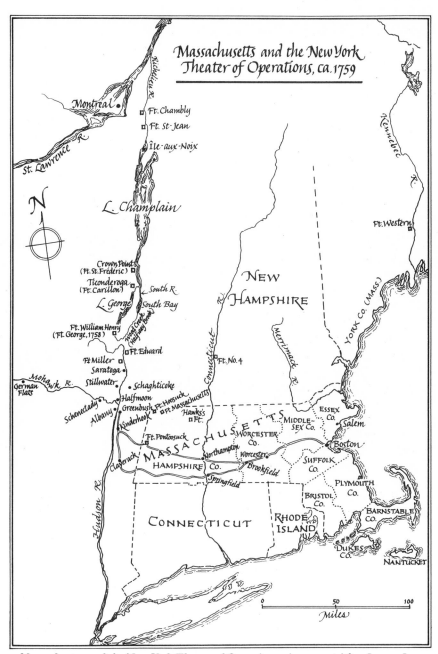

Massachusetts and the New York Theater of Operations, circa 1759. After Lester J. Cappon *et al., Atlas of Early American History: The Revolutionary Era, 1760–1790* (Princeton, N.J., 1976), 2, 4. Drawn by Richard Stinely

Reimbursement cost Great Britain dearly—over a million pounds sterling in the course of the conflict—but Parliament's grants by no means enabled Massachusetts to avoid paying for its share of the war. Only about two-fifths of the Bay Colony's total expenses for the war were reimbursed, and the government borrowed so much money that province taxes remained at wartime levels until 1770.[11] Pitt's transfusions of specie and credit merely allowed the government of Massachusetts to continue the fight without going bankrupt. So precarious were provincial finances in September 1758 that the province was teetering on the brink of default when the reimbursement for expenses incurred in 1756 arrived and allowed the government to pay its short-term debt.[12] Pitt's new policy of decentralization and subsidy marked a major divide in the political history of the Seven Years' War.

Militarily, too, the years after 1757 were quite different from the previous ones. The new commander in chief, Major General James Abercromby ("a heavy man," according to a subordinate officer, and "an indifferent soldier" in the estimation of Francis Parkman)[13] had been Loudoun's second in command. Pitt limited Abercromby's authority so strictly that Pitt himself became de facto commander in chief, exercising direct control over Abercromby's chief subordinate officers. When Pitt dispatched Major General Jeffery Amherst and Brigadier James Wolfe to besiege Louisbourg in 1758, he allowed Abercromby no part in directing the operation. When Pitt ordered Abercromby to attack the French at Ticonderoga, he even included detailed instructions on how to deploy his troops. Pitt steadfastly refused to delegate any authority to his subordinates; with equal self-assurance he overrode the aversion of regular officers to employing large numbers of provincials. He was convinced that only vast numbers could decisively beat the French and thus insisted that the colonies raise large bodies of provincials every year, even though his regular field commanders regarded them as a burden.

The seven thousand troops Massachusetts raised in 1758 were posted primarily to Abercromby's command, where most participated in the expedition against Ticonderoga. At least twelve thousand men, the largest

11. Jack P. Greene, "The Seven Years' War and the American Revolution: The Causal Relationship Reconsidered," in Peter Marshall and Glyn Williams, eds., *The British Atlantic Empire before the American Revolution* (Totowa, N.J., 1980), 98. For tax levels, see Joseph B. Felt, "Statistics of Taxation in Massachusetts," American Statistical Association, *Collections*, I (1847), 211–581.

12. Thomas Pownall to William Pitt, 30 Sept. 1758; copy in Parkman Papers, XLII, 282–288, Massachusetts Historical Society, Boston (a transcription of the same from State Papers, America and West Indies, Vol. LXXI, Public Record Office, London).

13. Parkman, *Montcalm and Wolfe*, II, 93 (quoting James Wolfe); II, 51.

assemblage of troops in New York during the war, took part in the attack on 8 July. Nearly five hundred of them never returned from the series of frontal assaults Abercromby launched against the French field works held by Montcalm and only about three thousand defenders. At the end of that botched and brutal day, Abercromby ordered a withdrawal that soon became a pell-mell retreat back to the head of Lake George. Anglo-American morale was shattered, and loss of confidence caused the rest of the summer to be spent in constructing a new post, Fort George, near the ruins of Fort William Henry.

Montcalm's successful defense of Ticonderoga was the last significant French victory of the war. Less than three weeks later, Louisbourg surrendered to Amherst. This effectively sealed off the Canadian interior from resupply. A month later, Lieutenant Colonel John Bradstreet delivered another blow that was almost equally damaging, and far more surprising. Bradstreet, a bullheaded man and an accomplished egotist, was an American-born regular officer who early in the war had commanded the provincial batteau service. This corps of rivermen ferried supplies along the waterways between British forts in New York, and, as their leader, Bradstreet had become obsessed with the idea of using them to mount an amphibious expedition against Fort Frontenac, on Lake Ontario. The principal French fur-trading entrepôt for the interior, Fort Frontenac lay on the northeast shore of the lake, opposite the ruins of Oswego, at so great a distance from the major British forts in the Hudson Valley and at Lake George that the French had deemed it secure, leaving it with only a small garrison. Bradstreet organized a force of men (mainly provincials) familiar with river navigation who were to travel from the Hudson to Lake Ontario via the Mohawk and Onondaga rivers, cross the lake, and lay siege to the fort using only small arms and light artillery. His little army surprised the French on 27 August, captured the fort, and seized an immense quantity of booty. The next day they sailed off in a captured brigantine and a schooner laden with furs, after burning seven other ships and destroying the fort.

Even more important than the central position of Frontenac in Canada's fur-trade network were its functions as the indispensable link in the resupply chain for France's western forts and as the base for French shipping on Lake Ontario. With Frontenac and the lake fleet gone, all the western forts—Niagara and Detroit on the Great Lakes, Duquesne and the others in the Ohio country—began to suffer shortages and soon became indefensible. When Brigadier John Forbes finally managed to cut through a road to Fort Duquesne, the French garrison was too poorly supplied to resist and withdrew without a fight. By the close of the 1758 campaign, the French had thus surrendered control of the trans-Allegheny

West, had lost all safe communication between Montreal and the Great Lakes forts, and were beginning to experience supply shortages caused by the closing of the Saint Lawrence. It was only too clear to Montcalm that Canada itself would soon become impossible to defend.

Abercromby was called home in the fall of 1758 to have his dubious achievements recognized by promotion to lieutenant general. His successor in the supreme command was Jeffery Amherst, the circumspect, competent victor of Louisbourg. Pitt's policies for 1759 continued to conform to the pattern established the year before. Massachusetts again responded enthusiastically. Initially the General Court voted to raise five thousand men and then granted a special bounty to recruit fifteen hundred more volunteers. These soldiers were intended in part to garrison Louisbourg and other Maritime forts, freeing regulars to participate in expeditionary forces. In addition to acting as garrison troops, the provincials would also participate in two of the year's campaigns, following James Wolfe up the Saint Lawrence to attack Quebec and aiding in Amherst's attempt to dislodge the French from Ticonderoga and Crown Point.

Amherst's force reached Ticonderoga on 22 July 1759. The defenders, strapped for men and supplies, held out for only four days before withdrawing. On the night of 26 July they blew up the fort's powder magazine, set fire to its buildings, and fled to Crown Point. Amherst cautiously decided to repair the damaged structure before pursuing the enemy; but when he sent scouts down the lake to Crown Point, he learned that the French had withdrawn from that fort as well. On 31 July the British accordingly took possession of the second post, also blown up and burnt by its retreating garrison. Amherst again decided to rebuild before proceeding after the enemy. In addition to ordering a whole new fort constructed, Amherst also sent men to build a road eastward from Crown Point to Township Number Four, on the Connecticut River in New Hampshire. Finally, he decided to build a small flotilla to keep the four French gunboats on Lake Champlain from menacing his troops' batteaux when the time finally came to set off for Canada. Amherst's great caution saved lives but cost him the rest of the campaigning season. In November he dismissed his provincials and sent the regulars into winter quarters without taking further action against the French.

More than two hundred miles to the north, Amherst's impetuous subordinate Wolfe was showing no such restraint. With a force of nine thousand he had sailed up the Saint Lawrence as soon as the passage was clear of ice and had proceeded to attack the French in the vicinity of Quebec. All summer long the two sides fenced for advantage. Finally, on 13 September, Wolfe managed to infiltrate forty-five hundred men through Montcalm's defenses and position them on a plateau called the Plains of Abraham outside the walls of Quebec. Montcalm immediately attacked with an equal number of regulars and militia. In the battle that followed, the less-disciplined French force lost heavily—1,400 casualties against 660 for the British. Both commanders suffered mortal wounds. Quebec capitulated five days later, and Brigadier John Murray settled in with a strong garrison to hold the city through the winter.

By the beginning of 1760, no one could doubt that the British had gained the upper hand. New France had been cut off from the Mississippi basin, and its advanced posts on Lake Champlain were gone. With Louisbourg in English hands, any attempt to resupply Canada via the Saint Lawrence was out of the question, and stocks of matériel were declining fast. Many men had been lost from the defending forces and could not be replaced. The ablest commander in New France lay dead; his successor, the chevalier de Lévis, was a good officer but no peer of Montcalm. Brigadier General Murray's garrison at Quebec was a dagger pressing into the very heart of Canada. Unless the severely weakened and demoralized French could dislodge Murray's force before reinforcements were shipped up the Saint Lawrence in the spring, New France would be at the mercy of the English.

The British campaign of 1760 was accordingly planned to deliver a massive coup de grace to French resistance. Pitt asked the colonial governments to duplicate their contributions of the previous year. Massachusetts once more responded with zeal, resolving to raise five thousand troops and to reenlist as many as possible of the men who had been serving over the winter in the Maritime forts. The expeditions planned for 1760 formed a three-pronged final assault on the territory remaining under French control. General Murray, reinforced from the Saint Lawrence, would ascend the river toward Montreal. At the same time, Amherst would proceed from Albany via the Mohawk to Lake Ontario and thence down the Saint Lawrence. Brigadier General William Haviland would lead a force from Crown Point over Lake Champlain, driving the French back from the line of forts they still held along the Richelieu River. All three armies would converge simultaneously on Montreal, where Canada's last defenders would be trapped.

The Massachusetts troops not assigned to garrison duty for the most part joined Haviland's thirty-four-hundred-man force, made up of two regular and three provincial regiments. They first encountered the enemy at Île-aux-Noix, a fortified island at the head of the Richelieu River. The British opened fire on 23 August. On the night of the twenty-seventh, the French fell back to Fort Saint-Jean and Fort Chambly on the lower Richelieu approach to Montreal. Haviland left his wounded at Île-aux-Noix and pursued, reaching Fort Saint-Jean on the twenty-eighth only to find it in

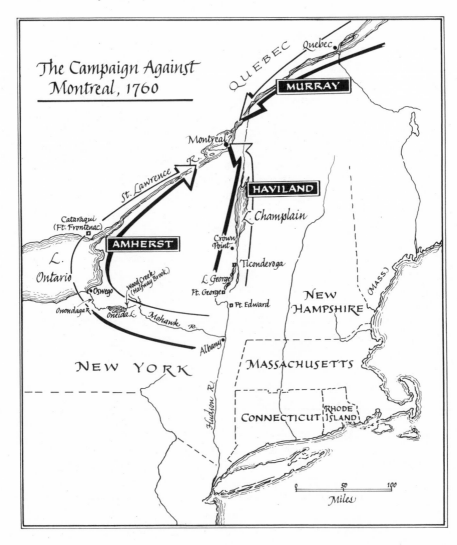

The Campaign against Montreal, 1760. After Lester J. Cappon *et al., Atlas of Early American History: The Revolutionary Era, 1760–1790* (Princeton, N.J., 1976), 2–4. Drawn by Richard Stinely

flames and its garrison retiring to Chambly. On 1 September, after brief resistance, Chambly's defenders surrendered, and the route to Montreal was left unobstructed. By 6 September Amherst's force lay above the city, and Murray's was encamped below it on the Saint Lawrence. With Haviland approaching overland against crumbling resistance, the governor-general of New France, the marquis de Vaudreuil-Cavagnal, had no choice but to ask for terms. On 8 September he surrendered, ending the war in Canada after six years of hard fighting.

Great celebration attended the arrival of the news in Massachusetts. "No where," wrote Thomas Hutchinson, was it "received with greater joy, no part of the king's dominions being more interested in it."[14] The men and women of the Bay Colony now anticipated unmolested peace and prosperity, with eventual relief from their astronomical tax rates. But as their newly appointed governor, Francis Bernard, hastened to remind them, the war was not yet won. Although fewer of their sons would fight in the coming two years, Massachusetts inhabitants would find that their cooperation and money were still essential to the war effort.

Phase IV: Nunc Dimittis, 1761–1763

Early in 1761 Pitt renewed his requests and his promises. The General Court responded by voting to raise three thousand provincials, who spent the year quietly manning forts, thereby releasing regular troops to campaign against France's New World possessions. By now Massachusetts merchants and politicians had become habituated to war and its benefits. Military contracts for the supply of garrisons were lucrative and provided merchants with assured income. Parliament's grants meant a measure of tax relief but, more important, they provided a steady inflow of specie—a vital item if Massachusetts' hard money economy were to continue to expand. But the grants acted as a stick as well as a carrot. Since the province's claims for any year were reviewed and paid only after about two years had passed, Massachusetts could ill afford to antagonize its parliamentary banker by becoming uncooperative. By 1760 or 1761 at the very latest, the Bay Colony's whole political and economic system had come to depend on the imperial war-making machinery.

Massachusetts provincials saw battle for the last time in 1762. The assembly had voted to raise thirty-two hundred men, again for garrison duty. In July, however, a small French force seized Newfoundland, making it necessary to recapture the island and its profitable fishery. Most of the redcoats were committed to the Caribbean, so a force was scraped to-

14. Hutchinson, *Mass.-Bay*, III, 60.

gether from regulars billeted at New York and a Massachusetts regiment stationed at Halifax, Nova Scotia. Under Colonel William Amherst, the supreme commander's younger brother, this makeshift expedition dislodged the French after five days of fighting in September. The Newfoundland gambit was France's last effort in North America to gain an asset to bargain away in the peace negotiations; it may also have represented an attempt to divert British attention from Havana.

Spain had entered the war on the side of France in early 1762 but was incapable of undertaking any offensive action in the New World. Havana was therefore added to the British program of conquest in the Caribbean as a means of making the Spanish come to terms quickly. The fighting in Cuba, though complicated by heat and disease, was not drawn out. Havana surrendered on 13 August. News of the conquest was greeted in Massachusetts with raptures almost as great as those that had followed the capitulation of Canada. A Boston diarist, John Boyle, recorded on 16 September 1762 the "public rejoicings on account of the reduction of the Havana":

> Sermon preached by Dr. Sewall; cadets mustered; bells rung; batteries fired; concert of music; the town illuminated; bonfires, etc. Many loyal healths drank: a vast quantity of liquor consumed, and General Winslow of Plymouth so intoxicated as to jump on the table, and break a great number of bowls, glasses, etc.[15]

Winslow's considerable bulk may have been at odds with his enthusiasm, but if ever there had been cause for dancing on tables in Boston, this was it. The Treaty of Paris only confirmed the totality of the British triumph. To many of the inhabitants of New England, the successful conclusion of the war heralded nothing less than the beginning of the millennium. Even the most worldly of colonists undoubtedly agreed that the elimination of New England's perennial antagonist and the accession of immeasurable tracts of virgin land could hardly fail to produce a thousand years of peace and prosperity in North America.

But the millennium, as we know, did not ensue. The American Revolution did, and with it came the most persistent problems in the interpretation of the period. As Francis Parkman observed a century ago, "It is the nature of great events to obscure the great events that come before them. The Seven Years' War . . . in America is half lost to sight behind the stormcloud of the War of Independence."[16] The era of the Seven Years' War, for

---

15. John Boyle, "A Journal of Occurrences in Boston," 16 Sept. 1762, MS at Houghton Library, Harvard University, Cambridge, Mass.

16. Parkman, *Montcalm and Wolfe*, I, 3.

better or worse, will probably always be identified in American historiography as the pre-Revolutionary period, and historians will no doubt go on looking there, as many already have looked, for harbingers of the Revolution. But there are dangers in this approach. The easily forgotten point is that at the close of the Seven Years' War no living soul in Massachusetts could foresee the coming separation from Great Britain, and no one desired it. With the conclusion of the war in 1763, American commitment to the empire reached its zenith. No less than other Americans, New Englanders were pleased to be part of the British system—more pleased, perhaps, than ever before—and were proud to have participated in the British triumph. They embraced British heroes as their own. In William Pitt and Jeffery Amherst they found symbols of martial statesmanship and statesmanlike generalship; in Viscount Howe and James Wolfe they saw fallen heroes of legendary valor. During the war and in its aftermath, settlements were named in honor of Amherst and Pitt in Massachusetts and New Hampshire. Wolfe had his memory secured in public media ranging from memorial eulogies to the signboards on country taverns. The normally parsimonious Massachusetts Assembly voted £250 sterling to place a tablet, in "Testimony to the . . . Services and Military Virtues of the late Lord Viscount Howe," in Westminster Abbey.[17] Examples could easily be multiplied of such admiration for British heroes and of enthusiasm for the triumphant empire. It is therefore puzzling to find this fund of good will exhausted in less than a decade and a half, and richly ironic to see veterans of the Seven Years' War taking up arms again in 1775, against the redcoats beside whom they had so recently served.

When New Englanders named towns and taverns after their British heroes, they were commemorating the Seven Years' War as a public event. But their personal experiences of the war were often at variance with the public memory, and these personal experiences ultimately proved more important as a guide to understanding their world in the perplexing years that followed the Peace of Paris. To people with no inkling of what the future might bring, the years from 1763 to 1775 were not a prerevolutionary, but a postwar period. They reasoned about events that they encountered then on the basis of their experiences and their beliefs. And their beliefs were formed, just as their experiences were dominated, by the greatest war the eighteenth century had yet seen.

Everyone who has known veterans of a war in the twentieth century has heard war stories told, and almost every veteran succumbs sooner or later to the temptation to reminisce. The impulse to talk about one's military

17. *Ibid.*, II, 391–394; John Shy, *Toward Lexington: The Role of the British Army in the Coming of the American Revolution* (Princeton, N.J., 1965), 140–148; Gipson, *Victorious Years*, 224–225 (Howe's memorial).

service proceeds in part from the sharpness of the impression made by shared adversity or danger, and in part from the critical time in men's lives that the impression is made—late adolescence or early manhood. Military service, especially when it occurs under harsh conditions, tends to promote a powerful sense of camaraderie among soldiers, a camaraderie that is perhaps the strongest emotional bond they have formed outside their families of origin. In later life, the experience and the community can provide common reference points, benchmarks of memory—shared recollections that inform the veteran's judgment about his world. Mention Pearl Harbor, Bataan, and Bastogne to a group of World War II veterans, for example, and chances are excellent that you will elicit a highly consistent set of responses that will have little to do with geography. Pearl Harbor, you will find, means sneak attack; Bataan signifies the extermination of the defenseless; Bastogne means fortitude and defiance. What were originally mere place-names have been transformed into powerful metaphors in the minds of a generation of American veterans. Identifications remain similar because the community within which they were first formed agreed so thoroughly on the events' significance.

More routine experiences, too, provide landmarks in the geography of veterans' memory. *C-rations, basic training, foxhole,* and *company punishment* are words that carry little more than abstract significance for civilians, but they can evoke vivid recollections among those who have eaten, endured, dug, or suffered. Not all soldiers experience the terrors of combat, and those who do may try for years to communicate its meaning, or perhaps to block out the memory. But no one who has seen battle can either forget it or completely describe it. It is an experience that remains fully accessible only to those who have undergone it, fully understandable only among those who have shared it.

This was as true for the veterans of the Seven Years' War as it is for veterans of modern wars. Like a modern recruit, a New England soldier of the 1750s or 1760s was most often a young man at the time of his enlistment. Unlike a modern recruit, however, the eighteenth-century provincial's frame of reference usually did not extend far beyond the region in which he had been born and raised. The province he served was a loose confederation of mutually suspicious towns, held together by a distrust of outsiders that was even more intense than their suspicion of each other and united by a narrow provincial culture. At the core of their outlook lay the assumption that New England was bound by covenant to God Almighty. Few institutions transcended the boundaries of individual towns; communication and transportation links between settlements were poor at best. Little currency circulated outside the few large eastern towns. Although literacy was fairly widespread, reading matter was limited mainly to religious publications and to such newspapers as reached the countryside from Boston. All in all, mid-eighteenth-century Massachusetts offered its inhabitants few opportunities for corporate experience that surmounted parochial bounds and concerns.

The wars of the eighteenth century were the great exceptions to this generalization, and the Seven Years' War was the greatest exception of all. The conflict did not, however, affect all New Englanders similarly. Merchants enterprising enough to obtain military contracts, for example, found that the war offered unrivaled opportunities for profit. Farmers capable of raising surpluses and getting them to the market shared the discovery of John Adams's satirical persona, Humphrey Ploughjogger: "In the war time I could sell my fatt ocksen, and sheep, and every thing I could raise on my place, for a pretty good round price in muney." At war's end such men might well agree with Humphrey that "the war did me some good," although they had run the risk of losing sons (Humphrey claimed to have lost two), and most would find themselves nearly unable to pay their taxes once the fighting stopped.[18] The largest group to be touched by the conflict, however, was the group with the most uniform wartime experience, provincial soldiers. Harsh months of campaigning, punctuated by an occasional, terrifying battle, became a profound part of their experience.

Because they were mainly young men who owned little real property, soldiers had scant influence in their communities during the war itself. By the time the great imperial crisis reached its climax in the mid-1770s, however, the men who had been soldiers in the Seven Years' War had grown into their late thirties and early forties and were coming into their own in towns throughout the province. Their fathers, for whom "the war did . . . some good," were passing from the political scene. The veterans on the whole were less likely than their fathers to remember the war favorably and were unlikely to be well disposed toward the redcoats with whom they had served. The Seven Years' War had been, in effect, the greatest educational experience in their lives. It had transformed them from a mere group of contemporaries into a generation of men, whose common knowledge included a powerful set of lessons about themselves, about the British, and about war itself. The rest of this book examines the content of the war's lessons and the conditions under which those lessons were learned: conditions that made them impossible to forget.

18. Humphrey Ploughjogger [John Adams] to the *Boston Evening Post*, 20 June 1763, in Robert J. Taylor, ed., *The Papers of John Adams*, I (Cambridge, Mass., 1977), 64.

Chapter 2 ❖ "Sons of Some of the Best Yeomen in New England"
Army and Society in Provincial Massachusetts

At the outset of the Seven Years' War, Massachusetts Bay's native military tradition stretched back a century and a quarter, to the founding of the colony. Dozens of laws dealing with military organization and discipline were on the statute books, and—at least in theory—its male inhabitants were universally trained in the arts of war. The Bay Colony's defense rested ultimately on its militia, which with certain exceptions (ministers, slaves, civil magistrates, Indians, the students and faculty of Harvard, and a few others) consisted of every able-bodied man between sixteen and sixty years of age.[1] Its very comprehensiveness, however, made the militia a problematic military tool. Because its regiments were basically identical to the male populations of whole regions, they could be used only briefly, in extreme emergencies—in response, for example, to an invasion.

Even in the seventeenth century, militia units, properly speaking, had seldom functioned in offensive roles. Since any attempt to pursue an enemy would have left the militiamen's homes defenseless, campaigns were carried out instead by battalions of volunteers, while militia regiments came to represent only the manpower pool from which the volunteers could be raised. After King William's War, during the governorship of the earl of Bellomont (1697–1701), laws were passed that brought the principles of Massachusetts' military organization into line with practical neces-

1. For a survey of colonial systems of defense which emphasizes Massachusetts, see Douglas Edward Leach, *Arms for Empire: A Military History of the British Colonies in North America, 1607–1763* (New York, 1973), esp. 8–40; and John Shy, "A New Look at the Colonial Militia," in Shy, *A People Numerous and Armed: Reflections on the Military Struggle for American Independence* (New York, 1976), 22–33. For the origins of the system, see also Jack S. Radabaugh, "The Militia of Colonial Massachusetts," *Military Affairs*, XVIII (1954), 1–18; and the interpretative essay of Timothy H. Breen, "The Covenanted Militia of Massachusetts Bay: English Background and New World Development," in Breen, *Puritans and Adventurers: Change and Persistence in Early America* (New York, 1980), 24–45. In addition, several dissertations deal with colonial military organization. The most useful of these are Archibald Hanna, Jr., "New England Military Institutions, 1693–1750" (Ph.D. diss., Yale University, 1951); John M. Murrin, "Anglicizing an American Colony: The Transformation of Provincial Massachusetts" (Ph.D. diss., Yale University, 1966), esp. chap. 3; and Richard Henry Marcus, "The Militia of Colonial Connecticut, 1693–1775: An Institutional Study" (Ph.D. diss., University of Colorado, 1965), esp. chaps. 5 and 6.

sity. The militia was defined thereafter not as an army per se, but as an all-purpose military infrastructure: a combination of home guard, draft board, and rear-echelon supply network.[2] Thus during the long series of wars with the French and Indians the real fighting was done not by the militia, but by provincial armies, which the colonial government created from men recruited for single campaigns and sent to the field under leaders who held their rank independently of the militia command structure. On its training days the militia continued to provide a modest degree of compulsory military practice for most of the men in the province. If the danger were great enough, militia units could conceivably take the field themselves, as several regiments did in 1757. But the most important function of the militia was to provide volunteers—or, if necessary, conscripts—for the provincial armies.

Annually recruited provincial armies thus formed the backbone of the Bay Colony's military capability during the Seven Years' War. Like armed forces in general, provincial armies were drawn from surplus manpower—those who could be spared from essential economic tasks to perform the job of fighting. In the mother country the rank and file of the regular army was composed of permanently marginal members of British society. Convicts, vagabonds, sundry social misfits, and natives of the impoverished backcountry of Scotland and Ireland traditionally constituted a great proportion of the king's troops. As the eighteenth century wore on, these were increasingly joined by people cast adrift by enclosure and industrialization: farmers and laborers from depressed rural areas, artisans whose skills were obsolescent, and other poor but respectable folk whose positions in society had been eroded in an era of rapid economic change. For such men military service offered an alternative to a bleak proletarian life—or even starvation.[3]

2. Murrin, "Anglicizing an American Colony," 72–90; Hanna, "Military Institutions," 121, 283–290, and *passim.*

3. Sylvia R. Frey, *The British Soldier in North America: A Social History of Military Life in the Revolutionary Period* (Austin, Tex., 1981), 6–16; Eric Robson, "The Armed Forces and the Art of War," in *The New Cambridge Modern History*, VII: *The Old Regime, 1713–63*, ed. J. O. Lindsay (Cambridge, 1957), 175–176. For arguments that American soldiers in the 18th century represented similarly marginal groups, see Shy, "A New Look," in Shy, *People Armed*, 30; William Pencak, "Warfare and Political Change in Mid-Eighteenth-Century Massachusetts," in Peter Marshall and Glyn Williams, eds., *The British Atlantic Empire before the American Revolution* (Totowa, N.J., 1980), 65–66; James Kirby Martin and Mark Edward Lender, *A Respectable Army: The Military Origins of the Republic, 1763–1789* (Arlington Heights, Ill., 1982), 18–19. Most generalizations about the social composition of 18th-century American military forces have been based on studies of the membership of units in the Continental army; see especially Edward C. Papenfuse and Gregory A. Stiverson, "General Smallwood's Recruits: The Peacetime Career of the Revolutionary War Private," *William and Mary Quarterly*, 3d Ser., XXX (1973), 117–132; John R. Sellers, "The Common Soldier

Massachusetts soldiers of the Seven Years' War, in contrast, were by no means colonial proletarians. Rather, they were products of a society and economy that constantly generated males who were *temporarily* available for military service. To understand how and why civilians became provincials, one must first comprehend the place and role of young men in the Bay Colony. Their position depended on two facts of overwhelming consequence: the province's economy was dominated by noncommercial family agriculture, and its population was growing with astonishing speed.

I

Nearly a quarter-million people lived in the Bay Colony when the Seven Years' War began, and the great majority of them made their homes on family farms. A small fraction—an eighth or a tenth—of the colonists resided in towns in which the majority of the householders supported themselves by some means other than farming. Only in such comparatively urban settings as Boston, Salem, the port section of Newbury, Gloucester, Charlestown, and perhaps Marblehead or Beverly did money circulate regularly. In most of the province's farming communities economic life proceeded along different lines and depended less on the direct exchange of currency. This is not to say, however, that the province was made up of individually self-sufficient family farms, each of which produced what its occupants needed for food, fuel, and clothing. Such farms, a persistent ideal in America's folk memory, may have existed somewhere, but not in eighteenth-century Massachusetts. The locus of subsistence production in the Bay Colony instead was in the farm town as a whole.[4] Local systems of exchange allowed families on farms that were not individually self-sufficient to produce goods and services in enough quantity and variety to make economic life possible within towns or parishes. As we shall see, these arrangements depended heavily upon the participation of young men.

Massachusetts' inability to produce any substantial staple crop was responsible for the predominance of town-based local exchange systems in

in the American Revolution," in Stanley J. Underdal, ed., *Military History of the American Revolution: The Proceedings of the Sixth Military History Symposium, United States Air Force Academy, 10–11 October 1974* (Washington, D.C., 1976), 151–156, 164–166; Mark Edward Lender, "The Social Structure of the New Jersey Brigade: The Continental Line as an American Standing Army," in Peter Karsten, ed., *The Military in America: From the Colonial Era to the Present* (New York, 1980), 27–44.

4. Bettye Hobbs Pruitt, "Agriculture and Society in the Towns of Massachusetts, 1771: A Statistical Analysis" (Ph.D. diss., Boston University, 1981), 7–21, 25–40; and Pruitt, "Self-Sufficiency and the Agricultural Economy of Eighteenth-Century Massachusetts," MS, Charles Warren Center, Harvard University, March 1983.

the provincial economy. The middle colonies might export flour and pork, and the southern colonies could sell their rice and tobacco overseas, but New England grew or manufactured no great commodity for markets abroad. Instead, Massachusetts produced goods (including rum, fish, ships, and livestock) and services (especially in maritime transport) that created the chance for widespread, though for most people infrequent, participation in markets outside their own communities. Almost every place in the province could produce something salable if the demand existed. But demand was seldom intense enough to permit many Bay colonists to specialize in the production of goods for the market. Among the country folk who composed the bulk of the population, almost everyone had *some* contact with commercial activity, both through the sale of occasional surpluses and in the purchase of items, like pins, gunpowder, and high-grade cloth, which could not be produced by local artisans. In comparison with the much more frequent exchanges of goods and labor within individual towns, however, such extralocal transactions were rare. In the more commonplace intracommunity exchanges cash seldom changed hands, and countrymen had to rely on credit for their daily economic activity.[5] In this they were not unlike urban merchants who also operated principally on credit in their relations with corresponding firms and retailers. But the small scale and rural setting of local exchange systems gave credit within them a different meaning than it carried in the world of business.

With no formal financial institutions to centralize them, local credit transactions took the form of debts contracted between individual community members. Such debts were precisely figured in terms of monetary equivalents according to accepted standards of value, and recorded as so many pounds, shillings, and pence owed "by" or "to" one's fellow townsmen. Within any given community, thousands of small obligations, carefully set down in scores of ledgers and pocket notebooks, reflected the complex interchanges of pasturage for household products, of stud service for farm labor, of virtually anything useful for whatever could be had in local goods and services. The resulting webwork of debts (which normally carried interest only if they involved the transfer of that rare commodity, cash) thus represented a formalization of family interdependence within communities. Local debts were always legally collectible, but in practice were carried on for years between families and individuals before they were reckoned and settled.

Labor was the item most frequently exchanged on the local level, and this made young men crucial to the functioning of town economies. The

5. Christopher M. Jedrey, *The World of John Cleaveland: Family and Community in Eighteenth-Century New England* (New York, 1979), chap. 3.

demand for labor in preindustrial agricultural communities was heavy, but sporadic; the number of workers within individual families was not constant, nor were their skills necessarily suited to all their families' needs. The presence in the community of young men with strong backs and diverse abilities, who could be hired when extra hands were needed for clearing fields, plowing, harvesting, or for other tasks, gave farmers flexibility and reasonable efficiency in running their farms. Labor often functioned as a virtual proxy for currency in the local economy, and individual debts often represented work contracts—promises to deliver productive effort at the future point when it would be required.

Any rural householder at any given time would owe and be owed by dozens of his neighbors. Moreover, few men possessed liquid assets sufficient to settle all, or even many, of their debts on demand. Participants in village exchange systems thus were never, technically speaking, far from insolvency. For them, economic survival meant not being called on to settle their obligations frequently (or worst of all, unexpectedly). The way to succeed within these cash-starved town economies was not to get ahead, but to be a patient creditor and a faithful debtor—the kind of good neighbor who would provide necessary commodities or labor when called upon, and not the sort of man who would increase his estate at his townsmen's expense.

When creditors were of markedly greater wealth and community standing than their debtors, the interactions between them tended to take the form of patron-client relationships, promoting what we now identify as deferential social behavior. When creditors and debtors were more nearly equal in status and wealth, their mutual indebtedness could act as a powerful social cement, creating what we in retrospect see as communal cooperation. In rural Massachusetts either circumstance discouraged individualism and open acquisitiveness and, instead, reinforced the models of neighborly behavior countrymen heard expounded from their local pulpits. But this is emphatically *not* to say that the participants in rural town economies were less calculating than their urban cousins or that they were unworthy of their reputation for Yankee shrewdness. Far from inhabiting bucolic utopias, country folk lived in communities in which economic opportunity was severely circumscribed. Precisely because their prospects were so limited, they had to think hard about their present and future estate, reckon their accounts closely, and plan ahead.

The operation of local exchange networks can be observed in the account books of men like James Emery, a yeoman of Biddeford, in the "Eastward Part" of Massachusetts, Maine.[6] From 1763, when he opened

6. James Emery Account Book, Agriculture MSS, Baker Library, Harvard Business School, Boston.

his ledger as a new household head, until his son closed it after his death in 1810, Emery kept accounts with seventy-five of his townsmen. James Emery was by no means unenterprising, nor was his town a backwater, untouched by the market: by 1770 he was engaging in small-scale trading ventures to the West Indies on the sloop *Mayflower*, in which he owned one-quarter interest. Such ventures remained only a small part of his total dealings, however, and the great majority of the transactions recorded in his account book involved only the exchange of local labor and goods produced in town. Emery's accounts with two of his neighbors show the dynamics of a local exchange economy at the most fundamental level.

Emery's account with Robert Cole ran from 1768 through 1776, and during that period was reckoned twice: on 2 August 1769, when Cole owed £2 8s. 6d. Old Tenor to Emery, and again on 14 March, 1776, by which time Cole's debt had grown to £2 19s. Old Tenor. These sums were only the artifacts of a long history of exchanges. Between the beginning of their cooperation and the first reckoning of the account, Emery supplied Cole with shoe leather, molasses, two felt hats, seventy-nine yards of home-woven cloth, a small amount of Indian corn, four and a half days of labor, and three days' use of his ox team: total value, £27 16s. Old Tenor. Cole earned his credit with Emery largely by supplying him with labor. Cole's sons worked thirty-two days on Emery's farm, and Cole himself worked two days during the period before the first reckoning. In addition, Cole hired his ox team to Emery for two and a half days and provided him with sixteen skeins of homespun yarn, three pounds of butter, and a few pints of corn. This arrangement made eminent sense, since Emery's trading ventures on the *Mayflower* and his weaving skills allowed him to barter what he had a surplus of—goods of his own making and manufactured wares obtained outside Biddeford—for what he lacked: help on the farm. Emery would not begin to record hiring out his own sons' labor until 1774, and it is clear that in 1768–1769 Emery saw Cole's most desirable assets as his boys, who could help make up Emery's labor deficit. Over the eight years their account ran, each accumulated more than £75 of credit in Old Tenor value with the other, but in all that time, currency changed hands only twice. In the fall of 1773, Cole paid Emery £2 8s. in cash; a little over a year later, Emery delivered £2 5s. in cash to Cole. In Cole's dealings with Emery, labor (provided mainly by Cole's sons) accounted for 75.2 percent of the credit he earned. Hiring his draft animals and farm equipment to Emery accounted for 12.3 percent, payment in kind for another 7.1 percent, and payment in currency for 3.2 percent, of Cole's total credit. (The remainder of Cole's credit was earned in unspecified transactions.) Labor was also the principal item by which Emery gained his counterbalancing credit with Cole, although it provided a smaller proportion, amounting to 39.7 percent of the total earned between 1769 and

1776. Payments in kind and the hire of oxen and equipment made up 26.3 percent and 28.4 percent of Emery's credit, and only 4.4 percent of the total came from payment in currency. (The remainder was earned in unspecified exchanges.)

The account of James Emery and Matthew Kissick ran for a much longer time, never involved the exchange of cash, and was reckoned for the last time nearly a decade after the final transaction occurred. Between 1766 and 1782, Emery (and eventually his sons) worked for Kissick in a variety of jobs, from general labor to shearing sheep, and from hewing timber to repairing his plow and cart. In addition, Emery and his sons worked on Kissick's behalf for a third party, John Davis, with whom Kissick had another account; Emery also supplied Kissick with goods and hired out his oxen and equipment. In return, Kissick made and repaired chairs for Emery, hauled his dung, framed his barn, repaired his milk house, built him a pair of doors, and sent his sons to work on Emery's farm. Emery earned credit with Kissick mainly by supplying him with labor (77.3 percent of the total value of his account), followed by payments in kind (10.4 percent), the rental of draft animals and farm equipment (6.7 percent), and unspecified transactions (5.6 percent). Kissick gained his offsetting credit with Emery by supplying labor and by sending his sons to work for him (87.7 percent of the value of his account) and by making payments in kind (12.3 percent). The two men first reckoned accounts in December 1768 and found that Emery owed Kissick 9s. The sum was not collected, but carried over as a credit on the new account they immediately began. Their next reckoning was made on 22 March 1792, just short of nine years after Emery had delivered Kissick two hundredweight of hay in their last recorded transaction. After nineteen years of mutual indebtedness, Kissick finally owed Emery £1 17s. in Massachusetts currency. It is probable, though by no means certain, that a cash payment settled their account at that point. If so, it was the first time that cash had changed hands between them.

It is clear from such cases as these that the labor of young men was indispensable in the operation of the hardscrabble farm economies of Massachusetts towns, but that alone did not guarantee them a permanent place in their hometowns. The average rate of population growth in the eighteenth-century Bay Colony was about 2.5 percent per year, enough to double its population every twenty-eight years. Farmland was a fixed commodity in the long-settled eastern towns where most people lived, however, and by mid-century this meant that most families could not settle all their sons within the boundaries of their birthplaces. Depending on the quality of the land, farms usually could not be divided into holdings smaller than forty or fifty acres; the executors of intestate estates in the period would generally refrain from splitting a farm into pieces smaller than that for fear of "spoiling the whole."[7] Thus the head of a family with four sons living on, say, ninety acres, faced a difficult decision when the time came to settle his estate. He could divide the land equally between his sons; in so doing, however, he would condemn each of them to a lower standard of living then he had previously known, perhaps dooming them all to poverty.[8] He might, on the other hand, settle all his land on a single heir, ensuring that the family line would not decline in wealth; but what then of his other children? By the middle of the eighteenth century fathers were tending to resolve such dilemmas by giving each son at least some land, while fixing on one or two principal heirs (determined in most cases by their positions in the birth order), in order to preserve the integrity of the estate.[9] The sons not favored with land enough for farming received the bulk of their portions in other forms: help in purchasing land elsewhere, cash, tools, a liberal education, and so on, in degrees determined by the financial condition of the family.[10] Sons who inherited more land were often given obligations to fulfill in completing the portions of their siblings, engagements that might take years to complete.[11]

However a family's estate might be divided, sons knew that the division would take place only when their father was ready to settle, or when he died. Until they received their portions, young men generally lacked the resources to set themselves up independently, marry, and begin their own households. Consequently, for most male youths the period from their middle teens to their middle twenties was a time of prolonged dependence—a kind of prelude to real manhood. This was also the point in their lives at which they were capable of contributing the most to the economic welfare of their families of origin. As one historian of the family in this period has observed, it was the labor of sons that allowed families to prosper: "The ten years of work between a young man's sixteenth birthday and the mean statistical marriage age of twenty-six made an important contribution to his father's wherewithal" and was therefore a major factor in enabling the father to provide adequate portions for all his sons and daugh-

---

7. Jedrey, *Cleaveland*, 82.

8. John J. Waters, "Family, Inheritance, and Migration in Colonial New England: The Evidence from Guilford, Connecticut," *WMQ*, 3d Ser., XXXIX (1982), 82–83; Jedrey, *Cleaveland*, 81–82.

9. Jedrey, *Cleaveland*, 83–84; Waters, "Family, Inheritance," *WMQ*, 3d Ser., XXXIX (1982), 78–85; Philip J. Greven, Jr., *Four Generations: Population, Land, and Family in Colonial Andover, Massachusetts* (Ithaca, N.Y., 1970), 227–228.

10. Greven, *Four Generations*, 227–254 (land); 158–160, 243, 246, 251–253 (trade); 143, 166–167, 243–244 (cash); 243–244, 251–253 (education). See also Jedrey, *Cleaveland*, 74–84.

11. Jedrey, *Cleaveland*, 90–94.

ters.[12] This point can hardly be overemphasized. Whatever tensions an extended period of dependence generated, it was indispensable to the functioning of the family economy.[13] Without the greater income generated by the labor of the children as they became young adults, there was no guarantee that a family's offspring would ever achieve independence. Lacking land or trades or marriage portions, they might simply be absorbed into other households as servants or be forced to eke out precarious existences as permanent wage laborers.

Because the interests of fathers and sons were both interdependent and opposed in this matter, as the fathers sought to build up the family holdings and the sons yearned to establish themselves as adults, young men during the dependency period worked not only for their familes but for themselves as well. The typical pattern seems to have been for youths to work primarily for the family in their teens, and increasingly for themselves as they grew into their twenties. The years before marriage, then, were years of work and saving, as young men (especially those who knew that they would not become their fathers' principal heirs) sought to accumulate the stake that, supplemented by parental aid, would allow them to start their own households.

A major consequence of such family behavior was the perennial production of surplus males, young men who had not yet acquired enough property to marry and settle down as householders. Such youths lived at home or remained nearby, worked for their fathers or hired out for wages, held most of the small estates on their towns' tax lists, and generally owned little real property.[14] But while they were undeniably poor and did represent a kind of surplus population, they were neither permanently poor nor

12. Waters, "Family, Inheritance," *WMQ*, 3d Ser., XXXIX (1982), 77. See also Greven, *Four Generations*, 206; Patricia J. Tracy, *Jonathan Edwards, Pastor: Religion and Society in Eighteenth-Century Northampton* (New York, 1980), 237–238, n. 27; Robert A. Gross, *The Minutemen and Their World* (New York, 1976), 210–211, n. 22; Kenneth A. Lockridge, "The Population of Dedham, Massachusetts, 1636–1736," *Economic History Review*, 2d Ser., XIX (1966), 330; Daniel Scott Smith, "The Demographic History of Colonial New England," in Michael Gordon, ed., *The American Family in Social-Historical Perspective* (New York, 1973), 406.

13. Tracy, *Edwards, passim*; Greven, *Four Generations*, 222–258.

14. John J. Waters, "Patrimony, Succession, and Social Stability: Guilford, Connecticut in the Eighteenth Century," *Perspectives in American History*, X (1976), 156; Gross, *Minutemen*, 207–209, n. 16; Jedrey, *Cleaveland*, 94, 204, n. 80. Social standing peaked only when men reached their 40s and 50s; see Waters, "Patrimony, Succession," 158; Jedrey, *Cleaveland*, 63–64, 94; James A. Henretta, "Families and Farms: *Mentalité* in Pre-Industrial America," *WMQ*, 3d Ser., XXXV (1978), 20; Jackson Turner Main, "The Distribution of Property in Colonial Connecticut," in James Kirby Martin, ed., *The Human Dimensions of Nation Making* (Madison, Wisc., 1976), 54–104, esp. 61–64. For a good example of youth-related poverty, see the case of Jonathan, Daniel, and David Chandler of Andover, described in Greven, *Four Generations*, 251–253.

permanently surplus: they were in no sense members of an agricultural proletariat.

Permanently poor people did exist in late-colonial Massachusetts, of course, in numbers that apparently increased during the eighteenth century. Although we know comparatively little about these people, we may be sure that local villagers did not regard them in the same light as the young men we have been discussing—even though they were equally bereft of property. The difference was that the young men were in expectation of some inheritance, a condition that would have been well known in any small town. While we cannot determine their relative numbers exactly, we do know that the permanent poor were far fewer than the population of temporarily poor young men and that age would have been a major factor in differentiating the two groups.[15]

Age was in fact one of the most reliable determinants of economic and social standing among New Englanders. For most men in the Bay Colony, landlessness was a function of either youth or old age.[16] Between marriage, in their mid- to late twenties, and retirement or death in their late sixties or seventies, farmers usually saw the amount of wealth they controlled rise in a curve that peaked when they were in their fifties and then slowly decline as they distributed more and more property among their offspring in the form of dowries and inheritance portions. Since the process of inheritance was often not complete until after the death of one's father, many men did not attain full standing in their communities until they were in their forties. Men seldom exercised local political leadership until they had reached middle life and the fullness of means that was associated with it. It was assumed that only those who had established a stake in society, whose property in principle ensured that their interest was at the command of no man, could be relied upon to direct the life of the community wisely. Thus "a dependent son [no matter what his age] could not be a leader, any more than . . . a servant could be a voter."[17] The men who were called the "fathers of the towns" were literally that. Younger men waited their turn—

15. Douglas Lamar Jones, "The Strolling Poor: Transiency in Eighteenth-Century Massachusetts," *Journal of Social History*, VIII (Spring 1975), 28; Gary B. Nash, *The Urban Crucible: Social Change, Political Consciousness, and the Origins of the American Revolution* (Cambridge, Mass., 1979), 184–185. For comparative size of the permanently impoverished population and the youthful poor in Essex County, see estimates in Fred Anderson, "War and the Bay Colony: Soldiers and Society in Massachusetts during the Seven Years' War, 1754–1763" (Ph.D. diss., Harvard University, 1981), II, 419–420. During the period of highest vagabondage in Essex County, 1760–1764, the number of vagrants (male, female, and children) was about 862, according to Jones, "Strolling Poor," *Jour. Soc. Hist.*, VIII (Spring 1975), 35; at the same time, the Essex County total of men in the dependency age-range, 16–26, was about 4,100.

16. Jedrey, *Cleaveland*, 63–70.

17. *Ibid.*, 121.

for independence, for wealth, for leadership—not because they particularly wanted to do so, but because the strict limitations of opportunity in the hardscrabble farming economy of most towns left them no alternative.

While the young men of Massachusetts waited to assume the prerogatives and responsibilities of adulthood, they pursued occupations that varied according to choices their fathers had made for them while they were still children and according to the opportunities that were locally available. They could, in effect, enter three lines of work: farming, artisanship, and laboring. The first required land, either rented or owned; the second implied the acquisition of a skill and the ownership of tools; the third meant working for a wage, either as a day-laborer or a servant. Farming required the greatest outlay, conferred the most in terms of independence and community standing, and represented the goal for which most men were compelled to wait and save. Artisanship necessitated a lower level of capital expenditure—time spent as an apprentice was the biggest investment —but it meant a greater degree of dependence for young practitioners who lacked the resources to set up their own shops. Such journeymen, if they were not wholly itinerant, might well find themselves working for a master and earning wages not much higher than those of laborers. Laboring required only a strong back; while carrying no stigma, it offered the least in terms of independence, compensation, and respectability.[18] In pursuing any of these livelihoods, young men were not necessarily following fixed careers. Colonial farmers often practiced trades in addition to farming; artisans might inherit or purchase enough land to make most of their living from it and begin to style themselves "yeomen"; laborers might save enough to buy a patch of ground, rent some more, and purchase a few cattle, thus becoming husbandmen. Even country pastors were usually also farmers, tending flocks both spiritual and woolly. It is thus most accurate to think of any young man who was not yet fully established as being only a temporary member of whatever occupational group he might claim.[19]

Great variations in population density reflected equally great disparities in the occupational opportunities open to young men in different parts of Massachusetts. The most populous part of the province was the region that had been settled by the Puritans during the Great Migration of the 1630s—the original Bay Colony, consisting in the eighteenth century of the counties of Essex, Middlesex, and Suffolk. Mean population density there at the time of the Seven Years' War was on the order of sixty persons

18. For discussion of occupational patterns among young men in Massachusetts, see Fred Anderson, "A People's Army: Provincial Military Service in Massachusetts during the Seven Years' War," *WMQ*, 3d Ser., XL (1983), 499–527. See also "War and the Bay Colony," I, 50; II, 420–421.

19. Jedrey, *Cleaveland*, 64, 66–68.

per square mile, distributed in the familiar nucleated pattern of New England towns. The three counties to their south, Plymouth, Bristol, and Barnstable, had roughly half the density of the Bay area, about thirty persons per square mile. Until 1692 these counties had been a separate entity, the Colony of New Plymouth, which was first settled a decade before the Great Migration. Locally they were still referred to as the Old Colony, and they had retained a distinct regional complexion. They had grown from a smaller initial population base, had not yet developed an urban center, and were made up of towns settled in a more dispersed pattern than those of the Bay. The counties of Worcester and Hampshire were Massachusetts' western frontier and had on average fewer than fifteen persons per square mile. The dozen settlements of York County, or Maine, comprised the province's other frontier. In mean population density, these maritime towns "to the Eastward" fell squarely between the western frontier towns and those of the Old Colony. The main occupation of household heads in all of these regions was, of course, farming. But for young men who typically were not yet householders, the variations in settlement pattern and population density meant substantial differences in the kinds of employment that were available.[20]

Each of the three principal kinds of livelihood—in farming, artisanship, and laboring—was strongly identifed with young men's occupational opportunities in a specific region of the province. Only in the western counties was land available in sufficient quantities to make farming the predominant occupation of young men. Those who lived in the Bay Colony counties, amid dense population and nucleated settlements, were most likely to make their way as artisans, particularly in trades based on wood, leather, and cloth. For the young men of the Old Colony, as for those of Maine, long-occupied areas of dispersed settlement, employment centered on agricultural labor.

Despite these variations in the *kinds* of occupation accessible to young men in the different parts of the province, however, the actual *level* of economic opportunity was roughly comparable from region to region. Migration offers an index to the availability of employment: men who can find no work near home will seek jobs further afield, in areas where they can earn their livings. Among more than two thousand Massachusetts-born provincials on the Crown Point expedition in 1756, about three men out of five, regardless of whether they were natives of the populous east or the undersettled west, had stayed within the precincts of their birthplaces until enlistment (an event which for most occurred in their late teens and twenties). The province-wide consistency in the proportion of men re-

20. See Anderson, "A People's Army," *WMQ*, 3d Ser., XL (1983), 510–513; "War and the Bay Colony," I, 51–69; II, 421–433.

maining in their birthplaces versus those leaving them indicates that the migrants were not moving to flee from untenable economic circumstances. For most young men in Massachusetts, choosing to move away from home or to remain, like settling upon a livelihood, represented a reasonable response to local, structural variations in economic opportunity.

The Seven Years' War, with its massive demand for soldiers, brought another kind of variation in opportunity, a temporal one. In its ordinary operation, the province's rural economy was given shape and movement by the decisions of thousands of families trying to perpetuate family lines by "distributing scarce resources from one generation to the next" in accordance with custom and common sense.[21] The actions of young men in entering occupations, in moving or staying put, were largely governed by parental decisions that they themselves could begin to influence only as they grew into their twenties. Parents' decisions, in turn, were intended to enable the rising generation to achieve independence for itself—gradually—and, in its turn, to care for the dependent elderly, thus sustaining and replicating the family-centered social order. This complex, infinitely varied set of family strategies achieved something like a dynamic equilibrium between a burgeoning population and the colony's available resources.

For young men, the price of this equilibrium was prolonged dependence—a stage that most, undoubtedly, hoped would end quickly. One could hasten that end by gathering enough capital to start out with a minimum of parental help. And one way of accumulating such a stake, in the years between 1754 and 1763, was through provincial military service. Although a young man contemplating enlistment could hardly expect to become rich, service in the provincial forces did confer financial benefits. In the first place, military duty (unlike civilian labor) was steady work, for which a man would be paid from enlistment until discharge, a period that usually lasted six to eight months. The provincial private's pay was high by eighteenth-century military standards—about twice as high as a redcoat private's net earnings—and was comparable to a civilian laborer's. A provincial private in 1756 received £1 12s. in provincial currency per month, plus subsistence officially valued at 8d. per day.[22] Thus the private's wage, "all found" (that is, the wage including food and lodging) was worth 52s. Lawful Money per month, the equivalent of a 2s. daily laborer's wage paid for each of the twenty-six working days in the same period.[23] In the years after 1756, the private's wage rose to £1 16s. all found,

21. Jedrey, *Cleaveland*, 70.

22. *The Acts and Resolves, Public and Private, of the Province of the Massachusetts-Bay*, XV (Boston, 1908), 442, 454–455, hereafter cited as *Acts and Resolves*.

23. William B. Weeden, *Economic and Social History of New England* (New York, 1963 [orig. publ., 1890]), II, 896–898, gives the agricultural laborer's wage as 14s.–16s. Old Tenor per day, a sum equivalent to 1s. 11d.–2s. 2d. Lawful Money.

or the equivalent of 2s. for each of the working days and 1s. for each Sabbath. Additionally, the province compensated its soldiers for enlistment by a bounty amounting at least to an additional month's pay and at most to a full eight months' pay. In 1756, a year with a comparatively low bounty, the minimum offered was an extra £1 16s. plus a blanket valued at 12s. The cash compensation for the average private soldier on that year's Crown Point expedition, then, was more than £15 Lawful Money. The pay increased above that in every subsequent year of the war and eventually almost doubled.[24] Moreover, provincial soldiers received their wages at the end of their enlistments, an arrangement that forced the soldier to save and gave him access to relatively large sums of cash, that scarcest of the countryside's resources. Fifteen pounds would not buy a farm, but it was a good start. In Andover in that period it would pay for 15 to 30 acres of unbroken land, and in Northampton it would buy as much as 150 acres of unimproved upland.[25]

From the private's perspective, military service was a reasonably lucrative proposition, providing cash income to hasten his attainment of independence. Although service inevitably brought danger, privation, hard work, and exposure to the elements, none but the first of these was far removed from his civilian experience. As recruiters undoubtedly assured potential soldiers, the army also offered the opportunity for plunder and adventure. Military service meant, moreover, a chance to see a different part of North America and to participate in the struggle against New England's historic antagonists, the papist French and the barbarous Indians. If the life of the average young New Englander was largely a waiting game, military service promised both a change from the accustomed routines and perhaps an accelerated entry into real manhood.

II

The provincial recruiting process was never so unpopular or disreputable as that of the redcoats. Regular-army recruiting before the arrival of Lord Loudoun as commander in chief in July 1756 was unregulated and characterized by abuses—enlistment under false pretenses, the intoxication and kidnapping of men—that deeply antagonized New Englanders.[26] Public

24. For wages and bounties of private soldiers in the Massachusetts provincial forces during the war, see Table 1.

25. Land prices from Greven, *Four Generations*, 128–130, 224, 227; Tracy, *Edwards*, 16. Tracy's Old Tenor prices were recalculated in Lawful Money using the depreciation table in Nash, *Urban Crucible*, 405–406.

26. Stanley McCrory Pargellis, *Lord Loudoun in North America* (New Haven, Conn., 1933), 106–109.

revulsion at the regulars' methods complemented the attractions of higher provincial pay and brief terms of service to make the colonial recruiter's job immeasurably easier than that of his red-coated counterpart.[27] In addition, the militia's regimental and company commanders cooperated by making local men aware of enlistment opportunities, which enabled provincial recruiting to be carried on more efficiently and economically than that of the regulars. The process worked as follows.

Late each winter, usually in February, the governor of Massachusetts formally appointed the colonels who would command the province troops in the coming year's campaign. Along with his new or renewed colonel's commission, the governor sent each appointee a packet of blank commission forms for ensigns, lieutenants, and captains, to be distributed as he saw fit. The subordinate commands within his regiment would be assigned thereafter in accordance with the prospective officers' success in attracting men to the service. In 1755, for example, a captain was expected to enlist fifty men; a lieutenant, twenty-five; and an ensign, fifteen.[28] Junior officers in turn made informal arrangements with prospective noncommissioned

27. The advantage of the provincial recruiter over his regular counterpart was a complex one, consisting not only in the greater appeal of the provincial armies but also in the provincials' greater ability to operate within community social structures and to secure the cooperation of local justices of the peace. An example helps illustrate this point.

Early in 1759, Capt. Francis Legge of the 46th Regiment, recruiting near Boston, reported difficulties to General Amherst:

I listed a man the other day who came voluntarily to my lodgings to enlist. I sent him before Justice [Richard] Dana of this town in order to have him sworn and attested, which the judge refused to do because the man had not been listed twenty-four hours. I have since found out that the justice's reason for not swearing the man was to give some people of the town who are employed to list for the provincials the opportunity to entice the man away from me; which they did and listed him for the provincials, first making him return the advance money I gave him and paying twenty shillings besides. [Legge to Jeffery Amherst, 18 Feb. 1759, quoted in Norreys Jephson O'Conor, *A Servant of the Crown in England and North America, 1756–61* (New York, 1938), 144–145]

In this case Dana was availing himself of a technicality in the Mutiny Act, which governed enlistment. A man could renounce his initial agreement to serve if he did not make an attestation, in not less than 24 hours and not more than four days, before a justice of the peace, saying that he understood the terms of enlistment and that he had taken the oath of fidelity. Any recruit who declined to make the attestation, returned the money paid him by the enlisting officer (usually a guinea, or a pistole and a dollar), and paid a 20s. fine was free to go. (See Pargellis, *Loudoun*, 117, 123.) By preventing the man from making the attestation, Justice Dana had enabled the provincial recruiters to have a soldier for the price of paying his 20s. fine. From the British point of view, this was theft; the colonials probably thought it was cooperation in a humanitarian cause.

28. William Shirley to John Winslow, 12 Feb. 1755, "Journal of Colonel John Winslow . . . ," Nova Scotia Historical Society, *Collections*, IV (1884), 117. See also Ephraim Williams to John Burk, 11 Apr. 1755, MS in the John Burk Correspondence, French and Indian War Collection, American Antiquarian Society, Worcester, Mass.

officers, promising sergeants' or corporals' billets in their companies in return for the enlistments of private soldiers.[29] Along with the commissions, the governor dispatched an authorization for the colonel "to beat his drum anywhere within this province for enlisting volunteers in his majesty's service, in a regiment to be forthwith raised for the service and defense of his majesty's colonies in North America," in the coming campaign. These "beating orders" also instructed local militia commanders "not to give the [newly appointed colonel] any obstructions or molestations herein; but on the contrary to afford him all necessary encouragement and assistance, for which this is a sufficient warrant."[30]

Militia officers mainly encouraged and assisted in raising troops by ordering musters of their units, at which recruiters would appear and solicit enlistments. If an insufficient number of men proved willing to volunteer, the governor could make up the shortage in his province's quota under the provisions of "An Act for Levying Soldiers" (passed 1754), which empowered him to issue a general impressment order. Upon receiving such an order, each militia colonel would muster his regiment, and subordinate commanders would again ask for volunteers. If none emerged, the requisite number of men, in theory to be drawn from the idle elements of each town, would be conscripted into service. Law and custom permitted any "pressed man" to hire a substitute to go in his place, providing he paid a five-pound fine to the province. Those who hired replacements struck whatever bargain they could with the men who took their places. The going rate in 1756 was evidently about ten pounds Lawful Money; by 1759 it had increased to somewhere between fourteen and fifteen pounds.[31] As this increase indicates, while some impressed men were indeed of the shiftless sort envisioned in the authorizing legislation, others were chosen from among the better-off elements in the community, simply because they could afford to pay for substitutes.

Managed within the authority structures of Massachusetts villages by

29. See, e.g., the arrangements made between Job Winslow and David Perry, in Perry, "Recollections of an Old Soldier," *Magazine of History*, CXXXVII (1928), 20; and those between Rufus Putnam and Captain William Paige in Putnam, *The Memoirs of Rufus Putnam* (Boston, 1903), 32. Indirect evidence also exists in the diary of David Holdin, entry of 16 Apr. 1760, "Journal of Sergeant Holden," Massachusetts Historical Society, *Proceedings*, 2d Ser., IV (1889), 387–409. All citations of soldiers' diaries and orderly books hereafter will be made according to the form given in Appendix B, i.e., by diarist's name and date of entry. See also Ephraim Williams to John Burk, 11 Apr. 1755, Burk Correspondence.

30. William Shirley, beating order for John Winslow, 10 Feb. 1755, "Journal of Winslow," Nova Scotia Hist. Soc., *Colls.*, IV (1884), 118.

31. "An Act for Levying Soldiers, and to Protect Soliders and Seamen From Being Arrested for Debt," passed 20 Apr. 1754: *Acts and Resolves*, III, Pt. ii, 734–738, 808. See also Pargellis, *Loudoun*, 113. For Rufus Putnam's experience as a hired substitute, see his *Memoirs*, 25, n. 1 (a copy of a receipt dated 2 Apr. 1759).

leaders who knew a great deal about their townsmen's affairs, the process of impressment for the provincial armies differed widely from naval impressment, which amounted to the virtual abduction of merchant seamen. Militia officers instead conducted the land impress in such a way as to conscript the required number with a minimum of social strain. Any number of expedients, as varied as the communities in which impressment took place, were used to achieve this result. A typical method was to impress more men than the local quota required—a practice that allowed pressed men to share the expense of hiring the substitute and kept the burden within reasonable limits for those forced to contribute.[32] This practice explains a cryptic entry in the diary of a provincial soldier, Joseph Nichols:

> March the 27th, 1758. I 'listed [in his] majesty's service against Canada, and myself to do a turn this year for Captain Belknap's two sons, *viz.*, Samuel Howard and Jeremiah Belknap.

Captain Jeremiah Belknap, Sr., commanded the Framingham militia company. He had responded to his colonel's call by impressing his son and his son-in-law, who pooled their resources and paid Nichols to serve their "turn."[33] Belknap thus managed to handle impressment equitably—no one could accuse him of favoritism—while spreading the cost to keep from taxing either of the pressed men beyond his means. Such informal arrangements were so much a part of the fabric of local society and daily life that few recognizable documentary traces survive.

Another important means of promoting enlistment, which has left somewhat more direct evidence, was the use of kinship connections to help secure recruits. A unique set of personnel records from 1756 preserves the names and ranks of 3,047 provincials in six Massachusetts regiments on the Crown Point expedition, and includes supplementary information on the ages, occupations, birthplaces, and residences of at least 70 percent of the soldiers as well. These lists reveal that surnames were very widely shared in the army: the 3,047 soldiers had only 1,443 family names among them. Men with the same last name, of course, were not necessarily relatives, but in 104 cases two or more men within the same company shared not only a surname but birthplace or residence at enlistment—a circumstance that much more strongly indicates family ties. Out of these 104 groups, 65 had a member (or two) who, as an officer or a noncommis-

32. Leach, *Arms for Empire*, 22–23.

33. On Belknap, see Nancy S. Voye, ed., *Massachusetts Officers in the French and Indian Wars, 1748–1763* (Boston, 1975), entries 492–493. Joseph Nichols was no drifter, but an apparently promising (though poor) young man, recently married and evidently in need of money. In his journal, additional notes dated Mar. 1762 indicate that he kept school at Holliston following his service—a job for which he was paid 40s. per month, about the same rate he had earned as a clerk in the army during the 1758 campaign.

sioned officer, would have been active in raising the company.[34] Typical of such groups were the three Coffins in Captain Jonathan Pearson's company, all from Newbury: the twenty-five-year-old Corporal Tristram and Privates Benjamin and Joseph, nineteen and twenty-one years old respectively. Typical, too, were the four Bullocks—a lieutenant, a sergeant, and two privates, all from Rehoboth—in Captain James House's company. Such cases afford strong evidence of kinship between the men, and enough instances exist in which men of higher and lower rank within the same companies were definitely related to confirm the instrumentality of kinship in recruitment. Sons enlisted under their fathers: Sergeant Joseph Clark of Mendon, for example, served with his seventeen-year-old son, Joseph Jr., in Captain Benjamin Thwing's company; Private Samuel Robinson, Jr., a seventeen-year-old man from Hardwick, served in the company his father commanded. Older brothers enlisted younger ones, uncles recruited nephews, and cousins signed up to serve under cousins. All three Boydens in Captain William Bacon's company were kinsmen: Ensign Elhanan Boyden of Walpole was the elder brother of Private Jonathan and the first cousin of Private Ebenezer, also of Walpole, and was evidently the officer who enlisted them. In Colonel Jonathan Bagley's company Corporal

34. Quantitative statements in this chapter are derived from my analysis of a unique set of "descriptive lists" (hereafter cited as Lists) made during the Crown Point expedition of 1756, now collected and bound as "Muster Rolls, 1755–1756," Vol. XCIV of the Massachusetts Archives, at the State House, Boston. These lists were mainly collected at Fort Edward and Fort William Henry by company clerks in late July and August. They record information including the name, age, birthplace, residence, civilian occupation, condition of service (voluntary, hired, or impressed), and rank of each man, along with other less consistently recorded data. This information exists in a fair state of completeness on approximately four out of every five soldiers in the six regiments Massachusetts fielded for the expedition. Although a number of descriptive lists were made later in the war, there was never another instance of such comprehensive coverage of the province's troops.

In early Oct., as the campaign was drawing to a close, the provincial commander, Maj. Gen. John Winslow, directed that another set of rolls be drawn up. These were to record the physical condition of each soldier, by unit, rank, and name. These rolls and descriptive lists are a combination unique among the documents surviving from the Seven Years' War in Massachusetts. The descriptive lists contain sufficient data to reconstruct a social profile of the more than 3,000 men in the regiments of 1756. (For an extended treatment of this topic, see Anderson, "A People's Army.") The additional information on soldiers' physical condition permits a correlation of health and other factors, such as age and rank, and offers the opportunity to estimate the deadliness of wilderness campaigning to the soldier and to the army as a whole. (The health and welfare of the army are discussed at length in chap. 3, below.) My analysis of these lists was made with the aid of an IBM 370/168 computer, utilizing the Statistical Package for the Social Sciences (SPSS), Version 6, as described in Norman H. Nie *et al.*, *SPSS*, 2d ed. (New York, 1975). Coding and methodological concerns are discussed in "War and the Bay Colony," app. III, "Methods of Quantitative Analysis." With additions from other sources as noted, quantitative statements hereafter (including all tables) are based on the analyzed descriptive lists.

Moses Lowell, a forty-five-year-old yeoman from Amesbury, apparently enlisted three of his nephews—John, Gideon, and Eliphalet, all sons of his eldest brother.[35]

Genealogies make it possible to identify such straightforward cases of blood relationship, but patrilineal ties would by no means have been the only form of kinship instrumental in recruitment: in-law relationships and collateral connections between families of different names must have been no less influential. The process of enlistment thus created unusually close ties between the army's leaders and its rank and file—ties incomprehensible to regular soldiers like the redcoats, who understood that a virtually unbridgeable chasm separated officers from other ranks. Rather than being held together like the British army with draconian discipline in a system that discouraged officers from even learning their men's Christian names,[36] the provincial regiments were in some measure bound by kinship ties. Such relationships both tended to diminish whatever awe an epaulet might inspire in a private's mind and to mitigate an officer's tendency to see himself as a different breed of human being from his subordinates.

Other recruiting strategies further undermined the development of professionalism among the provincials. The growth of personal bonds during service and the undertaking of informal agreements relating to enlistment were central to the annual re-creation of the Massachusetts forces. Again, these were the sort of relationships and understandings likely to escape documentation, but two veterans' memoirs, written in the early nineteenth century, unmistakably show the process at work.

In the spring of 1758, David Perry, a sixteen-year-old shoemaker's apprentice who had recently joined the Dighton militia company, attended a drill session on a day when "there were officers on the parade-ground, to enlist men for the next campaign."[37] He signed on as a soldier in Colonel Jedediah Preble's regiment and saw service under Captain Job Winslow in the abortive Crown Point expedition. He liked soldiering enough to sign up again in 1759; this time he was recruited by a Dighton man, Lieutenant John Richmond. Perry expected, he wrote, "to join Capt. Nathan Rogers' company with the lads that enlisted with me." Lieutenant Richmond was

35. Source of information of Coffins, Bullocks, Clarks, and Robinsons: Lists. On the Boydens: Wallace Clarke Boyden *et al.*, *Thomas Boyden and His Descendants* (Boston, 1901), 12–13, 20–21, 38–40. On the Lowells: Delmar Rial Lowell, *The Historic Genealogy of the Lowells of America from 1639 to 1899* (Rutland, Vt., 1899), 312–313, 315, 318, 331.

36. See John Keegan, *The Face of Battle* (New York, 1976), 186–187. Although Keegan writes specifically here of Wellington's army, he is describing a system of discipline that had existed a half-century earlier, probably in an even more intense form, among the redcoats in North America. See also below, chap. 4; and Frey, *British Soldier*, chap. 4, "Crimes and Courts."

37. Perry, "Recollections," *Mag. Hist.* CXXXVII (1928), 8.

unexpectedly transferred to another regiment, however, and this momentarily confused the situation. Richmond urged Perry to accompany him to the new assignment as his "waiter," or servant, promising that the young soldier would "live as well as he [the lieutenant] did." Captain Rogers, the company commander, refused to release Perry from his unit, and a vigorous wrangle resulted. The regiment's major finally settled the dispute by ruling that only Perry could decide with whom—Richmond or Rogers—he would serve. Perry chose Richmond, and on the way to Boston, where they were to embark on the Saint Lawrence expedition, the lieutenant proved "a[s] good as his word as to my fare," Perry recalled: "I rode his horse as much as he did, until we gained the company."[38] At the end of the 1759 campaign, at Halifax, Perry fell in again with Job Winslow, his previous year's captain, who had been promoted to major. Perry spent most of the winter with him, apparently acting as his servant. He returned home in February.[39]

Perry had been back at his trade only a month when Winslow contacted him with an offer: "If I would enlist what men I could, and go back to Halifax with him, I should have a sergeant's berth . . . ; and if no vacancy occurred, I should be cleared from duty through the season." Perry soon collected "eight or ten likely young men"; but "there being no vacancy for a sergeant's berth, I lived with the Colonel, Major, and Chaplain of the regiment, and fared very well."[40] In the fall of the year he returned once again to Dighton, where he remained until he completed his indenture.

Perry served for the last time in 1762, when Job Winslow, by that time a lieutenant colonel, renewed the offer of a sergeant's billet. Once again Perry raised "a number of recruits" and marched them off to Boston. This time Winslow was able to make good on his offer, and Perry became a sergeant. In 1762 he saw action in Newfoundland, fell gravely ill, and barely survived. When he returned to Dighton for a long convalescence, he was not far past his twenty-first birthday.[41]

The most striking aspect of Perry's 1819 memoir, "Recollections of an Old Soldier," is the vividness of his memory, after six decades, of the promises made to him and of the precision with which those undertakings were fulfilled. By his account two commissioned officers made him three promises relating to recruitment. Fulfillment of two of the promises entailed fraternization between himself and his superiors—personal associations so close as to be unthinkable in any professional military force. Yet it is equally clear that such arrangements and the existence of close relations

38. *Ibid.*, 12.
39. *Ibid.*, 19.
40. *Ibid.*, 20.
41. *Ibid.*, 22, 30.

across ranks were crucial both to the recruiting process and to the routine functioning of the army. Rufus Putnam's memoir of the war, written at about the same time as Perry's, offers further instructive examples, since it also turns on the themes of promise and fulfillment.

Rufus Putnam first enlisted in 1757 at the age of nineteen. More ambitious than Perry, he wished to distinguish himself as a soldier and found great satisfaction in his promotion to sergeant in 1759, during his third tour of duty.[42] Almost immediately thereafter, however, things began to go wrong. Because he had been trained as a millwright, Putnam was detached from his regiment to build a sawmill—an order he resented, since it would take him away from his sergeant's duties. He submitted to reassignment only when Timothy Ruggles, a provincial brigadier general, personally ordered him to do so. (Putnam finally complied, he wrote, because "the brigadier knew me very well, and I had known him for many years . . . ; nor did I like to offend an officer whom I so highly respected.") Putnam's skill so impressed the regular engineer supervising the mill construction that he offered Putnam a dollar a day (about four times his sergeant's salary) to stay on as the operator of the sawmill after the release of his regiment. When Putnam applied for his pay at the end of November, however, he was astonished to receive three dollars, rather than the thirty or so he had expected. He had understood that he was to earn a dollar a day from the time of his regiment's release, but the engineer instead insisted that he was entitled to be paid only for the three days he had served past the expiration of his enlistment.[43] Putnam, feeling cheated, resolved "never to engage again as a soldier." He moved to New Braintree, where he had bought land, and set to work as a farmer.[44]

Putnam remained a civilian only until March 1760. At that point, Captain William Paige of Hardwick appeared with recruiting orders and a personal request from Brigadier Ruggles that Putnam raise troops for the coming campaign in return for a lieutenant's commission in Ruggles's regiment.[45] Still stinging from his encounter with the British engineer, Putnam hesitated. He hesitated, too, because he knew that several of the "older settlers" in New Braintree had sought commissions in the regiment and had been refused. The rejected applicants "appeared very angry, and complained that the town was insulted by my appointment. Therefore," he thought, "I had very little reason to expect much success in recruiting among them." Soon, however, he found himself sought out by men who wished to serve under him and accepted the recruiting orders despite his

42. Putnam, *Memoirs*, 31.
43. *Ibid.*, 27, 28.
44. *Ibid.*, 31.
45. Cf. *ibid.*, 32, and Voye, ed., *Officers*, entries 4204–4206.

misgivings. He recruited a number of soldiers but unwisely allowed Paige to enlist them personally in his company. Paige was miserably ineffectual as a recruiter in his own right, but enjoyed an inestimable advantage in his lack of scruples. In order to preserve his claim to a captaincy, Paige took credit for enlisting the troops who thought they were signing on to serve under Putnam. When the troops discovered his action, it was "much to their disappointment," Putnam wrote; "and to my own," he added, since "I was left to go a-begging." [46]

Brigadier Ruggles was in Boston and Putnam could find no one able to redress his grievance. Eventually another regimental commander, Colonel Abijah Willard, offered Putnam an ensign's commission, which he accepted. He tried to raise a few more men; "but," he recalled, "I had very little success, as might well be expected after what had taken place respecting the men I had enlisted." He came up with only three new recruits. [47]

Rufus Putnam set down these complicated disappointments in detail when he was an old man, following a distinguished career as a general officer in the War of Independence. He did it, he said, so that "all, but especially those unexperienced youth such as I was, [might] be cautioned how far they trust the friendship of those [in] whose interest it may be to dupe them." [48] Putnam and Perry agreed that the system was supposed to be based on informal agreements and understandings. Both men's accounts indicate how thoroughly the operation of the provincial forces depended on personal contacts between officers (even officers of high rank) and enlisted men. In Putnam's case, however, the system failed to function according to expectation, and he brooded over the failure ever after.

Putnam's decision to go to work on the sawmill depended on the intervention of a brigadier general, whom Putnam obeyed *not* because of his military authority, but because they had previously been acquainted and because Putnam personally respected Brigadier Ruggles. In the following year, despite his disillusionment, Putnam finally agreed to raise soldiers in large part because Ruggles specifically requested that he try. His hesitation demonstrates the extent to which recruiting depended on the recruiter's standing and reputation in the community. Putnam believed he would have little luck recruiting New Braintree men so long as the older settlers—the logical candidates for leading soldiers from the town—had not been recognized as leaders. The troops he initially enlisted understood that they would serve under him, since they were "much" disappointed to be mustered into Paige's company without Putnam as their lieutenant. It would be difficult to overestimate the importance of the recruits' personal

46. Putnam, *Memoirs*, 32–33.
47. *Ibid.*, 33.
48. *Ibid.*

confidence in the man who persuaded them to enlist. After Putnam's original recruits suffered their "disappointment," he could find few men who were willing to risk following him, even though his position as an ensign was already formally secure. Their reluctance hardly surprised him. Putnam had lost face as well as recruits and knew very well that his reputation could no longer justify many recruits' confidence. For the common soldier, the decision to enlist was much more than merely agreeing to serve: it meant choosing a leader.

We can understand the apparently erratic behavior of provincial armies in the field only by first recognizing that intense personal loyalties and expectations of reciprocity between men and officers suffused the process by which these armies were created. In its institutional ideal, a provincial army was a human pyramid, hierarchically organized and held together with chains of command, authority, and obligation, extending from the commander in chief at its peak down to the individual soldiers at its base. But the reality of recruitment gave the lie to the superficial orderliness of the provincial armies' organization. Rather than a uniform hierarchy of officers and men, a provincial army was in fact a confederation of tiny war bands, bound together less by the formal relationships of command than by an organic network of kinship and personal loyalties.

III

Only once during the war did a provincial general order the collection of a large body of information on the personnel under his command. In late July 1756, at Fort William Henry, Major General John Winslow had the clerks in his six Massachusetts regiments compile "descriptive lists" of each unit, recording data that could be used to identify deserters.[49] The result was, in effect, a census which affords two valuable opportunities. First, it provides a unique organizational snapshot of the Massachusetts provincial army, not in the ideal form envisioned in its authorizing legislation, but as it was realized in the field. Second, it permits an analysis of the social composition of the army, a glimpse into the civilian backgrounds of the great majority of its three thousand–plus soldiers.

In its formal organization the provincial army represented a scaled-down copy of the British regular establishment. Its fundamental component was the company, a unit of forty to one hundred men, led by three commissioned officers (a captain assisted by a lieutenant and an ensign) and seven noncommissioned officers (three sergeants and four corporals).

data on provincial force

49. "Muster Rolls," Massachusetts Archives, XCIV.

Ten companies made up a battalion, the basic tactical unit of the army. The army's principal administrative echelon was the regiment, which could consist of from one to four battalions. The Massachusetts regiments under Winslow's command had only one battalion each. Just as the company was commanded by three "company officers," the regiment was headed by three "field officers"—a colonel, a lieutenant colonel, and a major. Besides the three field and thirty company officers who together constituted its "line officers," each regiment had a six-member "staff" to perform administrative functions. Staff officers included the adjutant, who supervised personnel matters; the commissary and the quartermaster, who were responsible for the acquisition, storage, and distribution of food and matériel; the chaplain; and the surgeon and surgeon's mate. (An armorer and armorer's mate were also attached to the staff, but were regarded as technicians rather than officers.) In total strength a single-battalion regiment might range from four hundred to a thousand men, plus officers.

As in everything else relating to provincial military organization, there was considerable disparity between the intention and its realization. The six Massachusetts regiments in 1756 should have totaled sixty companies; instead, there were fifty-six. Only two regiments had their full complement of ten companies; the rest had nine apiece.[50]

According to the authorizing legislation the 1756 provincial companies were supposed to have thirty-eight "centinels," or private soldiers, plus a drummer and a clerk.[51] The actual composition of the units varied greatly, but over the course of the campaign each company averaged fifty-four men, including replacements.[52] Of this number, approximately twenty-five or thirty were present and on duty at any given time; only rarely would as many as forty men be on hand and fit for service in a typical company. Nor were all companies led by captains. As a traditional perquisite the three field officers of each regiment also commanded their unit's first three com-

50. For regiments that the army comprised and their strengths, see Table 2.

51. The ideal strengths of provincial units and the complements of men at each rank can be inferred from information in the acts by which money was appropriated for the provincial establishment: in this case, *Acts and Resolves*, XV, 311–312, which stipulates one captain for each 50-man company and one colonel for each 500-man regiment. Subtracting the 3 officers, 7 noncommissioned officers, the drummer, and the clerk of each company gives an expected centinel strength for each company of 38 in the army of 1756.

52. By 11 and 12 Oct., according to the lists, 366 replacments had arrived; as many as 500 were dispatched from Boston. See Loudoun to the duke of Cumberland, 3 Oct. 1756, in Stanley Pargellis, ed., *Military Affairs in North America, 1748–1765* (Hamden, Conn., 1969; [orig. publ., New York, 1936]), 240–241; and Shirley to Loudoun, 23 Aug. 1756, Loudoun Papers, LO 1563, Henry E. Huntington Library, San Marino, Calif. Hereafter material from the Loudoun Papers will be identified by date and LO document number; quoted material from the Loudoun Papers appears by permission of the Huntington Library.

panies, in which case each company was assigned an extra lieutenant (called a captain-lieutenant or a first lieutenant) who performed the actual tasks of command. The net effect of this practice was to swell the number of lieutenants above the authorized level and to funnel some extra pay into the pockets of the field officers.

One of the provincial regiments of 1756—the one commanded by Colonel Richard Gridley of Boston—departed from the organization stipulated by the General Court in having an artillery train attached. This unique unit, twice the size of a normal company, was commanded by Gridley himself, aided by seven lieutenants (among whom was Paul Revere). Its enlisted personnel consisted of matrosses, privates who sponged the cannon bores, rammed the charges, and positioned the guns; gunners, specialists who aimed and fired the pieces; and another set of specialists called bombardiers, who served the train's mortars.

With the exception of the members of the train, all the Massachusetts provincials in 1756 were infantrymen. The provincial establishment thus lacked not only the size but also the complexity of the British army; there were no functionally specialized units such as cavalry, grenadiers, dragoons, or light infantry.[53] The province's single-battalion regiments were never brigaded together, and its officer corps consequently lacked both brigadiers and brigade-majors. The only general officer among the Massachusetts provincials in 1756 was their commander in chief, Major General John Winslow, who was compelled to command his colonels directly, without even the assistance of aides-de-camp. In the later years of the conflict, Massachusetts' provincial forces did become somewhat more complex. Two brigadier generals (Timothy Ruggles and Jedediah Preble) eventually commanded regiments made up of two battalions each, and a light-infantry battalion was organized under Lieutenant Colonel Oliver Partridge in 1758. But despite a passing resemblance, provincial forces never managed to do more than mimic the regulars. In their functioning, as in their recruitment, great disparities persisted between the ideal and the actual.

One of the most important differences beween regular and irregular organizations was that the provincial army was never a permanent body. An officer corps was freshly commissioned every year and raised new troops to fill the army's units. Men enlisted not for a term of years or for the duration of the war, but for a campaign that they understood would last eight months. By law, none of the enlisted men could be compelled to serve longer than twelve months. Service was further limited by explicit statements built into commissions and enlistment agreements. In 1756, for ex-

53. For a numerical breakdown of the army of 1756 by rank, see Table 3.

ample, the men enlisted specifically in, and officers were commissioned explicitly for, "an expedition against Crown Point whereof John Winslow, Esquire, is commander in chief."[54] Both soldiers and governments took the limitations on service implied or expressed by such agreements seriously.[55] While soldiers might reenlist (and often did) and officers might be recommissioned (and often were) from year to year, the provincial army itself was perennially a new creation. Any continuity it enjoyed was accidental. The General Court recognized the hazard and the inefficiency of annually fielding forces that were largely composed of inexperienced troops. In the later years of the war it tried to remedy the problem by offering increasingly larger bounties to induce reenlistment. The very growth of these bounties, which eventually surpassed the equivalent of a year's salary for a centinel, indicates the difficulty of securing reenlistments.[56]

Officers were apparently more willing to serve multiple terms; but here, too, discontinuity posed a severe problem. Captains, for example, usually served more than one term. Among the forty-five captains who commanded companies on the Crown Point expedition in 1756 and whose careers can be traced from 1754 through 1763, thirty-seven (82.2 percent) were members of the army for more than a single campaign.[57] Almost half (twenty-two, or 48.9 percent) participated in three or more campaigns, and one—Captain Abel Keen of Pembroke—actually served in every year from 1755 through 1763. Yet of the thirty-seven officers who served several terms, only fourteen served their terms successively. Among the twenty-two who served in three or more years, only five served without interruption. Furthermore, only two managed to serve repeatedly under the same commander; the twenty-five captains whose successive regimental commanders can be ascertained served under from two to four different colonels.[58] Among field officers, the same patterns held. They too tended to repeat service, but usually only for two or three campaigns. Moreover, the higher their initial rank, the less likely they were to repeat their service.[59] The tendency for men whose initial appointment was as lieutenant

54. Copy of commission, in A. W. Lauber and A. C. Flick, eds., *The Papers of Sir William Johnson*, 13 vols. (Albany, N.Y., 1921–1962), IX, 484.

55. See below, chap. 6.

56. See Table 1.

57. Voye, ed., *Officers*, provides an alphabetical listing of all commissioned officers reflected in the Massachusetts Archives, Vols. XCI–XCIX, with separate entries for each officer's name, his dates and length of service, his residence (when known), and his unit commander's name. These were analyzed for service records of all captains who served in 1756 and all field officers who served during the war as a whole. For summaries see Tables 4–7.

58. See Table 4.

59. See Tables 5–7.

colonel or colonel to serve for only a single year would have exacerbated the problem of provincial continuity even if these officers had had experienced troops to lead every year.

The military problems engendered by lack of continuity and by short-term service reflected one of the provincial army's core characteristics, its exceptional voluntariness. This was an aspect of provincial military organization that puzzled and frustrated British officers, who were accustomed to an army that (although technically voluntary itself) relied upon long-term enlistments and freely applied physical coercion. One of the few coercive tools that the province could bring to bear was impressment, but even that, as we have seen, was managed in such a way as to minimize actual compulsion. The practice of hiring substitutes astounded and outraged British officers, who believed that it was more widespread—and more demoralizing—than in fact it was. The earl of Loudoun, for example, added it to his litany of complaint against New Englanders. "Affairs here," he reported from New York late in the summer of 1756, "are in a very bad situation; . . . the New England men, by all accounts, [are] frightened out of their senses at the name of a Frenchman; for those are not the men they use[d] to send out, but fellows hired by other men who should have gone themselves."[60]

As usual, Loudoun overstated the case. In 1756 fewer than ten men in a hundred among the Massachusetts forces were hired. By far the largest number of provincials were volunteers: nearly nine-tenths of all the Bay Colony's troops had enlisted of their own free will. Only 2.2 percent had been drafted out of their home militia units.[61] The 247 hired men *did* generally differ from the rest of the army. They tended to be older, to rank lower, to be more often born outside the Bay Colony, and to be more frequently unskilled in their civilian occupations. They were also likelier to die, fall ill, or desert by the end of the campaign than their volunteer counterparts. In short, hired men, at least in 1756, had more the look of a permanently marginal group than did the volunteers.[62] But the single most important characteristic of such men was surely their rarity. Voluntary recruits chiefly accounted for the army's social complexion. The provincials' manifest shortcomings as soldiers cannot be blamed on a prevalence of hireling, second-class manpower in the ranks.[63]

60. Loudoun to Cumberland, 29 Aug. 1756, in Pargellis, ed., *Military Affairs*, 232. Cf. Abercromby to Loudoun, 25 Feb. 1758, LO 5668, cited in Shy, *People Armed*, 265, n. 22.

61. Conditions of enlistment are summarized in Table 8.

62. Comparisons of the men in the three enlistment categories by various characteristics are summarized in Table 9.

63. Cf. Shy, "A New Look," in *People Armed*, 23–33, esp. 30–32.

The soldiers of Massachusetts Bay were generally young men, younger than the age at which men in their province usually married. The median age was 23 and the modal age 18, but the presence of a small group of older men raised the mean age to 26.3 years. Nearly three-quarters of all soldiers were under 30 years old.[64] The overwhelming majority of them had been following a manual occupation of some sort before joining the army, typically a job related to agriculture. These men either worked for themselves and were called "farmers," "yeomen," and "husbandmen," or they worked for someone else as "laborers." The last formed the largest single occupational group in the army, over a third of the men whose occupations are known. Farmers, yeomen, and husbandmen formed a smaller but still substantial group, just over one-fifth of the soldiers. "Husbandmen"—an appellation that implied the ownership of at least some part of one's farm—predominated among them. With the exception of eighty-one sailors and mariners, the rest of the soldiers with manual occupations—two out of five men—were artisans of some sort. Soldiers had been following fifty-seven different trades before enlistment, among which woodworking was the most common, followed by leather-, metal-, and cloth-based crafts. Fewer than two in every hundred soldiers—just 42 of the 2,175 with known occupations—had nonmanual occupations. Seven of them, all officers, called themselves "gentlemen"; most of the rest had been pursuing such modest commercial callings as victualler, tobacconist, and trader.[65]

Soldiers had been living in every part of the province at the time they enlisted and, essentially, mirrored its distribution of population. Over 90 percent of the provincials were residents of Massachusetts; the rest included residents of New Hampshire, Connecticut, and Rhode Island. Five out of every eight Massachusetts residents had been living within thirty miles of Boston when they enlisted. Just over half had been living in the three counties (Essex, Middlesex, and Suffolk) that the central area of the seventeenth-century Bay Colony comprised; about one-fifth were living in the Old Colony region of Bristol, Plymouth, and Barnstable counties, and another fifth were residents of the undersettled western counties of Hampshire and Worcester. The remaining 5 percent had made their homes in the handful of maritime towns that constituted York County (Maine). More men were residents of Boston at enlistment than of any other single town—229 in all.[66]

The great majority of the army's Massachusetts residents—more than

64. Age distribution of provincials by five-year cohort is summarized in Table 10.

65. Occupational structure of provincials in 1756 is discussed in Anderson, "A People's Army," *WMQ*, 3d Ser., XL (1983), 506–512; see also "War and the Bay Colony," I, 92; II, 449–451.

66. Residences at enlistment of provincials of 1756 are summarized in Tables 11, 12.

eight out of every ten—had been born in the province. Of the 429 soldiers who were *not* natives, roughly half came from each side of the Atlantic: 212 from Great Britain and the European continent, 217 from various colonies in the Western Hemisphere (mostly New England). Unlike these long-distance migrants, the Massachusetts natives were a home-prone lot. Nearly three-fifths of them were still living in their town of birth when they enlisted, and more than three-fourths of them still lived in their native county. Of the one-fifth who had moved beyond the borders of their native county, most were originally from Suffolk, Middlesex, and Essex; and the majority of these had settled in the western counties of Worcester and Hampshire.[67] How far a man tended to move from his hometown, once he left, depended on how densely his native region was populated and how close to Boston it lay. Migrants born closest to the capital, in the most heavily peopled part of the colony, usually moved the furthest; those born in the more lightly settled regions of the province, less far.[68]

Among the various occupational groups represented in the army, no single one had been especially footloose or especially persistent in its prewar experience. It is clear, however, that soldiers from areas in which one variety of occupation predominated among young men tended to remain close to home if they shared the dominant vocation, and mobile if they did not. Among soldiers from the area of the original Bay Colony, where most young men claimed an affiliation with a trade, artisans were the group most likely to persist in their birthplace until enlistment. Among men from the Old Colony region, where laboring was the principal occupation of young men, laborers tended to be the most persistent; and among men born in the west, where farming was the young man's most frequent vocation, farmers were likeliest to remain in their hometown until they joined the army.[69] This pattern reflected men's efforts to match their ambitions to opportunities. In an area as heavily populated as Essex County, for example, a young man who wanted to become a farmer would have found it difficult to acquire the necessary land locally, except by inheritance. Farming was thus an ambition facilitated by movement, most likely to the west or (for men born in Essex) to New Hampshire. Following a trade, on the other hand, represented an ambition more easily fulfilled at home, or nearby.

67. Birthplaces of provincials: see Tables 13–15.

68. Levels of movement for men born in Suffolk, Middlesex, Essex, Plymouth, and Bristol counties were calculated for their various hometowns as a function of distance from Boston. For a complete discussion, see Anderson, "War and the Bay Colony," I, 94; II, 453–456.

69. Levels of persistence by region of birth, for men in various occupational categories in the provincial troops of 1756, are summarized in Table 16.

The soldier's age was the single factor most strongly related to his movement or persistence before enlistment. In general, the youngest men in the army (who were also the most numerous) were the ones most often living in or near their birthplace when they enlisted. Immigrants into the province were uniformly the oldest, and transatlantic immigrants the oldest of all. On average, they were more than four years older than soldiers who still lived in their hometown at enlistment—28.9 as compared to 24.3 years of age.[70] Among all the age- and nativity-groups the British were on the whole both the oldest and the farthest from home; they also followed different occupations than native recruits, trades that reflected their origins in Great Britain rather than conditions in the Bay Colony.[71]

Because of its temporary, voluntary nature, the provincial army broadly corresponded in composition with the makeup of its parent society. The army was not heavily weighted with vagrant or marginal elements; while such men clearly made up a segment of the organization, they composed only a small minority of its membership, probably not much greater than their share of the population at large. The rank structure of the provincials further reinforces the impression of representativeness, since the army's impermanence precluded the development of a systematic promotion system. Officers who served several terms could in no way expect advancement. Among the thirty-seven captains from 1756 who served in more than one campaign, twenty-one retained their original rank. Nine captains had been or would be promoted; seven either were demoted or fluctuated in rank during later service.[72] Thus while previous experience could lead to higher rank, it offered no guarantee; civilian social standing was a more powerful determinant of military rank.

The most notable characteristic of rank in the provincial regiments was the lack of any clear-cut division between the occupations of officers and enlisted men. Among the regulars, the line between enlisted and commissioned personnel was sharp, if not impassable; the purchase system ensured that most men who entered the officer corps would at least be men of means, and probably gentlemen.[73] In the Massachusetts forces, by contrast, over half of the company officers identified themselves with manual occupations, and in fact followed the same livelihoods as private soldiers, although in different proportions. All that can be said about differences between ranks on the basis of occupation is that some ranks drew more of

70. Levels of movement, by average age and cohort, for soliders of 1756: see Tables 17, 18.

71. Occupational patterns of British-born versus Massachusetts-born provincials of 1756: see Tables 19, 20.

72. See Table 4.

73. The cost of an ensign's billet in the regular army in 1759 was between £200 and £400 sterling, according to Pargellis, *Loudoun*, 308, n. 36.

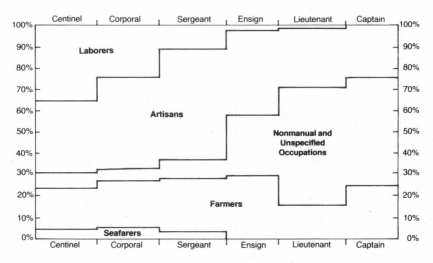

Figure 1. Occupational Distribution, by Rank, of Provincial Forces, 1756.
N = 2,309. See also Table 21. Drawn by Richard Stinely

their members from certain occupations than other ranks did. For example, centinels were most closely associated with the civilian occupation of laborer: centinels made up 75.1 percent of the army, but comprised 87.5 percent of the laborers. By comparison, only 51.2 percent of men with nonmanual occupations were centinels. Officers, on the other hand, were most strongly allied with husbandry and nonmanual pursuits. Company officers made up 5.9 percent of the whole army, yet 7.2 percent of the husbandmen and 21.9 percent of the nonmanual workers in the army held commissions. Overall, the picture is of rather gradual occupational shadings from rank to rank, from private to captain.[74]

The ages of the soldiers were also continuously graded: seniority in the provincial army was often literally that. Private soldiers averaged 25.8 years of age; noncommissioned officers, 27.8; and officers, 32.8.[75] When broken down into individual ranks and ages and compared with occupations, it appears that the relationship of rank to age was a highly consistent one. Among farmers in the army, those who served as privates had a mean age of 26.5, while those who became captains averaged 37.1 years of age; among laborers, privates had a mean age of 25.8 and the two officers 38.5; among seafarers, privates averaged 27 and sergeants 28.4; among artisans, the privates' mean age was 24.9, and that of captains was 33.4 years.[76] The

74. Occupational distribution of provincials by rank is summarized in Table 21.
75. Age averages of provincials by rank: see Table 22.
76. Mean ages of provincials by rank and occupation: see Table 23.

army was not, of course, exclusively graded by age, any more than Massachusetts society was: a few centinels were in their fifties and sixties. The most telling exception to strict age gradation was the average age of the highest enlisted rank, sergeant (29.8 years), as compared to that of the lowest commissioned rank, ensign (28.1 years). Sergeants were generally older than ensigns in every occupational division as well, except in the case of laborers. A number of factors affected the assignment of rank, particularly family connections, previous military experience, and political finagling. The strength of age gradation and the lack of occupational discontinuities between ranks, however, demonstrate that the army's strongest correspondence was not to any military ideal, but to the society from which, each year, it was drawn.

The correspondence between army and society, finally, is evident in the patterns of nativity and migration among officers and enlisted men. Men native to the Bay Colony were almost twice as likely to become noncommissioned officers and three times as likely to become officers as men born in Great Britain—a tendency equally pronounced with respect to other immigrant groups.[77] Among natives of the province, however, there was little difference in general level of mobility between men of various ranks. Officers were only slightly more likely than privates to have remained in their birthplace until entering military service.[78] Such similarities point once again to broad continuities in social standing, from rank to rank. The break was not obvious or abrupt between men who became soldiers because they were young and not yet settled, and men who became soldiers because they were permanently impoverished and lacked any better prospect in life. For older men in the provincial forces, it was generally true that the higher their rank above centinel, the more successful they were

77. If the provincial army had perfectly reflected the intended establishment as stipulated in the legislation that authorized its organization, its six regiments would have consisted in all of 3,072 men. Of these, 74.2% would have been centinels, 13.7% would have been noncommissioned officers, 5.9% would have been company-grade officers, and 6.2% would have held other ranks (3.9% drummers and clerks, 2.3% staff and other officers). If this is taken as the norm and compared to the men who actually held the ranks by their nativity, considerable divergence is evident, suggesting that men from outside Massachusetts on the whole held lower ranks than natives of the province:

Place of Birth	N	Centinels	NCOs	Officers	Others
Norm	3,072	74.2%	13.7%	5.9%	6.2%
Massachusetts	2,013	70.9	16.1	5.9	7.0
Other New England cols.	183	79.8	13.1	1.6	5.4
Great Britain	192	77.1	8.8	2.1	11.9
Other cols.	34	88.2	5.9	0.0	5.9
Europe	20	90.0	0.0	5.0	5.0

78. Levels of movement, by rank, of Massachusetts provincials: see Table 24.

likely to have been in civilian life. Men past their middle thirties—about a decade beyond the average marriage age—who were still serving as private soldiers were more likely to represent permanently marginal or unsuccessful members of New England society.

Massachusetts soldiers of 1756 reflected both the geographical distribution and the social structure of the province's population. One consequence of this was that the war touched every town directly—not just through the taxes it paid, but through the experiences and sufferings of its sons. The year 1756 was not marked by severe casualties—only six battle deaths occurred—but at least 71 towns in Massachusetts lost men. In 138 out of the 176 towns that sent soldiers, some milder form of injury occurred among the residents, such as wounds, disease, or lameness.[79] Given the low recovery rate from serious illness in the eighteenth century, it is quite probable that many of the sick and wounded, when discharged, went home to die. Indeed, the growing number of petitions answered each year of the war by the General Court, from relatives and others asking compensation for the maintenance of sick soldiers who had died under their care following campaigns, testifies to the commonness of such service-related deaths. At the very least, in 1756 alone 2 out of every 5 towns in Massachusetts suffered a death among their residents in the army, and 4 towns out of every 5 sustained some casualty. Even in its least active year, the war was felt everywhere in the Bay Colony.

The impact of military service can also be estimated in terms of Massachusetts' population. In 1756 approximately 2,080 provincials were Bay Colony residents born betwen 1727 and 1740. This amounts to about 9 percent of all Massachusetts males in their age cohort—about one man in twelve.[80] As a proportion of the whole, this vastly exceeds the mid-

79. No town suffered more than six deaths. In the case of Stoughton, a town that six deaths did befall, the dead constituted 13.3% of all the soldiers resident in the town at the time of enlistment.

80. Robert V. Wells, *The Population of the British Colonies in America before 1776: A Survey of Census Data* (Princeton, N.J., 1975), holds that the total reported in the census of 1764, 245,698 inhabitants, represents an undercount. J. Potter, in "The Growth of Population in America, 1700–1860," in D. V. Glass and D.E.C. Eversley, eds., *Population in History: Essays in Historical Demography* (London, 1965), 638–639, provides a higher estimate; working from his charts (a) and (d), one can interpolate a 1764 population of 259,000. (I.e., his estimates for 1760 and 1770 are 235,000 and 299,000, respectively, and his decadal growth for 1760–1770 is consequently 27%, or 2.43% annually.) Regarding 245,698 as the lowest possible population for 1764 and Potter's 259,000 as an upper limit, and taking an annual growth rate for the period 1750–1760 of 2.7% (from Potter's decadal increase for the period of 31%), the total population in 1756 would have been between 198,000 and 210,000 people. Applying West model life tables for mortality levels between 6 and 15 and an annual growth rate of 25/1000, between 24.7% and 25.5% of the male population would range from 16 through 29 years of age at any given time. (See Ansley J. Coale and Paul Demeny, *Regional Model Life*

eighteenth-century ratio of redcoats to the British population.[81] Yet 1756 was a year of light military engagement for Massachusetts; two years later more than twice as many men would serve in its army, a number nearly matched in the following year as well. All in all, Massachusetts counted 30,000 enlistments in its provincial forces during the war, a number that does not include terms served by artificers, batteauxmen, and rangers; nor does it include terms served aboard the province frigate or privateers, or enlistments in the regular army.[82] Even if we assume that every man who enlisted in the provincial army served an average of two terms, so that all 30,000 enlistments involved only 15,000 men, and if we apply the same proportions of residence and age observed in the 1756 army to the whole,

---

Tables and Stable Populations [Princeton, N.J., 1966], 132–150, 180–198.) Taking into account the sex-ratio imbalance reported in the 1764 census, the male segment of the estimated 1756 population would number between 96,030 and 101,850; applying the Coale-Demeny percentages yields a population in the 16–29 range of from 23,719 to 25,972.

Now, the army in 1756 had 2,391 men of known ages, 1,741 of whom (72.8%) were from 16 through 29 years old; if the same percentage is applied to all 3,047 men in the army, the total in the range is 2,220. Of all men with known residences, 93.8% lived in Massachusetts at enlistment; thus the total number of residents from 16 through 29 would have been on the order of 2,080. This is from 8.0% to 8.8% of the total number of men estimated to be in the range 16–29.

The order of magnitude, at least, of this estimate can be confirmed from an independent source. In 1763, Gov. Francis Bernard reported to the Board of Trade that Massachusetts, in 1759, had had approximately 35,000 "fencible men" (i.e., service-eligible militiamen)—a category including men in the ages 16–50. (Bernard to the Lords Commissioners for Trade and Plantations, 5 Sept. 1763, quoted in Joseph Henry Benton, Jr., *Early Census-Making in Massachusetts, 1643–1765* [Boston, 1905], 502.) Within the army of 1756, approximately 2,790 men were Massachusetts residents aged 16 through 50; this amounts to 8.0% of Bernard's "fencibles"—or, if one reduces the number to compensate for population growth, to approximately 32,500 in 1756, this amounts to 8.6%.

81. This comparison is decidedly on the conservative side. At its 100-regiment peak, the regular army would have numbered 70,000 men. This number represents something like 1.1% of the total population of England and Wales in the period. (See population estimates in D. V. Glass, "Population Movements in England and Wales, 1700 to 1850," in Glass and Eversley, *Population in History*, 240; these approximate 6.5 million. These estimates omit Ireland and Scotland, the source of many redcoats, so the proportion for the British Isles as a whole would be even lower.) The total of all Massachusetts residents in the army of the province, about 2,860 men, amounted to about 1.4% of the highest estimated population of the colony.

82. Enlistments in each year of the war for Massachusetts provincials were as follows:

1755	1,200 men	1759	6,800 men
1756	3,000 men	1760	4,000 men
1757	1,800 men	1761	3,000 men
1758	7,000 men	1762	3,200 men

Thus a total of 30,000 enlistments (Thomas Hutchinson, *The History of the Colony and Province of Massachusetts-Bay*, ed. Lawrence Shaw Mayo [Cambridge, Mass., 1936 (orig. publ.

then *at least* 30 percent of all Massachusetts men who were between six-teen and twenty-nine years of age during the war would have served in the provincial army.[83] Such a figure would scarcely have surprised the Bay colonists themselves. One contemporary noted that "one-third part" of Massachusetts' eligible males had served during the war.[84]

The significance of such a proportion for a province populated by large families was immense. If one-third of the men born between 1725 and 1745 became provincial soldiers, it would have been possible for every family in the province to be represented in the army. Large families, more-over, mean extensive kinship networks, so that even families not directly touched by military service certainly had relatives who became soldiers.

London, 1828)], III, 30, 34, 45, 59–60, 69, 76, 78, 80, 95, 99). The number of Massachusetts men with the "general service" was as high as 3,000 in a given year. According to Thomas Pownall, in 1758 Massachusetts supplied, along with its provincials "in the king's service and the king's ships, transports, batteaumen, carpenters, and rangers under the general service in all above 2,500 men," so that for the year the provincial levy of 7,000 "together with those employed in other parts of his Majesty's service is a draught of near 10,000 men out of the effective fighting men in this province." (Pownall to William Pitt, 30 September 1758, in Parkman Papers, XLII, 285, Massachusetts Historical Society, Boston; a copy made from State Papers, America and West Indies, LXXI, Public Record Office, London.)

83. This is as low an estimate as can reasonably be made. During the years 1755–1763 the Massachusetts population grew from approximately 205,650 to 254,500, extrapolating from Potter's estimates ("Growth of Population," in Glass and Eversley, eds. *Population in History*, 638–639). Applying the Coale-Demeny life tables, the number of men in the 16–29 age group would have grown from 25,434 to 30,648 during the same period, which is to say that approximately 34,000 men all told were included in this age-range at some point during the war years. Reducing the 15,000 hypothetical enlistees first by 6.2% to dismiss nonresidents of Massachusetts, then by 27.2% to eliminate men outside the 16–29 age group, the total of Massachusetts residents 16–29 years old from this group would amount to 10,243 men. This number is 30.1% of all 34,000 Massachusetts males that fell within the age bracket 16–29 at some point during the war.

The figure of 15,000, furthermore, must be taken as a minimal estimate. There was, of course, a good deal of reenlistment among provincials from year to year (although we do not yet know how much); but each campaign reduced the number of troops capable of reenlisting considerably. In the 1756 campaign, as we shall see, at least 5.7% of the original recruits were dead by the end of the year, and 22.6% were either sick or wounded; just over half of the original enlistees were still present and fit for duty. If we assume that 1756 was a bad year—which it seems *not* to have been—and estimate that only 15% of each year's soldiers were incapable of reenlistment, even this removes some 4,500 men from the pool of potential re-enlistees over the course of the war. This in turn suggests that a number larger than 15,000 probably served with the provincials; indeed, if the enlisted men conformed to the pattern of the captains of 1756 in repeating service, approximately 16,000 would have served during the war. If as many as 20,000 men served the 30,000 enlistments, the percentage of men aged 16–29 from the province who served would probably have approximated 40%.

84. William Bollan's memorial to the king, 11 Apr. 1764, claimed that "one-third part" of the eligible men in Massachusetts had "become your Majesty's soldiers" in the course of the war (quoted in Nash, *Urban Crucible*, 243).

Even a long lifetime after the Peace of Paris, the war's pervasiveness was well known in Massachusetts. In 1835 Nathaniel Hawthorne reminded his readers in the second of a series of sketches called "Old News" for the *New-England Magazine* how fully, "in the heat of the Old French War," New Englanders could "be termed a martial people. Every man was a soldier, or the father or brother of a soldier; and the whole land literally echoed with the roll of the drum either beating up for recruits among the towns and villages, or striking the march towards the frontiers. . . . The country has never known a period of such excitement and warlike life, except during the Revolution—perhaps scarcely then; for that was a lingering war, and this a stirring and eventful one." [85]

Regular officers in America, who were personally unfamiliar with American social conditions, misunderstood the nature of the provincial soldiery. Applying regular army notions of efficiency, organization, and discipline, redcoat officers saw the provincials as hopelessly disorganized, badly disciplined, and prone to desertion or mutiny. The reason for this, they concluded, was that the provincial soldier himself was a poor specimen. Major General James Abercromby believed that the provincial army of 1756—the one we have been examining—was made up of "riff-raff," the "lowest dregs of the people, both officers and men." [86] Judging from the information now at hand, Abercromby's estimate was far from accurate, but it aptly expressed the prevailing British opinion.

Not surprisingly, New Englanders saw their soldiery in a much more favorable light. In 1755, an imperious British commander tried to recruit men from among two battalions of New Englanders in Nova Scotia. The ranking provincial officer, Lieutenant Colonel John Winslow, was outraged at the attempt to entice men who had not been informed that they were being enlisted for life in the king's troops. "Sure I am," Winslow protested to the governor of the colony, if such enlistments were to be countenanced,

> that it will be a most impolitical step, as these men are sons of some of the best yeomen in New England, who encouraged them to undertake this expedition, . . . and on like occasions the men have been returned at the end of the time limited, and [it] was expected by governor and people [that this] would have now been the case. And if [they are] disappointed and their children [are] kept, there will be an end put to any future assistance, let the extremity be what it will. [87]

85. Roy Harvey Pearce, ed., *Nathaniel Hawthorne* (New York, 1982), 261.
86. Quoted in Pargellis, *Loudoun*, 99.
87. John Winslow to Charles Lawrence, 27 Oct. 1755, in "Journal of Winslow," Nova Scotia Hist. Soc., *Colls.*, IV (1884), 180.

In a similar tone of warning the governor of Massachusetts wrote to William Pitt three years later. Thomas Pownall, who had governed the Bay Colony since mid-1757, was trying to explain the immense pressure the war had put on the province's financial and human resources and was pleading for relief in the form of a subsidy. In passing, Pownall also characterized the provincial army:

> I beg leave, sir, to inform you that most of these soldiers in the ranks are freeholders, who pay taxes; that these are the sons of some of our representatives, the sons of some of our militia colonels, and the sons of many of our field officers and other officers [who are] now doing duty as privates in the number I have this year raised. And that the sons of some of our principal merchants, one who pays £500 sterling *per annum* [in] taxes, were impressed for the same.[88]

When Massachusetts fielded a provincial force during the Seven Years' War, as Winslow and Pownall were trying to make clear, it was sending forth its sons in more than a metaphorical sense. The provincials represented a kind of image of the colony's society at large; they were Everyman's sons and were expected to return to normal civilian livelihoods after their military interlude had ended. To a degree that may be unique in American history, social and economic conditions had made the Seven Years' War for the Bay Colony into a people's war and virtually guaranteed that it would be fought—voluntarily—by armies of the people.

88. Pownall to Pitt, 10 Sept. 1758, Parkman Papers, XLII, 285.

Part Two ❖ The Experience of War

Chapter 3 ❖ "Hard Service and Poor Keeping"
Everyday Life in the Provincial Army

In March 1759, a twenty-one-year-old stonemason from Salem, Gibson Clough, volunteered for duty "in the service of my king and country in the . . . intended expedition against Canada." Clough found himself assigned instead to Louisbourg, the great French fortress that had fallen the previous year to Wolfe and Amherst. It was only the first of Gibson Clough's many disappointments. It seemed initially as if assignment to a post like Louisbourg would merely deprive him of the adventure and plunder he might have had with an expeditionary force. At the end of the year, however, he discovered what the really significant difference was between garrison duty and service with an expedition: garrison troops were much more liable to be coerced into serving past the ends of their enlistments. Clough had gone off on what he had understood would be a tour of "six months . . . [and] to be dismissed by the first of November or as much sooner as his majesty's service would admit." [1] When he returned to Salem almost two years later, he was bitterly aware that stone walls meant more than protection from the enemy. They gave the garrison commandant a monumental advantage over the soldiers stationed, as securely as if they were prisoners, within them.

We know of Private Clough's sorrows at Louisbourg because he kept a diary from the day he left Salem until the day he finally came home. More than seventy other New England soldiers maintained similar journals during the war. Several men acquired pocket books expressly to record their military experiences. [2] Some, like Samuel Morris and Thomas Moody, used the same small volumes to record successive years of service; one man, Seth Pomeroy, actually recorded his participation in the 1755 Crown Point campaign in the notebook he had used a decade earlier at the first siege of Louisbourg. An occasional diarist, like James Hill in 1755 and John Cleaveland in 1758, would try to carry on his journal after he returned home; but those who tried all gave up the effort after a few entries. In no case did a man begin his diary *before* enlistment. The writers apparently intended to record their military experience as a distinct episode in

1. Gibson Clough, "Relation to his Kind Reader" (initial entry), 1759. This and subsequent references to soldiers' diaries refer to sources listed in Appendix B, cited by author's name and date of entry.
2. E.g., Luke Gridley (1757), William Henshaw (1759), Jonathan Procter (1760).

their lives—a separate story that began with enlistment and ended with homecoming. The pocket notebooks, like James Hill's and Joseph Nichols's, were often used subsequently to record debts and memoranda, but later notations usually consisted of undated jottings, entirely unlike the disciplined daily entries made during campaigns. The very way in which soldiers recorded their military experience thus suggests that they saw it as discontinuous with their civilian lives and worthy of special note, or at least of a complete record.

Through their journals, we can examine provincial soldiers' daily lives from their own perspective and in considerable detail—something impossible to achieve with their redcoat counterparts, since "the almost universal illiteracy . . . of the [European] common soldier of any century before the nineteenth" renders the regular privates' experiences largely irrecoverable.[3] In addition to the provincials' military journals, a few autobiographical accounts written in the early nineteenth century, a scattering of soldiers' correspondence, and several orderly books survive. These sources help validate and amplify the diaries, but it is the diaries that provide the richest record of daily life in the provincial camps. They reveal that whether soldiers served in garrisons as Gibson Clough did, or participated, as most did, in expeditions, their experiences of military life followed similar patterns in the war's successive campaigns. Although no two years were identical, the *structure* of life remained basically unaltered. Using the soldiers' journals, we can reconstruct the pattern of their lives from enlistment in the springtime to homecoming in the fall. It was a harsh experience, but it was a broadening one as well: and it was, at any rate, unforgettable.

I

When a man enlisted, usually in March or April, he received a sum of cash as an installment on his bounty. This initial payment (which like the bounty tended to increase as the war went on) made enlistment legally binding on the recruit and gave him money to live on until he accomplished the next step of the process, "mustering-in."[4] When each regiment was recruited up to a reasonable approximation of its authorized strength —usually in mid-May—the colonel notified his subordinates to march the

3. John Keegan, *The Face of Battle* (New York, 1977), 32.
4. Initial payment rose from two dollars in 1755 to five in 1758. "Journal of Colonel John Winslow . . . ," Nova Scotia Historical Society, *Collections*, IV (1884), 116; "Establishment of the Forces on the intended Expedition against Canada," broadside dated Boston, 17 Mar. 1758, Massachusetts Historical Society, *Proceedings*, 2d Ser., VI (1890), 31.

men they had enlisted to a central point of rendezvous, where they would begin their active duty. At this rendezvous the men received the rest of their bounties, in addition to blankets, clothing, cooking supplies, and weapons, if such gear had not already been issued.[5] Because they would not be paid again until the end of the campaign, this payment was important to the men; unless they had brought spending money from home, it would furnish their funds for incidental purchases until the summer was over.[6]

The principal gathering point for units being transported by sea to the Maritimes or to the Saint Lawrence was Boston, while regiments marching overland to serve on the New York frontier gathered at Worcester or Springfield. Mustering-in—the formal enrollment of men in units, the administration of oaths of allegiance, and the reading of the Articles of War—marked the first time the provincial companies existed as real military organizations.[7] The men knew the process as "passing muster," since those deemed unfit would be dismissed by order of the "muster master" (or the "commissary of musters"), the administrator responsible for authenticating each unit's membership roll.[8] Not everyone passed muster: in 1758 David Perry worried that he might be rejected because he was small for his age of sixteen, though in the end that proved no hindrance.[9] In 1760, a year of lower demand for provincial soldiers, a substantial weeding-out took place. Sergeant David Holdin noted in that year that out of the eighty-five original recruits in his company "seventy-five passed muster and ten only was rejected"—suggesting that the expected failure rate was even higher than one in eight.[10]

At the rendezvous point the provincials met the other members of their regiments and began, perhaps for the first time in their lives, to create a community that was defined by common purpose rather than by geo-

5. *Ibid.*; William Sweat, 29 May 1758; Joseph Holt, 25 May 1758; Lemuel Wood, 2 May 1760; John Frost, 26 May 1760; Moses Dorr, 25 May 1758. In some cases, supplies were not issued until the troops had reached the rear echelon of the army, however (e.g., at Albany): William Henshaw, 24 May 1759; Amos Richardson, 13 June 1758.

6. On the effects of this, see Loudoun to Cumberland, 2 Oct. 1756, in Stanley Pargellis, ed., *Military Affairs in North America, 1748–1765* (Hamden, Conn., 1969 [orig. publ. New York, 1936]), 236–237.

7. See, e.g., David Holdin, 5, 7 May 1760.

8. Before 1757, the Massachusetts commissary of musters was a civilian appointee, Byfield Lyde; thereafter, provincials mustered before a regular officer—in most cases, Capt. Anthony Wheelock, muster-master at Worcester and Springfield. (Lyde: Mass. Archives, XCIV, *passim*; Wheelock: David Holdin, 30 Apr. 1760; William Henshaw's journal, 12 May 1759; Lemuel Wood, 28 May, 9 Sept. 1758.)

9. David Perry, "Recollections of an Old Soldier," *Magazine of History*, CXXXVII (1928), 20.

10. David Holdin, 30 May 1760.

graphical accident. The scale of their most immediate community was familiar, since the average regiment had about the population of a rural parish. In its makeup, however, the military community differed markedly from the soldiers' civilian environments. Although regiments were recruited around geographical centers that more or less coincided with their colonels' residences, they were not strictly territorial units, and usually included residents of several counties plus men from a neighboring province or two.[11] Even individual companies showed surprising diversity: in the provincial regiments of 1756, the average company had among its members men who had been living, at enlistment, in nine different Massachusetts towns, located in two or three counties, as well as a few men from outside the province altogether. In some units, of course, all the soldiers came from a single community, but such cases were rare. Seldom could even half of the men in a company call the same town home, and there were instances of truly impressive diversity. Captain William Peabody's company, for example, numbered among its forty-five members the residents of twenty-two Massachusetts towns, located in five counties. The impression of diversity grows even stronger when nativity is taken into account: the average company had among its members men born in four Massachusetts counties, one or two neighboring provinces, and at least one overseas area.[12]

Although soldiers also served in locations to which they were transported by sea, the majority marched westward across Massachusetts, following what became a standard route. Most companies were raised in eastern Massachusetts and therefore converged on Worcester as their point of rendezvous. From there they followed the Boston-Springfield post road, the main east-west artery in the province. At Brookfield the route divided; many took the northern fork to Northampton before striking out for five days' march through the wilderness via Pontoosuck (or Pentusuc) Fort, on

11. For a breakdown of the six regiments of 1756 by the residences of their members, see Table 25.

12. Only 3 companies in service in 1756 were composed solely of men born and raised in Massachusetts. Of the 56 companies raised for Crown Point in that year, 48 had members who were born abroad. The range of backgrounds could be quite wide: Capt. George Hanners's company numbered among its soldiers 4 Englishmen, 6 Irishmen, a German, and a Swiss; Capt. Benjamin Williams's unit included an Englishman, 3 Irishmen, a German, and a Dutchman; and Capt. John Nixon's company boasted a Scot, 3 Irishmen, a Channel Islander, a German, and a Portuguese. In one case, the foreign-born were even numerous in absolute terms: Capt. Richard Atkins's company, although it was made up entirely of Boston residents, had 17 foreign-born members, who accounted for 32% of its strength.

For a summary of residence and nativity, by regiment and company, of the soldiers in the army of 1756, see Fred Anderson, "War and the Bay Colony: Soldiers and Society in Massachusetts during the Seven Years' War, 1754–1763" (Ph.D. diss., Harvard University, 1981), II, 471–473.

the site of modern Pittsfield. This path had been laid out by Colonels William and Joseph Williams, powerful Connecticut Valley gentlemen known as "River Gods," who were widely suspected of trying to profit from the route. This way was somewhat shorter than the more southerly route, which kept to the post road. Despite its greater length, the common soldiers greatly favored the latter, because it required them to march less than twenty miles through an uninhabited region, "Green Woods," located in the modern town of Otis. Companies lucky enough to take the southern route could lodge at inns all the way to Albany.[13] Whatever path the men took across the province on the way to New York, the trip was a gradual transition from civilian life to soldiering. At the same time, it was for most provincials the longest migration they had yet experienced, one which offered them the chance to see a great deal of New England countryside.[14]

The distance from eastern Massachusetts to Albany by the roads the provincials took was on the order of two hundred miles and could be traversed on foot in as little as ten days; that was how long, at least, it took James Hill to walk there with his company in early June 1755.[15] In most cases the journey was more leisurely, interrupted by several days spent mustering and fitting out at the rendezvous. Two weeks seems to have been a quick trip and three weeks more like the average for men who started in eastern Massachusetts.[16] Whenever possible, soldiers stayed at inns. They could afford to do so because the province paid each man "billeting money" of 1s. 6d. Lawful Money per diem, a sum that a regular officer once complained was sufficient to support five or six men.[17]

Soldiers knew that their billeting subsidy was generous and relished spending it whenever they could. In 1758, for example, William Sweat and two comrades set off in advance of their company on the way to Worcester, choosing "to keep few together, it being more to our profit as to

13. On the nature of the route, see Caleb Rea, 16 June 1758.

14. The prewar migration careers of the soldiers who left a record of their march overland approximates quite closely the experience of the soldiers on the descriptive lists collected at Fort Edward and Fort William Henry in 1756. Of the 10 soldiers who kept journals whose places of birth and residence can be determined, 6 were still living in their towns of birth; 2 were still living in the same county, but outside their towns of birth; one had moved out of his native county but had remained within Massachusetts; and one was a man born in Connecticut who had moved to the Bay Colony before enlisting.

15. James Hill, 29 May–8 June 1755.

16. See, e.g., William Henshaw, 10–24 May 1759 (15 days from Leicester to Albany); William Sweat, 24 May–10 June 1758, (16 days from Salisbury to Albany); David Holdin, 24 Apr.–15 May 1760 (22 days from Groton to Albany); Lemuel Wood, 24 May–12 June 1759 and 24 Apr.–13 May 1760 (20 days from Andover to Albany, both times); Joseph Holt, 24 May–9 June 1758 (17 days from Andover to Albany).

17. Loudoun to Cumberland, 22 Nov.–26 Dec. 1756, in Pargellis, ed., *Military Affairs*, 276–277.

victuals and drink." The march, punctuated by pauses in which "we refreshed ourselves with a bowl of toddy" now and a "dram of clough water" then, was not at all unpleasant. At Worcester, Sweat remarked, "We live very well now, as long as the money last[s]," although he realized that he and his comrades "must soon expect worse," since they were, after all, bound off on an expedition.[18] Sweat's experience was not exceptional: others also noted good meals and lodging, and pauses when "[we] drank our beer."[19] Sometimes the soldiers fared uncommonly well, as did Lemuel Wood and seven of his fellows at Sheffield: they found they had a little extra money and took themselves "to the tavern and drunk a gallon and a half pint of wine and there we lodged that night as merry as milord."[20] Not all landlords along the way offered such satisfactory accommodations as that—Colonel Abraham Williams, an innholder and militia officer in Marlborough, was notorious for the stinginess of his board—but the majority seem to have been hospitable.[21] Hospitality was, after all, in their interest: to men like Captain John Curtis of Worcester, Nathan Walcott in Brookfield, and John Downing in Ware River Parish, the thousands of soldiers marching past their doors each year must have looked like a river of gold.[22]

As the provincials moved westward, they took note not only of towns and villages, of inns and landlords and meals, but of distances traveled, of the countryside and the people who inhabited it. In a rudimentary form, their journals thus became travelogues, which fact suggests that from its very beginning military service was a broadening experience for the small-town boys who made up the bulk of the provincials. Distance itself was clearly important to the soldiers: assiduously they noted the length of each day's march, and occasionally cumulative distances too, as if to take account of how far they had come since leaving home.[23] The recording of distances and directions ("We have steered, for this two days' march, about northwest and by north") provided points of reference for men whose educations provided little in the way of geographical training.[24] Soldiers took careful note of their surroundings, and even the least reflective

18. Refreshments: William Sweat, 24, 25 May 1758; coming changes: *ibid.*, 28, 29 May 1758.

19. Joseph Holt, 29 May 1758. See also, e.g., Samuel Chandler, 2 Oct. 1755, and *passim*; Stephen Cross, 27 Mar. 1756.

20. Lemuel Wood, 5 June 1759.

21. See, e.g., Thomas Moody, 19 May 1760; Lemuel Wood, 26 May 1759.

22. The overflow from this stream of soldiers could mean extra income for private householders as well. See, e.g., William Sweat, 24, 25, 28, 30, 31 May 1758; Stephen Cross, 27 Mar. 1756.

23. See, e.g., James Hill, 30, 31 May, 2 June 1755; see also Luke Gridley, entry following 23 Nov. 1757; Caleb Rea, 19 June 1758; Samuel Jenks, 18 July, 15 Nov. 1760.

24. Quotation from William Sweat, 1 June 1758; see also Nathaniel Dwight, 29 Sept. 1755, and *passim*; Samuel Chandler, 30 Sept. 1755, and *passim*.

of them evaluated the towns and countryside passed through. James Hill noted simply that he "came to Westfield, a good town,"[25] but the Reverend Samuel Chandler commented at length: "Westfield [is] a very fine, populous town. Large intervale, many miles over. Handsome buildings. Here and two parishes in Springfield, clocks on the meeting house. Brick schoolhouses."[26] Chandler, like many other soldiers, also had a countryman's eye for appraising property. Some of the soldiers' most detailed descriptions are of soil conditions and characteristics. It is clear from observations as careful as William Sweat's on the terrain in Ware River Parish—"This land is very uneven and woodsy, yet it is a springy ground and a good soil"—that men from the populous eastern parts of the province were taking careful note of the agricultural potential of lands in the undersettled west.[27] Such observations suggest that some soldiers were considering the possibility of moving permanently; at least one soldier meditated forthrightly on taking up residence in Canada.[28] Very good evidence exists, in fact, that New Englanders understood military expeditions in part as reconnaissances to spy out new Canaans for themselves and their increase. In Nova Scotia in 1755, John Winslow wrote from Fort Beauséjour to the governor of the province at Halifax for permission to pay an official call—a visit that meant Winslow would have to undertake a hundred-mile overland journey. Winslow said that on his way he hoped to "observe the country through which I pass, [so] that in case it should be thought convenient to settle any part of this province by people from New England, *which by them is expected*, I might be able to say somewhat about it on my return."[29] The governor never gave Winslow permission to make his junket, but the determined New Englander sent others to observe on his behalf.[30] Reports

25. James Hill, 3 June 1755; see also, e.g., Joseph Holt, 28 May, 7 June 1758; John Frost, 30 May 1760; Moses Dorr, 11 June 1758; William Sweat, 5, 6, 9 June 1758; Lemuel Wood, 3 June 1759.

26. Samuel Chandler, 3 Oct. 1755; see also Stephen Cross, 9, 20, 23 Apr. 1756, and *passim*; Caleb Rea, 21 June 1758; John Cleaveland, 20 June 1758; William Sweat, 3, 4 June 1758; Moses Dorr, 26 June 1758.

27. William Sweat, 1 June 1758; cf. Samuel Chandler, 1–4 Oct. 1755, and *passim*; Nathaniel Dwight, 17 Nov. 1755; Stephen Cross, 23 Apr. 1756, and *passim*; Caleb Rea, 9 July 1758; Thomas Moody, 28 Aug. 1760; John Barber, 8 Aug. 1754; David Holdin, 28, 31 Aug., 9 Sept. 1760; Archelaus Fuller, 11 June 1758; John Thomas, 8 July, 6–8 Dec. 1755; Seth Pomeroy, 31 July 1755; Nathaniel Knap, 10 Aug. 1758; Joseph Nichols, 25, 28, 30 June 1758; Samuel Jenks, 15 June, 8, 9, 12 Sept. 1760; John Winslow, 20 June, 3 Sept. 1755; Perry, "Recollections," *Mag. Hist.*, CXXXVII (1928), 21–22; Moses Dorr, 2, 3 Aug. 1758.

28. Samuel Jenks, 12 Sept. 1760.

29. Winslow to Lawrence, 23 July 1755, "Journal of Winslow," Nova Scotia Hist. Soc., *Colls.*, IV (1884), 210 (my emphasis). See also Winslow to Lawrence, 18 Aug. 1755, *ibid.*, 244.

30. Entry of 3 Sept. 1755, *ibid.*, III (1882–1883), 91. See also John Thomas, 6–8 Dec. 1755.

of returning soldiers undoubtedly influenced the decisions of New Englanders to settle in Nova Scotia in the years following 1758.[31]

Throughout the war New Englanders proved inveterate sightseers. Stephen Cross of Newbury, a shipwright who traveled to Fort Oswego via the Hudson and Mohawk rivers in 1756, recorded that he and his party stopped at New York and at Albany specifically to "view the city."[32] Others described, sometimes in detail, Albany's decorated stone and brick houses, situated with their gable ends ("notched like steps") toward the rough-paved streets, their roofs adorned with fantastic weather cocks of "horses, lions, geese, sloops, etc., etc." and settees at their doors "kept scoured very neat."[33] In addition to the unfamiliar Dutch styles, formal architecture (especially that of the Vauban-style fortifications the French had erected), churches, and unusual structures of all sorts attracted special notice. Soldiers sometimes made side trips to see well-known attractions. Lieutenant William Henshaw took his company to Kinderhook, where they "stopped and viewed their meeting house. Their pulpit [is] like a cupboard, [with] pews round it and seats all about. The roof runs up in a four-square peak."[34]

Such careful notation of unusual sights suggests the rubbernecking of previously untraveled men. Even the provincial chaplains, who were typically college-educated and presumably had a more cosmopolitan frame of reference than most soldiers, fell back on localist analogues when they described what they saw. John Cleaveland, for example, the pastor of a rural parish of Ipswich, wrote that he was "surprised to find" that Albany was

31. Lawrence Henry Gipson, *The Great War for the Empire: The Years of Defeat, 1754–1757*, 335; *The Victorious Years, 1758–1760*, 322, in Gipson, *The British Empire before the American Revolution* (New York, 1936–1969), VI, VII; Perry, "Recollections," *Mag. Hist.*, CXXXVII (1928), 20–21.

32. Stephen Cross, 17 Mar. (New York), 26 Mar. (Albany); cf. Nathaniel Knap, 11 Apr. (Dartmouth, Nova Scotia), 30 July 1758 (Louisbourg).

33. Samuel Chandler, 6 Oct. 1755—one of Chandler's longest entries. Cf. similar descriptions in Joseph Nichols, 15–19 June 1758; Caleb Rea, 11, 19–21 June 1758; John Cleaveland to Mary Cleaveland, 26 June 1758, John Cleaveland Papers, III, 160–161, Essex Institute, Salem, Mass., hereafter cited as JCP.

34. William Henshaw (journal), 22 May 1759; see also Samuel Chandler, 5 Oct. 1755. Cf., on Catholic churches, Lemuel Wood, 11 Sept. 1760; Samuel Jenks, 12 Sept. 1760. For the very detailed attention paid to fortifications (especially the works built by the French) see, e.g., Lemuel Wood, 15 Aug. 1759; Jonathan Procter, 1 Sept. 1760, and *passim*; Samuel Chandler, 6 Oct. 1755; Stephen Cross, 14 May, 17 Nov. 1756; Samuel Jenks, 3 July, 28 Aug. 1760; Nathaniel Dwight, 2–3 Nov. 1755; David Holdin, 31 Aug., 2, 7 Sept. 1760; Thomas Moody, 6 Sept. 1760; William Henshaw, 7 Aug. 1759; John Thomas, 19 June, 8 Dec. 1755; Seth Pomeroy, 13, 20 Aug. 1755. Another attraction was the "melancholy sight" of the ruined Fort William Henry: e.g., Obadiah Harris, 22 June 1758; William Henshaw, 7 Aug. 1759.

"a city beautifully situated [and] full as large as Salem." When he saw Schenectady, he observed that it was "very pleasantly and compactly situated [and] according to my judgment it is as large as Charlestown near Boston."[35] In a similar vein, when the Reverend Samuel Chandler of Gloucester reached Springfield, he noted its situation "on the great river Connecticut which is much larger than Merrimack." Two days later he crossed the Hudson at Albany and wrote, "the river larger than Connecticut."[36] Chandler's perspective was widening: he would surely never again see the Merrimack in the same light. A like expansion of horizons occurred for any provincial who left his home town and trekked off to the wilds of northern New York; he, too, would never see his home quite as he had before the war. He would, however, have acquired a set of reference-points in common with thousands of other veterans who had made the same march as he.

Movement to join the army was for most soldiers a relatively gradual transition from civilian to military life. Yet for men who marched overland, and particularly for the soldiers who marched via Northampton and Pontoosuck Fort, the last few days of the trek left no doubt that service could be arduous. "Very much fatigued and wet," wrote Ensign Moses Dorr in 1758 near the western border of Massachusetts, "by reason of the bad traveling over miles, through swamps and rivers. Such traveling I never seen."[37] David Perry, who passed over the same route, recalled sixty years later, "We had no other road than marked trees to direct our course" after leaving Northampton, "no bridges on which to cross the streams: some of which we waded: others we passed on trees felled by our men; and for five successive nights we lay on the ground."[38] Another private recorded that the result of such "exceeding bad going" was "the chief [part] of our company was very weary and lame" when they arrived at the Hudson.[39] Caleb Rea, the surgeon of Colonel Jonathan Bagley's regiment in 1758, observed that the difficulty of the route was compounded by the fact that "many companies hadn't one-fourth [of their] allowance of Bread, nor any rum for four or five days" and tried to speed up in the hope of arriving sooner. In marching "very fast," however, "many, through [the] difficulty

35. John Cleaveland to Mary Cleaveland, 26 June 1758, JCP, III, 160–161; John Cleaveland, 20 June 1758.

36. Samuel Chandler, 3 Oct. 1755; 6 Oct. 1755. For other examples of diarists' comparisons using local reference-points, see John Winslow, 20–22 June 1755, "Journal of Winslow," Nova Scotia Hist. Soc., *Colls.*, IV (1884), 176; Seth Pomeroy, 5 Sept. 1755; Samuel Jenks, 1, 10, 20, 22 July 1760; Caleb Rea, 28 July, 15 Sept., 13 Oct. 1758.

37. Moses Dorr, 11 June 1758.

38. Perry, "Recollections," *Mag. Hist.*, CXXXVII (1928), 8.

39. William Sweat, 9 June 1758. Cf. Samuel Morris, 22 June 1759.

of the way, got broken shins, sprained joints, bruised feet, and other accidental wounds, by falling over stones [and] stumps, into quagmires, etc."
Rea noted that "among all the Bay regiments" the route was reputed to be
"so bad that it is become a proverb. No one," he concluded, "need pass
muster or any other proof of their fitness for a campaign but to march
through these woods."[40] For the provincials this last stretch of the approach march was a taste of things to come: discomfort, short rations, and
hard going.

II

When they emerged from the woods east of the Hudson, the footsore provincials were astonished to see the number of men preparing to begin a
year's campaign. "I arrived at Greenbush," wrote Samuel Morris in June
1758, "and here I found men as thick as trees."[41] Just a month later, some
twelve thousand of these soldiers would take part in the attack on Ticonderoga led by Major General James Abercromby. On 5 July 1758, the
biggest cities in North America could boast populations only a thousand or
two greater than the number of luckless soldiers rowing batteaux down
Lake George toward their rendezvous with defeat.[42] It was an extraordinary concentration of troops, so great that witnesses believed that as many
as twenty thousand men were taking part in the expedition.[43] No other
single effort made during the war quite matched it, at least in northern
New York; but even smaller concentrations of troops could powerfully impress the small-town-bred provincials. Amherst's invasion force in 1759
numbered only about eight thousand, but to Samuel Morris, it seemed
immense:

> Thursday, the twenty-first of June 1759. This day the whole of the
> army struck their tents at the break of day. . . . The number of those

40. Caleb Rea, 15 June 1758.
41. Samuel Morris, 10 June 1758.
42. Strength of Abercromby's expeditionary force: Gipson, *The Victorious Years*, 217–
218; the populations of Boston and Philadelphia in the same year were both on the order of
15,000 (Gary B. Nash, *The Urban Crucible: Social Change, Political Consciousness, and the
Origins of the American Revolution* [Cambridge, Mass., 1979], 408–409). The total population
of a military camp, furthermore, was always larger than its strength of soldiers; there were
regular camp followers (authorized usually at a level of 40 or 50 per regiment), plus sutlers
and their families, plus unauthorized camp followers of various sorts—Indians, refugees,
hangers-on, seekers after commissions, and so forth.
43. Moses Dorr estimated 18,000 on 6 July 1758; Joseph Holt, 5 July 1758, put the number at 20,000; Caleb Rea, 3 July 1758, thought there were 16,000 men at the Lake. Cf. Amos
Richardson, 5 July 1758.

that marched, as near as I can judge, was about 9,000 men, the biggest number of men that [I] ever saw march on foot in all my life.[44]

To control and sustain such numbers of men required regimentation on a level entirely outside the previous experience of most New England soldiers. Had they been redcoats, such regimentation would largely have been accomplished as a consequence of instruction in the intricacies of infantry drill. For the provincials, however, that was not the case.

Formal training among Bay Colony troops was always scanty, even though they obviously needed a great deal of it. Orderly books and journals indicate that provincials were frequently ignorant of rudimentary maneuvers and, indeed, were sometimes barely familiar with firearms. On 16 June 1759, a month before departing on the expedition that would finally succeed in capturing Ticonderoga from the French, Lord Jeffery Amherst found it necessary to order that "the commanding officers of the provincials' regiments examine what number of men they have who are not marksmen; some perhaps may not have fired a musket. [Measures are to be taken immediately so that] the whole may be ordered out to fire at a mark."[45] At most, the regular commander expected that each provincial would fire three to five rounds in practice and have some experience in firing platoon volleys.[46] In addition, provincial officers were "upon all occasions to practise their men in going through their motions, that they may [be] more ready when they come on more actual service."[47] This was fine in theory; the problem was that the provincial officers were to understand that "this is not to hinder their furnishing such men for work as may be ordered"—and regular commanders leaned heavily on provincial units for fatigue assignments.[48] As a result, in a provincial regiment that was probably a bit above average in proficiency, there were only eight days spent in training between the time the unit joined the expeditionary forces on 29 May 1759, and 21 July when the army set out to besiege the French fort at Ticonderoga.[49]

44. Gipson gives Amherst's strength as 8,000 in *The Victorious Years*, 360; Samuel Morris, 21 June 1759; see also Robert Webster, 21 June 1759. For other examples of witnesses' being greatly impressed with the scope of expeditionary preparations, see Moses Dorr, initial entry, 1758; Stephen Cross, 27 Mar. 1756; Amos Richardson, 22 June 1758; Asa Foster, 27 June, 3 July 1758; Obadiah Harris, 6 July 1758; John Noyes, 7 July 1758; Benjamin Bass, 14 Aug. 1758; Lemuel Wood, 20–21 June 1759; Constantine Hardy, 20 June 1759; David Perry, "Recollections," *Mag. Hist.*, CXXXVII (1928), 9; Joseph Nichols, 3 July 1758.

45. Wilson's orderly book, 16 June 1759, 30.

46. *Ibid.*, 17 June 1759, 33; 28 June 1759, 50; 29 June 1759, 51.

47. *Ibid.*, 29 June 1759, 51–52.

48. *Ibid.*, 8 July 1759, 63.

49. Robert Webster, 29 May, 8, 16, 18, 28, 29, 30 June, 9, 13, 21 July 1759. During the same period, Webster's company did fatigue duty on at least 20 days, spent 12 days in march-

Light as this training schedule was, many units had the benefit of even less. In the 1758 campaign, Private Amos Richardson, a member of Colonel Ebenezer Nichols's regiment, had only a single day's training, just before the army's departure for Ticonderoga.

> Tuesday, the fourth day [of July, 1758]: . . . in the afternoon, we all had leave to shoot off all our guns, and we did. And there was a fine firing of them for a spell. And some of our men did shoot one of the regulars through the head, which killed him dead.

That ended the regiment's target practice for the day and, indeed, for the rest of the year. When the army embarked for Ticonderoga, Nichols's regiment—perhaps because of its utter ineptitude—was left behind to garrison the camp at Lake George. Yet the provincial regiments that did accompany the expedition were not significantly better prepared than Nichols's. On 3 July, for example, Colonel Jonathan Bagley's regiment was drilled "in the exercise of brush fighting" before General Abercromby and Lord Howe, the expedition's leaders; the performance was so lackluster that "the sergeants were all ordered to draw up in a rank by themselves and be exercised by the adjutant, who was ordered thus to teach 'em twice a day till he had learned them their duty." [50] On the same day, which can only have been a trying one for Abercromby, "the Connecticut regiment [was] embodied for to learn how to form your front to the right and left, for General Abercromby and his aide-de-camp to view." [51] In other words, two days before the expeditionary force was scheduled to embark, the Massachusetts noncommissioned officers were still uncertain how to execute commands, and the Connecticut troops were trying to learn how to deploy from a column to a line. Within a week these provincial battalions were among the troops that saw action near Ticonderoga. Private David Perry was there, as a soldier in Colonel Jedediah Preble's regiment, and his initial reactions were probably typical. When the first engagement began, he wrote:

> The whistling of the balls and the roar of the musquetry terrified me not a little. At length our regiment formed among the trees, behind which the men kept stepping from their ranks for shelter. Col. Preble, who, I well remember, was a harsh man, swore he would

---

ing and recovery from marching, and 3 days on guard duty. For other indications of provincial training and proficiency, see Luke Gridley, 2–24 May 1757, *passim*; Constantine Hardy, 28 June 1759; Lemuel Wood, 5, 6 July 1758, 5 July 1759; John Hawks, 17, 21, 22 June, 11 July 1759; Samuel Jenks, 15–23 July 1760; Samuel Merriman, 30 June 1759.

50. Caleb Rea, 3 July 1758.

51. Lemuel Lyon, 3 July 1758.

knock the first man down who should step out of his ranks which greatly surprised me, to think that I must stand still to be shot at.

The next day, when Preble's regiment tried to storm the French entrenchments in front of the fort, there were no tactical subtleties: "Our orders were to 'run to the breast-work and get in if we could.'"[52]

The almost complete absence of drill from the provincials' daily routine meant that they went into battle with none of the steadying habits that drilling inculcated.[53] What was true of the exceptionally disorienting environment of combat also applied to the less dramatically stressful but scarcely more familiar life of the camp. Although daily routine began to emerge soon after provincial soldiers joined the other forces taking part in a campaign, soldierlike habits were a long time in forming. The painful process by which provincials learned soldierly behavior can be traced in regimental and general orders.

Early in any given year, procedural orders were most frequent, dealing in detail with matters that would have been controlled by custom, habit, or standard procedure in a professional military organization. Such concerns as how many men each battalion should assign to the picquet guard, for example, were covered in military manuals like Humphrey Bland's *Treatise of Military Discipline;* yet they constantly cropped up in general orders directed at the provincials, who were unaware of the conventional practice.[54] Similar matters, like the enforcement of conformity in dress or instruction in sanitary practices, were prescribed at length in the provincials' regimental orders. Procedural directives tended to become less frequent as campaigns progressed, a fact that suggests they were becoming less necessary and that, by late summer at least, provincials had become more or less habituated to life in camp. Unfortunately for the martial reputation of the New Englanders, however, the best time to advance against the French was in the spring or the early part of the summer, before the French fleet could resupply Canada via the Saint Lawrence. Thus the most was required of the provincials at the time they were least able to function as soldiers, as they struggled to learn the unfamiliar rules of military life.

Because each year's provincial force was a new creation, deficiencies in behavior that would have been routinely corrected by experienced, low-ranking leaders went unremedied until they had to be confronted as group

52. Perry, "Recollections," *Mag. Hist.*, CXXXVII (1928), 9.

53. For a discussion of the benefits of precision in drill, as well as other elements of professional competence, to men under fire, see John Keegan's discussion of British behavior at the battle of Waterloo (*Face of Battle*, 175–195, also 34).

54. Cf. Humphrey Bland, *A Treatise of Military Discipline*, 6th ed. (London, 1746 [orig. publ. London, 1727]), 206, and Hawks's orderly book, 21, 22 June 1759.

problems, in regimental orders. The directives issued in one typical provincial battalion during the first six weeks of the campaign of 1759 show the regiment's commanding officer trying to bring order out of chaos. His troops wander out of camp after retreat, wear outlandish hats (sometimes two of them at a time), ignore rudimentary sanitary rules, neglect to wash themselves and their clothes, disturb the camp with boisterous singing and shouting until long after midnight every night. Even his officers are troublesome: they fail to wear any insignia to distinguish themselves from their men, refrain from inquiring into their troops' behavior, wrangle with the adjutant on parade over what duties they should be assigned.[55]

About half of the orders issued in this initial phase of the campaign were addressed to subaltern and noncommissioned officers and were clearly aimed at compensating for their lack of experience. In part they were intended to instruct the junior leaders on their duties, promoting their technical proficiency and the health or performance of their troops. Most of all, however, they were oriented toward teaching the proper roles to officers and men. Soldiers were told that they could not dress to suit themselves; they could not sleep or cook or defecate where they pleased; they could not sing or halloo or gamble late into the night. The orders thus defined the limits of a soldier's personal freedom. At the same time, the orders directed to the leaders instructed them on the behavior appropriate to their station. They were to distinguish themselves from their men, restrain their passions, consistently inquire into the most personal details of their soldiers' lives. Soldiers, these orders held, are men who lead thoroughly circumscribed existences and whose behavior is subject to the scrutiny of their superiors. Officers, the orders informed them, are men of another order, who have the duty and the unquestionable right to inquire into any subordinate's affairs. The orders limited the privacy of the soldiers and the personal freedom of officers and men alike and limited them in such a way as to reinforce the authority of commissioned over enlisted personnel. The army desperately needed orderliness and subordination in order to withstand attack, to resist disintegration under the pressure of disease and internal disruption: to function as a military body, not a mob. Yet these attempts to bring provincial soldiers under control were never entirely successful. At their best, provincial camps remained unsatisfactory examples of how armed forces live on campaign.

Since training occupied little of the soldier's time, the aspect of his life that was most orderly, in the sense of being the most completely regulated and controlled by his leaders, was his work. While a few provincials participated in "scouts," or raiding and reconnaissance patrols, these re-

55. Hawks's orderly book, 29, 31 May, 7, 9, 12, 16, 21, 22, 24–26 June, 2, 3, 6, 8 July 1759.

mained principally the function of Rangers, or of Indian auxiliaries. For the great majority, daily life was divided between fatigue and guard details. Guards in camp, according to common practice in the eighteenth century, consisted of "guards extraordinary" and "guards ordinary." The former were units detached to do duty at outposts, to escort wagon trains, or to provide security for supply batteaux—assignments that might take them away from camp for several days, or even weeks, at a time. Guards ordinary were considered "such as are fixed during the campaign, and are relieved regularly at a certain hour every day." [56]

Generally speaking, there were five kinds of ordinary guard details on which provincials served. Each battalion provided security for its own part of the camp compound with a "quarter guard"—usually a subaltern officer, a drummer, two sergeants, and forty men who performed local police functions, confined prisoners awaiting regimental punishment, and patrolled the unit area at night. Each quarter guard was based in a small cluster of tents located across the parade ground from the front of its battalion. Battalions also maintained "picquet guards" individually composed of a captain, two subalterns, three sergeants, and fifty men. The "body of men . . . [was] to be always ready to march at a moment's warning, either to sustain out-posts, foraging escorts, or, in case the enemy should endeavor to surprise . . . [the] camp, to march out and attack them, in order to give the army time to draw up." [57] The soldiers of the picquet remained under arms, on alert for a twenty-four-hour period. When an alarm did sound, they would assemble under their captain on the regimental parade ground; he would then conduct them to a rendezvous point where the field officer of the day would take command and march what amounted to a temporary regiment off to meet the enemy.

In addition to the picquet and the quarter guard, which were on duty with their units at all times, each battalion periodically contributed troops to various guards assigned to the encampment at large. The most important of these was the "main guard," which provided the camp's external security. This duty passed from regiment to regiment and required a considerable number of men. The smallest main guard consisted of a company, under the command of a captain. Its men were posted for a twenty-four-hour period as sentries around the camp perimeter and also watched over the artillery park, baggage and transport trains, the boats, and the cattle. The camp also had a "provost guard" which provided police functions beyond those supplied by the quarter guards of each battalion. The provost guard detail was usually a detachment of forty-five men under a subaltern officer. Its main responsibility was to secure any prisoners being

56. Bland, *Treatise*, 206.
57. *Ibid.*, 213.

held for trial by general courts-martial or for punishment; it also supervised all major punishments, including executions. Finally, general officers and certain staff members were entitled to personal guards: a lieutenant general, for example, had a guard of thirty-three men; a major general was entitled to twenty-three, and a brigadier to fifteen.[58]

At any given time, perhaps a quarter of the troops in a camp were engaged in guard duties; indeed, it was regarded as a pernicious practice to have any fit man mount guard less often than every fourth day.[59] Since guards were detailed for twenty-four-hour periods and since none of the duties allowed men to sleep normally, frequent guard mounts interfered substantially with soldiers' circadian cycles. Men who recorded guard duty also recorded relief at the end of their tours. "I came off [main] guard, and glad was I," wrote Amos Richardson in 1758. "And after I came off, I went and lay in my tent and slept almost all day."[60] Richardson and his comrades were not always so lucky as to have a day off after guard duty; John Woods, for instance, performed alternating fatigue and guard details in late August and September 1759 and noted his occasional release from duty as "a rare thing."[61] Guard duty, furthermore, subjected men to more stresses than those induced by lost sleep. Jumpy sentries fired at real or imagined noises, and guards sometimes mistook stray livestock for enemies moving about in the dark.[62] Heavy guard duty schedules thus promoted order in the camps both by their regimentation and by keeping half of a camp's soldiers either occupied or worn out from a previous tour. Another effect was to erode the soldiers' resistance to disease by compounding physical and mental stress with frequent deprivation of sleep.

The other half of the soldiers' usual occupation, fatigue duty, had simi-

---

58. For the duties and other specifications of these guards, see *ibid.*, chap. 15, "Consisting of Camp-Duty"; for orders to mount the various guards see, e.g., Wilson's (1759) or Hawks's (1759) orderly books, *passim*. Bland authorized more guards than these; these, however, are the only ones spoken of in the diaries and orderly books.

59. Bland, *Treatise*, 153. In fact, they seem to have mounted guard rather more often than every fourth day. Amos Richardson, a private in Colonel Nichols's regiment at Lake George in 1758, stood guard 25 days between 17 Aug. and 17 Oct. During this time he was ill for 13 days and unable to perform his duties, so Richardson was in effect on guard 25 out of a possible 49 days: main guard and picquet guard 9 times each and quarter guard 7 times. For similar frequencies, see, e.g., Anonymous, 9 Sept.–21 Oct. 1758; John Woods, 5 Aug.–27 Sept. 1759.

60. Amos Richardson, 8 Oct. 1758; cf. Richardson, 17–18, 21–22 Aug., 24–25 Sept. 1758; John Woods, 31 Aug.–7 Sept. 1759; Lemuel Lyon, 2 Oct. 1758.

61. John Woods, 27 Aug. 1759; cf. 4 Aug. 1759. See also *ibid.*, 3, 20 Sept. 1759.

62. See, e.g., Obadiah Harris, 8 Aug. 1758; Lemuel Wood, 27 Aug. 1759; Gibson Clough, 18–20 July 1760; Jonathan Procter, 19, 20 July 1760; Obadiah Harris, 1 Aug. 1758; Robert Webster, 5 July 1759; Samuel Chandler, 5, 7 Nov. 1755.

lar effects. Immense amounts of labor were required to keep an army functioning in the wilderness, and provincials, far more than the highly trained and hard-to-replace regulars, supplied the muscle that built roads, dug trenches, cut wood, constructed vessels, and hauled supplies. Regulars employed provincials, Colonel James Robertson bluntly explained to his regiment's agent in England, "to work our boats, drive our wagons, and fell our trees, and do the works that in inhabited countries are performed by peasants."[63] This comment was not entirely accurate, since provincials also handled jobs that the regulars were incapable of performing for themselves, jobs that required skills and expertise not readily available among men who had always been soldiers. Colonel Robertson himself had engaged Sergeant Rufus Putnam to operate the sawmill that Putnam had built in 1759. He thus could hardly have been unaware of skilled provincial contributions, even if he forebore to acknowledge them.[64] Orders requiring provincial regiments to send in the names of artisans—as when Colonel John Bradstreet called for a list of "carpenters, smiths, masons, joiners and brick layers, millwrights, [and] wheelwrights"—attest to the redcoats' reliance upon provincial skills as well as provincial brawn.[65] Regulars, indeed, behaved as if they assumed an unlimited supply of skilled workers among the provincials. Rather than organizing artisan-soldiers into special units, regulars preferred simply to call for workers whenever the need arose. Private Obadiah Harris, for example, a carpenter from Wrentham, was employed at the beginning of the 1758 campaign in constructing a hospital at Fort Edward and in erecting a stockaded fort near Lake George. Neither he nor any of his fellow workers were permanently detailed as carpenters; Harris spent most of the campaign with his battalion, building and maintaining roads between Albany and Fort Edward.[66] Other provincials performed not one or two, but a variety of tasks. Private John Woods, for example, hauled supplies during the siege of the French at Ticonderoga in July 1759. In late July and August he worked as a batteau-portager, a woodcutter, a clearer of brush, and a carpenter; from

63. Robertson to John Calcraft, 22 June 1760, Loudoun Papers, LO 6251, Henry E. Huntington Library, San Marino, Calif., cited in Alan Rogers, *Empire and Liberty: American Resistance to British Authority, 1755–1763* (Berkeley, Calif., 1974), 67, 156, n. 31. Hereafter material from the Loudoun Papers will be identified by date and LO document number; quoted material from the Loudoun Papers appears by permission of the Huntington Library.

64. Rufus Putnam, *The Memoirs of Rufus Putnam* (Boston, 1903), 28.

65. Williams's orderly book, 11 Aug. 1758; cf. similar orders in Moneypenney's orderly book, 16 Apr., 27 May 1758; Hawks's orderly book, 11 June 1759; Wilson's orderly book, 5 July, 31 Aug., 1, 5 Sept., 2 Oct., 1759.

66. Obadiah Harris, 12–21, 23–29 June 1758 (construction work); 15–30 July, 7–17 Aug., 20–25 Sept., 9 Oct. 1758 (other duties).

the end of August through October he built dams, maintained roads, loaded and unloaded wagons, carried clapboards, worked on a sloop, and acted as a stevedore.[67]

Keeping men at work on fatigue duty—especially when provincial soldiers and officers alike were convinced that they were doing more than their share—was accomplished both by threatening punishment and by offering incentives.[68] Troops were paid additional wages for certain kinds of fatigue work. Beyond his normal compensation a provincial working as a common laborer would be paid 1s. a day in New York currency. Employed as a semiskilled artificer—for example, as a sawyer—he earned 1s. 3d. When he worked at a task requiring special skills, like those of a carpenter or mason, he made an additional 1s. 7d. daily.[69] Although road mending, the construction of fortifications, and the digging of entrenchments were considered normal duty and were not formally compensated, a tot of rum a day for such work was the custom until the practice was curtailed in 1760. (Thereafter rum was allowed, at the rate of a gill a day, only when "the weather be wet and bad.")[70] Though hardly munificent, the extra pay was welcomed. Amos Richardson once griped at a spell of hard fatigue, cutting timber at Halfway Brook: "We worked all day as hard as we could work, and we did as much as we did in two day[s] before or more"; but he was pleased when he was paid a week later. "I went to the pay master for to get my pay for my work, which I did at the Halfway Brook," he wrote, "and I got one whole dollar and a quarter."[71] Fatigue pay could accrue to a sizable sum if a soldier were steadily employed "on

67. John Woods, 23–27, 30–31 July, 1–3, 13, 26–30 Aug., 13–15, 19 Sept., 1–21, 31 Oct. 1759. Cf. James Hill, who built boats (4 July–4 Aug. 1755), cut timber (18 Aug.), built a storehouse (4 Sept.); then worked again on boats (6 Sept.), a powder house (12 Sept.), more boats (13–16 Sept.), and worked on fortifications (30 Sept.–15 Nov. 1755). See also Luke Gridley, who mainly worked on roads and acted as a woodcutter (28–31 May, 1–23 June, 18 July, 14–28 Oct. 1757); Josiah Peary, who cut and hauled wood, mowed hay, herded livestock, and hauled stores (28, 29 May, 14 June, and *passim*); Lemuel Lyon, who herded cattle and sheep, worked on fortifications and roads, cut fascines, dug ditches, and performed a variety of miscellaneous tasks (23 Aug., 6, 8, 13, 16 Sept., 2, 8, 13, 16, 20, 26 Oct., 1–4 Nov. 1758); Samuel Morris and Robert Webster, who did batteau duty, worked on fortifications, helped build a hospital, cut fascines, dug trenches, cut timber, herded livestock, and built a road (10, 12, 13, 24–26 June, 1, 5, 10, 25 July, 7, 9, 11, 14, 15 Aug., 1, 3, 5, 10, 14, 24 Sept., 3 Oct., 26 Oct.–10 Nov. 1759).

68. Samuel Jenks, 1, 27, 31 Oct., 14 Nov. 1760.

69. Hawks's orderly book, 4 June 1760.

70. *Ibid.* For examples of payment in liquor for road work and fortification work, see, e.g., Lemuel Lyon, 24 Aug., 8 Sept., 19 Oct. 1758. Under adverse circumstances, the compensation could be considerable; Lyon, for example, once received a quart of rum for keeping sheep on a "wet and raw cold" night, 26 Oct. 1758.

71. Amos Richardson, 25 June, 4 July 1758.

the king's works." [72] Such was the case with Jonathan Procter, who was posted at Louisbourg during the destruction of the fortifications in 1760. For his work as a carpenter he received £8 3s., a sum that nearly doubled his private's pay while he was engaged in the extra duty. [73]

III

Much of the fatigue work that provincial troops performed, especially the building of roads, was done away from the major English forts and hence at some distance from supply magazines. This stretched the provisioning capabilities of the command to its limits, and sometimes beyond. Soldiers constantly complained of food shortages whenever they were detached for service away from a fort for periods of a week or longer. At the least, hunger cut into the men's capacity to work efficiently. Amos Richardson found himself in such a situation when he confided in his diary, "I went to work; and I worked part of the day. And I was so hungry that I could not work any more, before I got some sustenance; for I had not took any allowance for eight day[s]. And I was almost starved." [74] On other occasions, short allowances contributed to mutiny and desertion. Sergeant Robert Webster, employed in constructing a road from Crown Point to Township Number Four, New Hampshire, described such a case. He and his men had been on short rations for a painfully long time by 11 November 1759, when he wrote:

> We are at work but we haven't any bread nor salt nor haven't had this eight days. We live on fresh beef and water and some Chakabra leaf broth. The day before yesterday four of our party went from us sick to go to Number Four and some [left] out of every party. Our men are weak living in this form. I am not well.

Two days later Webster complained that now they were reduced to water and broth only:

> Tuesday, the 13th. Encamped on the road. It hadn't pleased the Major to give us any meat yesterday nor today as yet so we lay still at

72. Obadiah Harris, 1 July 1758; Enoch Poor, 14 June, 17 Oct. 1759.

73. Jonathan Procter, 5 July (£1 9s.), 10 Aug. (£1 16s.), 7 Sept. (£1 9s.), 14 Oct. (£1 12s.), 6 Nov. (£1 7s.), 16 Nov. 1760 (10s.). These payments were apparently recorded in the Lawful Money of Massachusetts, in which Procter customarily reckoned. Procter's total earnings for 20 months at Louisbourg amounted to £63 5s. L.M.; in addition to the £8 3s. above, he received £32 10s. as his private's wage, £6 12s. as an enlistment bounty in 1759, £12 as a reenlistment bounty in 1760, and £4 as compensation for wintering at the fort.

74. Amos Richardson, 6 July 1758.

present. This day at twelve o'clock they gave us two days' allowance of beef so we went to work.[75]

Victualing, like work and discipline, was a matter of constant concern to the provincials. Diet, furthermore, was a critical determinant of the provincials' health, behavior, and even state of mind.

After the regular command finally took control of their supply system late in the 1756 campaign, provincial troops drew rations identical to those provided to the redcoats. The principal items of the weekly allowance were seven pounds of beef or four pounds of pork, either fresh or in salted form; seven pounds of bread, or flour sufficient to bake it; three pints of peas or beans; a half-pound of rice; and a quarter-pound of butter.[76] If all these articles were delivered, properly prepared, and eaten, the resulting diet was high in protein and more than adequate in carbohydrates and fats. Depending upon whether salted or fresh provisions were issued, and whether the meat was beef or pork, the ration probably provided the average soldier between about twenty-two hundred and three thousand calories daily.[77] Three thousand calories is about the daily intake recommended for modern soldiers doing garrison duty; when the United States Army places men on heavy work details, however, it allows up to about forty-five hundred calories a day. Modern soldiers are of course taller and heavier than their eighteenth-century counterparts, but even allowing for major differences in size (and hence in dietary needs), provincial troops on fatigue duty can only have been a lean and hungry-looking lot.

In most cases it is impossible to correlate diet with provincial behavior, because the information in soldiers' journals is usually inadequate to indicate caloric levels. In September 1758, however, Obadiah Harris made a series of entries in his journal that document both his unit's ration level

75. Robert Webster, 11, 13 Nov. 1759.

76. Winslow to Loudoun, 3 Sept. 1756, LO 1937. The provincials' diet in Massachusetts had hitherto been somewhat more generous. They received, weekly, six pounds of pork or seven of beef; six pounds of bread; a half pound of sugar; two ounces of ginger; a pound of flour; a pint of Indian meal; four ounces of butter; a pint of molasses; seven gills (about one-fifth of a gallon) of rum; and three and a half pints of pease or beans (*The Acts and Resolves, Public and Private, of the Province of the Massachusetts Bay*, XV [Boston, 1908], 455, hereafter cited as *Acts and Resolves*).

77. For the nutritional content of foods, see Robert S. Goodhart and Maurice E. Shils, eds., *Modern Nutrition in Health and Disease*, 6th ed. (Philadelphia, 1980); and World Health Organization [R. Passmore *et al.*], *Handbook on Human Nutritional Requirements*, World Health Organization Monograph Series, 61 (Geneva, 1974). Nutritional data is accurately summarized in a form convenient for calculation in Richard Ashley and Heidi Duggal, eds., *Dictionary of Nutrition* (New York, 1975), 17–27, and *passim*. Precise values are impossible to obtain because of the general dearth of information on food-preservation techniques, the uncertain fat content of the meat, and the unknown age of the provisions. Nonetheless, the

and his comrades' behavior. In the middle of the month, Harris and his battalion were on road-mending duty near Stillwater, north of Albany. On the nineteenth he noted, rather acidly: "We drawed stores for seven days. We had four pounds of pork, six pounds of flour, three gills of rice, [and] three ounces of butter. That is all the provision for seven days." Apparently this was typical of what his unit had been receiving for most of the summer, since Harris had recorded drawing a full allowance only once. While the pork, flour, rice, and butter issued on the nineteenth represented less than a full ration, they were not a great deal less. The four items could have yielded somewhat more than 2,250 calories a day, about the same level as a full ration. The items listed, furthermore, would have provided over 110 grams of protein a day, about twice the modern recommended daily allowance.[78] Harris's ration also contained sufficient carbohydrates and fats, plus adequate levels of phosphorus, iron, niacin, and vitamin B₁—and probably enough iodine as well.[79] The most noticeable

---

following probably approximate, on the generous side, the caloric values of the various species of victuals:

Item	Quantity	Calories	Calories in Daily Portion
Salt beef	1 lb.	990	990
Salt pork	1 lb.	1,300	745
Fresh beef	1 lb.	1,500	1,500
Fresh pork	1 lb.	1,520	870
Bread	1 lb.	1,075	1,075
Peas	1 pt.	250	110
Beans	1 pt.	500	215
Rice	1 lb.	1,600	115
Butter	1 oz.	200	115

Incidental items were sometimes supplied and added on occasion to the daily intake; these included ginger—used as a seasoning and as a water purifier (see, e.g., Loudoun to Cumberland, 17 Oct. 1757, in Pargellis, ed., *Military Affairs*, 401)—sugar, molasses, spruce beer, rum, and Indian meal. The supplements, however, were not part of the standard issue. (The previous provincial ration, supposing regular delivery of each item in the allowance specified above, n. 76, had provided approximately another 750 calories per day, hence a daily range of from 2,950 to 3,750 calories.)

78. Ashley and Duggal, eds., *Nutrition*, 25. The National Academy of Sciences–National Research Council's Food and Nutrition Board recommends 54 g of protein per day for men 19–20 years old of average height and weight (69 inches, 147 pounds); it also suggests 3,000 calories per day, however.

79. Obadiah Harris, 19 Sept., 12 Sept. 1758. The daily content of this day's ration was approximately as follows: protein, 114 g; carbohydrates, 345 g; fats, 77 g; niacin, 31 mg; vitamin B₁, 4 mg; phosphorus, 2.5 g; iron, 22 mg. These all meet or exceed the recommended daily allowance of the National Academy of Sciences for adult males of 19–22 years of age. Also present, but in insufficient amounts, were vitamin A, 400 IU; vitamin B₂, 1 mg; calcium, 220 mg. (RDA levels of these substances, respectively, are 5,000 IU, 1.8 mg, 800 mg.)

effect this fare had on the men building the road was to keep them hungry. They would not have noticed the subtler changes induced by the diet's heavy deficiencies in the other B-complex vitamins, vitamin C, and several necessary minerals. Yet these deficiencies almost certainly weakened the men's health, perhaps affected their mental states, and probably influenced their behavior.

The soldiers' first response to the short rations was to try to obtain food from the farmers who lived near Stillwater. Early in October the ration had not changed; Harris complained that "our allowance for a week is not sufficient for four days" and noted that otherwise he and his unit had "nothing to eat but what we get of the Dutch people." [80] But the Dutch charged high prices, and the soldiers could ill afford to provision themselves at the going rate. The result was preoccupation with food and money, dual concerns that surfaced in a poem Harris had penned earlier in the campaign. A total failure of supply had then brought the regiment to a standstill: a mass desertion was narrowly averted by the timely arrival of provisions on 22 August. Harris celebrated the event in "fourteeners," the meter of popular ballads:

> And now provisions come again,
>> And we have some to eat;
> Blest be the man that got the pease
>> And he that got the meat!
> The bread also to us is come,
>> And rice enough, in store;
> And some fresh beef for our relief:
>> What can we wish for more?
> Now we begin to live again—
>> The butter, it is come,
> And for our money we can have
>> Our bottles filled with rum.
> Yet some of us, they do complain,
>> Are all filled up with evil;
> For of [their] money they do spend,
>> And the Dutch they beat the d——l.
> Their sauce unto us they will sell,
>> Their price, it is so bad,

Absent altogether were vitamins C, D, E, folic acid, B_6, and B_{12} and the minerals magnesium and zinc. Although none of the items of the ration contained iodine, of which 140 mcg are thought to be the daily requirement, it seems possible that this very small amount would be present in the brine within which the pork was packed. (Nutritional requirement source: Ashley and Duggal, eds., *Nutrition*, 25, 27.)

80. Obadiah Harris, 2 Oct. 1758.

For squash and beans and pursley, too,
    Which makes us very mad.
The sutler he will 'tend full fast
    And for our wages call;
When we get home, we shall have none—
    For we shall spend it all.

The first half of Harris's poem offers a grateful recitation of the standard ration. The last half concerns the dietary supplements that the soldiers provided for themselves. The item they clearly preferred to buy was rum, which had anesthetic and caloric, though no nutritional, value. The sauce (or "sass," the New England dialect term for garden greens) that the Dutch sold so dearly, helped to alleviate both the monotony of the ration and several of its vitamin deficiencies. The poem indicates that the soldiers' desire for fresh vegetables was about as great as their desire for rum, and the anxiety expressed in the last couplet concerns the effect of spending to buy both liquor and greens. Their hunger for elements absent from the diet recalls the cravings experienced by pregnant women in a condition called opsomania; here it is aggravated by worries over money. The result, Harris records, was that the soldiers were "very mad" at the "Dutch."

Fresh vegetables could have made up a substantial amount of the vitamins missing from the provincials' fare, but they could not have been of much help in supplying calcium and magnesium. Deficiencies in these minerals are known to produce irritable, nervous, and belligerent behavior of the sort Harris had been steadily describing in his unit.[81] In addition to being "very mad" at the local farmers, the men of his battalion were "so cross and touchy that they can't speak to one another," as Harris put it on 21 August.[82] A few days earlier, he had recorded a "fray" between his unit and a group of regulars—a fight occasioned by the provincials' attempt to supplement their fresh meat supply.[83] Less than a week later, Harris described another set-to, this time between members of his regiment and a farmer, which resulted in the theft of the farmer's entire apple crop.[84] Mineral deficiencies and chronic hunger thus shortened tempers enough to promote disorder among the provincials even as shortages of B-vitamins lowered their resistance to disease and encouraged digestive disorders, especially the diarrhea that plagued soldiers in every campaign of the war.[85]

81. *Ibid.*, 145, 151–152. The relatively high phosphorus concentration may in part have aggravated the calcium deficiency, since these elements must be present in a constant ratio: see *ibid.*, 152–153.
82. Obadiah Harris, 21 Aug. 1758.
83. *Ibid.*, 13 Aug. 1758.
84. *Ibid.*, 27 Aug. 1758.
85. Ashley and Duggal, eds., *Nutrition*, 243–244, 247–251, 253–254.

Like the men of Harris's battalion, soldiers of every provincial regiment constantly tried to supplement their diet, although they were usually too far from farmers to deal directly with them. Instead they resorted to gardening, to hunting and fishing, and to buying from sutlers. For expeditionary troops, the latter method was the most common, and certainly the easiest. The diarists' frequent mentions of sutlers indicate that these small traders were highly important in the life of the camp. The absence of a sutler was regarded as a special hardship, since their supplies helped alleviate temporary shortages and generally relieved the monotony of camp fare. "My heart was grieved," wrote the Reverend Daniel Shute after seeing Colonel Thomas Doty's regiment in 1758, "to find the men so greatly fatigued, and nothing comfortable to take. No sutler, no doctor, no chaplain with them."[86] Another soldier complained in much the same vein when his regiment's sutler failed to arrive when expected: "Our army [is] very much uneasy with their manner of living. Our allowance at present is only flour and pork. No rum or sugar to be had in our regiment, for our sutler is not come, and we labor under a great disadvantage."[87] Necessary as the sutlers were, the relationship between them and the soldiers was always strained, as witness Obadiah Harris's fears of the sutler who "will 'tend full fast / and for our wages call" at campaign's end. "Our sutlers are fell much in the price of their stores," observed Joseph Nichols as the army decamped from Lake George in 1758. "Rum that a few days [ago] was sold for half a dollar for [a] quart is sold for half the money, and much of their stores they gave away. It is justly come upon them for their extortion," he concluded, "for they have very much imposed upon our people in this campaign."[88]

Officers suffered less than enlisted men in the field both because their work was less physically taxing and because they received more food from the commissary. Each colonel was permitted to draw six times the amount of an enlisted man's daily allowance; captains were entitled to a treble, and subalterns to a double, ration. Whatever was left over the officers could sell back to the commissaries at four pence sterling per ration.[89] Officers thus had a greater quantity of victuals available or, if they chose, a cash subsidy that they could spend at the sutler's tent. Because their lives were less regimented than those of their men, they could also go hunting or fishing more easily.[90] Finally, officers had servants who prepared their food and supple-

86. Daniel Shute, 11 Aug. 1758.

87. Joseph Nichols, 17 July 1758.

88. Joseph Nichols, 23 Oct. 1758. Cf. William Sweat, 4 Oct. 1758.

89. Stanley McCrory Pargellis, *Lord Loudoun in North America* (New Haven, Conn., 1933), 293. A general in chief could draw 18 rations; the understanding was that higher-ranking officers had to feed not only themselves but households of servants as well.

90. See, e.g., John Cleaveland, who went fishing himself, 19 July 1758, and also recorded

mented the ration with industry and ingenuity. "This morning observed Col. Williams's waiter pass by me," wrote Joseph Nichols on a day when he had drawn a nearly complete ration, though "scanty of pork." The man was carrying "squashes and carrots. Col. Bagley's waiter caught several dozen of pigeons with a net. I could not but think of the Israelites longing for the fruits of Egypt." [91] The culinary distance between the provincials and their regular superiors, however, was easily as great as that which separated provincial privates from provincial colonels. The Reverend John Cleaveland, a man who could appreciate a good meal, dined with Major General Abercromby only once during the campaign of 1758, and was most impressed by the "sumptuous dinner" he had. "Soup first, boiled beef, roast beef, boiled fish and fried fish all fresh, sodden venison and new potatoes, a plum pudding, apple pie and cheese!" [92] Girth, as surely as age and uniform, must have distinguished officers, especially regular generals, from the other ranks in the army. Such distinctions did not go unnoticed by men who often had cause to "think hard of their usage." [93]

At the very least, thoughtful provincials connected their diet with their performance as soldiers. "The spirits of men seem to fail," wrote a worried and hungry Joseph Nichols after the army's defeat at Ticonderoga in 1758. "We are losing our [*illeg.*] courage that in years past we had the credit of. It is a common saying that money makes the man to go, and I make no doubt if in case our natures was refreshed with diet agreeable to what we are used to, our strength and courage would come to us like an armed man: I would be understood, in a natural cause." [94] A month later he picked up the same explanation again and once more amplified it with a

---

officers who went hunting: see 30 Aug., 19 Sept., 11–13 Oct. 1758. See also William Henshaw, 4–5 Aug., 11 Aug., 1 Sept., 2 Oct. 1759; Lemuel Wood, 20, 29, 31 Aug. 1758; Samuel Chandler, 27–28 Oct. 1755; Moneypenney's orderly book, 16 July 1758; Luke Gridley, 13 Oct. 1757. Enlisted men hunted when they could, but were generally discouraged from doing so because of the great potential for ammunition wastage, the exposure of hunters to enemy Indians lurking in the woods, and the difficulty of distinguishing men who were hunting from deserters. See, e.g., Lyman's orderly book, 16, 18, 24 May, 30 Aug. 1757, for measures directed against uncontrolled hunting by privates. Even so, private soldiers did repeatedly manage to hunt—and fish—to supplement their rations; see James Hill, 20, 21, 22, 30 Aug., 2 Dec. 1755; Luke Gridley, 30 Apr., 5, 16, 19, 24 May 1757. Often game was killed simply when it happened to appear rather than as a consequence of hunting, but these windfalls also provided welcome additions to the allowance of provisions. See, e.g., Amos Richardson, 9 June, 19 Aug., 24 Aug. 1758; Enoch Poor, 30 Sept. 1759; Caleb Rea, 11 Aug. 1758.

91. Joseph Nichols, 10 Aug. 1758.

92. John Cleaveland, 10 Sept. 1758. Earlier he had written to his wife describing a much scantier daily fare: John Cleaveland to Mary Cleaveland, 25 July 1758, JCP, III, 162–164. See also Seth Pomeroy, 27, 28 Aug. 1755; and Caleb Rea, 27 Oct. 1758.

93. Joseph Nichols, 30 Oct. 1758.

94. Joseph Nichols, 17 July 1758. For the significance of Nichols's curious final clause, see chap. 7, below.

proverb. "Much complaint among our men concerning their allowance, and they have good reason for it. For four days [of provision] will but just answer for three [of consumption]. Our scouting, fatiguing, and guarding is very hard. Hard service and poor keeping makes Jack a dull boy."[95] Such complaints were increased by the inadequacy of shelter in the wilderness encampments. If his hard work and stingy diet made the provincial soldier dull, his leaky tent ensured that he would often be wet and miserable, and his crowded, dirty camps multiplied the chance that he would fall prey to disease as well.

IV

Throughout the war provincial camps never approached the geometrical order of the regulars' encampments. In its purest drill-manual form, the redcoat camp perfectly expressed the army's hierarchical ideals. Laid out in a grid composed of rectangular battalion areas each a hundred yards wide and three hundred yards long, the regular camp separated officers and men, allowed easy movement along avenues that intersected at right angles, and located sanitary facilities well away from troop kitchens. Within each battalion block, the arrangement of tents replicated the pyramid of command. The colonel's quarters stood in the heart of the area, at the apex of a broad triangle of officers' tents. Below the baseline formed by the subalterns' billets, the enlisted men pitched their tents in a compact rectangle, along parallel company streets. Shelters reflected the rank of their occupants. Common soldiers slept five to a tent in tents that measured about seven by nine feet; captains lived individually in tents of about nine feet by ten. At the top of the regimental scale, the colonel slept in a "bedchamber-tent, about the size of a captain's"; in addition, he had a "dining-tent, . . . commonly twelve foot broad and fourteen deep." Even the allocation of the camp's surface area precisely reflected rank. The billets of a battalion's seven hundred enlisted men covered an area only about forty yards long by a hundred wide; the tents of the thirty-six company officers were pitched next in line on an identical plot of ground; and bordering this, just seven field and staff officers occupied an area fully sixty yards by one hundred.[96] (See Figure 2.)

Provincial camps were chaotic by comparison. This was especially true early in the war, but considerable irregularity persisted even after 1756. Little attention was paid to order when a provincial unit went about setting up camp; days or even weeks might pass before orders would be is-

95. Joseph Nichols, 22 Aug. 1758.
96. See Bland, *Treatise*, 241–249.

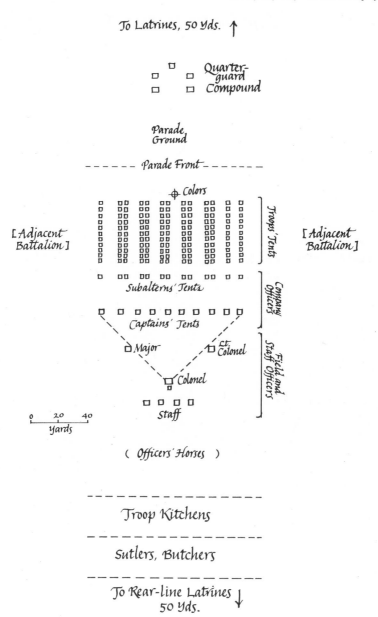

To Latrines, 50 yds. ↑

Quarter-
guard
Compound

Parade
Ground

– – – – – – Parade Front – – – – – –

Colors

[Adjacent
Battalion]   [Adjacent
Battalion]

Troops' Tents

Subalterns' Tents

Company
Officers

Captains' Tents

Major   Lt.
                Colonel

Colonel

Field and
Staff Officers

Staff

0   20   40
yards

(Officers' Horses)

Troop Kitchens

Sutlers, Butchers

To Rear-line Latrines ↓
50 yds.

Figure 2. Layout of a Regular Battalion Area. After Humphrey Bland, *A Treatise of Military Discipline,* 6th ed. (London 1746 [orig. publ. London, 1727]), 244. Drawn by Richard Stinely

sued requiring troops to clear the ground "of all the stumps and rubbish
. . . and pitch their tents regular in straight lines." [97] The differences
between a typical provincial campsite and one occupied by regulars can
be inferred from Caleb Rea's account of a reshuffling of troops at Lake
George camp in July 1758. In the relocation process Colonel Jonathan
Bagley's regiment was shifted from one side of the encampment to the
other and had its old spot taken by a regular battalion. [98] "Removed our
encampment through the whole forces, general and all," wrote Rea. As the
unit left, he lingered to watch "the regulars employed in cutting up the
stumps where our regiment moved from. Their method was to dig around
the stumps with mattocks, cutting off the side roots; then fastening it to a
tackle, fifteen or twenty men would haul it up or break it off some depth
underground. Thus forty men cleared off about twenty stumps a day,
making all smooth." [99]

That the officers and men of Bagley's regiment had willingly coexisted
with stumps for which the redcoats had no tolerance signifies more than
mere provincial slovenliness or regular compulsiveness: it reflects fundamental differences between provincial and regular attitudes toward camp
life. Provincial practices, in turn, had important implications for their
health and welfare in the field.

The housing of soldiers in camp was one of the most obvious points of
divergence between regular and provincial practices. Early in the war,
New Englanders campaigning on the New York frontier found themselves
chronically short of tents and improvised a variety of shelters. Robert
Treat Paine, the chaplain of Colonel Samuel Willard's regiment, described
the provincial camp at Lake George as it looked near the end of 1755 in a
letter home. Who, Paine mused rhetorically, could

> describe the various accommodations and conveniences of living used
> in this place? In one part you might behold rows of habitations ap-
> pearing like whited sepulchres, the same stuff that among us proves
> fatal to villains, here screens them from trouble; in another part you
> might see a cave or hole in the rocks; some huge poles of brush and
> dirt served to fend off the cold and rain—others had long rows of
> buildings that much resemble meeting-house sheds; but the better
> sort of people built according to certain rules of architecture in prac-
> tice here; the doors are low and the roofs level, some spread them
> with hides and sheep-skins, though others neglect it for the benefit

97. Hawks's orderly book, 16 July 1759, continuation of battalion orders. Cf., e.g., Constantine Hardy, 5, 6 Aug. 1759; Nathaniel Dwight, 27 Nov. 1755.
98. The order to move is in Moneypenney's orderly book, 16 July 1758.
99. Caleb Rea, 17 July 1758.

of the light—their windows are made lengthwise and some reach from side to side; there are very few that wainscot, paper, or plaister their rooms, by reason they prefer the pine scented balsam their timber affords. Their lodging is various, some using an artificial couch and others preferring the feathers the land produces, so that truly it may be said of some that their houses are fir and their bed is green.[100]

Despite his mock-heroic tone, Paine conveyed a fair impression of the variety of tents, burrows, longhouses, and bow-houses that made shift for housing in the provincial camp. Such an agglomeration diverged in several important respects from the regular ideal. In the first place, brush houses were scarcely portable: if the army moved, it had to move without its shelter.[101] If the army gave in to inertia and stayed put, the ground beneath the huts could not be dried, as could the earth under tents, by striking them temporarily or by turning up their sides. In good weather, this doubtless made huts less comfortable and perhaps less healthy than tents were.[102] But most of all, brush and wood shelters prevented the achievement of the order and subordination so assiduously sought in the regular camp arrangement. Unfortunately for the cause of discipline, such shelters generally resisted rain better than tents and were easily constructed when necessary. For example, after a "very rainy" night that "set some afloat," John Woods and his tentmates "contrived about building a house"; two days later it was finished, a "fine house, the biggest in the regiment."[103] From the standpoint of uniformity, the uncontrollable impulse to build was bad enough; but the competitive individualism implicit in wanting to build "the biggest in the regiment" was potentially much worse. Predictably enough, the desire for outsize houses did not stop with privates. In 1758 Colonel Jedediah Preble employed thirty men to build his house at Lake George. More surprising even than that, however, is an observer's aside that Preble was building a new dwelling because he had *sold* his old one.[104]

The more substantial huts might require considerable investments of time and labor, as John Cleaveland noted of his dwelling: "With Mr. Beckwith, Mr. Johnston, Mr. Eels, and brother [Ebenezer Cleaveland] this afternoon raised our house at Lake George, built of sawed planks. Twelve feet long and ten feet wide, and though it is of some expense to build it, I

100. Quoted in Ralph Davol, *Two Men of Taunton in the Course of Human Events, 1731– 1829* (Taunton, Mass., 1912), 122–123. The letter was written in November, according to Davol, 120; he gives no further information.

101. Brush huts could in fact be moved, but only with difficulty. See Samuel Jenks, 7–10 July 1760.

102. See, e.g., Wilson's orderly book, 8 Aug. 1759; Luke Gridley, 29 June 1757.

103. John Woods, 8, 10 Aug. 1759.

104. William Sweat, 30 Aug. 1758.

should gladly leave all here to return to my family and people." [105] Cleaveland's account implies several other problems that such semipermanent housing bred. While the chaplain observed that he would gladly leave his newly built abode to return home, it is much less likely that he would gladly have forsaken it to make another sally against the French at Ticonderoga. Furthermore, the five chaplains who built the house lived there together, rather than with their respective regiments. While this arrangement effectively addressed the housing shortage, it greatly diminished the integrity of the five regimental staffs to which the chaplains belonged, since staff members were supposed to live next door to their colonels. Finally, the chaplains built the house with their own hands. This was a good, practical response to the problems of building, but clearly violated the proscription of manual labor for officers. [106]

Faced with the manifold abuses that hut-building engendered, from nonuniformity to the creation of de facto real estate markets within their camps, regular commanders tried to prohibit such practices. "When the Assisting Deputy Quarter Master General has marked out the lines of the encampment, the several regiments are to pitch their tents," ordered Major General Daniel Webb at Fort Edward on 28 June 1757. "Accordingly the commanding officer of each corps is to be answerable to the general that their regiments encamp proper, and on the ground assigned to them by Mr. Lesley. And any tents pitched irregular will be ordered to be struck. No huts will be allowed . . . on any account within the lines. And the men's kitchens are to be built in the front, without the lines." [107] Such commands were of little avail, however. Four months after General Webb's prohibition, without any intervening order to countermand it, directives were issued at Fort Edward that make it clear the provincials had been busy building huts anyway. Moreover, the shelters had proven useful enough that sanctions had to be threatened to prevent the departing provincials from tearing the huts down as they left: "G[eneral] L[yma]n's O[rder]. That the men belonging to the provincial troops take particular care not to pull down or destroy any of their huts, upon penalty of staying here all winter." [108]

The fact was that, no matter how unmilitary, potentially unhealthful, and unquestionably irregular soldier-built housing was, it offered at least

105. John Cleaveland, 6 Sept. 1758. Two weeks later, Cleaveland moved into a better hut with the regiment's lieutenant colonel, John Whitcomb; this one had a fireplace and chimney (John Cleaveland, 20 Sept. 1758; cf. John Cleaveland to Mary Cleaveland, 26 Sept. 1758, JCP, III, 176–178.)

106. Other officers, of course, also built their own shelters; see, e.g., Samuel Jenks, 7–10 July 1760.

107. Lyman's orderly book, 28 June 1757.

108. *Ibid.*, 8 Nov. 1757; an amplification of the same, 10 Nov. 1757.

as much protection as the tents. Even when there were enough of the "osnaburg tabernacles"—as one soldier called the canvas shelters—to house the troops on an expedition, a single thunderstorm or the onset of cold weather was enough to reveal their deficiencies. The Reverend Daniel Shute, who was thankful that he had remained dry in a hut on 28 August 1758, was nonetheless grieved to see the effects of a heavy rain that left soldiers "very much soaked in their osnaburg tents." The provincials' virtual obsession with weather conditions seems almost understated in view of such conditions as this: "This forenoon cold and cloudy with a northeast wind. The afternoon a cold rain. At night the storm increased. Our tent was worn out. We was very much exposed." [109] Joseph Nichols reflected on camp conditions in much the same vein after the ninth man in his regiment died from disease:

> The bloody flux prevails in our regiment very fast. Several of our company reduced very low. It's imputed to the season of the year's changing: the nights and mornings begin to be cold and we often have cold rains. Our tents begin to be of but little service, for they will not shed rain, but let it through very fast. These things is very detrimental to people's health. And our allowance is bad. And no provision made for the sick, which is very hard indeed. [110]

Few soldiers linked disease and camp conditions as explicitly as Nichols did, but there can be no doubt of the connections. Regular officers were quicker to remark on the provincials' state of health as a function of their living conditions, and their portraits of the provincials' way of life were never flattering. In 1756, for example, Lieutenant Colonel Ralph Burton wrote to Lord Loudoun describing what he had recently seen among the New England troops. "At Fort William Henry," he remarked, were

> about 2,500 men, 500 of them sick, the greatest part of them what they call poorly. They bury from five to eight daily, and officers in proportion. Extremely indolent and dirty to a degree [that] the fort stinks enough to cause an infection. They have all their sick in it. The camp nastier than anything I could conceive. Their necessary houses, kitchens, graves and places for slaughtering cattle, all mixed through the encampment.

109. "Osnaburg tabernacles" is from Samuel Jenks, 4 Sept., 15 Nov. 1760; Obadiah Harris, 15 Aug. 1758. Cf. Nathaniel Dwight, 4 Oct. 1755.

110. Joseph Nichols, 17 Sept. 1758. Mentions of inadequate shelter in tents were common; see, e.g., Samuel Jenks, 22 Oct., 15 Nov. 1760; Thomas Moody, 9 Nov. 1760; John Woods, 8 Aug. 1759; John Thomas, 31 Oct. 1755; Abijah Willard, 29 Aug., 4, 18 Sept., 15 Oct. 1755; Samuel Chandler, 23 Nov. 1755.

> At Fort Edward about 2,500 men, between five and six hundred sick. Bury daily from five to eight men, and officers in proportion. Their camp much cleaner than at Fort William Henry, but not sufficiently so to keep the men healthy.[111]

Sanitary conditions may have improved after 1756 as a result of joint service with the redcoats, but provincial camp life was not noticeably more pleasant at the end of the war than it was when Burton made his complaint. In 1760, for example, Captain Samuel Jenks recorded taking walks as long as "five or six miles, in order to keep out of the smell of the camp."[112] By the beginning of October the excursions had become "usual" for himself and others who hoped "to get a better air than we have in camp, which is almost infectious [from] such numbers of sick and dead men [being] always in camp."[113] A fellow officer described another camp, in September 1760, even more graphically: "The imagination of man cannot form to itself a place more stinking and loathesome [than this,] where our poor men lie groaning and gasping [out] their lives daily."[114] Such conditions seem to have been common, in provincial encampments, throughout the conflict.

Commanders repeatedly issued orders to promote sanitary measures among the provincials—often enough to suggest that the soldiers persisted in unsanitary practices despite the instructions. Even so, regular officers criticized provincial leaders for paying too little attention to the cleanliness of their troops. In addition to general indictments like Burton's, these surfaced as peevish asides in regular orderly books. Six weeks after the New England battalions arrived in Nova Scotia in 1755, for example, Colonel Robert Monckton pointedly "observed" in an order directed at the two New England colonels that "many of [their soldiers] have not changed their shirts since their first putting them on at Boston."[115] As provincial officers gained in campaigning experience, they came to issue standing orders, without being prompted, for "the non-commissioned officers and privates . . . [to] make it their daily practice to wash and keep their face and hands clean, and their weekly practice to wash their shirts, that they

111. Lt. Col. Ralph Burton to Loudoun, 27 Aug. 1756, LO 1599. Upon receiving Burton's report, Loudoun wrote to Winslow advising him on sanitary measures: drying the ground under shelters, burying refuse, constructing a slaughterhouse—and creating a cemetery out of sight of the camp (Loudoun to Winslow, 4 Sept. 1756, LO 1706).

112. Samuel Jenks, 23 Sept. 1760.

113. Samuel Jenks, 7 Oct. 1760. See also, e.g., 19 Sept., 10, 12 Oct., 7 Nov. 1760.

114. Thomas Moody, 14 Sept. 1760. The post he described was the camp at Île-aux-Noix.

115. "Orders of the Day, Fort Cumberland Camp," 7 July 1755, "Journal of Winslow," Nova Scotia Hist. Soc., *Colls.*, IV (1884), 197.

may have a clean one to put on every week."[116] It would seem, however, that practice among the men lagged well behind official policy. Two soldiers who carefully recorded the performance of routine duties, Lemuel Lyon and William Sweat, noted in 1757 and 1758 that they washed their clothing six and four times during the respective campaigns.[117] John Woods, who was in every discernible respect a typical private, noted washing only twice during the campaign of 1759, and his pragmatic practice may have reflected that of most provincials. His second laundry occurred only after he made an unpleasant discovery: "Washed my jacket and shirt, and boiled them out to kill the lice, for I found several about me; so I gave them a dressing."[118]

If provincial troops were slow to understand the need for personal hygiene, they were even harder to convince of the necessity for other sanitary measures. Since most were country men with little experience of life in large, dense settlements, this is hardly surprising; practices the commanders deplored would not have been so bothersome and potentially dangerous among a dispersed rural population. "It is observed that the Soldiers are not so exact as could be wished in regard to cleanliness in the Camp," wrote John Winslow in late August 1755, "leaving their cabbage leaves, pease pods, etc., among their tents which, in a little time, will become noisome." As a remedy, he ordered the creation of a garbage dump thirty feet from the entrance to the encampment. In his journal entry for that day he noted, "[We] began . . . to clear ourselves of one of the Egyptian plagues."[119]

Equally difficult to control and of even greater peril to the health of a camp was the soldiers' tendency to disregard latrines. These "necessary houses" they learned to use only slowly, if at all. As late in a campaign as August, provincial commanders would still be issuing procedural orders concerning the use of privies. This was the case, for example, when Colonel Joseph Williams, in the hope of lessening "infections, steams, etc." in

116. Regimental order for Frye's regiment, 23 June 1759, in Josiah Peary, 23 June 1759. See also, e.g., Hawks's orderly book, 27 June, 13 July 1759.

117. Lemuel Lyon, 29 June, 11, 13, 17 July, 4, 19 Aug. 1757; William Sweat, 7, 17 July, 22 Sept., 10 Oct. 1758.

118. John Woods, 11 Oct. 1759. (The other occasion was 25 Sept.) Another private who served in 1759, Robert Webster, wrote on 10 July, "I washed and this was the first time that I washed since I came from home." Webster had left Woodstock on 13 May, so he had gone nearly two full months without a washing.

119. "Journal of Winslow," Nova Scotia Hist. Soc., *Colls.*, III (1882–1883), 78. Winslow evidently referred to the fourth plague, flies. For other examples, see, e.g., Josiah Peary, 6, 23 June 1759; Hawks's orderly book, 26–28 June 1759; Lyman's orderly book, 20, 28 June, 5 Sept., 8 Oct. 1757.

his camp, "strictly forbid" his troops from "going to stool in other places [than latrines] near the encampment." Their present practice, he explained, had the pernicious "tendency to nauseate the water or infect the air with a disagreeable stink."[120] As Robert Treat Paine coolly put it in describing the camp at Fort William Henry in 1755, "The land here is not tilled, though it is excellently manured."[121]

The effects of irregular sanitation and poor personal hygiene were compounded by the necessity of concentrating troops, for reasons of security, into the smallest possible camp areas. Captain Nathaniel Dwight, a surveyor in civilian life, measured the camp at Fort William Henry on 2 November 1755 and found that slightly more than twenty-three acres were enclosed within the breastwork.[122] At the time, the camp held about four thousand men, of whom twenty-five hundred were healthy enough to perform their duties.[123] The camp thus had a population density at least *nine times as high* as Boston's and was undoubtedly one of the thickest patches of settlement in North America. Robert Treat Paine was straining for irony when he called it a "wonderful city," but he was not far wrong.[124] Besides Boston, only three towns in Massachusetts—Salem, Newbury, and Marblehead—had populations equal to or larger than that of the camp in the fall of 1755. Nor was that particular gathering of troops especially large: the encampment that stood on the same ground in 1758 had a perimeter "counted nigh three miles circulation" and at times held more than fourteen thousand men.[125]

Although military service took place in the midst of a wilderness, camp life was paradoxically more like an intense urban experience than anything most provincials had ever known. By concentrating its soldiers in tightly packed cantonments the army also introduced them to two other characteristics of city life: a dangerous disease environment and very high levels of mortality. Disease and death were so common that, like the density of population, they exceeded all but the most wretched urban conditions. Especially as campaigns neared their ends, everyday existence in the camps assumed a nightmarish quality, more and more resembling life in rank and pestilential slums.

120. Williams's orderly book, 7 Aug. 1759; see also *ibid.*, 10 Aug. 1759; Hawks's orderly book, 24 June 1759.

121. Quoted in Davol, *Two Men of Taunton*, 121.

122. Nathaniel Dwight, 2 Nov. 1755. The measurements he gave were 42 perches by 89 perches, or approximately 700 by 1,500 feet. Robert Treat Paine's letter confirms this with his own estimate of about "22 acres compactly settled and the inhabitants strictly confined within these narrow limits" (quoted in Davol, *Two Men of Taunton*, 122).

123. Samuel Chandler, 13 Nov. 1755.

124. Quoted in Davol, *Two Men of Taunton*, 121.

125. Joseph Nichols, 25 Aug. 1758.

V

The last three months or so of a campaign, from mid-August through dismissal in November, formed a distinct and perilous phase of military service. Governor Francis Bernard in 1763 reported to the Board of Trade:

> In the beginning of the late war many perished by the sword, but much more by the diseases incidental to a campaign. In 1760, when I came to this government, I was surprised to [s]ee what havoc disease alone made among the provincial soldiers in the course of, and especially towards the end of, a campaign. And yet I remedied this mischief by three provisions only: having them well clothed, keeping them from rum, and supplying them plentifully with spruce beer. If these regulations had been established in the beginning of the war, many hundreds (I may say some thousands) of lives would have been saved.[126]

The results of Bernard's prophylactic measures were very likely more dramatic in his correspondence than in the field, but he was quite right about the havoc wrought by diseases. As the weather worsened and shelter began to prove wholly inadequate, the soldiers' cramped and unsanitary living conditions exacted a heavy toll in lives lost to various "camp distempers": dysentery, diphtheria, typhus, typhoid fever, smallpox, and other virulent disorders.

In 1756, levels of mortality in the late campaign can be measured with some precision for all six Massachusetts regiments on the Crown Point expedition. Late in July of that year the names of 2,681 men serving in the Bay Colony's battalions were recorded; on October 11 and 12 a second muster was conducted, which revealed that in the interval 154 provincial soldiers had died and 606 more had fallen ill or been badly hurt.[127] This represents a crude death rate, for less than three months, of 57.4 per thousand, and total casualty rate for the same period of 283.5 per thousand.[128]

126. Bernard to the Lords Commissioners for Trade and Plantations, 5 Sept. 1763, in Joseph Henry Benton, Jr., *Early Census-Making in Massachusetts, 1643–1765* (Boston, 1905), 55.

127. For a summary of the physical conditions of Massachusetts provincials as of 11 and 12 Oct. 1756, see Table 26.

128. The death rate of 57.4/1000 represents a most conservative figure, since the 154 deaths are verifiable ones, noted as "killed," "died," or "deceased" on the rolls. The 278 men who simply vanished from the lists between the musters of July and Aug. and the survey of conditions on 11 and 12 Oct. may very well have included at least some dead. Moreover, mortality tended to increase heavily in the final weeks of any campaign. The Massachusetts regiments were in the field for another full month beyond the time the condition rolls were collected. If the incidence of infection and death was indeed growing, many more men would have fallen ill or died before the end of the campaign.

The same pattern is evident in soldiers' journals of other years, and insofar as these documents can be used to establish the incidence of mortality within individual units, they tend also to indicate that the death rate of 1756 was not unusually high. Four diaries are sufficiently complete for death rates to be computed for the units they describe. Because the frequency of death varied considerably between regiments, these rates cannot be taken as reliable indicators of army-wide mortality in the three years covered. Nonetheless, they do offer evidence concerning the *range* of service-related mortality and, together with other journals, show something of how soldiers reacted to the appalling conditions around them.

Two provincials recorded, with apparent completeness, the total number of deaths within their battalions: Luke Gridley for Phineas Lyman's Connecticut regiment in 1757, and John Cleaveland for Bagley's Massachusetts regiment in 1758. Gridley noted on 11 October 1757 that about 50 men had so far died in his regiment; 10 more died before the organization was disbanded in early November. The unit consisted originally of 900 men; this suggests a late-campaign mortality level of 66.7 per thousand.[129] In Colonel Jonathan Bagley's regiment the following year, according to John Cleaveland's account, 32 men died in a little less than five months, between mid-June and mid-October. Bagley's regiment was a smaller organization than Lyman's, numbering about 800 men; its campaign death rate thus stood at 40.0 per thousand.[130] Cleaveland's letters to his wife tend to suggest that Bagley's regiment was an unusually healthy one.[131] Neither Bagley's nor Lyman's regiment suffered substantial battle casualties.

Evidence from two companies which served in different regiments in 1760 indicates that much higher death rates could also occur. Captain Samuel Jenks commanded a company in the first battalion of Brigadier Timothy Ruggles's regiment; over the six months between 28 May and 26 November, 10 of his approximately 80 men died, all of disease. This translates into a campaign death rate of 125 per thousand.[132] Finally, Captain John Wentworth's 80-man company, in Colonel John Thomas's regiment, sustained 11 deaths among its members between 20 May and the end of November. This yields a campaign death rate slightly higher than that of Jenks's company, 137.5 per thousand.[133] In the three diaries from which

129. Luke Gridley, 11, 12, 21, 22, 27, 29 Oct., 3 Nov. 1757.

130. John Cleaveland, table of deaths from disease, following 26 July 1758 entry; see also entries for 10 July, 15 Oct. 1758. Twenty-six men died of illness; another six from wounds sustained at Ticonderoga. For the total size of the unit, see Joseph Nichols, 31 May, 1 Oct. 1758, and John Cleaveland (1758), postscript entry.

131. John Cleaveland to Mary Cleaveland, 3 Aug. 1758, JCP, III, 164–165.

132. Samuel Jenks, 11 Nov. 1760, and *passim*.

133. Thomas Moody (1760), postscript entry.

dates of death can be determined, covering Bagley's 1758 regiment and the two 1760 companies, virtually all deaths from disease took place during the late campaign, between the end of August and the beginning of November.[134]

If these figures are taken to represent the upper and lower limits of campaign death rates among the provincials, the dimensions of military mortality and its meaning for the soldiers begin to emerge. In Winslow's army of 1756, Lyman's regiment of 1757, and Bagley's regiment of 1758, covering a period of only three to five months in each case, soldiers died at almost twice the rate citizens of contemporary Boston did, during the same *entire* years. At its worst, in Jenks's and Wentworth's companies in 1760, disease carried off soldiers in half a year at about four times the city's annual rate.[135] This, however, measures campaign mortality against urban conditions, which were markedly deadlier than those in the countryside; and it was from the country that the great majority of the recruits came. Annual mortality in rural Massachusetts seems seldom to have exceeded twenty or twenty-five per thousand, and even in epidemic years it may not have reached one hundred per thousand.[136] Thus the typical provincial private, raised in a small community, experienced a disease environment in which (if he was lucky) he was about four times likelier to meet death, in a matter of months, than he was in a whole year spent in his hometown. At its worst, life during the late campaigns was routinely riskier than it had been during the worst epidemics in New England's history.

134. By Cleaveland's account (1758), in Bagley's regiment 6 deaths occurred at the unsuccessful siege of Ticonderoga, in July; 6 deaths occurred in Aug.; 14 in Sept.; and 6 in Oct. In Jenks's company, 3 deaths occurred in Sept.; 5 in Oct.; and 2 in Nov. In Wentworth's company, by Moody's (1760) record, one soldier apparently died in June or July; 4 in Sept.; and 6 in Oct.

135. According to the five-year averages in John B. Blake, *Public Health in the Town of Boston, 1630–1682* (Cambridge, Mass., 1959), app. II, 249, the annual crude death rate for Boston in the period 1756–1760 was 34/1000; in the preceding five-year period, it had been 39/1000. (Gary Nash recomputed the figures for a slightly different level in *Urban Crucible*, 444, n. 10.) The worst year for mortality in 18th-century Boston was apparently 1721, the year of the smallpox epidemic; mortality then rose to 103/1000 (Blake, *Public Health*, 248).

136. See, e.g., Philip J. Greven, Jr., *Four Generations: Population, Land, and Family in Colonial Andover, Massachusetts* (Ithaca, N.Y., 1970), 196–197, n. 14; annual rates in Andover in the first half of the 18th century were, by Greven's estimate, as follows: 1715, 16/1000; 1725, 19/1000; 1735, 9/1000; 1740, 15/1000; 1745, 21/1000. The highest death rate he recorded was in 1738, the year of the "disastrous epidemic" of throat distemper, when the crude death rate rose to 71/1000 (see also p. 199). Kenneth A. Lockridge, in "The Population of Dedham, Massachusetts, 1636–1736," *Economic History Review*, 2d Ser., XIX (1966), 332–333, opts for a maximum in Dedham of 27/1000 annually, and for an average on the order of 20–23/1000. (These figures, for reasons that Lockridge explains on p. 332, are so estimated as to overstate mortality.)

Such comparisons can give only a rough impression of how awesome such mortality seemed to the soldier. If it was his first campaign, he simply had no experience that could compare adequately to what was going on around him. The recruits' bewilderment at the dangers of camp life emerges clearly in a notation Joseph Nichols made in his diary early in August 1758—two days before the first man in his regiment died of the camp distemper.

> Our provincial forces die more or less, almost every day; but people who are used to camps tell me that they never knew a more healthy time in an army. May what we daily see and experience take good effect, and all the dispensation of divine providence be sanctified for the good of all our whole army![137]

Seven weeks later, when nearly a score of soldiers from his regiment lay dead of disease, the personal "effect" of this "dispensation" was clear to Nichols: a vivid awareness of the uncertainty of life. "How near all of us be to death we know not," he wrote, "for many in our camps are well, and dead in four or five day[s]. Oh, how we ought to be constantly preparing for our great and last change!"[138] For Nichols and his comrades, it was not merely the intensity of the late-campaign mortality, but the suddenness of death that mattered. In the army, life was literally here today and gone tomorrow—gone in some cases so abruptly that a man might have no last chance to repent of his sins or to make amends to those he had wronged.[139]

Conscious of their peril and of the worsening camp conditions, soldiers during the last months of campaigns showed special concern for their personal states of health and for the health of their comrades; they sometimes kept rosters of those who died. The tensions of the late campaign can be seen with special clarity in the writings of several soldiers at Lake George in 1758. Sometime in August, the Reverend John Cleaveland started to keep a running account of the members of Bagley's regiment who had died of disease. As late as 3 August the chaplain had written home that there had been no deaths as yet, although Bagley's was the "only regiment exempted" so far.[140] In the space of fifty days, however, from the last week of

137. Joseph Nichols, 8 Aug. 1758.

138. *Ibid.*, 27 Sept. 1758.

139. Conversations with sick and dying soldiers noted in Cleaveland's diary tend to suggest the importance placed by those in danger of death on the last chance for repentance and amendment of the spirit. See his account of the death of Ebenezer Ransome, 18 Sept. 1758, which is also a good example of a venerable New England genre, the death narrative. (See David E. Stannard, *The Puritan Way of Death: A Study in Religion, Culture, and Social Change* [New York, 1977], chap. 4, for a full discussion.) Ransome evidently intended to meet his end in accordance with well-understood norms of deathbed behavior.

140. John Cleaveland to Mary Cleaveland, 3 Aug. 1758, JCP, III, 164–165. The deaths Cleaveland recorded occurred between 10 Aug. and 15 Oct. 1758.

August through the chaplain's departure in the middle of October, twenty-three of Bagley's soldiers died—eight during the week of 17–23 September alone.

Cleaveland's journal for the period, his letters home, and the diaries of others in the camp manifest considerable concern and apprehension. "My dear," Cleaveland wrote on 3 September, "I have but just a moment of time to write in, and cheerfully embrace it to let you know I am in health at present . . . but God only knows how long I shall enjoy it. People begin here to be taken down with very malignant fevers. We lost three or four last week and many are ailing with one disorder or another."[141] On 5 September he availed himself of a courier's departure to send his wife another letter, even though he averred: "I have nothing new to write that I omitted two days ago. Only this: that it is more mortal here I think every day. Col. Whiting lost four yesterday out of his regiment," and others several more.[142] In his daily journal entries during the period, Cleaveland noted deaths as they occurred, recorded cumulative totals of men who had died to date, described his visits to the sick, recounted conversations with dying soldiers. On occasion his anxieties surfaced in spontaneous prayer: "The Lord stay the Destroying Angel and pity us, for we are but dust and can't stand before the blow of his angry hand."[143] At other times his notations suggested the virulence of the diseases, their shocking suddenness. "Twenty-nine men are sick, were taken ill Tuesday night. The Lord preserve my health for a blessing and heal the sick among us, and prevent the spread of mortal diseases. Amen."[144] Cleaveland's entries also indicate the extent to which pestilence was a staple of camp rumor. "This evening the post lad, just going out of the camp, informs me that three provincials, having each of them wrote a letter to send by him to their friends, dropped down dead suddenly. And the letters were in their pockets dated the same day, in which they say they are in health. A solemn warning this, to be always ready."[145]

Cleaveland's diary in August, September, and October reveals a man worried about illness, living in a camp that, if anything, was even more anxious than he was. While the chaplain was unusual in his clerical per-

---

141. John Cleaveland to Mary Cleaveland, 3 Sept. 1758, *ibid.*, 170–172.

142. John Cleaveland to Mary Cleaveland, 5 Sept. 1758, *ibid.*, 168–169. Col. Nathan Whiting commanded a Connecticut battalion.

143. See, e.g., *ibid.*, 10, 15, 28, 29, 31 Aug., 2, 7, 16, 18, 21, 22, 23, 24, 28, 29 Sept., 1, 9, 13, 15 Oct. (entries recording deaths within the regiment); 10, 15, 29 Aug. (entries recording cumulative totals of deaths); 7, 22 Aug., 18, 21, 28 Sept., 3, 5 Oct. (visits to the sick); 18, 28 Sept., 3 Oct. (conversations with the sick recorded); 23 Aug., 21, 23 Sept. 1758 (ejaculatory prayers; the last is the prayer quoted).

144. *Ibid.*, 21 Sept. 1758.

145. *Ibid.*, 6 Sept. 1758.

spective and his articulateness, the writings of other contemporary witnesses bear out the impression. Ensign Archelaus Fuller, another member of Bagley's regiment, fretted over his health and that of his comrades during what he called "a very sickly time with the provincials."[146] Private William Sweat, who belonged to another unit, noted late September as particularly bad, "a very dying time." Besides his own worrisome health, Sweat was acutely aware that "our men dies very fast and suddenly, for they fall down dead as they are traveling."[147] Joseph Nichols also expressed concern, as we have seen above, at the catastrophic course of disease: "Some are about one day and another day I hear of their death, inasmuch as our lives is so uncertain!"[148] Bagley's regimental surgeon, Caleb Rea, was so busy with the care of the sick by mid-September that he found it hard even to set aside his duties long enough to attend divine services, a development he found especially distressing. Then he fell ill himself with dysentery and remained "weak and feeble" in his tent for more than a week.[149] By the time Rea recovered, the camp's medicine supply had been exhausted, and the only way left to deal with the sick was to send them home and hope for the best.[150] Thereafter invalids were sent off twice a week, as soon as surgeons could certify that they were no longer fit for service.

Early dismissal of the sick was distasteful to commanders, who thought the practice invited malingerers to desert under the guise of evacuation. (As Rea observed, the dismissals made "many well and others sick.")[151] The early release of the provincial invalids, which occurred in every campaign of the war, marked a kind of surrender, an admission that the sick had grown too numerous for the army to handle. Many soldiers commented on the "great numbers" of departing invalids; Caleb Rea noted simply, "Invalids sent home by wholesale."[152] Discharge could be dangerous. Samuel Jenks, for example, noted that out of a "party of eighty

146. Archelaus Fuller, 17 Sept. 1758; see also 21, 22, 24 Sept., and *passim*.
147. William Sweat, 18, 25 Sept. 1758; see also 15, 30 Sept. 1758.
148. Joseph Nichols, 3 Sept. 1758.
149. Caleb Rea, 17 Sept., 20–29 Sept. 1758 ("weak and feeble," 25 Sept.).
150. Caleb Rea, 19 Sept. 1758; John Cleaveland, 1 Oct. 1758.
151. Caleb Rea, 10 Oct. 1758. For similar sentiments in other years, see Samuel Jenks, 21 Oct. 1760; Loudoun to Winslow, 21 Oct. 1756, LO 2056; Winslow to Loudoun, 23 Oct. 1756, LO 2069; Loudoun to Abercromby, 4 Nov. 1756, LO 2151; Loudoun to Winslow, 5 Nov. 1756, LO 2159.
152. "Great numbers": Obadiah Harris, 26 Sept. 1758; Caleb Rea, 11 Oct. 1758; see also, e.g., Seth Pomeroy, 3, 11 Oct. 1755; Samuel Chandler, 13, 22–24 Nov. 1755; Nathaniel Dwight, 20 Oct., 19, 24 Nov. 1755; Luke Gridley, 25 Oct. 1757; John Cleaveland, 10 Oct. 1758; Joseph Nichols, 1 Oct. 1758; William Sweat, 30 Sept., 1, 13 Oct. 1758; Lemuel Lyon, 13, 22 Oct. 1758; Archelaus Fuller, 28, 29 Sept., 9 Oct. 1758; Samuel Morris, 7 Oct. 1759; Samuel Jenks, 28 Sept., 7, 23 Oct., 4 Nov. 1760; David Holdin, 23, 24 Oct., 12, 13 Nov. 1760; Thomas Moody, 3, 23, 24 Oct., 12 Nov. 1760.

sent by Major Hobble to Albany, I hear seventy of them are dead; and another small party sent that way since, I hear eighteen of them are gone the way of all flesh. So frail a creature is man!"[153] The best that a seriously ill man could hope for, apparently, was to be released when he was still strong enough to survive the journey home, or at least get to an inn or a private house where he could be nursed back to health. Such was the case, for example, with Colonel Seth Pomeroy, who was sick with a high fever at the time of his release. He managed to reach an inn near Albany before he collapsed; there he lay close to death for ten days before the fever relented, and he convalesced for two weeks more under the innkeeper's care before he was able to travel once again.[154]

In the troop hospitals care was a good deal more haphazard than what was available even at an inn. Regimental surgeons and their mates were primarily responsible for the treatment of the sick and wounded from their own units; in addition, enlisted men were detailed from each regiment to act as nurses. Eighteenth-century therapeutic techniques were limited in scope and effectiveness: soldiers who received treatment and lived to tell the tale were mainly bled, purged, or given emetics. Considering in addition the rudimentary extent of the contemporary materia medica,[155] recovery from serious diseases depended primarily upon each individual's constitution and his body's ability, with rest and adequate diet, to recuperate naturally. Army hospitals provided little enough, even in the way of shelter and reliable diet, to promote healing. There were permanent hospitals, notably at Fort Edward, Albany, and Halifax, Nova Scotia, but these were never adequate to house all the sick; many other temporary expedients supplemented them. When Obadiah Harris fell sick in 1758, he was left, along with other invalids of his unit, "at a Dutchman's barn" near Halfmoon which served "as an hospital for the sick of our [i.e., Ruggles's] regiment."[156] The diet of the sick was no better than that of the healthy

153. Samuel Jenks, 4 Nov. 1760. When a party of 500 set off on 23 Oct., he observed that there were "some so bad I think they will never reach New England"; he was pleased to hear word, two weeks later, that only one or two had died on the first leg of their homeward journey (4 Nov. 1760).

154. Seth Pomeroy, 23 Oct.–17 Nov. 1755.

155. The military pharmacopoeia apparently consisted in its basics of the drugs Caleb Rea borrowed of another surgeon when the arrival of his chest was delayed: "I borrowed some medicine of Doctor Price, viz., Pul. Rhei one dr., Crm Tartar one oz., Laud Liquid one oz., Diascord one oz., Pil Cochia one oz., Pul. Corte one oz." (1 July 1758). "Pul. Rhei" probably meant pills of pulverized rhein, or rhubarb root, a purgative and astringent agent; "Crm Tartar" was cream of tartar, used as an emetic; "Laud Liquid" was laudanum, an opiate; "Diascord" was an astringent herbal preparation based on the leaves of germander, *Teucrium scordium*; "Pil Cochia" was apparently a coca extract, possibly a form of cocaine; "Pul. Corte" probably refers to pills made from powdered Peruvian bark, or chinchona, a febrifuge.

156. Obadiah Harris, 9 Oct. 1758.

soldier, and no more predictable: "We have nothing to eat but meat for all the sick," Harris complained in September 1758.[157] A few weeks later, at the Lake George camp, Joseph Nichols mourned that there was "no provision made for the sick, which is very hard indeed."[158] Sanitation in the hospitals was as inadequate as in the camps themselves. Lieutenant John Frost briefly visited the hospital at Crown Point in 1760. The only impression he recorded was of the stench: "Of all the smell that I ever smelt, there was none that ever smelt so bad."[159] Care of the bedridden did not even extend to providing them with clean linen. When Sergeant David Perry contracted "the nervous fever" in 1762, he was hospitalized at Halifax. He remained delirious most of the time, but at one point, he later recalled, "I came to myself so much as to know that the body lice were eating me up, and told one of those who waited on me, to heat a tailor's goose which was in the room, and iron my blanket on both sides; which he did, and it turned red as blood."[160] To make matters worse, when Perry finally recovered, months later, he found that he had "spent or lost" all his wages, "by reason of sickness & c.," and indeed had even lost his "clothes, except those [he] had on at the hospital."[161] Observers sympathized with the sick, prayed for them, and—cautiously—visited them; but there was little more they could do. "After dinner visited the Sick," wrote John Cleaveland in 1758, "some [I] found under very pitiful circumstances. One his lip eat off in about a day or two with the mortification."[162]

The mortality and illness that beset the late campaign subjected even those soldiers who remained healthy to sustained stress, since no one knew who the next victim would be. What the soldiers did not fully understand was that late-campaign mortality was in fact rather selective, that death by disease did not threaten all of them equally. There was, for example, some variation by rank: the 1756 crude death rate among private soldiers, 67.1 per thousand, was higher than that for noncommissioned officers (41.2 per thousand) and officers (28.7 per thousand).[163] The most telling variation, however, was by the age of the soldier. Men aged fourteen to nineteen came through relatively well, with a three-month death rate of 37 per thousand. At the opposite end of the spectrum, men of fifty-five years and older suffered dreadfully: over the three-month interval from late July

157. *Ibid.*, 3 Sept. 1758.
158. Joseph Nichols, 17 Sept. 1758.
159. John Frost, 11 July 1760.
160. Perry, "Recollections," *Mag. Hist.*, CXXXVII (1928), 20.
161. *Ibid.*, 30.
162. John Cleaveland, 5 Oct. 1758.
163. The physical condition of Massachusetts provincials as of 11 and 12 Oct. 1756 as well as their death rate are summarized by rank in Tables 27, 28.

through early October they died at a rate of 275.9 per thousand.[164] As we have seen above, the provincials likeliest to represent socially marginal elements were the older privates, those in their late thirties and beyond. The physical effects of campaigning on the average soldier—that is, on the private in his early twenties—were less severe than the psychological effects. Jittery as they were in the last months of a campaign, most of these soldiers would make it home, while older men bore the brunt of suffering from disease. The experiences of the typical provincial recruit with illness were harsh and frightening enough to make a permanent impression, but not likely to be permanently damaging. They were, moreover, *shared* experiences: a part of the common groundwork of memory for all those who served in the provincial armies.

VI

Soldiers eagerly anticipated their discharge from the army and return to civilian life—a function at least in part of the dreadful health conditions and the worsening weather of the late campaign. When word came that departure was imminent, usually in late October or November, it was greeted as "joyful news" by men who had been monitoring the camp rumors carefully for indications that the campaign was ending.[165] Preparations for the march were quick; turning in tents and equipment and drawing marching rations and billeting money were typically accomplished in a day or two.[166] Returning soldiers marched as units until they reached a dis-

164. The physical condition of Massachusetts provincials as of 11 and 12 Oct. 1756 as well as their death rate are summarized by age cohort in Tables 29, 30.

Compounding the problem of mortality for the army was the fact that nearly four times as many men were absent from duty because of sickness as had died. Considered from the commander's perspective, only slightly over half of the men who had been present in July and August 1756 were still fit for duty in mid-October. Under these circumstances, the provincial army was hovering on the verge of military impotence. Although it could still garrison forts, such an army could hardly be expected to do more than defend itself if called into battle; only a steady stream of replacements could rebuild an organization suffering such attrition. Following the fall of Fort Oswego to the French in late Aug., and in response to the badgering of Lord Loudoun, Massachusetts did in fact send replacements totaling 366 men to New York. At least three times that number, however, would have been necessary to compensate for the losses the provincials had suffered. (For an account of Loudoun's difficulties in persuading Massachusetts to reinforce its troops and his similar problems with other colonies, see Pargellis, *Loudoun*, 171–183.)

165. David Holdin, 17 Nov. 1760.

166. James Hill, 26, 27 Nov. 1755; Luke Gridley, 30, 31 Oct. 1757; Seth Metcalf, 18 Dec. 1757; William Sweat, 23 Oct. 1758; Robert Webster, 18 Nov. 1759; David Holdin, 17, 18 Nov. 1760; Thomas Moody, 10, 17, 18 Nov. 1760.

persal point, where they were mustered one last time; they then took their separate ways, traveling home in small groups.[167] The soldiers' return seems to have had a much more hurried, or at least a more purposeful, aspect than their approach march in the spring. Soldiers who kept diaries recorded distances traveled, weather, lodging, food—but wrote little, now, of the countryside they passed through, and seldom took side trips. Most men who were healthy at the time of discharge usually managed to march home from the New York frontier in less than two weeks, often at a rate of thirty or more miles a day.[168]

The provincials' transition from military to civilian life, then, was a quick one, faster than their initial transformation into soldiers. In a sense, they had been in fairly close touch with civilian life all along: letters were frequently received or sent, carried mostly by men who happened to be traveling between the army and New England on business, or by petty entrepreneurs who ran postal services. The total volume of mail was impressive: a chaplain who returned to New England from Flatbush (near Albany) accumulated "at least half a bushel of letters" to distribute on the trip.[169] Some soldiers were particularly heavy correspondents—John Cleaveland wrote at least thirty letters in 1758, and Joseph Nichols more than a dozen in the same year; Jonathan Procter sent about twenty in as many months during 1759 and 1760, and Samuel Jenks wrote at least a score in six months of 1760 alone.[170] Even those provincials who sent few or no letters still managed to maintain contact with home. When the militia company from his hometown arrived at Fort Edward as reinforcements after the alarm of 1757, Lemuel Lyon noted that it was "with great joy we received them, and much more the things that were sent us."[171] Similarly,

167. These seem to have been determined by unit commanders. The process was brief, not at all the equivalent of the mustering-in, which had taken place generally at Worcester. Capt. Samuel Jenks, for example, performed his last muster at Fort Number Four, in New Hampshire, where he remained briefly after his men dispersed (Samuel Jenks, 25, 26 Nov. 1760); other commanders apparently used Albany or Greenbush as dispersal points (Joseph Nichols, 3 Nov. 1758).

168. Samuel Chandler, 27 Nov.–17 Dec. 1755; James Hill, 27 Nov.–12 Dec. 1755; Luke Gridley, 30 Oct.–10 Nov. 1757; Seth Metcalf, 20 Dec. 1759–3 Jan. 1760; John Cleaveland, 16–25 Oct. 1758; William Sweat, 23 Oct.–7 Nov. 1758; Archelaus Fuller, 1–11 Nov. 1758; Obadiah Harris, 15–23 Oct. 1758; Robert Webster, 18–23 Nov. 1759; Samuel Morris, 14–26 Nov. 1759; David Holdin, 18–29 Nov. 1760; Thomas Moody, 18 Nov.–1 Dec. 1760.

169. Caleb Rea, 12 June 1758.

170. John Cleaveland, 12, 17, 26 June, 4, 11, 25 July, 3, 17, 21, 30 Aug., 3, 8, 16, 22, 23, 26 Sept., 3, 11 Oct. 1758; Joseph Nichols, 24 Sept. 1758 (a notation that he had written 12 letters home thus far in the campaign); Jonathan Procter, 15 May (initial entry, recording all letters sent in the previous year of service at Louisbourg), 9, 22 June, 15 July, 28, 29 Oct. 1760; Samuel Jenks, 29 May, 12, 20, 21, 30 June, 6, 12, 20, 31 July, 5, 8, 24, 29 Aug., 18, 19 Sept., 9, 19 Oct. 1760.

171. Lemuel Lyon, 20 Sept. 1758.

Seth Metcalf apparently wrote no letters, but a kinsman visited him at Fort Edward in 1757, bringing him "some conserve[s], cheese, sugar, and dried apple," as well as news from home.[172]

Soldiers who wrote letters home were men likely to be firmly rooted in familial networks and in the lives of their communities. Given the position of young men in provincial society and economy, it would be somewhat surprising if most veterans returning to rural communities (so long as they were healthy enough to work) had any considerable difficulty reintegrating themselves into civilian life. The information available about several soldiers' postservice experiences tends to bear out this impression. James Hill arrived in his hometown, Newbury, on Friday, 12 December 1755; the next Tuesday he "went to work for Master Shute" at his old occupation, shipbuilding.[173] Several provincials mentioned returning to the homes of relatives. Obadiah Harris's last entry of the campaign records that he traveled "seven mile to Medway and dined, and from thence five miles to my father's house at Wrentham."[174] He went back to farming; his next entry speaks eloquently for his subsequent life:

> Wrentham, April the 20th, 1785:
> Where I am yet and ever like to be.

On that same day, he recorded a note due him of £178 6s. 4 3/4d., so the quarter-century that intervened between entries had evidently been a fairly prosperous one.[175] Like Harris, most soldiers whose postwar careers can be traced remained for the rest of their lives in the towns they had called home at the time of their service.[176] Those who moved evidently followed the same careers they had followed before the army and by no means lost contact with family and community. Samuel Jenks, for instance, became a partner in his father's blacksmithing business, moving to Boston. Samuel Morris farmed and kept school in the Sturbridge-Dudley

172. Seth Metcalf, 14 July 1757. Other soldiers also had visits from relatives; see, e.g., Archelaus Fuller, 27–28 Sept. 1758.

173. James Hill, 12, 15 Dec. 1755.

174. Obadiah Harris, 23 Oct. 1758. Other diarists who conclude by describing a return to their own or a relative's house include Luke Gridley, 10 Nov. 1757; Seth Metcalf, 3 Jan. 1758; John Cleaveland, 25 Oct. 1758; William Sweat, 7 Nov. 1758; Archelaus Fuller, 11 Nov. 1758; Enoch Poor, 12 May 1759; Samuel Morris, 26 Nov. 1758; Robert Webster, 23 Nov. 1758; John Burrell, 22, 23 July 1760; David Holdin, 29 Nov. 1760; Thomas Moody, 1 Dec. 1760; Perry, "Recollections," *Mag. Hist.*, CXXXVII (1928), 30, 31; Putnam, *Memoirs*, 21.

175. Obadiah Harris, 20 Apr. 1785.

176. Of 16 whose later careers can be traced, 10 apparently remained in their residences at enlistment for the rest of their lives: Samuel Chandler, Seth Pomeroy, Seth Metcalf, John Cleaveland, William Sweat, Archelaus Fuller, Obadiah Harris, Gibson Clough, Jonathan Procter, Thomas Moody. Six moved: Rufus Putnam, David Perry, Samuel Jenks, David Holdin, Samuel Morris, Joseph Nichols.

area, to which he moved (from Woodstock) with his new wife. David Perry took his cordwainer's expertise to Killingly, Connecticut, where he married and raised a family.[177] None of these men was spectacularly successful; but none of them slipped into indigence, either. This is not to say that movement back to civilian life was always so easy or successful: it was most certainly *not* so in every case, and must have been particularly troubled for men who had been disabled in service. Yet for the soldiers we know through the surviving diaries, the transition from soldier to civilian was not traumatic. They had, for the most part, been the sons of middling men; they themselves became men of the middling sort, indistinguishable from the run of farmers and artisans across the province. Only one thing set them apart: the shared experience of war.

When they marched home from campaigning, provincial veterans had seen much more of the world than they had known before enlistment. In the midst of the wilderness they had seen a miniature representation of their whole, surprisingly diverse, province—a community united in common cause against New England's historic enemy. At the same time, military service afforded them the chance to see British regulars at close range. In their encounters with the regulars, the provincials discovered a great deal that surprised them, both about the British and about themselves. Whether they fully appreciated it at the time or not, the war caused the young men of the Bay Colony, at a crucial point in their lives, to experience their identity as a distinct people.

177. Samuel Jenks (1760), introductory note; Samuel Morris (1758), final entries; Perry, "Recollections," *Mag. Hist.*, CXXXVII (1928), 30–31.

Chapter 4 ❖ "There Is No Spare Here of the Whip"
Interactions between Provincial and Regular Troops

Of all the British officers who appear in the diaries and memoirs of provincial soldiers, only Brigadier General George Augustus, Viscount Howe, seems to have evoked consistently favorable responses from the New Englanders. Rufus Putnam called Lord Howe "the idol of the army" and thought it "not extravagant to suppose that every soldier in the army had a personal attachment to him." His popularity sprang from personal qualities exactly the opposite of those that provincials found repellent in other redcoat officers. Howe made it a point to circulate among common soldiers and artificers, "and his manner was so easy and familiar, that you lost all that constraint or diffidence we feel when addressed by our superiors, whose manners are forbidding."[1] In other words, Howe was the exception that proved the rule: a regular officer admired by the provincials because he behaved as the provincials wanted officers to behave—which is to say, not at all like a redcoat officer.

One of the most important legacies of the Seven Years' War was the creation among the provincials of this general sense of what could be expected of redcoats. The war offered New Englanders and Britons a chance to take each other's measure with an intimacy and on a scale unprecedented in colonial history. Such intercultural contact—for that is what it was—largely took place through the operation of the British military justice system, and it gave the colonial soldiers an unflattering, disturbing impression of their comrades in arms.

I

When provincial enlisted men had direct contact with redcoat officers, it was the regulars' mercilessness and haughtiness that they were most likely to note. Joseph Nichols recorded with distaste an example of regular mis-

---

1. Rufus Putnam, *The Memoirs of Rufus Putnam* (Boston, 1903), 23. Howe's death on 6 July 1758, during a skirmish with the French on the approach to Ticonderoga, "struck a great damp on the army," as Putnam put it. The event was reported by virtually every diarist on the campaign. See, e.g., William Sweat, 6 July 1758; Moses Dorr, 9 July 1758; Caleb Rea, 6 July 1758; John Cleaveland, 6 July 1758; Joseph Nichols, 25 Aug. 1758; Obadiah Harris, 6 July 1758; Amos Richardson, 7 July 1758; Samuel Morris, 6 July 1758; Thomas Haynes,

treatment of provincial troops and the provincials' reactions, which occurred at the close of the 1758 campaign. At the end of October, as the
redcoats were going into winter quarters, Nichols's unit, a Massachusetts
regiment under the command of Colonel Jonathan Bagley, was detained at
Fort Edward to help send supplies down the Hudson River. On 31 October, the day that the men of the regiment understood to be the very last of
their enlistments, at "about sunrise, the chief officer of the fort came to
our regiment and ordered all our men up to the falls to meet the wagons
and teams. Our men seemed to be loath to go before they eat. Those that
refused to turn out, he drove out, and some he struck with his staff, which
caused a great uproar among us. Our people in general declare in case we
are so used tomorrow, blows shall end the dispute."[2] As it turned out, the
regiment was dismissed later in the day, and the crisis was averted. The
incident only reinforced impressions of the British that already existed
among the provincials. Around the middle of the summer it had been
widely believed in Bagley's regiment that Colonel Thomas Doty's battalion
at Halfway Brook had been so "affronted by Capt. Crookshanks, a Regular, [that] the great part deserted: near or quite half the reg[iment]."[3] The
rumor was in fact wildly exaggerated; but the provincials who passed it
along were capable of believing that a regular captain could indeed give
such offense that "near or quite half" of a provincial regiment might desert in response.

Even more than did their enlisted men, provincial officers resented the
regular leaders' hauteur. John Winslow's journal of the Nova Scotian campaign in 1755 bristles with animosity toward his superior, Colonel Robert
Monckton—an enmity heightened by Winslow's repeatedly frustrated
ambition to command a regular regiment of his own.[4] Along with the rest

"Memorandum of Collonial French War, A.D. 1758–," Fort Ticonderoga Museum, *Bulletin*,
XII (1966), 150. References to soldiers' diaries refer to sources listed in Appendix B and are
cited by author's name and date of entry.

2. Joseph Nichols, 31 Oct. 1758. The "chief officer" was probably Col. James Prévost, a
man acknowledged even among the regulars to be peremptory (see Loudoun to Cumberland,
25 Apr.–3 June 1757, in Stanley Pargellis, ed., *Military Affairs in North America, 1748–1765*
[Hamden, Conn., 1969 (orig. publ. New York, 1936)], 354–361). For a similar episode, recorded at great length by a diarist who rarely made lengthy entries otherwise, see Samuel
Greenleaf, 12 Nov. 1756.

3. Caleb Rea, 24 July 1758. Capt. "Crookshanks" was Capt. Charles Cruikshanks, a Royal
American [60th] Regiment lieutenant who from 1757 commanded one of the New York Independent companies. Loudoun thought him a "diligent Officer" (Loudoun, "List of Commissions" [Apr. 1757]; Loudoun to Cumberland, 25 Apr.–3 June 1757, in Pargellis, ed., *Military Affairs*, 334, 347). Apparently about 60 men deserted from Doty's command, according
to a fragment of Abner Barrows's diary, published with Williams's orderly book (1758), 214.

4. Winslow to King Gould, 16 June 1755, "Journal of Colonel John Winslow . . . ," Nova
Scotia Historical Society, *Collections*, IV (1884), 177. Winslow to Thomas Lane, 26 June
1755, in *ibid.*, 178; Winslow to the earl of Halifax, 27 June 1755, in *ibid.*, 180.

of his New England colleagues, Winslow believed that Monckton and the governor of Nova Scotia were conspiring to deprive the New Englanders of the honor they knew they deserved for driving the French forces from Acadia.[5] Moreover, Winslow and his comrades thought that Monckton took advantage of every opportunity to disregard and snub them, to harass them, and even personally to humiliate Winslow. The last of these Monckton undeniably did when he assigned Winslow to a remote location, at the head of an insignificant detachment, and then publicly deprived him of the regiment's colors just as he was leaving.[6] By the end of the campaign of 1755, the New England officers' early enthusiasm had been transformed into animosity. The estimate they had formed of regular behavior contributed heavily to the New England assemblies' insistence upon strict division between regular and provincial forces in the campaign proposed for the following year.[7]

The distaste of provincials for haughty regulars runs like a litany through officers' diaries during the rest of the war. Caleb Rea retailed story after story of provincial officers who had been affronted, slighted, or abused by regulars. The provincials had regarded it as "an imposition" when a portion of Colonel Ebenezer Nichols's regiment was posted to an insignificant detail at Halfway Brook. Nichols had been ordered to lead the detachment himself, while one of his subordinates was placed in command of the main body of the regiment at Fort Edward. When Nichols was finally relieved from his backwoods post, the British command saw fit to replace him not with another field officer, but with a regular captain. The New Englanders

---

5. See, e.g., extract dated 29 July 1755, *ibid.*, III (1882–1883), 189–190.

6. Winslow noted that "acquaintance" between regulars and provincials "greatly dropped" after the surrender of Fort Beauséjour (31 July 1755, *ibid.*, IV [1884], 215). Incidents in which the provincials felt their characters aspersed and themselves to be discriminated against in assignments followed the drop-off (see 11–14 Aug. 1755, *ibid.*, 228–229, 230, 237–238); these incidents culminated in Monckton's peremptory taking of the colors from Winslow on 14 Aug. (see 14–15 Aug. 1755, *ibid.*, 238–240). Winslow deemed the latter most offensive—"the most ungentle ill-natured thing that ever I saw, and as such I set it down in my book" (15 Aug. 1755, *ibid.*, 240). After Winslow was detached with a small force, Monckton continued to offer affronts to the junior New England officers (Jedediah Preble to Winslow, 5 Sept. 1755, *ibid.*, III [1882–1883], 100–101; Winslow to Monckton, 19 Sept. 1755, *ibid.*, 131–132; Winslow to Preble, 19 Sept. 1755, *ibid.*, 132–133; Monckton to Winslow, 23 Sept. 1755, *ibid.*, 150–151; Preble to Winslow, 24 Sept. 1755, *ibid.*, 151–152). The whole increasingly nasty affair culminated with Monckton's attempt to enlist soldiers from among the New England battalions at the end of the year—an act regarded as deeply offensive to colonial dignity and charter privileges (Winslow to Gov. William Shirley, 20 Oct. 1755, *ibid.*, 175–176; Winslow to Lt. Gov. Charles Lawrence, 27 Oct. 1755, *ibid.*, 179–180; Winslow to Monckton, 3 Nov. 1755, *ibid.*, 182–183; Preble to Winslow, 10 Oct. 1755, *ibid.*, 187; Winslow to Shirley, 19 Dec. 1755, *ibid.*, 190–191).

7. Lawrence Henry Gipson, *The Great War for the Empire: The Years of Defeat, 1754–1757*, 206, in Gipson, *The British Empire before the American Revolution* (New York, 1936–1969), VI.

believed that this and similar slights were calculated insults, aimed not just at the individual who happened to be singled out for humiliation but at provincial officers as a group. Rea also resented the way in which regular leaders consistently ignored their provincial colleagues and failed to include them in councils of war. On 23 August, for example, he noted: "This day at a general council, Colonels Lyman and Preble was called as members. Mark, two provincials with perhaps twice or thrice the number of regulars."[8] In the same vein the Reverend John Cleaveland grumbled in a letter to his wife from Lake George that provincial colonels were never consulted "and know no more what is a-going to be done than a sergeant till the orders come out."[9] Both Rea and Cleaveland, along with other provincial officers, came to worry before the end of the 1758 campaign that the regulars—who were responsible for the failure of the expedition against Ticonderoga—would contrive a means of blaming the defeat on the provincials.[10]

In the campaign of 1760, Captain Samuel Jenks suffered a disillusionment parallel to that which Winslow had experienced in 1755. Although he began the campaign with singular enthusiasm, Jenks soon came to resent the discriminatory treatment he and his comrades received from their regular commander, Brigadier General William Haviland. Following the capitulation of the French garrison at Île-aux-Noix, for example, he wrote that "several of our officers" had tried to view the fortifications, only to be "prevented by the regulars. [This] is looked upon [as] a very high affair, when we have done most part of the fatigue during the siege, and our men have been more exposed than they, [that we] must now be denied the liberty to go and see what [we] have fought for." He fiercely resented the assignment of provincials to fatigue details, at which "no honor is to be got." After the defeat of the French he concluded that the redcoats were intentionally detaining the provincials in Canada "to get all they possibly can out of us before they dismiss us. I think this parallel with the devil's rage, when he knew his time was short to plague mankind in; so I know their time is short, like their master's."

Discrimination against the provincials became especially pronounced, and Jenks grew increasingly bitter, as the campaign finally neared its end. "This morning the snow is about six inches deep on a level, and extreme cold and windy," he wrote on 14 November. "Yet our good friends the regulars turned out the provincials on fatigue sooner than usual, and kept

8. Caleb Rea, 25 July 1758 (Nichols's humiliation); 23 Aug. 1758 (exclusion from councils of war).

9. John Cleaveland to Mary Cleaveland, 25 July 1758, John Cleaveland Papers, III, 162–164, Essex Institute, Salem, Mass. (hereafter cited as JCP). Cf. William Williams to Israel Williams, 11 July 1755, quoted in Alan Rogers, *Empire and Liberty: American Resistance to British Authority, 1755–1763* (Berkeley, Calif., 1974), 72, n. 52.

10. Caleb Rea, 31 Aug. 1758; John Cleaveland, 15 Sept. 1758.

their own men off the works." By the end of the campaign, Jenks had spoken companionably with a regular officer only once. The rest of his contacts had been wholly impersonal, and mostly unpleasant.[11]

The differences between British and New England goals, expectations, and views of military service all tended to strain relations between the groups when the regulars were exercising their authority. There were other kinds of interactions, too, between redcoats and provincials, interactions not complicated by the exercise of authority and the envy or resentment that it generated. These situations, as much as any, were the ones by which the provincials took the measure of the British. Insofar as most New Englanders, before the war, had had little opportunity to observe Britons at first hand, military service provided them with their first real chance to form immediately verifiable impressions. Provincials' diaries allow us in effect to watch as they form their images of the regulars—perceptions both favorable and unfavorable, by which the New Englanders came to know more about the British and more about themselves.

Many of the interactions between the groups consisted merely of curious observation, as when Joseph Nichols strolled around the encampment of Gage's regiment, whom he identified as "the Leather Caps who are called the Light Infantry." They were, he noted, "a mixed nation, even of all sorts."[12] Sometimes what the New Englanders saw was more disturbing than that: one observer noted that the redcoats of the Fiftieth Regiment were "Scotch Irish and English and by their manners and behavior we suppose[d] were convicts."[13] Most observations, however, were of behavior that the colonists found curious rather than threatening. One of these was the discovery that the regulars kept different holidays than the New Englanders did. Provincials unofficially observed Election Day—"Our people made it a day of mirth and joy" at Louisbourg in 1760, wrote Gibson Clough—and, despite the active discouragement of their commanders, also kept up the tradition of disorder on Pope Day.[14] Regulars, on the other hand, as a matter of official policy, observed the king's birthday, and kept Saint George's Day as well (or Saint Patrick's, or Saint Andrew's Day, depending on the composition of the regiments).[15] "This day," wrote

11. Samuel Jenks, 28 Aug. 1760 (Île-aux-Noix); 1 Oct. 1760 (fatiguing); 31 Oct. 1760 ("the devil's rage"); 14 Nov. 1760 (work during snowstorm); 21 July 1760 (conversation with redcoat officer).

12. Joseph Nichols, 26 Aug. 1758.

13. Stephen Cross, 15 Nov. 1756. These men had been enlisted in the southern colonies; Cross suspected the lot of them to be transported felons.

14. Election observation: Gibson Clough, 28 May 1760; Luke Gridley, 12, 13 May 1757; John Burrell, 28 May 1760. Pope Day disorders: Samuel Jenks, 6 Nov. 1760; David Holdin, 5 Nov. 1760; Thomas Moody, 5 Nov. 1760.

15. William Henshaw, 10 Nov. 1759; Gibson Clough, 22 Apr. 1760.

Jonathan Procter, who was amused by such antics, "is called here [at Louisbourg] Saint George's Day, and the English draw up and walk round the walls of the garrison, and carry Saint George's cross in their hats. This is a Day for the English to acknowledge their country as Saint Patrick's Day is for the Irish. These days are observed in garrisons and camps where soldiers are kept."[16] Provincials noted other redcoat peculiarities, too: their officers fought duels, for instance, a practice in which New Englanders seem not to have engaged.[17] Regulars were also known to commit suicide—an act that was evidently rare or unknown among provincials. Insofar as the recorded suicides were committed by men awaiting punishment, it seems likely that this tendency was a consequence of the harshness of regular discipline.[18]

Provincials found much to admire in the redcoats and noted especially their courage under fire, their ability to remain healthy on campaign, and their greater disposition to orderliness and teamwork—all functions of their more effective discipline.[19] Provincials were also aware that they were being unfavorably compared to regulars, apparently a habit of British officers. When "a regular soldier drowned [and] two others [were] shot by accident" on a single day in 1758, Caleb Rea responded that "this brings to my mind their reflections on our provincials, as there has been four or five [provincials] killed by accidentally firing their pieces."[20] The provincials' consciousness of such comparisons led them to compete avidly with the regulars. On 20 July 1760, for example, at Lake George there was "a race of two whale boats between the provincials and regulars. The latter six oars, the former eight paddles. The provincials beat the regulars forty-two minutes running six miles."[21] Such impromptu contests, which included shooting matches and wrestling ("the Lobsters and our men hopped and wrestled together to see which would beat, and our men beat"), reflected the provincials' desire to prove themselves the equals of the redcoats in strength and skill.[22] The provincials' evident interest in these events per-

16. Jonathan Procter, 23 Apr. 1760; cf. entry of 8 Nov. 1760.

17. Samuel Jenks, 18 July 1760.

18. See, e.g., William Sweat, 14 Aug. 1758; Gibson Clough, 27 June 1759, 6 Feb. 1760, 15 June 1760; Jonathan Procter, 15 June 1760.

19. For admiring mentions of the redcoats, see, e.g., Archelaus Fuller and John Cleaveland, 8 July 1758 (intrepidity in battle); Joseph Nichols, 6 July 1758 (ability to keep order under pressure), 26 Aug. 1758 (healthiness in camp); Caleb Rea, 16 July 1758 (bravery), 17 July 1758 (efficiency and orderliness).

20. Caleb Rea, 14 Aug. 1758. John Cleaveland was similarly sensitive to unfavorable comparisons and avidly accumulated stories that showed the provincials to be as good as regulars at soldiering, or better. See, e.g., 2 Oct. 1758.

21. Thomas Moody, 20 July 1760.

22. Shooting matches: Lemuel Lyon, 25 Aug. 1758; Caleb Rea, 23 Aug. 1758. Wrestling

haps betrays a certain anxiousness to establish their prowess as soldiers, even as it suggests that they regarded the regulars as martial models, of a sort. But it is also clear that the New Englanders entertained no doubt that they were the moral superiors of the redcoats, and this conviction colors most of their perceptions of the British.

The most common depiction of the redcoats, officers and men alike, was as inveterate breakers of the Second and Third Commandments, matters of no small concern to many provincials. "Sad! sad! is it to see how the Sabbath is profaned in the camp!" mourned Caleb Rea, who went on to observe that "many that seem pious" did their best to rebuke the defilers of the day, even though they could do little because the real problem lay with the regular leaders, who refused to enforce proper Sabbath order.[23] "It is a melancholy thing that the Lord's Day should be so little regarded," Joseph Nichols observed, adding that it was nonetheless "much more regarded by the provincials than the regulars."[24] Samuel Jenks, too, found the habit irksome: "No regard is paid . . . to sacred time. This day I heard a band of music at the commanding officer's tent while [a group of officers] were dining which was very delightful, though in my opinion not so seasonable on such days of sacred appointment."[25] Such complaints were strongly related to concern over the frequency with which the redcoats took the name of the Lord in vain. To the Reverend John Cleaveland, who might have been expected to have a tender sensibility about such matters, swearing seemed to be "the naturalized language of the regulars in general," including their Anglican chaplain, at Louisbourg in 1759.[26] But laymen, too, were quick to complain of redcoat profanity. Following the defeat of Abercromby's army at Ticonderoga in 1758, Caleb Rea was moved to reflect on what "horrid cursing and swearing there is in the camp, more especially among the regulars; and," he shuddered, "as a moral cause I can't but charge our defeat on this sin, which so much prevails, even among the chief commanders."[27] Joseph Nichols commented repeatedly

---

matches: Lemuel Lyon, 4 Sept. 1758. (Wrestling was common enough that it became a problem; it was sometimes forbidden, as by a 14 July 1759 order at Lake George [Hawks's orderly book].)

23. Caleb Rea, 11 June, 23 July 1758, and *passim*.

24. Joseph Nichols, 10 Sept. 1758, and *passim*.

25. Samuel Jenks, 22 June 1760; see also 29 June, 6, 13 Aug., 21 Sept., 12 Oct., 2 Nov. 1760. See also Luke Gridley, 19 June 1757; Jonathan Procter, 29 Apr. 1760, and *passim*; John Graham, 17 Aug. 1756 (attributing a profaned Sabbath to the influence of visiting regulars).

26. John Cleaveland to Mary Cleaveland, 22 Aug. 1759, JCP, III, 194–195. He had made similar observations the year before: see John Cleaveland to Mary Cleaveland, 3 Sept. 1758, JCP, III, 170–172.

27. Caleb Rea, 10 June 1758.

on the language of his comrades and noted, typically, that he "observed but little profaneness among our provincials, but among the regulars, much profaneness."[28]

Such comments illustrate a point of cultural divergence between the two groups and show how the provincials perceived it. Most New England soldiers had grown up in a land where those who took the Lord's name in vain or who traveled on Sundays could be—and often were—brought to book for misdemeanor before the local justice of the peace.[29] As soldiers, the natives of the Bay Colony not only found it disturbing that such flagrant breaches of good order occurred; they were bothered even more by the fact that the leaders of the army did nothing to stop them. Indeed, the regular officers' own behavior seemed to encourage further breakdowns in decency. Provincial commanders, on the other hand, issued orders against swearing and orders compelling attendance at divine services.[30] Regimental courts-martial among the provincials attempted, whenever possible, to enforce both.[31] While orders were occasionally issued among the regulars for divine service, there was little attempt to compel attendance, and it clearly mattered much less to British commanders than the maintenance of routine camp order.[32] Profanity does not seem to have bothered the regular leaders at all. Like their unfamiliar holidays, the regulars' attitudes toward casual oaths and amusement on the Sabbath derived from a cultural milieu that was unexpectedly alien to the colonists. Unlike holiday-keeping, however, provincials could not interpret swearing and Sabbath desecration simply as curiosities, because these were not merely neutral traits: they were moral defects, sins.

Other aspects of redcoat behavior excited similarly adverse reactions. The provincials found, for example, that they were lewd. Unlike New Englanders, who did not permit women to follow their regiments into the field, regulars were accompanied by, and consistently identified with, camp women. Female camp followers in fact performed valuable services to the army, including laundry and care of the sick. Some were undoubt-

---

28. Joseph Nichols, 3 July 1758; cf. entries of 5, 8 June 1758.

29. On prosecutions for profanity and Sabbath-breaking, see William E. Nelson, *Americanization of the Common Law: The Impact of Legal Change on Massachusetts Society, 1760–1830* (Cambridge, Mass., 1975), 15, 38.

30. Orders against swearing: see, e.g., Caleb Rea, 23 June 1758, citing an order issued by Col. Jonathan Bagley; also Hawks's orderly book, 4 July 1759; and "A Good Advice from a Gentle Man [Col. Joseph Frye?] to the Soldiers in Fort Cumberland," Boyd's orderly book, 6 Oct. 1759. On compulsory attendance at divine service, see, e.g., Williams's orderly book, 1 July 1758.

31. Lemuel Wood, 16 Aug. 1759; "Journal of Winslow," 2 Aug. 1755, Nova Scotia Hist. Soc., *Colls.*, IV (1884), 219; David Holdin, 11 July 1760; John Barber, 2 July 1754.

32. Wilson's orderly book, 10 June 1759.

edly prostitutes, but this was by no means true of all, or even many of them. Camp women were regulated by general orders, were subject to military justice, and were provisioned by the command, along with the soldiers; thirty or forty were allowed to accompany each regiment.[33] As far as the provincials were concerned, however, they were loose women. Scarcely a favorable or even a sympathetic reference to them exists in any provincial diary, and most mentions reflect badly both on the women and their soldier sponsors. In a typical reference one soldier noted on 18 October 1758 that "this afternoon there was a Lobster corporal married to a Rhode Island whore."[34] At least the event was a peaceful one; David Holdin's account of an altercation involving regulars and a camp woman was altogether more violent and sinister. "A mighty discord amongst the regulars this night," he wrote in 1760, "disputing who had the best right to a woman and who should have first go at her, even until it came to blows, and their hubbub raised almost the whole camp."[35] Other incidents that the New Englanders set down, like the expulsion of women for carrying "an infectious distemper . . . very common to the sex in these parts," the involvement of women in violent wrangles, and the subjection of women to whipping for various infractions, indicate that the provincials saw regulars and their consorts as equally unsavory beings.[36]

Aggressiveness was the final touch in the provincials' portrait of the redcoats. As long as the war went on, violence punctuated relations between the groups, and if the provincials are to be believed, it was the regulars who started fights. There is no reason to suppose that it was so one-sided; the antagonism was mutual and expressed itself in escalating intensity from name-calling to fistfights to riots. *Lobster* was a favorite provincial epithet, and the British seem to have responded in kind. Incidents were frequent enough to elicit reactions like Lieutenant Colonel John Bradstreet's:

> As all reproachful and reflecting speeches or epithets are scandalous between soldiers engaged in the same cause, subjects of the same

33. For the exclusion of women from provincial camps, see, e.g., Seth Pomeroy, 19 Aug. 1755; for evidence of their services as nurses, see Moneypenney's orderly book, 14 May 1758; as laundresses, Samuel Jenks, 10 Aug. 1760; victualing and control of camp women by general order, Moneypenney's orderly book, 19 May 1758, and *passim*, also David Holdin, supplementary entry dated 31 May 1760.

34. Lemuel Lyon, 18 Oct. 1758; cf. Henry Lyon, 18 Oct. 1758.

35. David Holdin, 4 Oct. 1760; cf. Lemuel Wood, 5 Oct. 1760.

36. Venereal disease: see Lemuel Wood, 19 Aug. 1759. (See also Moses Dorr, 23 Sept. 1758: "About three o'clock the whole town of Sodom was pulled down and set on fire, *viz.*, where was a number [of] womens' huts; which made great disturbance.") Violent encounters involving camp women: e.g., Samuel Jenks, 24 July 1759; whipping: Lemuel Lyon, 1 Sept., 6 Oct. 1758.

prince, and who ought to be united in one common interest: This is
therefore to forewarn all the soldiers of the several corps not to cast
any reflection or utter any language that is affronting or abusive to
each other, on pain of being punished with the utmost severity for
disobedience of orders.[37]

The abuse in this case was clearly mutual, but to judge from the provincials' journals, New Englanders were constantly suffering under the jeers
and blows of the redcoats. In a typical episode, a lieutenant of Ruggles's
Massachusetts regiment at Crown Point in 1760 arrested a regular enlisted
man for "abusive language" and confined him to the quarter guard, or regimental calaboose. As the guardhouse detail was changing, a witness recalled, "there came about forty of the grenadiers with clubs and forced our
quarter guard, and took away the prisoner. The guard pursued as fast as
possible, and the picquet was turned out, and all pursued, and recovered
two of the mob. They fired two guns at the grenadiers; I believe wounded
some. This affair put the whole of the line in commotion."[38] In this account, it is worth noting, the witness put the regulars at fault not once but
twice: first for abusive language, and again for cudgeling their way in
to free the prisoner. The fact that the provincials fired on the mob, apparently as it was fleeing, was mentioned almost incidentally, without
censure.

Although the provincials' impression of redcoat aggressiveness was
probably exaggerated, British soldiers were an unlovely lot, and the New
Englanders' opinion of them was unquestionably founded in reality.
Within the British army itself the assumption ran that the typical enlisted
man was at best a rascal, at worst a brute: "Only a savage discipline, it was
believed, could hold together men who were inspired by no great or common ideal."[39] The ferocious disciplinary system through which regular
leaders attempted to control the men under their command was the principal medium through which provincials had contact with redcoat officers.
Provincial soldiers consistently commented on the harsh physical punishments of the British army—particularly so after 1756, when provincial
troops who served jointly with the regulars were subject to the British
Rules and Articles of War—the code of military justice that the provincials
called "the martial law."

37. Williams's orderly book, 28 July 1758.

38. Samuel Jenks, 13 July 1760. Cf. John Frost, 13 July 1760; David Holdin, 13 July
1760. A similar incident, again in which the provincial diarist attributes the riot to British
aggression, is in Obadiah Harris, 13 Aug. 1758. For other examples, see William Henshaw,
23 June 1759; John Woods, 30 Oct. 1759; Stephen Cross, 15 Nov., 17 Dec. 1756; William
Sweat, 10 Oct. 1758; David Holdin, 24 Nov. 1760; Samuel Greenleaf, 13 Nov. 1756.

39. Eric Robson, "The Armed Forces and the Art of War," in *The New Cambridge Modern
History*, VII: *The Old Regime, 1713–63*, ed. J. O. Lindsay (Cambridge, 1957), 175.

II

The ability of regular officers to inflict drastic punishments on enlisted men who had violated military law was the basic fact of life for the eighteenth-century redcoat. It provided the means by which leaders secured obedience to their commands and rested on the assumption that soldiers had to be made certain that, however much they might fear the enemy, they had more to fear from their own leaders if they disobeyed orders. Regular officers enjoyed a reputation for disciplinary rigor that was clearly deserved, one which struck awe in the hearts of the provincials. Yet regular officers, although they administered an intentionally harsh system of military justice, were not sadists. English military law and its application during the Seven Years' War reflected the suppositions that underlay the English criminal law in general. Like civilian courts, military tribunals emphasized capital punishment as the mainstay of order.

Eighteenth-century English criminal law, it has been argued, was an ideological system that relied for its effect upon the interaction of three key principles: justice, terror, and mercy.[40] The law itself was understood to possess an independent life, above every interest and influence; it was eternal, immutable, and incorruptible. The law, moreover, was believed to apply impartially, blindly. Regardless of their social status or wealth, all evildoers were liable to precisely the same penalties for transgressions of the law. The magistrates who applied the law delivered and carried out their decisions in such a way as to emphasize the law's majesty, the criminal's helplessness, and the terrible finality of judgment. Sentences were carried out publicly to provide a morally edifying and terrifying spectacle for the onlookers. Executions in particular attracted huge crowds of spectators and offered what amounted to a vast object lesson to the audience.

Within this system, the criminal was ideally a kind of tragic actor whose brief hour upon the stage ended in a scaffold speech condemning his conduct and warning against similar transgressions before he plummeted, contrite, into eternity. In the solemnity of sentencing, the drama of the gallows, and such hideous postmortem rituals as the dissection and the hanging in chains of malefactors—in these lay the law's terror. Justice decreed, and the state exacted, irrevocable penalties for crime.

Yet justice and its terror could be tempered with mercy, for it was the prerogative of the crown to pardon any criminal, up to the very moment of

40. This brief discussion closely follows the findings of Douglas Hay, "Property, Authority and the Criminal Law," in Hay *et al.*, *Albion's Fatal Tree: Crime and Society in Eighteenth-Century England* (New York, 1975), 17–63. See also E. P. Thompson, *Whigs and Hunters: The Origin of the Black Act* (New York, 1975), esp. 245–269; and David J. Rothman, *The Discovery of the Asylum: Social Order and Disorder in the New Republic* (Boston, 1971), 5–56.

execution. Apparently about half of the capital sentences handed down in eighteenth-century English courts ended not on the gallows, but in transportation to the colonies or imprisonment.[41] This enhanced the drama of punishment, making every execution a cliffhanger in which the culprit might be pardoned at the last second. Pardons, as sovereign acts of grace, reinforced the reverence of common folk for the crown and for its agents, the magistrates. Because the typical pardon would be granted in response to a petition written in behalf of, say, a condemned laborer by a local gentleman, pardoning also formed an important "part of the tissue of paternalism, expressed in the most personal terms."[42] Thus the law, in its panoply of justice, terror, and mercy, was an important agent in maintaining the control of the ruling class in England and expressed the very nature of English social relations. Because England's rulers also believed that the law had a life of its own, they never managed to transform the jurisprudential system into a mere agency of their class interest. Yet they clearly understood that the law perpetuated their influence and facilitated the task of governance.[43]

Regular officers were overwhelmingly drawn from the ruling class, and they dispensed military justice in a way that reflected the strategies and functions of their nation's jurisprudential system. Within the limits of military law, property and life were safeguarded with as much rigor as they were in the civil system. Yet the army had at its disposal a wide range of auxiliary punishments, too, by which it could compel submissive behavior among the common soldiers. Insubordination, for example, a uniquely military crime that was defined ad hoc by officers using personal, subjective criteria, could be punished as severely as theft, with hundreds of lashes from a cat-o'-nine-tails.[44] Outright defiance of a superior officer carried the death penalty.

The function of courts-martial in maintaining order, like that of civilian courts, depended upon the trinity of justice, terror, and mercy. The second element carried particular weight in the military context, since punishments were swiftly meted out after sentencing, appeals were impossible, and soldiers were compelled to witness the administration of the lash or noose at punishment parades. Mercy, too, was dispensed with a prac-

41. Hay, "Property, Authority," in Hay *et al.*, *Albion's Fatal Tree*, 43.

42. *Ibid.*, 47.

43. This is a point upon which E. P. Thompson is especially eloquent; see *Whigs and Hunters*, 258–269.

44. Cf., e.g., the penalties for theft described in Wilson's orderly book, 8, 10 July 1759, with those for insubordination in the same, 18 July, 1 Aug. 1759: in cases of minor theft, in which the offender was not deemed a chronic thief, and insubordination, the penalties assessed approximated 400–500 lashes with a cat-o'-nine-tails.

ticed hand: Jeffery Amherst pardoned half of the men sentenced to heavy flogging by courts-martial under his command in 1759 and commuted the sentences of just under a third of the men sentenced to death.⁴⁵ Under the closer control commanders could exercise over the administration of justice, pardons could be withheld until the very last instant and create an especially touching spectacle as the condemned man broke down and sobbed in gratitude.⁴⁶ Such a situation could be exploited for immediately practical ends as well. Lord Loudoun once observed that a properly managed pardon provided the ideal means of inducing a man to enlist for life or to volunteer for service in the West Indies as a token of his appreciation.⁴⁷

Regular officers thus used military justice to promote discipline in the army in much the same way that civilian magistrates in England employed the law to promote social order, protect the interests of property, and provide justice as they understood it. But New Englanders did not share the regular officers' assumptions; nor was the distinctive structure and composition of provincial armies, which fostered close ties between leaders and enlisted men, conducive to the exercise of British-style military justice. Following Loudoun's unification of regular and provincial commands in 1757, Massachusetts provincials were governed by the Rules and Articles of War and by the British Mutiny Act, just as the regulars were. In the years before 1757, however, and in certain isolated commands thereafter, Massachusetts soldiers served under their own version of military law—a system that reflected, as surely as Britain's did, the structure and suppositions of the surrounding society.

The cornerstone of provincial military justice was a brief law, the 1754 Mutiny Act. Mutiny acts were passed by the General Court only in wartime and were limited in operation to one year, or until the year's provincials were discharged from service.⁴⁸ The act dealt with offenses which

---

45. Wilson's orderly book (1759), *passim*. There were 32 sentences of flogging (300–1,500 lashes) handed down by Amherst's general court-martial boards between 23 May and 30 Oct. 1759; 16 whippings were carried out. During the same period there were 10 death sentences pronounced, 7 of which were performed. Cf. Loudoun's and Webb's policies in 1757, which were comparable in terms of sentencing and in severity and frequency of execution. (Lyman's orderly book [1757], *passim*; Luke Gridley, 1757, *passim*.)

46. See, e.g., John Cleaveland, 26 Aug. 1758; Anonymous soldier, Louisbourg, 20 Jan. 1760.

47. Loudoun to Winslow, 12 Sept. 1756, Loudoun Papers, LO 1784, Henry E. Huntington Library, San Marino, Calif. Hereafter material from the Loudoun Papers will be identified by date and LO document number; quoted material appears by permission of the Huntington Library.

48. The following discussion is based on the Mutiny Act of 1754: *The Acts and Resolves, Public and Private, of the Province of Massachusetts-Bay*, III (Boston, 1908), 753–754, hereafter cited as *Acts and Resolves*.

were strictly military: mutiny, sedition, and desertion, as well as incitement to any of those three crimes. It authorized specially convened eleven-member courts-martial to impose capital sentences on those guilty of such offenses. The act was silent on other crimes but specifically added that nothing in it should be construed as exempting soldiers "from the ordinary process of the law." In case a court-martial should actually hand down a death sentence, the penalty had to be approved by the governor of the province, acting as commander in chief, before it could be carried out. The assumption behind the Mutiny Act, like the Press Act (a provision of which stipulated punishments for soldiers who tried to sell or pawn the province's arms), was that minor aberrations in discipline would be adjudged by courts-martial and "punished by riding the wooden horse, running the gauntlet, and other like military punishment."[49] Soldiers who committed major crimes, as comprehended in the law of the province, might be whipped, expelled from the army, and bound over to the civilian authorities; but further punishment could only be exacted by magistrates. Although the traditional military punishment of flogging was not specifically covered, the law of the Bay Colony was understood to govern the permissible number of strokes. Under all but extraordinary circumstances the civil and Biblical limit of thirty-nine lashes was observed by provincial courts-martial until the junction with the regulars in 1757.[50]

The limitations that the Mutiny Act placed on military courts, especially with regard to executions, suggest that the assumptions underlying the provincial military justice system were quite different from those of justice, terror, and mercy. These provincial assumptions drew heavily upon a literal application of the traditional distrust of standing armies. Nowhere was this clearer than in the preamble to the Mutiny Act itself.

> WHEREAS this government have judged it necessary that a number of forces should be raised and levied for the safety and defence of this province, and of his majesty's subjects and interest therein; *and whereas* no man may be forejudged of life or limb, or subjected to any kind of punishment by martial law, or in any other manner than by the judgment of his peers, and according to the known and established laws of the province; *yet, nevertheless*, it being requisite for retaining such forces as are or shall be raised for his majesty's service

49. *Acts and Resolves*, III, 737.

50. There was, to my knowledge, only one instance before 1757 in which the number of strokes imposed by a court-martial exceeded 39: at Lake George in 1755, a soldier was whipped 100 lashes and drummed out of camp with a noose around his neck for "profane swearing and a sodomitical attempt" (Seth Pomeroy, 6 Aug. 1755). The severity of this whipping may well have stemmed from outrage at the attempted sodomy; such heavy flogging was not, strictly speaking, legal under the Massachusetts Mutiny Act.

on the present occasion in their duty, that an exact discipline be observed, and that soldiers who shall mutiny or stir up sedition, or shall desert his majesty's service be brought to a more exemplary and speedy punishment than the usual forms of law will allow. . . .[51]

The act that followed, as we have seen, in fact did very little to assure either speedy or exemplary punishment of military criminals, at least if the example intended was a speedy death by hanging. There is no evidence, however, that provincial leaders felt disadvantaged by this or that they desired a more stringent law. The punishments inflicted upon soldiers in 1754, 1755, and 1756 by provincial courts-martial were actually lighter than they might have been, even under the restrictive provisions of the Mutiny Act. Moreover, surviving sources suggest that provincial discipline, unlike that of the regulars, depended not on the ability of commanders to make horrifying examples of criminals, but on consistency, solidarity, entreaty, and instruction. These in turn reflected the character of provincial culture and the norms of New England society. The discipline they produced, of course, looked to professional soldiers like no discipline at all; yet there can be no doubt that it approximated the intentions of its custodians, the provincial officers. A few examples will serve to illustrate the nature of the system.

In 1755 the New England Regiment of two battalions, commanded by John Winslow and raised principally in Massachusetts, spent seven months in Nova Scotia campaigning against the French and deporting the Acadian population. During this period, fourteen courts-martial and two courts of inquiry were held in the regiment, deciding cases that ranged from that of "Peter, an Indian," who was accused of "fighting with his mess mate and biting a piece off his arm," to instances of theft, insubordination, and mutiny.[52] Twenty-three cases, involving twenty-eight defendants, were heard; six men were acquitted, and the rest suffered various punishments. The most common sentence was for the offender to be whipped "upon his naked back with a cat, well laid on."[53] No whipping exceeded thirty lashes; that sentence was awarded to three men who were guilty of stealing from civilians and to another who had been grossly abusive to his officers. Insubordination and other breaches of military responsibility, including desertion of one's guard post and petty theft within the camp, earned the offenders only fifteen or twenty lashes. About a third of the men found guilty were punished not by whipping, but by being "set upon the wooden horse" for periods ranging from thirty minutes to an hour, a punishment

51. *Acts and Resolves*, III, 753–754.
52. "Journal of Winslow," 24 July 1755, Nova Scotia Hist. Soc., *Colls.*, IV (1884), 211.
53. *Ibid.*, 11 Aug. 1755, 226.

in which the criminal straddled the spine of two slabs of wood nailed together in an inverted *V*. (In some cases a musket would be suspended from
each ankle to increase the victim's discomfort.)[54]

By eighteenth-century professional standards, such punishments were
ridiculously mild. While riding the wooden horse for an hour and suffering thirty lashes from a cat-o'-nine-tails were painful and humiliating experiences, they were comparatively nothing beside the savage floggings
handed out by regular courts-martial. Thirty lashes, at any rate, was not
sufficient to deter Private William Mitchell from indulging his penchant
for "sauciness to his officers and . . . profane cursing and swearing" only a
week after he had been whipped twenty strokes for the same offense.[55]
There was, then, comparatively little terror in the provincial punishments;
but there was not much mercy either. In no case during 1755 was a man
pardoned after sentencing—the standard British means of keeping soldiers both grateful and submissive. Far from creating the climactic scene
in a drama of magisterial justice and mercy, provincial punishments were
predictable, workaday penalties. Justice in the provincial armies did not
kill, even though under the law it could. It relied instead for its effect on
comparatively mild, commonplace, consistent retributions. Because it was
by nature less lethal, provincial justice was of necessity less spectacularly
merciful.

The relatively smooth gradation of social status between privates and
commanding officers and the complicated connections between ranks in
the provincial forces also mitigated the penalties imposed. As the case of
one of Winslow's captains suggests, provincial officers early in the war
were not necessarily even aware of the great gap that was supposed to divide commissioned from noncommissioned personnel. Early in July 1755
John Winslow presided over a court of inquiry to determine whether the
character of one of his officers, Captain Nathan Adams, had been "aspersed" by a Lieutenant Noyce and one Sergeant Brewer of the regiment's
other battalion. The court found that both Noyce and Brewer—who had
called the captain "a damned coward"—were guilty of the slander and required both men to acknowledge their error publicly, begging Captain
Adams's pardon before their assembled regiment. They did so, Captain

54. Theft from civilians and abuse of officers: 2 Aug. 1755, *ibid.*, 219; 4 Sept. 1755, *ibid.*,
III (1882–1883), 92; 15 Sept. 1755, *ibid.*, III (1882–1883), 123. Insubordination: 3, 25 July
1755, *ibid.*, IV (1884), 190, 212. Desertion of guard post: 11 Aug. 1755, *ibid.*, IV (1884),
225–226. Petty theft: 10 July 1755, *ibid.*, IV (1884), 200. Punishments: 1, 24, 31 July 1755,
ibid., IV (1884), 187, 211, 214; 18 Sept. 1755, *ibid.*, III (1882–1883), 130; John Thomas,
7 July 1755.

55. "Journal of Winslow," 24 July, 2 Aug. 1755, Nova Scotia Hist. Soc., *Colls.*, IV (1884),
211, 219.

Adams forgave them, and the matter was settled.[56] This ritual of public confession, apology, and reconciliation was also practiced among the regulars, as when a court-martial on 1 August 1759 sentenced a captain of the Seventeenth Foot to apologize on parade to his lieutenant colonel for "disrespectful behavior."[57] The significant difference between these instances is that Adams—and Winslow and the rest of the provincial court of inquiry—thought that a *sergeant's* apology could make sufficient satisfaction to an officer whose honor had been affronted. Among the regulars, with their more finely honed conceptions of status, only officers' apologies could matter; noncommissioned officers had too little standing to make such amends meaningful. Regular noncommissioned officers could be reduced to the ranks if they gave offense—as when Corporal Samuel White of Gage's Light Infantry regiment was broken for a similar insult—but whatever apologies they might wish to make could not be heard across the social gulf that separated them from their leaders.[58]

Maintaining order in the camps was a major concern of both regular and provincial officers, but they employed very different methods to do so. Whenever a regular commander wanted to correct a breach of camp discipline, he would issue an order identifying the practice he wanted to suppress and specifying the punishment that would be levied on offenders if they did not immediately desist. These orders were terse and peremptory. The following examples, issued at Fort Edward in 1758, are typical:

[3 June.] All soldiers and followers of the army who are found gaming in camp, shall immediately receive three hundred lashes without a court martial.

[3 June.] The Article of War, which forbids, on pain of death or such other punishment as shall be ordered by a general court martial, if any person [is] to occasion false alarms in camp by discharging of firearms, by drawing of swords, by beating of drums, or by any other means whatsoever, will, for the future, be strictly put in execution.

[15 June.] Any sutler who is convicted of selling or giving any rum to a soldier will immediately receive two hundred lashes, [have] his liquors seized, and [be] banished [from] the camp.[59]

56. 4–6 July 1755, *ibid.*, 195–197.
57. Wilson's orderly book, 1 Aug. 1759, 109.
58. *Ibid.*
59. Moneypenney's orderly book, 3, 15 June 1758 (Fort Ticonderoga Museum, *Bulletin*, XII [1966–1970], 345, 350). The second of these orders reinforces the impression of the mildness of the sentences imposed by Winslow's court-martial boards. A man under the Rules and Articles of War might be subjected to the death penalty for falsely alarming a

Provincial orders, on the other hand, took the form of admonitions and rarely included the explicit threat of punishment. In 1755, for example, when Winslow's men began to violate restrictions on leaving their encampment at Grand Pré, Winslow did not threaten; instead, he issued an order "to remind the soldiers of this camp of the former orders" against passing beyond the picquet line without permission.[60]

At isolated posts staffed only by provincial troops, striking examples of the provincial tendency to remind and exhort occurred even after the unification of command in 1757. This was the circumstance at Fort Cumberland, Nova Scotia, in 1759 and 1760, where Colonel Joseph Frye commanded a garrison of approximately four hundred Massachusetts soldiers. Early in July 1759, Frye noted a growing problem with troops stealing "clothing and other things out of the province stores" and exchanging them for the sutlers' liquor. Instead of decreeing a penalty for pilferage and then making an example of an offender or two, Frye chose to make a long admonitory address, a kind of sermon, on the abuse. This "practice," he wrote on 7 July,

is not only a violation of the Articles of War, which exposes such offenders to corporal punishment; but destroys the design of that government in sending them under the care of gentlemen to relieve the wants of the soldiers; and not only so but will be attended with other bad consequences to those guilty of such irregularities. For most certainly rum will not defend them from the inclemency of the weather, nor the stinging of the insects with which this country very plentifully abounds, as clothing will; and besides, too much strong liquor intoxicates the brain and renders those that take it in that degree unfit for military duty or anything else. And if they are posted as sentries as sometimes has been, ten to one but they are catched asleep, put under guard and brought to punishment; for the avoiding of which they'll plead they never did so before, nor should they have done so then, only they happened to be a little in liquor—a pretty name for drunkenness. For remedy in this case it's Col. Frye's orders that no sutler person licensed for selling spiritous liquors sell or let any of the soldiers above mentioned have any rum, wine, brandy or any other sort of spiritous liquors on any account whatever, till they have leave to do so.

---

camp, but the only penalty assessed for this infraction by the provincials was an hour's ride on the wooden horse ("Journal of Winslow," 1 July 1755, Nova Scotia Hist. Soc., *Colls.*, IV [1884], 187).

60. "Journal of Winslow," 13 Oct. 1755, Nova Scotia Hist. Soc., *Colls.*, III (1882–1883), 171.

Colonel Frye's experiment in prohibition lasted only four days. On the eleventh of the month he restored permission for the sutlers to sell liquor to the troops. "But," he added, "with caution that they receive no sort of clothing of said troops as pay for said liquor or for anything else they may purchase of them. And that if the sutlers, or others in trade, credit those troops for anything whatever, [they] must run the risk of getting pay for the same, as the soldiers receive no pay till they return to New England again." In none of this was there any threat. Frye mentioned the Rules and Articles of War and corporal punishment almost as theoretical possibilities. He did not promise to invoke the punitive regulations, nor did he threaten to stave the liquor kegs of sutlers who disobeyed his order not to sell to the soldiers. Instead, he instructed his men on their own best interest.[61]

During the rest of his tenure at Fort Cumberland, Frye continued to admonish his troops for wrongdoing, rather than to coerce or threaten them. In late July the men took to misusing the molasses they had been issued. Instead of using it to brew antiscorbutic spruce beer as they were supposed to, they were eating the molasses straight, "to the damage of their health." Frye's response was to halt the molasses issue, but again his measures proved temporary. On 2 August he restored the ration with the warning that "if the soldiers in spite of all preventions will eat it and bring themselves into a bad habit of body, they must own it is their own fault."[62] At the beginning of November, the privates began refusing to unload firewood from supply ships, maintaining that their sergeants had no right to order them about after the expiration of what they had understood to be the term of enlistment. Rather than whipping a few recalcitrant privates as encouraging examples to the rest, Frye merely remonstrated: winter would soon be upon them, he said, and without a supply of firewood, there would be great suffering. The following spring members of the garrison began to desert on about the anniversary of their enlistments. Instead of hunting down deserters and court-martialing them, as a regular commander would have done, Frye lectured the remaining soldiers on the importance of loyalty and listed with approbation the names of the thirty-five soldiers who had so far shown no disposition to leave for home.[63]

In all of these instances, Colonel Frye threatened his men with nothing more painful than the knowledge that what they were doing was wrong. He was concerned less with maintaining high levels of conformity and efficiency than with making his soldiers aware that he would not be held responsible for their misbehavior. They had, after all, been warned: they

61. Josiah Peary, 7, 11 July 1759; Boyd's orderly book, same dates.
62. Josiah Peary, 2 Aug. 1759; Boyd's orderly book.
63. Josiah Peary, ca. 1 Nov. 1759, 17 May 1760.

would have to accept the consequences in the form of ill health, suffering, or dishonor.

Joseph Frye's orders demonstrate the persistent provincial assumption that discipline did not necessarily require the free application of physical coercion. Instead of linking promises of punishment to his directives, Frye tried to explain the reasons behind them. He addressed his men paternally, as if their refractoriness was somehow the product of childishness or misinformation. His mildness cannot be explained as the consequence of inexperience, stupidity, or weakness. Frye had led troops in the previous war; he had served in Acadia in 1755 as a combat commander and had fulfilled his duties with great coolness and competence at the siege of Fort William Henry in 1757. He was obviously intelligent: his account of the atrocities that followed the capitulation of Fort William Henry stands as a model of clarity and precision.[64] And he was not incapable of applying force, since he did approve at least one whipping—a fifty-lash sentence for a member of his artillery train, on 8 June 1759. The only satisfactory explanation of his aversion to threatening physical punishment is that he did not believe such a policy was necessary to secure the cooperation of his troops. The rambunctiousness of his garrison at Fort Cumberland indicates that exhortations and explanations were not in themselves sufficient to create tight discipline. Yet Frye's perseverance in using such tactics suggests that he was able to tolerate a relatively high level of disorder among his troops, and perhaps that he even expected it. At any rate he never became sufficiently disillusioned with his persuasive, paternalist methods to abandon them. He evidently assumed to the very last that the men under his command were susceptible of instruction, that once they came to understand what was expected of them, and why, they would do their duty.

For officers who assumed that such methods could be made to work, discipline depended less on any commander's acts and policies than on the character of his troops, and character was largely outside his control. To change the behavior of miscreant soldiers depended less upon restraining them than upon reforming their morals. Hence Frye's patient instructions on right behavior; hence his willingness to wash his hands of his troops' misbehavior if they persisted in it. For regular officers, creating good discipline was analogous to the teaching of good manners. Provincials, who assumed that conduct reflected character, tended to conclude instead that either men were good soldiers or they weren't. If a man proved refractory and unresponsive to exhortation or repeated chastisement, provincial of-

64. Nancy S. Voye, *Massachusetts Officers in the French and Indian Wars, 1748–1763* (Boston, 1975), entries 2107, 2117–2119, 2121, 2125; Joseph Frye, 3–10 Aug. 1757; Francis Parkman, *Montcalm and Wolfe* (Boston, 1901 [orig. publ. Toronto, (1884)]), I, 517–528; II, 444–445.

ficers consequently preferred to expel him from camp, not to make a gruesome spectacle of him. To hang or brutally beat an offender would not make the virtuous more virtuous or make the corrupt less corrupt.

The difference between the provincial and the regular approach to disciplining habitual offenders emerges in an exchange between John Winslow and Lord Loudoun in 1756. In September Winslow found himself faced with a minor dilemma: a provincial general court-martial, acting under the authority of the Massachusetts Mutiny Act, had condemned an infamous deserter to death at Fort William Henry. Normally Winslow would have ordered the man to be drummed out of the camp with a noose about his neck to symbolize his commission of a capital crime. Now, because of his new subordinate relationship to Loudoun, he was unsure whether he had the authority to grant a pardon. He decided to ask for guidance: "I am not clear in hanging matters and, if your lordship thinks proper, in lieu thereof will drum the fellow out of the regiment as he is, it seems, a common disturber of the camp." [65] Loudoun was astonished at Winslow's proposal. Merely to expel the man, he replied, would be looked on by the soldiers "as no punishment at all" and would set a bad example. He suggested that Winslow go ahead with the reprieve, but to manage it in such a way as to induce the man to enlist for life in a regular regiment, thus providing a salutary example for the other soldiers even as he secured a new soldier for the king's troops. [66]

Seventeen fifty-seven, the first year of a fully combined command, brought an end to routine provincial leniency, since loyalty compelled provincial officers serving jointly with regulars to uphold royal disciplinary regulations. Most colonial officers, however, apparently tried to moderate the severity of punishment, or at least to explain to their men what the consequences of disorderly conduct could be under the new regime. The latter was the course that Phineas Lyman, Connecticut's chief officer throughout the war, followed at the outset of the campaign of 1757. Lyman was very nearly professional in attitude and did his best to fulfill the expectations of his superiors; yet he also recognized the potential consequences of a precipitate shift to harsh discipline. At the beginning of the year he took advantage of a regimental court-martial to make a personal statement to his troops concerning crime and punishment. According to a private in one of the Connecticut companies, on 19 May

> Teuset [an Indian private] was put under guard for not obeying orders, and a whipping post [was] set up. We was all brought round in

65. Winslow to Loudoun, 5 Sept. 1756, LO 1710.
66. Loudoun to Winslow, 12 Sept. 1756, LO 1784. For an example of such induced enlistment, see David Holdin, 16 Oct. 1760.

a body. His sentence was to be whipped twenty lashes. Upon his begging favor and promising reformation, his honor [Lyman], with good advice and strict directions to us all, reprieved him.[67]

Thereafter General Lyman was not particularly inclined to spare the rod in chastising his troops. The "advice and strict directions" he gave on this occasion, however, indicate that he also assumed his men were capable of understanding an exhortation on discipline as fully as they could comprehend the infliction of pain.

Another response was less conventionally ethical and thus left fewer documentary traces. It involved manipulating the court-martial system so as to lessen the likelihood that provincial offenders would be tried by courts composed, even in part, of regular officers. There were two kinds of military courts, corresponding to different levels of command authority. Regimental courts-martial exercised jurisdiction over relatively minor crimes such as neglect of duty, within individual regiments only. These were convened by order of the unit's colonel and consisted of a president (usually a captain) and three or four junior members (lieutenants and ensigns). Regimental tribunals among provincials serving under regular command seldom passed sentences in excess of two or three hundred lashes; most were for fewer than fifty.[68] Crimes carrying heavier penalties and all capital cases were referred to the next level of military justice, the general court-martial.

The general court-martial was a much more elaborate and formal affair than its regimental counterpart. It was convened by a commanding general and made up of a colonel (acting as president) and twelve other officers. Whenever possible, a fourteenth officer was assigned as deputy judge-advocate, or prosecutor. In mixed forces of regulars and provincials, general courts-martial "of the line" included both regular and provincial members, with regulars usually in the majority. These determined most cases involving provincial soldiers. General courts-martial "of the regulars" were convened when the accused men were redcoats, although on occasion they settled provincial cases as well.[69] Except in the case of officers, whose status protected them from corporal punishment, the lightest

---

67. Luke Gridley, 19 May 1757.

68. The most informative sources for the operation of regimental courts-martial are the orderly books, in combination with the diaries of officers who served on the boards themselves. See, for example, William Henshaw's orderly book and diary (1759), *passim*; "Journal of Winslow," Nova Scotia Hist. Soc., *Colls.*, III (1882–1883), 71–196; IV (1884), 113–246, *passim*; Samuel Jenks, *passim*.

69. The composition of general court-martial boards in Amherst's expeditionary force of 1759 is summarized in Table 31.

sentences that general courts-martial assigned were on the order of three hundred lashes with a cat-o'-nine-tails.[70]

Thus after provincials and regulars finally joined forces in 1757, the only hope that provincials accused of serious wrongdoing had of escaping a rough handing by a redcoat-dominated general court-martial was to have their cases heard at the regimental level. Regimental courts could try only minor crimes, however, and an accused man had no control over the wording of the charge against him—the factor that determined the court in which he would be tried. As a consequence, the sympathy of the officer who ordered a man arrested was crucially important, since that officer was also responsible for drawing up the charge.

Provincial officers who entertained reservations about regular-style discipline therefore could mitigate the possible punishment by softening their charges—in effect conspiring on behalf of the accused to circumvent the military justice system. The diary of Captain Samuel Jenks preserves a clear example of this provincial response to regular discipline.

In 1760, Samuel Jenks commanded a company in the first battalion of Brigadier General Timothy Ruggles's regiment. From the very beginning of the campaign, his diary entries show that he was an enthusiastic soldier, capable of taking pride in even mundane assignments, such as gathering boughs for the brewing of spruce beer. He admired his colleagues and was actively concerned for his company's welfare. It came as a real shock to this eager, earnest young officer to discover on 12 July that two of his men had committed a serious crime; he found that —

> James Casey and William Delarue had got up orders on the sutler and forged my name to them, and taken a considerable [amount] up. I immediately sent them under guard, and acquainted Colonel Saltonstall [the battalion commander] of their crime, who advised me not to send their crime in as forgery, because then they must come to a general court martial and be tried for their lives; and it is death for a soldier to counterfeit his officer's hand. But [he] told me to send in their crime as ill behavior and insolent treatment, which I accordingly did, and by that means hope their lives will be saved by trying them by a regimental court-martial.

The next day Jenks investigated further and found that two more of his men had also used forged orders. Straightaway he ordered the two, Henry Bony and Jacob Hasey, arrested. All four were tried the following day.

70. Stanley McCrory Pargellis, *Lord Loudoun in North America* (New Haven, Conn., 1933), 330–332; Wilson's orderly book (1759), *passim*.

> *Monday, July 14th.* This day, about 7 o'clock A.M., there was a regimental court martial held at the president's tent, who was Captain Chadbourn. After the prisoners were brought and examined, Casey and Delarue confessed they were guilty of the facts, but the other two pleaded not guilty. But Hasey owned he saw Delarue sign his order, but it appeared Bony knew nothing of his [Delarue's] signing his. The court sentenced Casey 250 stripes, Delarue 150, and Hasey 50; which the Brigadier [Timothy Ruggles] approved of as just.

Later that day the punishment was administered.

> I ordered the sergeants to turn out all my company to see them go through the operation, to deter any from such vile practices. I had rather lost twenty dollars than such affairs should [h]a[ve] happened in my company.

Perhaps the sight did indeed deter Jenks's men from further misbehavior; at any rate, no more members of his company came before courts-martial during the rest of the campaign.[71]

Two aspects of Jenks's account bear special attention. First, turning in the men on a lesser charge than forgery was not Jenks's own idea, but the suggestion of his battalion commander, Lieutenant Colonel Richard Saltonstall. Unlike Jenks, who was campaigning for the first time, Saltonstall was a veteran officer from a family with a long martial tradition. Saltonstall's contact with things military had been literally lifelong, and he evidently had settled opinions on the nature and importance of military discipline.[72] Nonetheless, he made sure that the case would stay with the regiment, guaranteeing comparatively lenient treatment and effectively subverting the intention of the British military judicial system. By approving the sentence "as just," Brigadier Timothy Ruggles, the regiment commander, also connived at the circumvention of the system. Lest it should be suspected that Ruggles was kept unaware of the real nature of the four defendants' offenses, it is clear that the actual crime was widely known in the regiment. A sergeant in the regiment's other battalion recorded that the men were accused *not* of "ill behavior and insolent treatment," but of "forging orders . . . and ill treatment." [73] Thus in at least one case, a novice captain, a veteran field officer, and the highest ranking officer in all of the Massachusetts forces conspired to keep men guilty of a capital offense

71. Samuel Jenks, 17 June 1760 (spruce beer); 5, 8 July 1760 (agreeable colleagues, concern for his men); 12 July 1760 (discovery of forgery); 13 July 1760 (arrest of Bony and Hasey); 14 July 1760 (court-martial and punishment).

72. Voye, ed., *Officers*, entries 4960–4970.

73. David Holdin, 14 July 1760.

from being tried for it, because they agreed that the penalty was excessively severe.

It is significant, too, that the incident produced a considerable reaction in Jenks himself. His vexation—"I had rather lost twenty dollars" (almost a month's pay)—suggests that he took it quite personally, as if the forgeries reflected dishonorably not just on the offenders but on his company and himself. Unlike a regular officer, who would have been likelier to take pride in seeing the forgers brought to justice, Jenks regarded the whole process with distaste. Had his sense of community been restricted to his fellow officers, Jenks would have had little cause for regret; since it apparently included his company, however, the episode entailed a personal loss of confidence—a disappointment in men whose loyalty he had hitherto assumed.

Provincial disciplinary practices and the assumptions that underlay them reflected traditional New England ideals of community life—that men ought to be knit together as one in the common pursuit of God's will. Nothing could have been less consistent with British conceptions of military order, or less understandable to most redcoat officers. The common soldiers of New England viewed the operation of the regulars' disciplinary system with equal incomprehension—bafflement alloyed, naturally enough, with the anxiety that they might at any time become the system's next victims.

III

The enlisted men who were the principal subjects of the disciplinary system did not see military justice from the vantage point of a court-martial board. For them it was a levy of pain: soldiers like themselves being flogged in a daily succession, irregularly punctuated by executions. Soldiers who served in 1757 and thereafter were intensely conscious of the coercive aspects of military discipline. It had not always been so: provincials who kept diaries in 1754–1756 rarely mentioned physical punishments. No soldier in the early years of the war, in fact, referred to corporal punishment more than a single time in his journal, and several made no mention at all.[74] The most detailed description in these early diaries is brief and rather flat and shows little sympathy for the criminals:

74. These were as follows:

Diarist, Year	Punishments Mentioned	Time Span Covered
John Barber, 1754	1 (2 July)	2½ mos.
John Thomas, 1755	1 (7 July)	9 mos.

2nd July [1754]. A court martial was called upon Morgan Dehortee and Richard Garrivan for cursing and wishing damnation to themselves and others, threatening men's lives, etc.; Captain [Eleazer] Melvin, president or chief judge. They were ordered to be punished accordingly. The next day they had pay: Morgan Dehortee was whipped thirty lashes and Garrivan [rode] the wooden horse. At which time the regiment were mustered, all in arms, to behold the sight.[75]

By comparison, at Fort Edward between 10 May and 3 November 1757, Private Luke Gridley recorded eighty-two punishments, including seventy-one floggings and six executions—on average, three to four sentences carried out per week. In his almost adverb-free diary, Gridley wrote of men being "whipped cruelly" and described this relatively mild punishment, one of the first he witnessed:

Day 25th [of May]. There was one Daniel Boake, one of Captain Gallup's men, run the gauntlet through thirty men for sleeping on guard. [He] cried "Lord God have mercy on me," the blood flying every stroke. This was a sorrowful sight.[76]

As the campaign wore on, Gridley grew accustomed to such sights, and the entries in his journal became less graphic, but with ritual precision he went on recording every punishment he saw and others that he heard about.

The eighty-odd instances of disciplinary action that Gridley noted probably did not exceed what the average soldier would have seen or heard de-

James Hill, 1755	0	8 mos.
Samuel Chandler, 1755	0	3 mos.
Seth Pomeroy, 1755	1 (6 Aug.)	5 mos.
Elisha Hawley, 1755	1 (6 Aug.)	2½ mos.
Nathaniel Dwight, 1755	0	3½ mos.
Isaac Wyman, 1756	1 (1 June)	2 mos.
Anonymous commissary, 1756	0	2 mos.

All these were unofficial journals—that is, they do not include orderly books, which recorded courts-martial within units. The single example of an orderly book from this period is Winslow's 1755 journal, which, as we have seen, records only about 20 relatively mild punishments. That the nine soldiers' journals above mention so few instances of punishment thus implies that such events did not much impinge on the lives of the diarists.

75. John Barber, 2 July 1754.

76. "Whipped cruelly": Luke Gridley, 19 Sept. 1757. (The punishment Gridley thought cruel is identified by the journal's editor [who had at his disposal another source, which he does not identify] as a multiple flogging of four men: one 500 lashes; another, 300; a third, 250; the fourth, 30 [F. M., ed., *Luke Gridley's Diary While in Service in the French and Indian War* (Hartford, Conn., 1906), 54, n. 3].) Gauntlet: Luke Gridley, 25 May 1757.

scribed during a single campaign. The punishments Gridley mentioned resulted from sentences passed by the regimental courts-martial in each of the seven regiments that garrisoned Fort Edward, plus the penalties assessed by the seven general courts-martial that sat during the summer.[77] In 1759, Amherst's expeditionary force held sixteen general courts-martial in just over five months' time. These produced seven executions and sixteen heavy floggings, about the same number of heavy penalties that Gridley witnessed.[78] In addition, each of the eighteen regiments in Amherst's force conducted its own courts-martial, generating large numbers of lesser sentences at the same time. The two Massachusetts regiments on the expedition held eleven regimental courts-martial between them; if they were typical units, there must have been at least ninety regimental boards convened during the campaign.[79] The total of all public punishments in Amherst's expeditionary army was thus at least as great as that which Gridley recorded at Fort Edward two years earlier.

From the soldiers' point of view, corporal punishment was one of the constants of life; moreover, they saw capital sentences exacted every month or two.[80] Officers, not personally threatened by the noose or the cat, could

77. Strength of Fort Edward: Pargellis, *Loudoun*, 235, n. 18, 244–45. Courts-martial: Lyman's orderly book (1757), *passim*. Lyman's regiment held nine regimental courts-martial, a fairly large number. These sat on 3, 18, 25, 31 May; 1 June; 19 July; 13, 19 Sept.; 17 Oct.

78. Wilson's orderly book (1759), *passim*.

79. These were Ruggles's and Willard's regiments, and at least half of the latter's courts-martial awarded penalties. Ruggles's regiment: Hawks's orderly book, 30 May, 29 June, 1, 7, 11, 16 July 1759 (no sentence recorded); Willard's regiment: Lemuel Wood, 16, 21, 26 Aug., 20, 25 Sept. 1759 (four penalties imposed: the reduction of two noncommissioned officers on 16 and 21 Aug., and the whipping of two privates on 20 and 25 Sept.).

80. The monthly distribution of severe punishments at Fort Edward in 1757 and with Amherst's expeditionary force in 1759 was as follows:

	Fort Edward, *1757*		Amherst's Expedition, *1759*	
	Executions	*Floggings of 100 or More Lashes*	*Executions*	*Floggings of 100 or More Lashes*
May	?	?	3	—
June	—	3	—	5
July	1	4	3	6
Aug.	—	3	1	3
Sept.	2	10	—	2
Oct.	2	4	—	1
Nov.	1	—	?	?

(Sources: Luke Gridley, *passim*, for Fort Edward. [Gridley specified the number of lashes only on about two-thirds of the sentences; on the rest he simply wrote "whipped," which introduces a conservative tendency into the above table.] For Amherst's expedition, Wilson's

observe the goings-on with a kind of sympathetic detachment. "There is almost every day more or less whipped or picqueted or some other ways punished," wrote Caleb Rea. For the enlisted men, however, the fall of the lash and "the shrieks and cries" of the afflicted were more than the cause of pity: they were perpetual reminders that soldiers under British discipline lived under a reign of terror. Punishments of provincials and regulars alike distressed New Englanders, for both groups were equally at risk. Even the most dispassionate observers among the New England soldiers were appalled to see a man "whipped cruelly" or "whipped till the blood came out at the knee of his breeches."[81] Diaries indicate that the horror of the floggings formed part of the currency of camp rumor: "This Day," wrote Samuel Morris on Sunday, 2 September 1759, "there was a man whipped to death belonging to the Light Infantry. They say he had twenty-five lashes after he was dead."

The feelings of resentment, fear, and powerlessness aroused by such punishments burned the sight into witnesses' memories. David Perry was looking back across almost sixty years when he recalled an episode that took place near Halifax, Nova Scotia, in 1762:

> Three men, for some trifling offense which I do not recollect, were tied up to be whipped. One of them was to receive eight hundred lashes, the others five hundred apiece. By the time they had received three hundred lashes, the flesh appeared to be entirely whipped from their shoulders, and they hung as mute and motionless as though they had been long since deprived of life. But this was not enough. The doctor stood by with a vial of sharp stuff, which he would ever and anon apply to their noses, and finding, by the pain it gave them, that some signs of life remained, he would tell them, "d——mn you, you can bear it yet"—and then the whipping would commence again. It was . . . by far worse than death. I felt at the time as though I could have taken summary vengeance on those who were the authors of it, on the spot, had it been in my power to do it.[82]

Hideous as eight hundred lashes was, it was far from being the worst a man could receive: a thousand stripes was the standard punishment for

---

orderly book [1759], *passim*, and Hawks's orderly book [1759], *passim*. [These floggings were in fact all in excess of 300 lashes, which seems to have been about the lower limit for a general court-martial sentence; many more 100-lash floggings probably occurred as the result of regimental court-martial decisions.])

81. Daily punishments: Caleb Rea, 25 July 1758; cf., for example, Samuel Jenks, 9, 15 July 1760. Cruelty: Seth Metcalf, 22 July 1757.

82. David Perry, "Recollections of an Old Soldier," *Magazine of History*, CXXXVII (1928), 23.

desertion, and sentences of as many as fifteen hundred were awarded for theft.[83]

But even more than floggings, executions exercised fascination and horror for the provincials. This was of course what the commanders who signed the death warrants intended, assuming that the drama of the gallows would deter potential criminals from mischief-making. The reactions of the witnesses, in their length and detail, bear out the commanders' expectations, for the provincials were paying close attention indeed. No commander could have wished for a more salutary reaction to a hanging, for example, than John Cleaveland's:

> This forenoon, about nine o'clock, one of the regulars was hanged for thefts. He confessed on the ladder that gaming, robbery, theft, whoring, bad company-keeping, etc. were [the] sins which brought him to this shameful untimely death, and warned his fellow soldier[s] against such vices. He desired the prayers of the people standing by for his poor soul, and [was] praying for himself [as he] was hove off the ladder. The Lord makes this sad spectacle a means of warning effectually all from the sad [sins] that the soldiery are much addicted to.[84]

It might be added that no commander could have wished for a more exemplary performance than that rendered by the hanged man, who played out his role in the best tradition of Tyburn theater. Not every man who met his end by execution did it in so obliging a manner. When the convict did not cooperate, however, the effect on the observer was no less powerful:

> The 20th [of July, 1759]. This morning the criminal that was condemned yesterday [a redcoat, and a notorious thief] was brought forth . . . to be shot. . . . When he came to the place of execution, he was very loath to die. They could not persuade him to kneel down to be shot. They then tied him hand and foot but could not make him stand still. They then took and tied [him] to an old log and he hung down underside the log. They then fired and killed him.[85]

83. Wilson's orderly book (1759), *passim*.

84. John Cleaveland, 25 July 1758. (Cf. John Cleaveland to Mary Cleaveland, 3 Sept. 1758, JCP, III, 170–172, for punishment as a means of restraining wickedness.) The parallel account of Cleaveland's friend, Dr. Caleb Rea, notes the name of the condemned man, one "Mr. Hone," and adds a good deal of gossipy detail. This suggests a secondary effect of executions: the word-of-mouth amplification, by rumor, of every aspect of the event. Shock waves of gossip carried to every corner of the camp, bringing each execution to the attention even of those who did not attend.

85. Lemuel Wood, 20 July 1759. James Henderson was also present and remarked on the execution in one of his journal's longest entries: "July 20. This day there was a regular shot to

The soldier who described this pathetic episode, Lemuel Wood, had witnessed his first firing squad execution just seven days earlier. He had described that event with equal precision:

> The 13 [th of July, 1759]. This morning at six o'clock a court-martial set for the trial of the deserter that was brought in yesterday. He was sentenced . . . to be shot today at twelve o'clock in the front of the quarter guard of Forbes's Regiment. Accordingly all the picquets of the lines was drawn up for the execution of the above prisoner. The provost guard brought forth the prisoner and marched him round before all the regulars' regiments [and] from thence to the place of execution. There was drawn out of the regiment to which the prisoner belonged [two] platoons of six men each. The prisoner was brought and set before one of the platoons and kneeled down upon his knees. He clinched his hand. The platoon of six men each of them fired him through the body. The other platoon then came up instantly and fired him through the head and blowed his head all to pieces. They then dug a grave by his side and tumbled him in and covered him up, and that was an end of the whole.[86]

Lemuel Wood was not yet eighteen when he described this scene. His clarity in depicting the ritual promenade of the prisoner, the size of the firing squads, and the last gesture of the condemned man's "clinched" hand all suggests the strength of the impression that the execution, and especially the gratuitous violence of the second volley, made upon him. If he did not remember these details into his old age—and he died an old man—all he needed to do was consult his diary to bring back the images. One suspects, however, that Wood had no need to refresh his memory: like David Perry's recollection of the barbarous floggings at Halifax, these were sights burned into his consciousness, memories that would live as long as the man.

Such descriptions vividly convey the effects of regular-style discipline on New England provincials. Punishments were unarguably successful in striking awe into the hearts of New Englanders; at the same time, however, they created a vigorously unfavorable impression of the regular officers. When David Perry recounted the brutal whipping at Halifax, he remembered it not just as an example of cruel treatment but as "a specimen of *British* cruelty."[87] Gibson Clough, as he arrived at Louisbourg,

---

death. He seemed to be very obstinant and would not kneel to be shot. They were obliged to tie him with a rope to a tree and then shot him. Oh, what a dreadful sight it is to behold men used after such a manner."

86. Lemuel Wood, 13 July 1759.

87. Perry, "Recollections," *Mag. Hist.*, CXXXVII (1928), 23, my emphasis.

noted darkly that "there is no spare here of the whip." [88] When he realized later that he would be detained beyond his enlistment, Clough reflected that "we now see what it is to be under martial law and to be with the regulars, who are but little better than slaves to their officers." [89] As the provincials realized, the regulars' unyielding disciplinary system forged an effective, efficient, fighting force, the product of a society and culture more different from New England's than the New Englanders had ever suspected. The provincials, who had only the most rudimentary understanding of cultural differences, could hardly have failed to explain the disparity between regular behavior and their own expectations in moral terms. When the New Englanders weighed their allies in the moral balance, they could only find the redcoats wanting.

The judgment that redcoats were deficient in moral character promoted intramural conflict, while it allowed the provincials to assume that it was the regulars who caused trouble. Furthermore, the conviction that the redcoats were morally deficient had its necessary counterpart in a self-congratulatory assumption of provincial moral superiority. This notion had two effects. First, it enabled New Englanders to discount the importance of mere technical proficiency as a criterion of military virtue: redcoats might be proficient soldiers, but if they were bad men, they could not be wholly admirable. Second, their feelings of moral superiority enabled the New Englanders to estimate their own importance in the struggle very highly—more highly, perhaps, than they should have. Such convictions, as we shall see, were of great consequence when the New Englanders came to interpret the meaning of the war. In the meantime, the provincials still had to face the struggle of daily life and a much more intense trial, battle: the army's ultimate raison d'être, the soldier's starkest confrontation with death.

88. Gibson Clough, 4 July 1759.
89. Gibson Clough, 30 Sept. 1759.

Chapter 5 ❖ "As Mournful an Hour as Ever I Saw"
Battle and Its Effects

In its broadest outlines, Britain's program of conquest consisted of pressing the French back from their frontier outposts on the Saint Lawrence River, the Great Lakes, and Lake Champlain, wearing away French manpower and matériel until British forces could pinion their adversary in the Canadian heartland. Early in the war, French sorties against outposts like Forts Oswego and William Henry had kept the Anglo-American forces off balance. By 1758, however, the French were becoming so hard pressed for men and supplies that holding actions were all they could manage. Montcalm successfully defended Fort Carillon (Ticonderoga) in that year; but the western and eastern anchors of Canada's long water axis—Fort Frontenac on Lake Ontario and Louisbourg on Cape Breton Island—were both lost under British sieges. Thereafter, Canada's defenders could only carry out a grudging withdrawal, in the hope that the problems of supplying its far-flung armies would prove too great for Britain. New England troops who saw combat in the early part of the war thus usually fought in defensive actions, resisting French raids or sieges. The exception to this was the successful British–New England offensive against Acadia in 1755, in which the French were successfully driven from Forts Beauséjour and Gaspereau. Later on, once the initiative had passed to the British, New Englanders helped attack the French as they retreated from strongpoint to strongpoint, toward home. With a few exceptions (most notably the celebrated encounter on the Plains of Abraham) combat took the form not of open-field pitched battles, but of fights for fortified positions along the main avenues of approach to Canada. These sieges were seldom extended: Louisbourg withstood the British for seven weeks, but most forts were abandoned after a few days.

Provincial soldiers were present at most of the major battles of the war in the north: in 1755, the battle of Lake George and the siege of Fort Beauséjour; the loss of Fort Oswego in 1756; the abortive assault on Ticonderoga and the successful siege of Fort Frontenac two years later; the taking of Ticonderoga and operations against Quebec in 1759; the next year's siege of Île-aux-Noix; and the recapture of Saint John's, Newfoundland, in 1762. In tactical terms, these engagements were straightforward clashes between infantry and infantry, or between artillery and infantry. Provincial troops played the major role as combatants only in 1755; in the later battles, they acted mainly as members of reserve corps and as support troops, digging trenches, hauling cannon, and the like. In these capacities they were by no means out of danger. Reserves were frequently posted close enough to battlefields to sustain losses from enemy fire, and as support troops the provincials were often more exposed than the regulars, who were kept under cover until the time came to assault the enemy fortifications. In the later sieges of the war—for example, those of Ticonderoga in 1759 and Île-aux-Noix in 1760—the French saved their opponents the trouble of storming the works by withdrawing rather earlier than was tactically necessary. This consideration spared the lives of a great many redcoats but did nothing to alleviate the suffering of the provincials who had been steadily exposed to the defensive cannonade. On the other hand, while New England troops were present as a reserve corps at the bungled assault on Ticonderoga in 1758, they were never committed wholesale to slaughter, as the regulars of the Forty-second and Forty-sixth regiments were. In the absence of reliable casualty statistics, the traditional assumption that the British suffered the greatest number of combat casualties can still be accepted. Yet there can be no doubt that New England soldiers participated widely in combat, sustained a great many casualties, and witnessed the destruction of many lives on the battlefield. The effects of such experiences can be examined in two stages: first, through a survey of the emotional and physical impact of combat as seen from the provincials' perspective; second, by analyzing the motivation of New England soldiers and the character of provincial leadership under stress.

I

New England soldiers generally anticipated battle with high spirits, even eagerness. "The troops seem to be exceedingly engaged to go forward," wrote John Cleaveland to his wife on 26 June 1758, less than two weeks before the disastrous fight with the French at Ticonderoga.[1] His contemporaries emphatically agreed: Joseph Nichols at the time thought the soldiers "zealous" to get into action, and Archelaus Fuller noted their "good health and high spirit."[2] Troops not included in the expeditionary force "took it quite hard because they could not go with the rest of the army down to the Narrows [Ticonderoga]."[3] These writers were describing the

1. John Cleaveland to Mary Cleaveland, 26 June 1758, in Howard H. Peckham, ed., *Narratives of Colonial America, 1704–1765* (Chicago, 1971), 137.
2. Joseph Nichols, 6 July 1758; Archelaus Fuller, 5 July 1758. References to soldiers' diaries refer to sources listed in Appendix B and are cited by author's name and date of entry.
3. Amos Richardson, 3 July 1758; see also Asa Foster, 3 July 1758.

army of 1758, but provincials writing before other battles described their comrades' morale in much the same way. In 1755 the provincials preparing to besiege Fort Beauséjour impressed Abijah Willard with their proud "soldierlike" appearance and their "lively" application to work.[4] The passage of years brought no appreciable loss of enthusiasm. The provincials were "all brave and hearty" before the successful siege of Ticonderoga in 1759; the next year, "the men [were] in high spirits" when the siege of Île-aux-Noix commenced and set to work "briskly" in constructing earthworks.[5] Such high morale can best be explained by the fact that provincial battalions seldom saw combat more than once in any given year. Although many veterans stood in the ranks, especially later in the conflict, no provincial regiment ever had a chance to become battle-hardened. It is unlikely that the majority of provincial soldiers in any unit that served during the war had a concrete idea of what lay ahead when they went into action.

No provincial witness, on the other hand, noted anything like high spirits after a battle. Whether the provincials won or lost made little apparent difference. The failure of the assault on the French at Ticonderoga in 1758 was a great and astonishing defeat, and the soldiers responded with a widespread depression. Archelaus Fuller felt "weak and outdone" and noted that the men fit to work "worked very dull."[6] Amos Richardson wrote that "a good many of our men was out of case" after the battle.[7] Joseph Nichols concurred: "Our people seems to be in a confused posture, and our men are very much discouraged and beat out with their late hardship."[8] In a letter written the day after the army's retreat John Cleaveland described the "universal dejection . . . in everyone's countenance" and admitted, "I am at a loss what encouraging arguments to use with the people to get their spirits up."[9] He attributed the dysentery that afflicted the camp—and himself—after the defeat to "dejection and discouragement arising from disappointment."[10]

Unlike this encounter, the battle of Lake George, on 8 September 1755,

4. Abijah Willard, 4, 5 June 1755; see also John Thomas, and "Journal of Colonel John Winslow . . . ," Nova Scotia Historical Society, *Collections*, IV (1884), 113–246, same dates.

5. Robert Webster, 24 July 1759 (Samuel Morris, 24 July 1759, makes a similar notation); Samuel Jenks, 16, 20 Aug. 1760. See also Thomas Moody, 10, 15 Aug. 1760.

6. Archelaus Fuller, 8, 13 July 1758.

7. Amos Richardson, 12 July 1758.

8. Joseph Nichols, 12 July 1758.

9. John Cleaveland to Mary Cleaveland, 11 July 1758, John Cleaveland Papers, III, 166–168, Essex Institute, Salem, Mass. (hereafter cited as JCP); also in Peckham, *Narratives*, 120–121.

10. John Cleaveland, 11 July 1758. See also David Perry, "Recollections of an Old Soldier," *Magazine of History*, CXXXVII (1928), 11: "We went over the lake . . . in high spirits . . . but returned back melancholy and still, as from a funeral. . . . While lying in camp . . . the men grew sickly."

had been a signal victory for General William Johnson's provincial army. Yet the reactions it inspired were strikingly similar to those of the defeat. Although the battle ended with at least two hours of daylight remaining, the New Englanders made no attempt to pursue the retreating French. Instead, they made a cursory inspection of the battleground and then, apparently, collapsed. It was the next day before they made any attempt to begin "the melancholy work of burying [the] dead," according to Seth Pomeroy's diary. "Melancholy," in fact, was the word to which Pomeroy most often resorted to describe the army's tasks and state of mind after the engagement. Three days after the battle, the burials continued: a "most melancholy piece of business." Following the victory, which Pomeroy as an acting regimental commander had done much to secure, he wrote not of pride and enthusiasm, but of listlessness. The camp, he thought, had become "a melancholy place [with] so many of our near friends taken away." [11] Sickness, which had been present but not severe before the battle, intensified afterward. Within ten days the sick had become so numerous that wagonloads of men were being furloughed home. When Pomeroy himself shortly thereafter fell into "an ill state of health," he noted that the condition "is now common in the camp." [12] The provincials' lethargy, the dramatic rise in the frequency of their physical complaints, and the drop in their morale should not be identified with the twentieth-century phenomenon of combat exhaustion, since the eighteenth-century response was clearly much milder and briefer in duration than the neuroses generated on the modern battlefield. Yet battle *did* leave marks on the men it touched. Victory and defeat were categories that mattered less in experience than in the abstract. Battles disoriented winners and losers alike, radically altered their moods, and evidently damaged their physical health as well. [13]

The act of writing about battle gave some provincial soldiers a means of gaining control over the event. Description allowed them to sort out events, to arrange in sequences and categories the chaotic occurrences of combat. Men who did not, or could not, write apparently accomplished the same result by talk: armies buzzed with rumor and war stories for days after battle. [14] The degree of personal participation conditioned men's descrip-

11. Seth Pomeroy, 9, 10, 12, 14 Sept. 1755.

12. Seth Pomeroy, 19, 20 Sept. 1755; James Hill, 19 Sept. 1755.

13. The connection between battlefield stress and subsequent illness seems likely, if not absolutely provable. Karen Ordahl Kupperman has persuasively suggested links between mental states and susceptibility to disease under other circumstances in "Apathy and Death in Early Jamestown," *Journal of American History*, LXVI (1979), 24–40. Modern instances of combat-induced psychoneurotic disorder are well known, and have been discussed in historical as well as technical literature; see, e.g., John Keegan, *The Face of Battle* (New York, 1976), 328, and *passim*; Eric J. Leed, *No Man's Land: Combat and Identity in World War I* (Cambridge, 1979), esp. 163–192.

14. See, e.g., Caleb Rea, 7–9 July 1758; Amos Richardson, 11 July 1758.

tions of combat. Those who did not actually fight in or witness battles recorded them briefly and rather drily. But men who actually took part in
even minor skirmishes generally left long and careful accounts of their ac-
tivities. Lieutenant Joseph Holt, Captain Asa Foster, and Private Amos
Richardson, all members of Colonel Ebenezer Nichols's regiment, exemplify this pattern.

Nichols's Massachusetts regiment garrisoned Fort Edward in July 1758
while the bulk of Abercromby's expeditionary force went to Ticonderoga,
so none of the three diarists saw the great engagement. All three recorded
its essential elements from reports that came back from the attackers; and
all three, being generally laconic chroniclers, used few words to describe
the battle. Holt's account is representative: the army, he wrote, "marched
against their [i.e., the French] breastworks; had a terrible hot fire, lost a
great number, killed and wounded." [15] On 20 July, however, Holt, Richardson, and Foster were personally involved in a skirmish with enemy
raiders near Halfway Brook, in which more than a score of soldiers were
killed. All three wrote detailed accounts, many times longer than what
they had written concerning Ticonderoga. It was, in Holt's account, as
"terrible a day as ever I saw. Early in the morning, as a party of ten men
were coming down from the lake, the enemy fired upon them, and killed
and took all but one. Sundry officers and men, to the number of about
thirty, sallied to the assistance of the scout, and many others directly followed. The enemy exceeding our number, they run upon us and beat us
off, and killed six commissioned officers, and took and killed many others,
a list of which follows." Holt appended the names, companies, ranks, and
hometowns of all twenty-seven known casualties, together with information about their injuries. [16] The accounts of the others agreed in detail on
the sequence of events; both named members of their companies who had
been killed or wounded. Foster added a description of the dead, "mangled
in a dreadful manner"; Richardson agreed that "they was all strip[ped]
and scalped and very much cut to pieces." [17] All three witnesses recorded a
reconnaissance conducted the next day to the site of the ambush, which
discovered several more dead soldiers and evidences of a very large enemy
raiding party. [18]

The detail and specificity with which the three men recorded their experiences stands in marked contrast to the brevity and abstraction of their
accounts of the battle of Ticonderoga, an event of altogether greater significance for the army as a whole. Abercromby's defeat at Ticonderoga, of
course, was heavily documented by its immediate participants. Indeed,

15. Joseph Holt, 8 July 1758 (a retrospective entry). Cf. Asa Foster, 9 July 1758.
16. Joseph Holt, 20 July 1758.
17. Asa Foster and Amos Richardson, 20 July 1758.
18. Joseph Holt, Asa Foster, Amos Richardson, 21 July 1758.

among the provincials it was the most written-about battle of the war, and personal accounts by six New Englanders have survived. Together these show, in microcosm, the range of provincial reactions to combat. Depending upon what the soldier was trying to record, these eyewitness accounts fall into two categories. The writers of the first tried to take in the battle as a whole and to establish a context for interpreting the experience. The authors of the second set of accounts depicted the battle in much more personal and fragmentary terms. To these men the meaning and even the shape of the battle were less immediately clear, though the impact of the event was perhaps more powerful for them than for the first group. For convenience' sake we can identify witnesses with the former perspective on the battle as having bird's-eye views, and the latter as seeing it from the worm's-eye level.

The two bird's-eye writers, Caleb Rea and John Cleaveland, initially wrote lengthy accounts of what they had seen personally and what they had learned from others. Then, for days afterward, they refined and supplemented their understandings with further information on the episode, trying to fix precisely the positions of units and their movements, making judgments about the tactics the regular commander had adopted.[19] Both made an effort after the return of the army from Ticonderoga to learn the number of casualties in the battle, and both finally obtained accurate totals.[20] The accounts they wrote on the day of combat were accurate and rather detached.

"This has been a most bloody fight," wrote John Cleaveland:

Our troops attempted to force the French entrenchment before the fort with small arms and met with very great loss on our side. Our men acted with the greatest intrepidity, and one or two companies of

19. Caleb Rea, 8, 13, 15, 16 July, 23 Aug. 1758; John Cleaveland, 8, 10, 12 July, 23 Aug. 1758; John Cleaveland to Mary Cleaveland, 11, 25 July 1758, JCP, III, 162–164, 166–168. For other examples of the same tendency, see Samuel Chandler, 17 Oct. 1755; Seth Pomeroy, 8–14 Sept. 1755; Seth Pomeroy to Israel Williams, 9 Sept. 1755, in Louis Effingham de Forest, ed., *The Journals and Papers of Seth Pomeroy, Sometime General in the Colonial Service* (New Haven, Conn., 1926), 137–139; "Journal of Winslow," 4, 8, 12–16 June 1755, Nova Scotia Hist. Soc., *Colls.*, IV (1884), 146–149, 152–158; also Winslow to Shirley, 6 June 1755, *ibid.*, 172–176.

20. The actual total of killed, wounded, and missing in the battle was 1,944 men. Cleaveland placed the sum, "according to the information I have had," at "eighteen or twenty hundred in the whole army, principally among the regulars and Highlanders" (10 July 1758). He was quite precise, in addition, about casualties in his own regiment. Rea also had a reasonably accurate total, although he transposed the numbers of killed and wounded; he estimated 1,600 by "the best account I've yet been able to get" (16 July 1758). Lawrence Henry Gipson gives the following breakdown for the battle: among the regulars, 464 killed, 1,117 wounded, and 29 missing; among the provincials, 87 killed, 239 wounded, and 8 missing (*The Great War for the Empire: The Years of Defeat, 1754–1757*, 231, in Gipson, *The British Empire before the American Revolution* [New York, 1936–1969], VI).

the Highlanders and regulars were almost entirely cut off. Many were slain, and many came in wounded. The number of both are not yet known, though it is conjectured that a thousand are among the killed and wounded!

He listed the officer casualties in his battalion, then evaluated the tactics of the British force:

The conduct [of Abercromby] is thought to be marvelous strange, to order the entrenchment to be forced with small arms when they had cannon not far off, and numbers sufficient to keep the enemy off till we had entrenched and placed our cannon and bomb mortars so as to play upon the enemy. Most of our forces retreated towards the landing where the batteaux lay!

Cleaveland buttressed his account with a carefully drawn map that showed the positions of British units at the beginning of the encounter and a hundred words more of explanation concerning their movements during the attack.[21]

Caleb Rea's account agreed in tone and substance.

[July] 8th. A clear day and not very hot; wind southwest. . . . This morning about nine or ten o'clock our army attacked the enemy in their advanced breastworks, and soon drove them out; and followed them to their entrenchments, which was strongly formed by art and nature and fortified with cannon, also under cover of the fort. It is said the regulars who gave the first attack were almost all swept off by grape shot from the cannon as well as by small arms. For when the enemy saw the intrepidity of our troops forcing the entrenchments with their bayonets, they retreated hoisting English colors, thereby decoying our men into the French; and then fired their cannon with small ball and grape shot slaying many hundreds. Notwithstanding all this, our men once and again got possession of different parts of the entrenchment, but at last was obliged to retreat with great loss. Why this was not attacked with cannon and mortars I know not. Many conjectures there are . . . but it seems it was absolutely necessary to reduce this [entrenchment] before we could attack the fort, as it lay before [the fort] and reached from lake to lake, half a mile or more in length. The fort [is] placed on the point or neck of land between the lakes and no coming at it but over this entrenchment. The battle lasted hot till three or four after noon, when our men only fired from the breastworks they first recovered of the enemy, and from trees, stumps, logs, etc. In the evening orders came

21. John Cleaveland, 8 July 1758.

to keep the ground till late in the night, and with all caution, and if possible undiscovered to the enemy, retreat to the landing, . . . which was according[ly] done.[22]

The accounts of the chaplain and the surgeon had important elements in common. Both men tried to make explicit the relationship between the British tactics—frontal assault on field fortifications, without artillery support—and the results—heavy losses of life. Rea added an incident that Cleaveland omitted in his description of the French ruse of raising an English flag. Here again, however, he attributed the result to the tactics: the French stratagem succeeded, and "many hundreds" of regulars were slain in consequence. Both writers commented on the "intrepid" behavior of the British troops under fire. Both characterized wounds and death on the battlefield only in general terms. Cleaveland wrote of companies' being "cut off" (by which he meant destroyed, not isolated) and of the "many [who] were slain and . . . wounded"; Rea spoke of men being "swept off" by cannon fire. Both men tried to make a preliminary estimate of the casualties suffered. Both were concerned to record the enemy position as precisely as possible: Cleaveland by drawing a map and Rea by a rather lengthy verbal description. Both closed their accounts with the British retreat to their boats; both recognized the foolhardiness of attacking entrenched troops with bayonets, unsupported by cannon. In these versions the battle was basically orderly. The action is embedded in causal relationships; wounds and deaths are employed as units of account; the encounter has an episodic structure with a definite conclusion, the retreat; the bad judgment of the British commander in failing to utilize artillery is clearly blamed for the losses suffered.

Subsequent historians have, reasonably enough, trusted Rea's and Cleaveland's coolly comprehensive accounts. Yet junior officers and enlisted men who kept journals that described the battle drew rather different, much less orderly pictures. After the battle these witnesses were less intent on gathering information about the big picture. Casualty estimates, when they made them, tended to be higher, and their descriptions of combat from the worm's-eye level communicate a much greater sense of personal involvement and danger. Lieutenant Archelaus Fuller, an otherwise terse writer, described the battle in what for him was a lengthy, "sorrowful account [of] this unfortunate day." After noting positions, he recorded impressions:

Before the regulars came up the fire began, very hot. The regulars hove down their pack[s] and fixed their bayonets; came up in order; stood and fought very courage[ous]ly. Our men drawed up very near

22. Caleb Rea, 8 July 1758.

and was ordered to make a stand. The fight came on very smart. It held about eight hours, a sorrowful sight to behold. The dead men and wounded lay on the ground, having some of them their legs, their arms, and other limbs broken; others shot through the body and very mortally wounded. To hear their cries and see their bodies lay in blood, and the earth trembled with the fire of the small arms, was as mournful [an] hour as ever I saw.

At sunset the engagement ended. Fuller's unit retired to a breastwork in the rear and was told to hold its ground. Many fell asleep, including Fuller, who awakened to find "that the army [was] chiefly gone." Hastily they retired to the boats at about daybreak on 9 July. Despite the fact that Fuller's company was not informed of the general retreat and despite the heavy casualties that he had witnessed in the unsupported infantry assaults, Fuller refrained from criticizing the command in his account.[23]

Obadiah Harris, a private in another regiment, also voiced no criticism in his version of 8 July, "a woeful day":

The men was ordered up before the breastwork to take it by force. And the French discharged their cannon upon us and cut us down in great numbers as the battle begun (about two of the clock in the afternoon and continued till sunset). At the beginning of the fight our men prevailed and got part of the breastwork. And the French, seeing our men prevail, made as though they would surrender, and ceased firing; pulled off their hats; set up an English flag. And our men thought that we had got the breastwork in [hand], and the French turned and fired upon us, and killed our men in great numbers, by which they was forced to retreat. And the enemy took full possession of the breastwork again, but our men tried the second and third time, but could not prevail, but was killed till the ground was almost covered with the dead bodies and we was forced to retreat. . . . And orders came for us to retreat to the boats, and we got back at the break of the ninth day, this. Came off as fast as we could and got to Fort William Henry at the sun setting.[24]

Joseph Nichols's account ran in the same vein as Harris's did but was rather more personal. He had "observed in the woods many slain men, an awful sight to behold," on the day before the battle. The dead, killed in previous skirmishing, had already moved him to reflect on the "heavy . . . judgment of war." The assault on 8 July, however, simply astounded him. "Our forces fell exceeding fast. It was surprising to me to think more of

23. Archelaus Fuller, 8 July 1758.
24. Obadiah Harris, 8 July 1758.

the regiments should be drawn up to the breastwork for such slaughter." He too recounted the French ruse of feigned surrender, then described the assault:

> Our enemies fired upon our men and cut them down like grass. The fire continued exceeding hot, and one regiment was drawn up after another. In about an hour, orders came for Colonel Bagley's regiment to march up directly. We marched up a small space and then orders came to halt. Several of the soldiers went up without order and was killed, and several wounded. Our captain took care to keep us back from going forward, and keep our ground good, so our company fell not a prey as many of other companies did. The engagement lasted from . . . [ten o'clock] till just as the sun set; then we carried off some of our wounded men, and I am apt to think many was left to the mercy of the enemy.

Nichols, like Fuller, emphasized the disorderly retreat to the boats, where

> news came that the enemy was coming to fall upon us. Oh, the confusion that we was in at that time; for we was in a poor situation for an enemy to attack us, being joined to a point of land, and the batteaux lay joining to one another fifteen deep from land. The cry of "Enemy" made our people cry out and make sad lamentations. We made the best of our way off, and received not hurt.

Two days after the return, Nichols mentioned that official estimates of casualties ran from two to three thousand, and added that he believed that they had to be more than two thousand.[25]

David Perry's narrative completes the set of soldiers' battle accounts. Though composed nearly six decades after the engagement, its vivid immediacy demonstrates the power of battlefield memories. Orders came to Colonel Preble's regiment on the morning of the eighth, Perry remembered, to advance

> in order to storm the enemy's breastworks, known in this country by the name of "the Old French Lines." Our orders were to "run to the breastwork and get in if we could." But their lines were full, and they killed our men so fast, that we could not gain it. We got behind trees, logs and stumps, and covered ourselves as we could from the enemy's fire. The ground was strewed with the dead and dying. It happened that I got behind a white-oak stump, which was so small that I had to lay on my side, and stretch myself; the balls striking the ground within a hand's breadth of me every moment, and I could

25. Joseph Nichols, 8–9, 11 July 1758.

hear the men screaming, and see them dying all around me. I lay there some time. A man could not stand erect without being hit, any more than he could stand out in a shower, without having drops of rain fall upon him; for the balls came by handsfull. It was a clear day—little air stirring. Once in a while the enemy would cease firing a minute or two, to have the smoke clear away, so that they might take better aim. In one of these intervals I sprang from my perilous situation, and gained a stand which I thought would be more secure, behind a large pine log, where several of my comrades had already taken shelter but the balls came here as thick as ever. One of the men raised his head a little above the log, and a ball struck him in the centre of the forehead, and tore up his scalp clear back to the crown. He darted back, and the blood ran merrily; and rubbing his face, said it was a bad blow, and no one was disposed to deny it, for he looked bad enough. We lay there till near sunset and, not receiving orders from any officer, the men crept off, leaving all the dead, and most of the wounded. We had two of our company killed, and a number wounded. Our captain ([Job] Winslow) received a ball in his wrist, which passed up the fleshy part of his arm, and he carried it there as long as he lived, which was a number of years; he was afterward raised to the rank of Colonel. Our Lieutenant was wounded by a shot in the leg, and one of our Sargents received a ball in his arm, which he carried with him to his grave.

We got away the wounded of our company; but left a great many crying for help, which we were unable to afford them. I suppose that as soon as we left the ground, the enemy let loose his Indians upon them: for none of those that we left behind were ever heard of afterwards. We started back to our boats without any orders, and pushed out on the Lake for the night. We left between 6 and 7,000, in killed and wounded, on the field of battle, which I believe is a greater number than ever was lost on our side, in one day, in all the battles that have been fought in America.[26]

There is of course no doubt that these four witnesses were describing the same encounter as Rea and Cleaveland; the divergences between the two sets of descriptions, however, help illuminate the nature of common soldiers' experiences of battle. The most notable distinction between the two efforts is in the authors' estimate of what merited description. Among the worm's-eye writers, only Harris attempted anything like a comprehensive picture. Fuller and Nichols were content to set down just what they could see from the edge of the battlefield. The only troop movement they noted, for instance, was their own regiment's short march forward to the

26. Perry, "Recollections," *Mag. Hist.*, CXXXVII (1928), 9–10.

position from which they observed the engagement. Perry, the one witness actually to come under fire, could see almost nothing but the ground and the men immediately next to him. He remembered the battle without any reference to orderly maneuver, solely in terms of his own desperate scramble for cover. Similarly, the four soldiers' narratives adverted to cause-and-effect relationships much less than did the accounts of Cleaveland and Rea. In the bird's-eye accounts, tactics produce results, and movement corresponds, in at least a general way, to orders issued. The worm's-eye views, on the other hand, do not clearly depict any tactics, except Harris's and Nichols's references to the French trick of feigned surrender. In their narratives, movements and events often take place with no reference to command or direction. All but Harris insisted that the retreat to the boats took place without being ordered; Nichols mentioned several men from his regiment rushing the French breastwork without being ordered to do so. When orders are recounted, their effects are anything but predictable. The only order mentioned in Perry's account was vague, impossible to execute, and gravely endangered anyone who tried to fulfill it.

The wide perspective of Cleaveland's and Rea's portraits of the battle virtually eliminated incidental detail, but the narrower accounts were thick with it. Archelaus Fuller did not describe the regulars' advance to the breastwork, but he noted the way that they "hove down their pack[s] and fixed their bayonets." Joseph Nichols described the congestion of the batteaux, "joining to one another fifteen deep from land," when the panicky troops arrived at the landing place on their retreat. David Perry recalled that he initially took cover behind a stump; but it was more than just a stump: "a white-oak stump, which was so small that I had to lay on my side, and stretch myself." When he sought better shelter, he headed not just for a log, but "a large pine log," which turned out to be already occupied. These closely focused accounts portray combat as anything but an orderly, comprehensible experience. The soldiers' battlefield was a world of vivid, frightening, confusing detail, made memorable by fear. Among the most important details to the soldiers were ones overlooked or dismissed by Cleaveland and Rea: the screams of wounded men, noise and concussion so intense that they made the earth tremble, lamentations of fear, dense palls of smoke, cries of warning, piteous appeals for help. Most of all, however, the soldiers' consciousness was dominated by death and wounds: the "slaughter" (a term of great concreteness to country folk) that left the ground in front of the French lines "almost covered with the dead bodies" of soldiers, "cut . . . down like grass" by enemy fire. In the more general narratives of Cleaveland and Rea casualties were present only in abstract form; the hideous wounds described by Fuller, Nichols, and Perry were absent.

The injuries mentioned—men's "legs, their arms, and other limbs broken, others shot through the body and very mortally wounded"—were principally inflicted by cannon smallshot and grapeshot, although volleys of musket fire were evidently great killers, too. Many wounds were incapacitating but not immediately fatal, leaving the victims to cry out for help after the battle. Rea and Cleaveland did not mention the wounded abandoned on the field, but the fact clearly disturbed Nichols and Perry, who assumed that the Indian allies of the French would kill or mutilate them. Finally, the soldiers' accounts of the battle lacked the clear-cut termination that Rea and Cleaveland both recognized in the retreat, which for them was an orderly occurrence. The soldiers' versions have ragged, indefinite endings; for them the retreat was a process, not a unitary event. Fuller's battle seemed to end with exhausted sleep and a confused awakening to find the rest of the army gone. Harris drew no clear line between the events of the eighth and the ninth. Nichols's account climaxed with the panic and "sad lamentations" of men stampeding for boats. Perry's battle in some ways did not end at all. He mentioned creeping off, then described wounds sustained in his company—injuries that lasted as long as the wounded men lived—and finally returned to speak of withdrawing from a field where the wounded were still begging, fruitlessly, for help.

Frightening and wrenching as the experience of battle was for its closest participants, the army's defeat did not necessarily lead them to blame their leaders. Only the writers with a comprehensive perspective, Rea and Cleaveland, immediately held General Abercromby responsible for ordering the brutal frontal assault on the French and for failing to use the artillery that was close at hand. The authors of the other accounts did not openly criticize. Fuller, Harris, and Nichols were silent on the subject, and for Perry and Rufus Putnam (who was also present, but a noncombatant and only an intermittent observer), judgment came only with the passage of years. "At the time," Putnam recorded in his *Memoirs*,

> I was uninformed of the situation of the [French] works or of the mode of attack; and had I been informed of all this, considering my youth and inexperience it would have been arrogance to have given an opinion. However, afterwards viewing the works and being informed of the mode of attack, I have judged it the most injudicious and wanton sacrifice of men that ever came within my knowledge, or reading.[27]

David Perry agreed, and for strikingly similar reasons:

> I was but a boy, and could have little judgment about it [i.e., Abercromby's generalship] then: but from later experience and reflection,

27. Rufus Putnam, *The Memoirs of Rufus Putnam* (Boston, 1903), 24–25.

I think it looks more like the conduct of a Hull, a Wilkinson, or a Hampton, than like that of an able General and firm patriot. We had artillery enough, and might have erected batteries; and it seems as though we might have taken the place.[28]

Putnam was twenty at the time of the battle; Perry was seventeen. Their initial reticence may reflect another aspect of battle's impact on the survivors: an unwillingness or inability to form any overall assessment of the event soon after its conclusion. Battle was so overwhelming, so devastating, that it evidently required a period of reflection to sort out its meaning. The process of reflection might take years, as it did for Putnam and Perry; but eventually judgment came. Putnam finally decided that Abercromby was a fool, and Perry concluded that he was a scoundrel. To reach these conclusions, they needed to decide what bad judgment and bad character were, and their memory of the battle heavily stamped their understanding of these traits. For them combat was the most intense manifestation of the processes at work in the rest of their provincial military careers. The whole of the military experience, while more easily comprehensible, functioned less dramatically to produce similar results: a common memory, a reference point, a shared expansion of horizons.

II

But what was it that motivated provincials to go into battle in the first place? How can we account for what has been called the "will to combat"—particularly since many injured soldiers would be abandoned on the battlefield and even the luckiest among the wounded might expect to be taken to a pestilential field hospital?[29] Iron discipline, as we have seen, cannot be the explanation, nor can the soldier's training. There is, in fact, no single reason why provincials were willing to risk their lives; instead, a combination of several factors was at work.

To a degree that cannot be determined precisely, religion formed an element of provincial motivation. Civilian ministers, whose preaching was

28. Perry, "Recollections," *Mag. Hist.*, CXXXVII (1928), 11. "Hull" was William Hull, who lost Detroit to the British in the War of 1812 and was cashiered by court-martial thereafter; "Wilkinson" was James Wilkinson, military adventurer and participant in unsavory intrigues from the Conway Cabal through the Burr Conspiracy; "Hampton" was Wade Hampton, widely held responsible for the failure of the American campaign against Montreal in the autumn of 1813.

29. "Will to combat" is a term employed by John Keegan, who has adopted it from the 19th-century French military theorist, Ardant Du Picq; it comprises an important analytical category in *Face of Battle* (see, e.g., 71, 113–116, 179–192, 269–279).

crucial to the articulation of public opinion, interpreted the war not so much as a conflict between Great Britain and France as between Protestant- ✓ ism and Popery. In this they mined the rich native vein of anti-Catholic sentiment and placed the struggle firmly in the providentialist tradition of New England historiography. Their interpretation, moreover, took on increasingly apocalyptic overtones as they came conclusively to identify the French king with Antichrist and the events of the conflict with the fulfillment of the last prophecies.[30] Army chaplains (who were, after all, civilian pastors in the army for a year or two) preached similar messages to the troops and whenever possible made special exhortations before battle. On the Sunday before the army's departure for Ticonderoga in 1758, for example, the various regimental chaplains preached with clear reference to the coming conflict. John Cleaveland wrote that his colleague, the Reverend Eli Forbes, had preached in the morning "from Exodus 17 . . . and an excellent sermon he preached, well adapted to the occasion."[31] Obadiah Harris was also in the congregation, and noted—unusually for him—both the citation and the text. "Exodus XVII and ninth verse: And Moses said unto Joshua, Choose us out men, and go out, fight with Amalek; tomorrow I will stand on [the] top of [the] hill with the rod of God in mine hand."[32] The sermon impressed Harris, as did the occurrences of the next day, when "the several regiments of the provincial[s] were called together . . . and the several chaplains agreed this day to offer up prayers in an extraordinary manner to engage the presence of God with us."[33] On Sunday,

30. For a more thorough discussion, see Nathan O. Hatch, *The Sacred Cause of Liberty: Republican Thought and the Millennium in Revolutionary New England* (New Haven, Conn., 1977), chap. 1, esp. 38–44; see also Thomas More Brown, "The Image of the Beast: Anti-Papal Rhetoric in Colonial America," in Brown and Richard Curry, eds., *Conspiracy: The Fear of Subversion in American History* (New York, 1972), 1–20; Sr. Mary Augustina Ray, *American Opinion of Roman Catholicism in the Eighteenth Century* (New York, 1936), 201–211, 221–242, and *passim*; Sacvan Bercovitch, *The American Jeremiad* (Madison, Wis., 1978), 115–118; James West Davidson, *The Logic of Millennial Thought: Eighteenth-Century New England* (New Haven, Conn., 1977), 196–212.

31. John Cleaveland, 2 July 1758.

32. Obadiah Harris, 2 July 1758. In the story, the children of Israel, wandering in the wilderness, are called upon to fight with the tribe of Amalek. After Joshua had chosen his force, Moses, Aaron, and Hur climbed a hill overlooking the battleground. When Moses held up his hands, Israel prevailed; when he let them fall with weariness, the battle turned in Amalek's favor. So Aaron and Hur positioned themselves on either side of Moses and held his hands steady until sunset: "And Joshua discomfited Amalek and his people with the edge of the sword." The Lord spoke to Moses after the battle, promising, "I will utterly put out the remembrance of Amalek from under heaven," so Moses built an altar, and named it Jehovahnissi, "Because the Lord hath sworn that the Lord will have war with Amalek from generation to generation" (Exod. 17:8–16). The text was indeed perfectly adapted to the occasion, as Cleaveland suggested.

33. Obadiah Harris, 3 July 1758.

in the afternoon, Cleaveland himself preached "to a large concourse from Eph. 6:18, praying always with all prayer and supplication in the Spirit, etc. . . . and there was remarkable attention in the assembly both parts of the day."[34] Cleaveland, too, impressed his auditory and adapted his discourse to the occasion. According to the observant Joseph Nichols, "He gave us a very good exhortation to pray and not fail; in particular when we are going to jeopard our lives in battle."[35]

Other forms of exhortation were also used to ready men for battle. Immediately before the French attack at Lake George in 1755, General William Johnson "harangued and did all in his power to animate our people," and so did his subordinate officers.[36] On the eve of the army's departure from Crown Point for Canada, 10 August 1760, members of Timothy Ruggles's regiment got a double-barreled exhortation, sacred and secular: "Mr. Crawford preached an excellent sermon, suitable to the occasion; and Brigadier Ruggles made a very glorious speech, which seemed to animate us."[37] Religion, however, seems to have been the predominant component in formal preparations for combat, and some evidence even suggests that there was an element of popular religious expression *during* battles. When the artillery batteries opened at the siege of the French fort at Île-aux-Noix in 1760, for example, the firing was supposed to be preceded "by all the drums beating a point of war, next by a band of musick, followed by all the provincials singing psalms."[38]

Together with whatever religious convictions propelled the average provincial was almost certainly another hope, drawing him to combat: plunder. Few witnesses failed to mention booty admiringly, including chaplains.[39] When Fort Frontenac fell to Colonel John Bradstreet's improvised

34. John Cleaveland, 2 July 1758. This verse ("Praying always with all prayer and supplication in the Spirit, and watching thereunto with all perseverance and supplication for all saints") is the climax of Paul's admonition, in extended martial metaphor, to "put on the whole armor of God"—"for we wrestle . . . against principalities, against powers, against the rulers of the darkness of this world, against spiritual wickedness in high places" (Eph. 6:18, 11, 12).

35. Joseph Nichols, 2 July 1758. Cf. Caleb Rea, 2 July 1758.

36. Captain Peter Wraxall to Henry Fox, 27 Sept. 1756, in Stanley Pargellis, *Military Affairs in North America, 1748–1765* (Hamden, Conn., 1969 [orig. publ. New York, 1936]), 139.

37. Thomas Moody, 10 Aug. 1760. "Mr. Crawford" was William Crawford of Shrewsbury, a ministerial candidate who later became a physician.

38. Samuel Jenks, 23 Aug. 1760.

39. Soldiers who made significant references to plunder include: David Perry, "Recollections," *Mag. Hist.*, CXXXVII (1928), 14, 16; Lemuel Wood, 27 July 1759, 28 Aug. 1760; Joseph Nichols, 5 July 1758; Archelaus Fuller, 5 July 1758; John Cleaveland, 8, 11 Sept. 1758; Benjamin Bass, 27, 28 Aug. 1758; John Burrell, 16 Aug., 11 Sept., 12 Oct. 1759; Enoch Poor, 17 July, 16 Aug., 9 Oct. 1759; James Hill, 9 Sept. 1755; Samuel Merriman, 26 July

expedition in 1758, the British captured what impressed the Reverend John Cleaveland as "a prodi[gi]ous quantity of furs and European goods"—the value of which was rumored at first to be seven hundred thousand pounds sterling, though the figure was later revised downward to eighty thousand pounds.[40] The twenty-seven hundred members of the expedition divided the spoil equally between them at Fort Bull, New York, on 8 September 1758.[41] Each soldier's share, even with the total value of the booty adjusted downward to the lowest estimate, would have been about thirteen pounds sterling.[42] Each of the nearly six hundred Massachusetts privates who had served with Bradstreet could have realized almost fifty pounds in Massachusetts currency by participating in the 1758 campaign, as the total of pay, bounty, and booty.

Bradstreet's troops were, of course, exceptionally lucky in plunder. Still, even a relatively small skirmish with the French could yield "a great deal of wine and brandy, sheep, turkeys, and hens"—no small reward for hungry troops.[43] In addition to the formal division of captured matériel, of course, there was the free-lance stripping of corpses in which nearly everyone seems to have engaged, even under conditions of considerable danger. David Perry, for instance, in 1762 took part in an infantry charge up Flagstaff Hill near Saint John's, Newfoundland. Thirty provincials and regulars were killed, but in the midst of the battle Perry paused to pick up "a good French gun" (which, he added, "I brought home with me").[44] After battles were over, pillage of a less daring sort was possible, although competition for spoil was heavy and pickings soon grew slender. "Our people and the Mohawks went out to plunder," wrote James Hill on the day after the battle of Lake George, "and got a great deal; but the Mohawks

---

1759; Moses Dorr, 12 Sept. 1758; William Sweat, 5 July 1758; John Thomas, 11 June 1755; John Winslow, 9, 19 July 1755; John Rous to Winslow, 15 June 1755, Winslow to Col. Robert Monckton, 17 June 1755 ["Journal of Winslow," Nova Scotia Hist. Soc., *Colls.*, III (1882–1883), 174, 176, 156–157, 159]; Caleb Rea, 6 July, 11 Sept. 1755; Samuel Jenks, 31 Aug. 1760.

40. John Cleaveland, 8, 11, 15 Sept. 1758.

41. [John Bradstreet], *An Impartial Account of Lieut-Col. Bradstreet's Expedition to Fort Frontenac . . . by a Volunteer on the Expedition (Seventeen Fifty-eight)*, ed. E. C. Kyte (Toronto, 1949 [orig. publ. London, 1759]), 25.

42. *Ibid.*, 24, n. 6, gives a very sober estimate, £35,000 sterling, for the total value of the Frontenac plunder—the lowest of which I am aware.

43. Archelaus Fuller, 5 July 1758. Joseph Nichols recorded the take as "considerable plunder and some plate . . . likewise turkeys and fowls in abundance" (5 July 1758). The skirmish that yielded this booty was the overrunning of the French advanced guard at the Ticonderoga sawmills, a preliminary of the battle of 8 July 1758. Cf. Obadiah Harris, Caleb Rea, 5 July 1758.

44. Perry, "Recollections," *Mag. Hist.*, CXXXVII (1928), 25.

got most of it." [45] If the battlefield were too long abandoned, results could be poor indeed, as Amos Richardson and several comrades found in 1758 when they "went out a-plundering" on a battlefield long grown cold. Richardson got only "a Dutch spoon and a handkerchief and a wormer to a gun and some more things which I would not keep account of." [46] The knowledge that participation in battle allowed the most profitable plundering very likely imparted a certain impetus to the provincial will to combat. [47]

Religious and pecuniary motivations readily coexisted in soldiers' minds. Another element, seldom mentioned in their journals but probably more important on the whole than either faith or greed, was peer pressure. Rufus Putnam articulated its meaning most clearly and honestly in his *Memoirs*. Putnam saw his first real fighting at Ticonderoga in 1758. After the initial skirmish with the French near the army's landing place, he wrote, "I was so panic-struck that I was willing to remain with the boat guard, which in the morning [before the skirmish] I should have been very unwilling to have been detailed for. However, I soon recovered, at least in a measure, so that I volunteered myself to join the regiment." Putnam's battalion was posted as part of the rear guard; on the afternoon of the battle, Putnam felt himself compelled to volunteer for the hazardous duty of carrying ammunition to the front. It was because he had been "feeling a little concerned lest my character might suffer for having willingly remained with the boat guard [that] I volunteered myself on this service. I have heard that some men should say they loved to fight as well as to eat. I

45. James Hill, 9 Sept. 1755.

46. Amos Richardson, 5 July 1758.

47. Only two provincials' diaries reflect the writers' concern that they might become the victims of plunderers themselves. Both Caleb Rea, in 1758, and Samuel Jenks, in 1760, delivered cash in the amount of one johannes (a gold coin worth 16 Spanish dollars) to intermediaries for safekeeping before expected combat (Caleb Rea, 4 July 1758; Samuel Jenks, 10 Aug. 1760). Enlisted men probably paid less attention to such arrangements because they had less to lose. Since they received only small advances on their pay, most probably went into battle with nearly empty pockets. This contrasts to European soldiers who were paid in the field and for whom "the only safe storage for valuables in an army without bankers was about the person" (Keegan, *Face of Battle*, 181). (Keegan refers to Waterloo soldiers here, but the same might have been said for the redcoats of a half-century earlier.) In a general way this is borne out by the inventories of personal effects taken at Halfway Brook on 24 July 1758 for 10 men who had been recently killed. The six privates who were killed owned clothing and goods— e.g., "half a pound of tobacco and bottle," "half a pound of chocolate," and "one pair of specks"—worth on average £8 17s. 1d. Old Tenor apiece, or only about £2 6s. Lawful Money. Only one private was listed as possessing a purse, which contained £11 5s. O.T., or slightly less than £3 L.M.; a captain who was killed, on the other hand, left a purse containing currency and notes to the amount of £51 2s. 10d. O.T., or somewhat over £13 12s. L.M. The personal effects of soldiers were sold at vendue by their officers, and the money was given to their next of kin. (See Samuel A. Green, "Capt. Thomas Lawrence's Company," Massachusetts Historical Society, *Proceedings*, 2d Ser., VI [1890], 21–31.)

never had any such feelings. So far as I am able to judge of myself it was pride and a wish to excel, or at least to come behind none, which influenced me at that period of my life to be among the foremost on all occasions that offered."[48]

Soldiers could experience such pressures in more overt ways, too. Two days before Sergeant Robert Webster and his unit left Fort George to advance on Ticonderoga in the 1759 expedition that finally captured the fort, he noted that one of his men, "Jonathan Corbin[,] confessed that he was afraid to go to Boges. Set his name down for a coward."[49] This evidently shamed Corbin into participation, for he served with his company during the siege and remained with the unit until he died of disease in late September.[50]

A final component in provincial combat motivation was the soldiers' faith in their leaders, a factor as variable as the character and behavior of individual New England officers. Soldiers' accounts indicate that even in the absence of a professional ideal of officer conduct, the provincials knew very well what they expected from their leaders. At the most rudimentary level, privates regarded the good officer as one who did not create useless work for his men, who knew his job and performed it without undue fuss, who cared properly for the welfare of his men.[51] A good officer did not expose his men needlessly to danger and remained calm under pressure.[52] The provincials expected their leaders to lead by example and to show as much courage as they expected from their men—to behave, in short, like Captain Samuel Peck. "Our captain was a bold man," wrote one of his soldiers. "I have seen him cock his piece, and walk promptly up to the enemy, face to face; and our men would never shrink from following such an officer, and they seldom followed him without success."[53] Bravery,

48. Putnam, *Memoirs*, 23, 24.

49. Robert Webster, 19 July 1759. *Boges*—pronounced *bogus*—and *Tantrabogus* were soldier slang for Ticonderoga. (By some unclear transformation, *bogus* also came to be the name for a favored soldiers' beverage, rum and molasses.)

50. Robert Webster, 27 Sept. 1758; cf. Samuel Morris, 27 Sept. 1758.

51. This set of attributes emerges most fully in the comments John Woods made on his officers in 1759. Woods was in almost every way a representative private, especially in his complaints. See especially entries for 7 Aug. (an ensign will not permit his men to eat for fear of breaking an apparently senseless rule); 27 Sept. (troops kept standing on parade for two hours because the officer of the day cannot be found to complete the inspection); 28 Oct. 1759 (an ensign creates extra work for his detail by too eagerly following mistaken orders).

52. See, e.g., Joseph Nichols, 8 July 1758, on his captain, who took care to keep his men in order, and out of the range of French fire; see also Lemuel Wood, 27 Aug., 25 Sept. 1759 (a description of a panicky pair of junior officers); and Rufus Putnam, 8–12 July 1758 (a panicky lieutenant abandons a patrol).

53. Perry, "Recollections," *Mag. Hist.*, CXXXVII (1928), 18. Peck was Perry's company commander in 1760.

however, was distinct from foolhardiness, and the leader was expected to take every possible precaution when encounters with the enemy were likely.[54] Officers who erred and then tried to make excuses for their bad judgment or bad conduct were disdained, since leaders were also expected to be dignified. "When an officer is brought to solicit his soldiers not [to] complain of him, he must feel small in his own eyes, as well as contemptible in the eyes of others."[55]

As these remarks suggest, provincial methods of leadership were primarily physical and personal—as indeed they had to be, given the general lack of training. In part this reflected the enlisted men's expectation that officers would share equally in danger and privation. Captain Samuel Jenks showed his commitment to this ideal of leadership when, despite conditions "not half so good or convenient as we generally provide for our swine at home," he "lay out with the picquet to keep them alert" and on guard against enemy attack.[56] Risk-sharing was, in a sense, the physical fulfillment of the recruitment promise that an officer would personally lead the men he had enlisted. Provincial volunteers had joined the army with the understanding that they would follow a specific man, not just any holder of a commission; hence the need for *personal* displays of courage, personal sharings of risk, for authority was in no sense an abstract conception, either to officers or to men. For provincial officers to be effective leaders, it was crucial to maintain a high level of solidarity with their enlisted men— precisely the opposite of the professional officer's prescription of rigorous separation.

Only one regular general, Viscount Howe, fully understood that if he gave provincial soldiers what they expected from their leaders, they would follow willingly, and perhaps even fight well. Howe's easy familiarity and robust physical courage quickly won the loyalty and respect of New England troops, and his death in the preliminary skirmishing before the battle of Ticonderoga shattered provincial morale. The effect of his death points up the fragility of provincial motivation, for the loyalty and faith accorded one leader would not necessarily be transferred whole to his successor. Provincial motivation in combat depended, to an extraordinary degree, upon individual willingness to cooperate. Leadership by personal example could be an effective way to elicit the soldiers' participation, but its highly individual focus made it as vulnerable as the human life upon which it ultimately turned.

54. Rufus Putnam called this caution "generalship" and reported that he first observed it in the conduct of his distant cousin, Israel Putnam, the Ranger—an example which "I recollect to have treasured up" (*Memoirs*, 13).

55. *Ibid.*, 12.

56. Samuel Jenks, 3 Sept. 1760.

Leadership, of course, was a quality as vital off the battlefield as on it. Because good leadership ultimately reflected no more than an officer's effectiveness in securing the cooperation of his soldiers, an examination of an able provincial leader in action can provide a close-up look at his soldiers' expectations, as well as at the leader's own understanding of the relationship between himself and his followers. Fortunately, Rufus Putnam's *Memoirs* offers a superb portrait of such an officer: Putnam's first company commander, Captain Ebenezer Learned. But there is a telling irony in the story, too: its main event is a desertion, which Learned very capably led.

From the time Captain Learned assumed command in April 1757, he participated actively in the communal life of his men. He "prayed with his company morning and evening." If no preacher was available, "on the Sabbath [he would] read a sermon," Putnam recalled, adding, "Oh! how the times have changed!" [57] Learned's men had enlisted to serve, at longest, until Candlemas (2 February 1758), although they expected to be dismissed at the close of the 1757 campaign. To their disappointment, they were not discharged in November, but kept on at Stillwater as the garrison of a small fortified outpost. In early January they concluded that they would be detained for the rest of the winter. Accordingly they began to plan their escape via the backcountry, avoiding the regulars posted along the main road. Learned was home on furlough, but when he returned on 5 January, his men immediately apprised him of their plan to depart on the day after their enlistments expired. Learned agreed that their cause was just and offered to request their discharge from the regular captain in charge of the post. If he failed to obtain it, he promised, he would lead them in their "retreat." The regular commander refused; so, early on the morning of 3 February, the entire company, with the exception of its invalids and its second lieutenant, left on snowshoes.

The party expected to reach Fort Hoosuck, on the western edge of Massachusetts, in two days' time. On the fourth day, with his men frostbitten, lame, and out of provisions, Learned realized that they were lost. He called the company together, Putnam remembered, and said: "It evidently appears that we are on a wrong stream, and we must be at least thirty mile north of Hoosuck Fort. But don't be discouraged, for my life on it, if the men hold out to travel four or five days, if I don't bring you to see the inhabitants of New England. However, if any man has a mind to turn back to Stillwater, he may go, in welcome. For my part, I will sooner die in the woods."

The men "all agreed to follow him." After three more days (during which time the soldiers finally grew hungry enough to eat their dog), the

57. Putnam, *Memoirs*, 11.

advance elements of the party finally struck what one man recognized as Pelham Brook. It was about sunset, and the men were strung out over a great distance from their day's march. The impulse was strong to follow the stream to the Deerfield River, on which they knew Hawks's Fort stood, no more than three miles ahead. At this point, however, "the captain conducted with great prudence, for not more than a dozen or fifteen of us were yet come up," Putnam wrote. "And although we might have gone in with safety, yet it must probably have been [with] the loss of some that were fallen in the rear on account of feebleness and frosted feet. The captain therefore ordered [a] corporal and two others to go on to the fort, and make provision for our arrival in the morning; and the rest to build fires for the night. Fortunately all the men came up." The next morning the deserters arrived at Hawks's Fort, "where we were kindly entertained." Although they had been marching through the winter woods for more than a week, not a man was lost.[58]

Captain Learned's cross-country navigation may have been weak, but his leadership was strong, well suited to the expectations of his men, and probably responsible for keeping them all alive. He never forgot that he was one of them. The men realized that he identified his interests with theirs, and reciprocated with their trust. When Learned returned from his furlough, they unhesitatingly announced their plans to desert and sought his cooperation. Learned clearly understood that his leadership was contingent on his men's continuing consent. When he realized that he had gotten them lost, he therefore offered the deserters an opportunity to retrace their steps to Stillwater. Two elements were present in his brief address to the men. First, he admitted his confusion and shared with them what information he had. Second, he expressed his personal commitment to continuing but made no further attempt to influence their choice. The decision of the group to continue thus represented a voluntary reaffirmation of confidence in Learned, a willingness to entrust their lives to a man who was ready to venture his own life on their behalf. Although he risked repudiation, such a renewal of consent was probably the only way he could have kept the group together much longer. While hardly the sort of gesture that would have recommended itself to a professional soldier, Learned's frank appeal to the men was a necessary symbolic act, one which met perfectly with their expectations.

The deserters' faith in Captain Learned was borne out when the leaders of the party struck Pelham Brook on 9 February. Learned's "great prudence" in pausing for the night ensured the continued integrity of the party and the survival of its stragglers. His decision to remain in the woods

58. *Ibid.*, 18–21.

that night, moreover, secured his moral position in the group. By demonstrating his willingness to undergo another hungry, freezing night with his men, he demonstrated that he did not place his own interest above theirs. Learned realized that the men relied upon his actions as a guide for their own conduct, and clearly grasped the sine qua non of provincial leadership, the primacy of loyalty to one's followers. As a result his style of command depended not on formal authority or enforced submission, but on group solidarity, personal example, mutual faith, and the periodically renewed consent of his followers. Learned was unquestionably a capable leader, and bringing his party through its ordeal was in its way a heroic achievement. Yet at every step his actions contradicted conventional, professional expectations of officer behavior.

Effective provincial leadership was not command in the regulars' sense, but something rather closer to negotiation. It required officers to furnish information and explain decisions to their men. It admitted the possibility that the men could withdraw their support from a leader who no longer enjoyed their confidence or shared their interests. So long as the soldiers remained knit together in a common cause, so long as their morale stayed high and they were convinced that their officers were worthy of their trust, provincial armies could function reasonably well, even in the absence of formal discipline. But stress, whether caused by combat, disease, short rations, or simple discouragement, severely challenged the cohesion of provincial armies. Ironically, it was only by accepting, and even promoting, the powerfully centrifugal voluntarism of the provincial soldiers that officers could lead effectively. Such an understanding was militarily nonsensical: it supposed that the survival of the army as a physical institution was somehow secondary to the existence of the army as an agreement—almost as a state of mind.

Part Three ❖ The Meaning of War

Chapter 6 ❖ "A Principle So Strongly Imbibed"
Contractual Principles and the Provincial Conception
of Military Service

British officers who served in North America never tired of reminding one another that American colonists made the world's worst soldiers. They saw provincial troops as overpaid and underdisciplined, a sickly, faint-hearted rabble led by men unwilling to exercise their authority for fear of losing favor with the mob. The populace was as bad as its soldiery: a greedy and small-minded people incapable of disinterested action in defense of the empire. The British largely formed these opinions in the course of their contacts with New England provincials. The unfavorable impression of New Englanders that regular officers brought home from North America in turn created the dominant British estimate of colonial military potential at the outset of the War of Independence.[1]

The British tended to conclude that New Englanders made bad soldiers because they were deficient in courage and moral fiber. That was a profoundly mistaken conclusion, but it was based on the indisputable fact that provincials often behaved unprofessionally and sometimes acted in ways detrimental to the war effort. Yet their behavior was neither unreasoned nor merely self-interested, as the British assumed. Instead, the unmilitary deportment of New Englanders reflected their tendency to base their actions and arguments upon contractual principles when confronted with the pretensions of their redcoat superiors. The agreement—amounting to consensus—among New Englanders over the contractual basis of military authority is nowhere more evident than in the disputes between regulars and provincials in the campaign of 1756. One of these conflicts, superficially over rank and precedence, between the supreme commander of the Anglo-American forces and the provincial field officers of Massachusetts, illustrates the application of contractual principles by members of a colonial elite. Another disagreement, between the supreme commander and Massachusetts elected officials concerning the provisioning of the troops, demonstrates the application of identical assumptions by a colonial government. Finally, a survey of mutinies and mass desertions among pro-

1. See, for example, Peter Wraxall to Henry Fox, 27 Sept. 1755, in Stanley Pargellis, ed., *Military Affairs in North America, 1748–1765* (Hamden, Conn., 1969 [orig. publ. New York, 1936]), 137–145; and Loudoun to Cumberland, 29 Aug. 1756, *ibid.*, 231–233.

vincial troops shows the same ideas at work in the minds of enlisted men and indicates the centrality of contract in popular understandings of the legitimate exercise of authority.

I

The year 1756 brought a French victory—the capture of Fort Oswego, Great Britain's main fur-trading post on Lake Ontario—and a change in the British command. In July, the earl of Loudoun, "a rough Scotch lord, hot and irascible," succeeded Major General William Shirley, the governor of Massachusetts who had been acting as commander in chief since the death of Edward Braddock.[2] The change produced an intermission in offensive military activity that left plenty of time for quarrels between regular and provincial officers. The first dispute concerned the rank of colonial officers and the extent of the supreme commander's authority over provincial troops. In the course of this argument it became clear that Loudoun and the provincial officers of Massachusetts espoused fundamentally antagonistic conceptions of military service.

The failure of Anglo-American initiative in 1756 was inevitable from the moment that the Newcastle ministry decided to relieve Shirley of supreme command by a complex, awkward method. Shirley was ordered to relinquish his authority to Colonel Daniel Webb, who was then to pass on the command to Major General James Abercromby, who would in turn surrender control to the newly appointed commander in chief, Loudoun. Webb arrived first, according to plan, but hesitated in taking over. Abercromby instead assumed command directly from Shirley on 25 June. He

2. Francis Parkman, *Montcalm and Wolfe* (Boston, 1901 [orig. publ. Toronto, (1884)]), I, 412. Historians who have addressed this campaign in addition to Parkman include Stanley McCrory Pargellis, *Lord Loudoun in North America* (New Haven, Conn., 1933), chaps. 2, 3, 5; Lawrence Henry Gipson, *The Great War for the Empire: The Years of Defeat, 1754–1757*, 231, in Gipson, *The British Empire before the American Revolution* (New York, 1936–1969), VI; Thomas Hutchinson, *The History of the Colony and Province of Massachusetts-Bay*, ed. Lawrence Shaw Mayo (Cambridge, Mass., 1936 [orig. publ. London, 1828]), III, 33–37; Douglas Edward Leach, *Arms for Empire: A Military History of the British Colonies in North America, 1607–1763* (New York, 1973), 379–391; and Herbert L. Osgood, *The American Colonies in the Eighteenth Century* (New York, 1924), IV, chaps. 15, 16. A more recent commentary on the events of 1756 consists of a portion of chap. 6 in Alan Rogers, *Empire and Liberty: American Resistance to British Authority, 1755–1763* (Berkeley, Calif., 1974); and an article by myself, which includes parts of this chapter: "Why Did Colonial New Englanders Make Bad Soldiers? Contractual Principles and Military Conduct during the Seven Years' War," *William and Mary Quarterly*, 3d Ser., XXXVIII (1981), 395–417.

proved unwilling to undertake any real action, however, before Loudoun's arrival. In the meantime, the campaign proceeded bumpily along the lines set down in the plan Shirley had devised during the previous winter, before he had been informed of his dismissal. By the time Loudoun appeared on the scene in late July, the course of the campaign could no longer be reversed.[3]

As we have seen in chapter 1, Shirley's plan for 1756 centered on an expedition against the French forts on Lake Champlain, to be undertaken entirely by provincial troops from New England and New York. To stimulate New England support, Shirley had awarded the command to John Winslow, who as a veteran of the Carthagena expedition (1740), King George's War (1744–1748), and the Acadia campaign, was one of New England's most distinguished and trusted soldiers. As a means of allaying the colonial assemblies' suspicions (aroused by Colonel Robert Monckton's attempts to enlist New Englanders as redcoats in Nova Scotia the previous year),[4] Shirley had promised that their troops would serve only under the officers who enlisted them, and only within a strictly limited geographical area. Commissions were issued and enlistment conditions announced accordingly. The various colonies responded by raising and equipping approximately seven thousand men.[5] In planning the campaign, Shirley's lack of experience as a professional soldier and his eagerness to solidify political support within the provincial assemblies led him to minimize the effect of the official British regulations, the Rules and Articles of War, on the troops Winslow was to command.

Among other things, the Rules and Articles of War stipulated that all provincial officers of company grade were to be junior to regular officers of similar rank; moreover, provincial field officers—majors, lieutenant colonels, and colonels—were to rank as "eldest captains" of the regular establishment. This meant that the addition of just one battalion of redcoats to a provincial army would reduce all senior provincial leaders to subordinate status. In a combined command, Winslow, a provincial major general, would be subject to the orders of the most junior regular major in the field. Beyond this, the Mutiny Act of 1754 made colonial troops serving in conjunction with regulars subject to British military law, not to the milder

---

3. This account follows the one in Osgood, *American Colonies*, IV, 377–378, 382–388; the same structure of occurrences can be found in any of the general accounts cited above, n. 2.

4. See above, chaps. 1, 2; also Gipson, *Years of Defeat*, 206.

5. On Winslow, see Parkman, *Montcalm and Wolfe*, I, *passim*, esp. 283; also a transcript of a letter from Winslow to Edward Holyoke, 20 Oct. 1749, setting forth his family's history and his own achievements to date, in behalf of his son's placement at Harvard: Massachusetts Historical Society, *Proceedings*, XXIX (1895), 6. On the plan and the number of men to be raised, see Gipson, *Years of Defeat*, 204; and Pargellis, *Loudoun*, 100.

provisions of provincial mutiny acts. As we have seen, this worried provincial soldiers, who feared redcoat discipline and the frequent death sentences handed down by regular courts-martial.[6]

Unlike William Shirley, Lord Loudoun came to North America with thoroughly conventional military ideas, which included a meticulous respect for the Rules and Articles of War. Thus the change of command made nonsense of Shirley's plans and promises, but only after the plans were already in effect and after the promises had been made to men who earnestly desired that they be honored.

Before Loudoun arrived, the interim commander, Major General Abercromby, called a council of war at Albany to consider the effect of placing the provincials under regular command, in accordance with regulations. On 16 July the council summoned Winslow from his camp near Lake George to ask "what effects he apprehended from the junction of his majesty's regular troops with the provincials." Winslow carefully replied that while he personally would be pleased to follow whatever orders were to be given, his men would undoubtedly desert in droves. Even supposing that mass desertions could somehow be prevented, he continued, the four New England assemblies would surely send no further reinforcements once the provincial forces became an arm of the regular command. Winslow then returned to his troops, promising to call a council of his own "principal officers . . . to know their opinions upon this point." Abercromby and his colleagues prudently concluded that to press for "a junction . . . [would be] extremely unadvisable and might be a fatal consequence to the public service."[7]

On 22 July, back at his Fort Edward headquarters, Winslow convened his promised council of war. It grew into a "grand debate" that lasted three days and ended in a resolution that seconded Winslow's opinion. The provincial officers held that their troops had enlisted expressly for the Crown Point expedition. In case of any alteration in that arrangement, they concluded, "it is our opinion that the effect will be a dissolution of the greater part of the army and have a direct tendency to prevent the raising [of] any provincial troops for his majesty's service for the future."[8]

6. Gipson, *Years of Defeat*, 205; Pargellis, *Loudoun*, 85–87; Osgood, *American Colonies*, IV, 387.

7. A. W. Lauber and A. C. Flick, eds., *The Papers of Sir William Johnson* (Albany, N.Y., 1921–1962), IX, 484–485 (minutes of a council of war, Albany, 16 July 1756).

8. Winslow characterized the council as a "grand debate" in a letter to Shirley of 2 Aug. 1756, Loudoun Papers, LO 1386, Henry E. Huntington Library, San Marino, Calif.; the response of the provincial council of war at Fort Edward is contained in "The Resolution of the Provincial Field Officers . . . ," 25 July 1756, LO 1352. Quoted material from the Loudoun Papers appears by permission of the Huntington Library. The Loudoun Papers will hereafter be cited by date and LO document number.

On 23 July, while Winslow and his officers were debating, Lord Loudoun arrived in New York. William Shirley and a remarkable array of Shirley's enemies were on hand for the occasion. The latter soon found that Loudoun was most attentive to their dissatisfactions with Shirley's leadership.[9] Even before Loudoun had left England, he had been poorly disposed toward Shirley, whom he regarded as a poseur. Now he heard tales of profiteering, maladministration, irregular commission purchases, and wholesale disregard for army regulations—and heard evidence, as well, of insubordination amounting to mutiny among the provincials at Lake George. Abercromby and the rest of Loudoun's staff quickly realized that the general intended to establish his authority by confronting Shirley and the provincials over the question of subordination, and their earlier disposition to accommodate Winslow and the provincial officers vanished. As one, Abercromby and the rest of the regular officers adopted Loudoun's new, harder line.

On the morning of 25 July, Loudoun summoned Shirley and accused him of allowing a situation tantamount to mutiny to arise among the provincial troops during his tenure as commander in chief. Shirley, unprepared for the attack, was unnerved.[10] The next day he recovered enough of his composure to send Loudoun a letter trying to explain the provincials' behavior and to dispatch an express to Winslow demanding to know exactly what had been said at Abercromby's council. He advised Winslow of the urgency of the situation and counseled him to mend his fences with the new commander as soon as possible.[11]

The provincial general remained unaware that anything was amiss until Shirley's dispatch arrived on 2 August. Aghast, Winslow replied that what he had said on 16 July was "so far from being mutinous that it has met with [Abercromby's council's] approbation." Nor, he wrote, was he "sensible of anything criminal, either in debate or otherwise. . . . What interpretation may be maliciously made by farfetched inferences . . . by designing persons, I don't know; but rest assured, it is impossible that

---

9. Douglas Edward Leach, *Arms for Empire: A Military History of the British Colonies in North America, 1607–1763* (New York, 1973), 383; John A. Schutz, *William Shirley: King's Governor of Massachusetts* (Chapel Hill, N.C., 1961), 238–239.

10. Loudoun also told Shirley he believed the governor and his confederates "would be looked on at home as little less than fomenters of rebellion, which struck him all of a heap; and there the conversation ended." Loudoun to Cumberland, 20 Aug. 1756, in Pargellis, ed., *Military Affairs*, 226.

11. Shirley to Loudoun, 26 July 1756, LO 1363; Shirley to Winslow, 26 July 1756, LO 1364 (see also printed version in Charles Henry Lincoln, ed., *Correspondence of William Shirley, Governor of Massachusetts and Military Commander in America, 1731–1760* [New York, 1912], II, 492–493, hereafter cited as *Corr. of Shirley*).

thinking people can believe that [the provincial officers] would countenance anything like mutiny."[12] He tried to explain the reasoning of his
officers to Shirley in refusing to operate jointly with the regulars:

> The grand debate with the officers in regard to the junction arises
> from the general and field officers losing their rank and command,
> which they were universally of opinion they could not give up, as the
> army was a proper organized body; and that they by the several gov-
> ernments from whom these troops were raised were executors in
> trust, which it was not in their power to resign. And even should
> they do [so], it would end in a dissolution of the army, as the privates
> universally hold it as one part of the terms on which they enlisted
> that they were to be commanded by their own officers; and this is a
> principle so strongly imbibed that it is not in the power of man to
> remove it.[13]

As Winslow understood the provincials' position, the army was a body
organized by the provincial governments to serve the provincial governments. Most important, it was organized on the basis of *contractual* understandings. Officers understood when they accepted their commissions that
they would hold specified ranks and exercise the authority granted by law;
the men similarly understood when they enlisted that they would be commanded by the officers who enlisted them. Such understandings made the
army "a proper organized body." If the conditions of the contract were
violated, the army would cease to exist. Appropriately, Winslow used an
everyday legal term to describe the officers' position: they had been made
"executors in trust," like the executors of an estate, men charged with con-
serving property in the community interest. Once made, the contract could
not be altered by any human agency, although it *could* be destroyed. Officers had it "not in their power to resign" their responsibility to the province, their "trust." Even the privates had "so strongly imbibed" the principle of service under "their own officers . . . that it [was] not in the power
of man to remove it" without dissolving the army along with the agreement. This was a homely frame of argument, and one especially resonant
in New England, a society fairly steeped in covenants: marriage covenants
binding husbands and wives, church covenants among the members of
congregations, the great covenant of salvation between God and his chosen
people.

When Shirley received Winslow's reply on 9 August, he forwarded a
copy to Lord Loudoun with a lengthy explanation of his own in the cover-

12. Winslow to Shirley, 2 Aug. 1756, LO 1386; also *Corr. of Shirley*, II, 496.
13. Winslow to Shirley, 2 Aug. 1756, in *Corr. of Shirley*, II, 497–498.

ing letter.[14] Then he replied to Winslow much as a country lawyer might argue a case, pointing out errors in the formulation of premises, defects in reasoning. The "root of the matter," Shirley explained, lay in the provincial officers' misperception of themselves as executors of a trust reposed in them by their provinces. Their "trust" was "the defence of the king's territories"—not the defense of a contractual arrangement. The provincial officers and men had misunderstood the true nature of their contract. In the first place, Shirley suggested, the contracting parties had never been capable of independent action, as Winslow had assumed; both provinces and soldiers fell under the king's dominion, and the king could command his soldiers as he saw fit in the defense of the realm. The crucial issue, Shirley maintained, was not one of contract, but of subordination to constituted authority. Ultimately the matter came down to sovereignty, an indivisible power that the king could not share with the provinces, and one to which they had no claim, whatever their pretensions. He drove home the point with a gibe. "As to the privates having imbibed the principle you mention: it can't be, sir, from the terms of their enlistment, and I can't but think it is in the power of their officers to set them right in this point."[15]

While Shirley and Winslow corresponded, Lord Loudoun was taking action. From the moment of his arrival, he had known that he would have to establish his authority firmly and now wasted no time in setting his erring subordinates straight. Loudoun was above all a direct man, unaccustomed to explaining himself and to repeating his orders. He wanted submission and was unwilling to settle for less.

Thus when Loudoun arrived at his headquarters in Albany on 31 July, one of his first acts was to summon Winslow from Lake George. Winslow had not yet received Shirley's letter of warning and thought he was merely being invited to make a social call on his new superior. He declined politely, explaining that he was busy with preparations for attacking the French forts. Loudoun understood this as willful defiance and summoned Winslow again on 5 August, this time peremptorily.[16] Arriving, as it did, on the heels of Shirley's warning of 2 August to "lose no time" in clearing up all suspicions of disloyalty, Loudoun's order rattled Winslow. Within two days he and his principal subordinates had ridden the sixty or so miles from their camp to Albany. On 8 August he appeared before his commanding officer to face the accusation of insubordination. He stood his ground, however, and on the ninth Loudoun sent him another written order:

14. Shirley to Winslow, 10 Aug. 1756, LO 1456 (also *Corr. of Shirley*, II, 510–515); Shirley to Loudoun, 10 Aug. 1756, LO 1455 (also *Corr. of Shirley*, II, 501–510).

15. Shirley to Winslow, 10 Aug. 1756, in *Corr. of Shirley*, II, 513.

16. Loudoun to Winslow, 5 Aug. 1756, LO 1415A.

I find myself under the necessity, from the conversation I had with you yesterday, to put the following questions to you. And as the situation of his majesty's affairs in this country make dispatch necessary, I expect an immediate answer.

. . . I desire to be informed by you, in writing, whether the troops now raised by the several provinces and colonies of New England, and armed with his majesty's arms, will in obedience with his majesty's commands, . . . act in conjunction with his majesty's troops and under the command of his commander in chief, in whose hands he has been pleased to place the execution of all those matters.[17]

On the following day Winslow made his respectful but obdurate reply:

I have advised with the chief officers of the several governments belonging to the army now with me here, who are ready and willing to act in conjunction with his majesty's troops and put themselves under the command of your lordship, who is commander in chief; so that the terms and conditions, agreed upon and established by the several governments to whom they belong and upon which they were raised, be not altered; all which they humbly submitted. And as to myself, your lordship may be assured I shall ever be ready to obey your commands.[18]

Winslow had given little ground. The following day, 11 August, he directed one of his colonels, Joseph Dwight, to write another letter to "acquaint" Loudoun "with the terms and conditions on which the provincial troops, now on their march towards Crown Point, were raised." The terms were that the commander in chief of the provincial expeditionary force was to be a general from Massachusetts; that the pay, bounty, and provisions of the men should be as set by the provincial assemblies; that the service should be neither south of Albany nor west of Schenectady; and that it should last no longer than twelve months from the date of enlistment.[19]

Loudoun now found himself in a difficult position. He could not drive or bully the provincials further, but he could not hope to defend the New York frontier without them either. Since his regular troops were already fully committed, he reluctantly decided to accede to the wishes of his stubborn auxiliaries. The next day (12 August) he extracted from all the provincial officers present a formal written submission to the king's authority. In return he promised that he would not attempt to bring about a junction for the time being and that the provincial campaign against Crown Point

17. Loudoun to Winslow, 9 Aug. 1756, LO 1450.
18. Winslow to Loudoun, 10 Aug. 1756, LO 1462.
19. Dwight to Loudoun, 11 Aug. 1756, LO 1471.

and Ticonderoga would be allowed to proceed under Winslow's command. By 19 August Winslow and his colleagues were back at Fort William Henry, overseeing preparations for the passage down the lake toward the French.[20]

Loudoun of course was hardly pleased with the modus vivendi he had been compelled to accept, and once the provincials were gone, he sat down to write a report to Whitehall explaining the state of affairs in North America. As he saw it, the dismal condition of the campaign resulted from William Shirley's meddling and the Massachusetts officers' obstructionism. Shirley, Loudoun wrote, had already erected a faction among his cronies in the army and was now endeavoring to build one throughout the colonies. Opposition to the principle of junction had even "been industriously raised among the private men" by designing members of the Shirley party. The problem, Loudoun explained, was that war as it was understood in North America was not war as it was practiced in Europe: "An expedition, as it has hitherto been managed in this country, has been looked on as a [ship]wreck, on which particulars find very good fishing." Shirley and his crew were little more than freebooters; realizing now that they were in danger of being exposed, Loudoun believed, they were doing their utmost to thwart him and the honest, efficient administration he was determined to inaugurate.[21]

The commander in chief was just finishing his report on 19 August when the post brought Shirley's long letter of the tenth, in which the governor tried to explain provincial actions and to justify his own conduct while supreme commander. Among the documents Shirley enclosed was a copy of Winslow's letter of 2 August—the letter in which Winslow explained the provincial officers' unwillingness as "executors in trust" to serve jointly with the regulars. Far from pacifying the general, as Shirley had hoped they would, the letters confirmed Loudoun's suspicions of conspiracy. Fearful now that Shirley, preparing to sail for England, would try to raise a party against him there, Loudoun hurriedly annotated the documents to point out the "fallacious Assertions" they contained and enclosed them in his report to Whitehall.

Lord Loudoun underscored the phrases in Winslow's letter that he found most offensive—particularly the section of Winslow's argument concerning the contractual understandings of the provincial officers and men.[22] But mainly Loudoun addressed himself to Shirley's letter, which he

20. Loudoun to Fox, 19 Aug. 1756, LO 1522; Winslow to Loudoun, 19 Aug. 1756, LO 1520.

21. Loudoun to Fox, 19 Aug. 1756, LO 1522.

22. Lincoln's version of the letter in *Corr. of Shirley*, II, 497–498, reproduces Loudoun's underscorings, which are absent from the secretary's copy in the Loudoun Papers, LO 1386.

edged with marginalia intended to demonstrate the governor's canting and treacherous ways.[23] One obvious indication of conspiracy, Loudoun noted, was the fact that his "principal, and almost the only," opposition was from the six Massachusetts colonels, all of whom were old retainers of Shirley's.[24] Loudoun saw the clearest indication of the governor's perfidy, however, in his explanation of how the provincials perceived the proceedings of Abercromby's 16 July council of war. This explanation was at the heart of Shirley's letter and constituted his chief defense of the Massachusetts officers' behavior. Loudoun's angry reaction to it makes clear why the general believed that provincial attitudes threatened the very essence of proper military relationships.

Shirley's version held that Winslow had in fact given honest, if misguided, responses to the council's questions; that his main concern had been to keep his force intact and able to proceed against the French; and that the council had not visibly disapproved of his opinions or his desire to operate independently. The members of Winslow's later provincial council of war had merely made their declarations, Shirley explained, "to avail themselves of the opportunity of preserving their rank and command among the provincial troops, by making that a condition of the proposed junction; and . . . [the provincial officers'] determination upon this matter hath rather proceeded from a notion of carrying their point by this means, than a general spirit of disobedience to the king's commands."[25] That was too much for Loudoun. "I shall only observe," he wrote,

> on this long passage, that most of the things advanced in it are false; and shall make no observations on the arguments made use of, either by Mr. Winslow or Mr. Shirley, to show their opinion of the king's order about the rank of provincial officers; or Mr. Shirley's notion that it was referred to them [i.e., the provincial officers] to determine, and by such means avail themselves, of settling the letter of the king's order and *carrying their point;* as the passages are too glaring to need a note. But I hope the king has a better opinion of Sir Charles Hardy, Mr. Abercromby and Mr. Webb [the principal personages at the 16 July council of war], than to imagine that they could ever think they had a right to refer his majesty's commands, to be debated in a provincial council of war.[26]

23. "Refutations of the Fallacious Assertions advanced by Maj. Gen. Shirley in his letter to the Rt. Hon. the Earl of Loudoun . . . ," LO 1461; see also parallel text version of the same in Shirley to Loudoun, 10 Aug. 1756, in *Corr. of Shirley*, II, 501–510.

24. *Corr. of Shirley*, II, 509, n. 10.

25. Shirley to Loudoun, 10 Aug. 1756, in *ibid.*, 506–507.

26. *Ibid.*, 505.

Loudoun made no serious attempt to refute Shirley's account by engaging it per se. Instead, he appealed to authority, in the form of the king's knowledge of the character of Hardy, Abercromby, and Webb—not one of whom, presumably, could have borne the humiliation of seeing royal dictates being hashed over in a bumpkins' council of war. That Shirley had had the audacity to attempt such an explanation offended Loudoun fully as much as the insubordinate declarations of Winslow and his council of war. Neither Shirley nor the provincials he presumed to defend, it seemed, had any sense of that subordination to authority which for Loudoun was absolutely fundamental to all military activity—indeed, to all proper social relations.

Ten days after his report to Whitehall, Loudoun wrote to the duke of Cumberland, his patron and direct military superior. By this time news had arrived that Britain's chief fur-trading station on Lake Ontario, Fort Oswego, had been lost after an embarrassingly brief siege. Moreover, the provincial campaign against the French forts on Lake Champlain had been abandoned in a shambles, and a violent dispute had sprung up between Loudoun and the civil authorities of Albany over the quartering of troops. His lordship was thoroughly fed up with Americans when he complained: "The delays we meet with in carrying on the service, from every part of this country, are immense. They have assumed to themselves what they call rights and privileges, totally unknown in the mother country, and made use of for no purpose but to screen them from giving any aid, of any sort, for carrying on the service." [27]

Loudoun's views, as an aristocrat and a professional soldier, and those of the officers of the provincial forces, proceeded from premises so different as to make them irreconcilable. When Loudoun thought of proper command relationships and of soldierly qualities, he thought first of subordination and obedience. He himself unhesitatingly obeyed his superiors, George II and the duke of Cumberland; it astonished him to think that the rustics of New England did not share his values. He drew the reasonable conclusion that they were perverse and self-interested. He failed to understand that the provincial officers had no firsthand experience with the two institutions that defined the world in which he had moved in Great Britain: a professional army and a highly stratified social system. English society, with its elaborate clientage networks and its vast distances between the great and the humble, operated on different assumptions and followed other rules than those of the smaller-scale societies of the colonies.

At about the same time that Loudoun was composing his report to Whitehall, he received a letter from Governor Thomas Fitch of Connecticut that made explicit some of the curious assumptions of the colonial

27. Loudoun to Cumberland, 29 Aug. 1756, LO 1626B.

world. Fitch had heard about the proposed junction between regular and provincial forces and was writing to register his concern. As the elected governor of what was (even by Massachusetts standards) a highly insular colony, Fitch was very much a product of the same small-time world as the provincial officers. The principles he articulated were the provincials' principles, too:

> Your lordship will see that these [provincial] troops were not raised to act in conjunction with the king's troops, as we were then [when the troops were raised] altogether unacquainted with his majesty's intentions respecting the operations that would be directed for annoying the enemy; yet are nevertheless raised for the same service and sent forth under the command of officers appointed and commissioned for that purpose. It therefore seems necessary that these troops be continued under the same command and employed agreeable to the design of their enlistments; otherwise the contract between them and their constituents, made for promoting his majesty's service in this particular, may be broken and their rights violated. The consequence of which may be greatly prejudicial not only to the king's interest and the safety of the country at this time but may prove a great discouragement on future occasions.[28]

Neither of the crucial terms that Fitch invoked—the "rights" of the soldiers and the "contract between them and their constituents"—had any great currency in a European professional officer's lexicon. Yet American provincial officers thought in precisely these terms. The governor was explaining that the operative relationship, so far as the provincial soldier was concerned, was between himself and the province that he understood to be his employer. Although he surely assumed that he was fighting on the king's behalf, the soldier did not regard himself as an employee of the king. It was, after all, the province that paid his wages and supplied him with food, according to the contract ("made for promoting his majesty's service") to which he had subscribed at enlistment. Within this contractual framework, the idea of the king's intervening, by virtue of his sovereign authority, to alter the terms of an agreement to which he had never been a party, made no sense. No contract could be changed without the mutual consent of the parties involved, and an enlistment contract was no exception. Any unilateral attempt to change the agreement simply nullified it and voided the soldier's contractual responsibilities. Such thinking produced an army that was wholly alien to Loudoun's experience: an army made up of men who assumed that soldiers' rights and the conditions of

28. Gov. Thomas Fitch to Loudoun, 3 Aug. 1756, LO 1407.

their enlistment had a real bearing on day-to-day operations, men who behaved as if they were actually the equals of their leaders.

William Shirley stood with one foot in Loudoun's world and the other in
the world of the provincial officers. First as a lawyer, then as North America's most successful royal governor, Shirley had dealt with the provincial
gentlemen of Massachusetts for two and a half decades. He knew their
world intimately; and as a client of the duke of Newcastle, he also understood the intricacies of British patronage networks. After he was relieved
of command, Shirley found himself caught between the provincial officers
and their aristocratic commander in chief, desperately trying to interpret
the actions of each to the other. He failed. Loudoun despised and dis-
trusted him from the start, and he never succeeded in making the provincial officers understand that the central issue in the dispute was one of sovereignty, not of contract. Loudoun and most of the other regular officers in
North America concluded that provincial troops were worthless as soldiers
and not to be trusted. In his plan for 1757, Loudoun resolved to request
fewer troops from the various colonies and to request them with only
company-grade leadership, circumventing problems of command by employing them under professional field officers.[29]

II

By mid-August, Loudoun had resolved to "drop all correspondence" with
Shirley, fearing that he would be drawn into a "paper war" for which, he
wrote, he had "neither time nor inclination."[30] Despite his disinclination
to deal with him, however, Loudoun found that William Shirley came increasingly to haunt his thoughts as the campaign drew to a close. Never a
man to mince words, the irascible Scot characterized his predecessor in
letters and reports as "the first contriver and fomenter of all the opposition
the New England men make, to be joined to the king's troops," accusing
him of "endeavoring to raise a flame all over the provinces," and of seeking
to make the supreme commander "personally ill [i.e., unpopular] with the
New England people."[31] Convinced that "all the evils" of opposition from
which he suffered had "their rise in one source,"[32] Loudoun strove to dis-
credit the governor at home by keeping Whitehall informed of the ways

29. Pargellis, *Loudoun*, 102–103, 212; see also Loudoun to Cumberland, 22 Nov.–26 Dec.
1756, in Pargellis, ed., *Military Affairs*, 279–280.
30. Loudoun to Fox, 3 Oct. 1756, LO 1961B.
31. Loudoun to Cumberland, 20 Aug. 1756, in Pargellis, ed., *Military Affairs*, 226.
32. Loudoun to Fox, 3 Oct. 1756, LO 1961B.

that he and his faction sought "to oppose and disappoint every scheme that can be proposed for the public service."[33] A good example of Shirley's determination to "retard the service,"[34] Loudoun believed, could be seen in the colonials' perverse refusal to cooperate with him in reforming the provincial system of supply.

Developments in early September had left Lord Loudoun a harried man. In addition to the irritations of dealing with his provincial officers, he had recently been informed of the loss of Fort Oswego, had seen the Crown Point expedition collapse, had found it necessary to bully the mayor of Albany into quartering his regular troops, and had discovered that the New England assemblies were reluctant to supply the emergency reinforcements he needed. Moreover, he had lately heard reports of rumors circulating in Boston that Massachusetts would soon try to withdraw its troops from the New York frontier.[35] To a man less besieged such rumors might have seemed inconsequential. But Loudoun's recent experiences had made him suspicious of provincial loyalty, and events soon convinced him that the rumors had a basis in fact.

On 9 September the chief provisions contractor for the regulars informed Loudoun that a provincial commissary at Lake George had offered him the chance to buy "a very considerable quantity of provisions" from the provincial stores at Fort William Henry.[36] The offer was not necessarily illegitimate, since the provincial and regular supply systems were quite independent, and the provinces would have no way of transporting the supplies remaining in their magazines back home once their soldiers were dismissed at the end of the campaign. At the same time, however, Loudoun received an urgent request from John Winslow, also at Lake George, for provisions. In preparation for the now-defunct Crown Point expedition, Winslow explained, provincial stores had been concentrated at the intended point of departure, Fort William Henry. In the process the magazine at Fort Edward, to the rear, had been stripped, and as a result the provincial garrison remaining there now had less than ten days' food supply remaining.[37]

Loudoun smelled a rat and knew at once its name was Shirley.[38] If the provincials were so short on food that they needed him to supply one of their garrisons, what were they doing trying to peddle supplies to the regular commissariat? If the provincials had been embezzling stores all along and had drawn provisions down to a dangerously low level, the situation

---

33. Loudoun to Cumberland, 2 Oct. 1756, in Pargellis, ed., *Military Affairs*, 236.
34. Loudoun to Fox, 3 Oct. 1756, LO 1961B.
35. *Ibid.*
36. *Ibid.*
37. Winslow to Loudoun, 5 Sept. 1756, LO 1710.
38. Loudoun to Fox, 3 Oct. 1756, LO 1961B.

was especially threatening. Loudoun had too few wagons and teams to supply the provincials indefinitely. Yet if the provincials ran out of food and he could not feed them, Massachusetts and the other province governments would have the perfect pretext for withdrawing their soldiers from the frontier. Here was plain evidence, Loudoun thought, that Shirley's henchmen were precipitating a logistical crisis in the hope of embarrassing him. Thus with characteristic determination, Loudoun resolved to meet his enemies head-on. He ordered supplies immediately forwarded to the hungry garrison at Fort Edward, then took steps to bring the provincial supply system under his personal control.

Up to this point the provincial army had been supplied by a complex and inefficient combination of civilian and military agencies.[39] Colonial assemblies every year appointed executive committees called committees of war, which were responsible for procuring food and matériel and seeing that they were transported to the main depot in Albany. There, resident civilian commissioners of supply received the goods; each commissioner then arranged for the provisions to be hauled up to his province's troops. Only when the stores actually reached the regimental commissaries did they come under military control. At no point did the provincial commanding general have any authority over the supplies that were delivered. He could ask, but not order, the commissioners to send what his men needed. Since Winslow's provincial army included troops from five provinces, his problems were compounded proportionally: his army had not one, but five roughly parallel systems of supply, each delivering a unique ration to the men of its colony, with varying success, on varying schedules, and with little reference to Winslow's needs or desires.

Loudoun proposed to rationalize the system. Calling together the commissioners at Albany on 10 September, he offered to take possession of all their supplies, paying for what was in usable condition. Henceforth he would supply the provincials at the same rate as his own troops, appointing his own commissaries to transport and issue the newly standardized rations. The commissioners could, if they wished, continue to provide the

---

39. The functioning of the system can be seen in Winslow's correspondence with Loudoun, particularly Winslow to Loudoun, 18 Sept. 1756, LO 1842; and in John Osborne, "An Account of the Cost and Charge of the several articles of Expence Arisen, in the Province of the Massachusetts-Bay, by means of the Expedition against Crown Point for the year, 1756, exclusive those of raising, Arming & Cloathing their Forces," 22 Nov. 1756, LO 2258. Osborne's account records expenditures of £36,070 4s. 14.5d. Lawful Money on the 1756 expedition, of which something over £20,000 was spent on foodstuffs. The account lists a few large expenditures—as to Green & Walker, Boston merchants, "for pork and other provisions, £1,754.1.10" and to "Messrs. Nicho[llas] and Isaac Gouvernour & Peter Vanburgh Livingston of New York for bread and flour, £2,066.13.4"—along with a multitude of small items, as to "Sarah Oxnard for cheese, £3.5.4." The bulk of the more than 200 suppliers listed were apparently from Massachusetts.

items that were not included in the regular allowance.[40] Loudoun's plan was a generous and efficient solution to a growing problem. But the commissioners of Massachusetts, Connecticut, and New Hampshire all balked at accepting it.

They explained that the purpose of their appointments had been to see that "a sufficiency" of supplies was "lodged at Fort William Henry ready for the army" to use. "We have discharged that trust," they maintained, and pointed out that the provisions were already in the hands of the regimental commissaries. The commissaries, furthermore, "have from their respective governments warrants for issuing the [provisions] . . . ; so that your lordship may plainly see we have no power to make any transfer of them without particular instruction from the several governments to whom we belong."[41] Loudoun must have been sorely fatigued at hearing provincial gentlemen lecture him—yet again—on their "trust," explaining that they could not comply with his wishes because their duties were governed by contractual agreements over which he had no control. Loudoun had been thinking, as a modern military commander would, in terms of his mission. The commissioners, however, were reasoning from much more legalistic premises.

At this point, realizing that he would make no more headway with civilians over whom he had no legal authority and aware that it would take weeks of correspondence with the provincial assemblies to gain their approval, Loudoun decided to appeal directly to Winslow and to Phineas Lyman, the Connecticut officer in charge at Fort Edward.[42] He proposed that they order their commissaries to sign over all remaining provincial stores to Winslow, so that Winslow could transfer them to regular commissaries, who in turn would take control of provisioning. It was a shrewd proposal because both Winslow and Lyman had been suffering agonies from the poor performance of the supply system. At Fort Edward, Lyman's troops had almost no food left and were growing restive. While Winslow's soldiers at Fort William Henry were in no danger of going hungry, they were out of their "small stores"—sugar, rice, ginger, butter, and rum. The New Englanders were particularly aggrieved at being deprived of their daily gill of rum (the equivalent of about three stiff shots per man),

40. Loudoun to Fox, 3 Oct. 1756, LO 1961B; Loudoun to the Commissioners of Massachusetts Bay, New York, New Hampshire, Connecticut, and Rhode Island, 11 Sept. 1756, LO 1768. For the variation between the king's allowance and Massachusetts' provincial ration, see Winslow to Loudoun, 3 Sept. 1756, LO 1937; or Fred Anderson, "War and the Bay Colony: Soldiers and Society in Massachusetts during the Seven Years' War, 1754–1763" (Ph.D. diss., Harvard University, 1981), II, 557.

41. John Foye, Benjamin North, and Peter Gilman to Loudoun, 12 Sept. 1756, LO 1780.

42. Loudoun to Winslow, 12 Sept. 1756, LO 1784; Loudoun to Lyman, 13 Sept. 1756, LO 1798.

and every day that went by without a rum ration added significantly to the threat of mutiny or mass desertion.[43]

Winslow was eager to have Loudoun take over the provisioning of his troops, but feared the consequences of assuming any personal responsibility for the stores. "I am sensible great loss has been sustained in removing the provisions" from Fort Edward to Fort William Henry, he wrote, "and every individual that has had any concern will be called to account. And should I make myself one, it may take me years to finish with the [colonial] governments."[44] To escape further pressure from his commander in chief, Winslow sent express messages to the provincial governments of Connecticut, New Hampshire, and Massachusetts advocating a modified version of Loudoun's proposal, whereby the commissaries of his regiments could transfer their supplies directly to Loudoun.

Winslow's letters gave the decision to the assemblies. That meant a long delay, during which Lyman's provincials at Fort Edward ran out of provisions and were compelled to rely on supplies that Loudoun forwarded to them from Albany. This created an unexpected and highly revealing result when the troops received orders to draw their first rations from the royal stores. As Phineas Lyman told the story, "Some vile fellow suggested that if they eat the king's bread they should become the king's soldiers." The idea so alarmed his provincials that a hundred and fifty of them—about a third of the garrison's effective soldiers—attempted to desert. Lyman tried to make light of the incident, saying that he had been "so lucky as to recover 'em"; but the discipline of his command had been gravely threatened.[45] The notion that the king's bread was the bait to a redcoat enlistment trap seems so bizarre that we might well pass over it as a manifestation of temporary mass hysteria. But when the responses of the provincial governments arrived, they expressed exactly the same concern.

None of the colonial governments would agree to relinquish control over provisioning arrangements until they had received assurances that supply by regulars would not place their troops under direct royal control. The Bay Colony's reaction was the most cautious of all. Because the fall session

43. Winslow to Loudoun, 18 Sept. 1756, LO 1842. Winslow described disciplinary problems resulting from rum shortages on several occasions: Winslow to Loudoun, 25 Sept. 1756, LO 1892; Winslow to Loudoun, 25 Sept. 1756, LO 1893; Winslow to Loudoun, 20 Oct. 1756, LO 2049. See also Loudoun to Cumberland, 3 Oct. 1756, in Pargellis, ed., *Military Affairs*, 241. The nature of these disturbances among the troops was described by an anonymous observer at the camp: "November 3. A very cold day with snow which so much affected the soldiers that they could not forget rum; insomuch as there was a continual calling out, 'O rum, rum! No rum! Strong rum! Home, home, home!' etc., from the morning till evening" (Anonymous commissary's diary, 3 Nov. 1756).

44. Winslow to Loudoun, 18 Sept. 1756, LO 1842.

45. Lyman to Loudoun, 6 Oct. 1756, LO 2855.

of the House of Representatives did not begin until 5 October, the first response to Loudoun's plan came from the Massachusetts Council, or upper house, on 21 September. The Council gave three reasons for not tampering with the status quo. First, the province's supply arrangements had been made by the whole General Court, and if they were to be undone, that would have to be accomplished by the same body. Second, the fall legislative session would soon begin, so there was no reason to rush into a change before the colony's elected representatives had duly deliberated the issue. Third, Loudoun's proposed alteration in the supply system might well be "construed to be putting [the provincials] under the sole power of his majesty's general to be continued in service during pleasure; which considering the privileges granted to the inhabitants of this province by the royal charter, the Board conceive that they have no right to advise to." [46] Although the Council was taking the high ground of constitutional principle by invoking the charter, its reasoning was not substantially different from that which led Lyman's provincials to desert. The Council's case rested on its understanding of contractual relationships, specifically of the inability of any person (or group) not a party to an existing pact to alter its terms. Loudoun concluded that this was all cant, and—worse—Shirley's cant: the Council's response, he believed, was "every word dictated by him." [47]

The Council and House of Representatives met in early October and debated Loudoun's offer, carefully weighing its potential risks and benefits before deciding to accept—with two reservations. First, they wanted to be sure that royal provisioning would not entail direct control of the provincials. "Before there was any intelligence of your lordship's appointment," they reminded Loudoun, "to encourage an enlistment, certain engagements were made on the part of the government, both as to the time of continuance of the men in service and as to the limits within which they were to be employed . . . ; and the Court are of [the] opinion that it is not in their power to depart from these engagements." Second, the General Court sought assurances that a previous offer of the home government to reimburse the province for its expenses in provisioning the troops would not be negated by Loudoun's supply scheme. Without the expected reimbursement, they wrote, "there seems to be no possible way for the government to procure money" to pay the troops at the close of the campaign. Because they needed to be sure that Loudoun's action in provisioning the provincials for a few weeks would not be regarded as fulfilling the minis-

46. Pargellis, *Loudoun*, 185; quotation from Massachusetts Council, "Minutes of a Meeting held . . . Boston," 21 Sept. 1756, LO 1608.

47. Loudoun to Cumberland, 3 Oct. 1756, in Pargellis, ed., *Military Affairs*, 241.

try's promise to supply them "at the expense of the crown," the General Court appointed a special delegation to meet with the commander in chief and make a full representation of Massachusetts' claims.[48] Only then would the Bay Colony agree to let Lord Loudoun feed its troops. The issue was not settled until the end of October, when the campaign was essentially finished.

The good soldier Loudoun had wanted to create a supply system that would function reliably and inexpensively. The long delay of the New England provinces, and especially of Massachusetts, in responding to his openhanded offer helped reinforce Loudoun's disdain for New Englanders and their ways. He concluded that America was a lawless country, a place where there was no rule "but the rule every man pleases to lay down to himself."[49]

Loudoun came closer to the heart of the matter in that assessment than he knew. Social relations in New England proceeded from a set of implicit assumptions that were voluntarist in the extreme. In the absence both of a strong governmental authority and a stratified social system, men *were* free to lay down rules to themselves to an extent that bewildered the commander in chief. But he was wrong in thinking that there was no locus of authority in colonial society. Such a locus did exist in that most voluntary of relationships, the contract. Loudoun did not understand that his proposals for provisioning, which were so obviously beneficial to provincial governments and provincial soldiers alike, were assessed initially not in terms of their potential benefit, but of the disadvantaging obligations they might impose if unwarily accepted. Like the soldiers who hesitated to eat the king's bread, the colonial assemblies thought it necessary to examine Loudoun's proffered loaves and fishes, to ensure that they were not stones and serpents in cunning disguise.

III

The sources for examining the disputes discussed thus far have been purely official, which is to say that they were written by relatively well educated men—members, by their own lights at least, of an elite. This means that whatever references were made to the enlisted men were made from a perspective that was not their own. But much evidence suggests that provin-

48. Josiah Willard to Loudoun, 13 Oct. 1756, LO 2015. (The commissioners delegated to consult with Loudoun were Thomas Hutchinson, Samuel Wells, and Sir William Pepperell. See Spencer Phips, "Commission . . . ," 22 Nov. 1756, LO 2269.)

49. Loudoun to Halifax, 26 Dec. 1756, LO 2416, quoted in Pargellis, *Loudoun*, 186.

cial enlisted men in fact agreed with their officers and their legislators about the centrality of contract, although they frequently disagreed with them over the application of the principle. A survey of the soldiers' writings demonstrates motivation by ideas of contractualism, from the beginning to the end of the war.

The act of keeping a diary can itself indicate a kind of consciousness of contracts in everyday life. The large number of pocket account books still extant testifies that the practice of recording personal debts and obligations was common everywhere in eighteenth-century New England, a practical necessity in a rural economy lacking formal financial institutions and chronically short of circulating currency. Military diaries, too, functioned as aids to memory, recording (for example) amounts of billeting money received and expended on the march, debts to sutlers, or the performance of extra duty for which extra compensation was expected.[50] Such account-keeping is not synonymous with the recording of contractual obligations, of course; but other characteristic features indicate that the diarists were indeed taking careful note of their own and the province's engagements.

Often the privates' journals begin with a formalized entry. For example:

> April 5, 1758. I, Lemuel Lyon of Woodstock enlisted under Captain David Holms of Woodstock in New England for this present Canada expedition. I received of Captain Holms £2 0s. 0d.[51]

Or this one, by Jonathan French of Andover:

> There being orders by the Great and General Court or Assembly to raise 1,800 men under the command of his excellency the right honorable the earl of Loudoun, for the defense of his majesty's colonies and for the annoyance of his majesty's enemies in North America; and upon consideration of six dollars bounty and some other articles I enlisted in said service, William Arbuthnot of Boston being

50. See, e.g., Samuel Chandler, 10 Oct., 4 Dec. 1755; Elisha Hawley, supplemental entries for 22 July–30 Aug. 1755; Seth Pomeroy, initial entry for June 1755 and records of various billeting charges due, 16 Apr. 1760; Luke Gridley, 3 July 1757; John Cleaveland, 21 July 1758; Obadiah Harris, 21–22 Aug. 1758; Caleb Rea, 28 June 1758; Joseph Nichols, accounts for June, 1759; Lemuel Lyon, 8 Sept., 26 Oct. 1758; John Noyes, 20 June, 3 Oct. 1758; Nathaniel Knap, 3 Aug., 1 Sept. 1758; Gibson Clough, 14 June 1759, 4 Dec. 1760; William Henshaw, 25 July 1759; Josiah Peary, 7, 11 July 1759; John Frost, 1760, additional entries headed "what I supplied the men with" (p. 9); John Burrell, 6, 10 June 1760; Samuel Jenks, 5 Aug. 1760. References to soldiers' diaries refer to sources listed in Appendix B and are cited by author's name and date of entry.

51. Lemuel Lyon, 5 Apr. 1758.

appointed captain of a company in the regiment commanded by Colonel Joseph Fry.[52]

Such entries record the undertaking of an agreement (enlistment), its parties (the soldier and the enlisting officer representing the province), and the receipt of consideration by which the contract was confirmed. The province, of course, kept muster lists and payrolls, official records that conveyed the same information, so the soldiers did not actually need to record these occurrences. That they did so with considerable consistency suggests that many soldiers were intent upon keeping track of the bargain between themselves and the province, in a document that could be produced as proof if their employer reneged on any part of its obligation. Thus the frequent notations in the diaries concerning the issue and quality of provisions take on additional significance, since the province agreed to supply the men with stated quantities of food and rum each week as well as specific articles of bedding and clothing.[53]

Of course, the province sometimes failed to keep its soldiers supplied with all the articles it had promised. Conveying huge quantities of food and other supplies across vast stretches of wilderness was always difficult, and occasionally impossible.[54] When the logistical system broke down, provincial troops frequently took concerted action in the form of mutiny or mass desertion to protest the failure of their employer to keep up its end of the bargain. The nineteen recorded instances of provincial mutiny and mass desertion, disorders that can be considered together as instances of conscious troop rebellion, show remarkable consistencies in the rebels' motivations and actions.

Soldiers who recorded troop rebellions ascribed causes that fall into three broad categories. In about 33 percent of the cases, the troops had become convinced that the army had failed to fulfill its obligations to them, specifically in providing food and rum; about 40 percent of the instances reflect the soldiers' conviction that they were being forced to serve more time than they had agreed to at the time of enlistment; and in the

52. Jonathan French (1757), initial entry. See also Luke Gridley (1757), initial entry; Joseph Nichols, 27 Mar. 1758; Obadiah Harris, 14 Apr. 1758; Samuel Morris, 4, 6 Apr. 1759; Gibson Clough, 4 Apr. 1759; Enoch Poor, 6 Apr. 1759; James Hill, 18 Apr. 1755; David Holdin, 20 Feb. 1760; Constantine Hardy, 2 Apr. 1759.

53. See, e.g., David Holdin, 16, 20, 26 May 1760; John Frost, 26, 27 May, 17 June 1760; John Burrell, 5 Aug., 1 Oct. 1759; Luke Gridley, 5 May, 2 June, 22 Sept. 1757; John Woods, 11, 28, 30 Sept. 1759; Obadiah Harris, 20–22 Aug. 1758; James Hill, 6, 9, 14 Nov. 1755; Lemuel Lyon, 16, 26 June, 4 July 1758.

54. For commentary on the problems of supply, see John Shy, *Toward Lexington: The Role of the British Army in the Coming of the Revolution* (Princeton, N.J., 1965), 88–89.

remaining disorders, provincials sought assurances that they would be additionally compensated for work not covered in their initial understanding.[55] In all but a single case the grievance was clearly a matter of contract, and in each collective action the soldiers showed concern for their compensation. This in turn reinforces the impression that provincial soldiers were motivated in part by the expectation of financial gain.

The intermingling of contractual and pecuniary concerns in the common soldiers' reaction to supply shortages comes through clearly in Obadiah Harris's description of a narrowly averted rebellion among Massachusetts troops belonging to Colonel Timothy Ruggles's regiment at Halfway Brook in August 1758:

> The 20th day, the Sabbath. Nothing remarkable, but full of fatigue and our provision grows short.

> The 21st day. We eat up clean all that was in our tents, and where to get the next mouthful we know not, but hope that Providence will provide for us. Now men are so cross and touchy that they can't speak to one another. "What shall we do for something to eat?" is the cry. The old saying is, "A day's life is hunger and ease." [We] used to compare it to a soldier's life; but hunger and toil is our present state.

Such grousing is common enough in soldiers' diaries; but Harris, uniquely, continued his complaint in fourteeners:

> And now when times are grown so bad,
> And our provision done,
> Let everyone take up his pack
> And make a march for home;

---

55. See Appendix C. In 6 out of 19 cases of mutiny and mass desertion, the cause ascribed by the diarists was a shortage of supplies; see John Thomas, 5, 7 July 1755; Elisha Hawley, 1 Sept. 1755; James Hill, 14–17 Nov. 1755; Samuel Chandler, 22 Nov. 1755; Lemuel Lyon, 22 July 1758; Caleb Rea, 22 July 1758; Robert Webster, 13 Nov. 1759.

In 8 cases, troop disorders occurred as a consequence of the expiration of the term of service as the soldiers construed it; see Nathaniel Dwight, 11, 20 Nov. 1755; Rufus Putnam, *The Memoirs of Rufus Putnam* (Boston, 1903), 16; John Woods, 27 Oct.–4 Nov. 1759; Samuel Morris, 1 Nov. 1759; William Henshaw, 29–31 Oct. 1759; Nathaniel Knap, 19–20 Mar., 17–18 June, 1–3 July 1759; Gibson Clough, 30 Sept., 31 Oct.–3 Nov., 22 Dec. 1759, 11 Feb. 1760.

In 4 remaining cases troops protested insubordinately by refusing to work unless paid additionally for extra duty: see Samuel Greenleaf, 2, 3 Nov. 1756; Obadiah Harris, 1 July 1758; Enoch Poor, 14 June, 17 Oct. 1759.

In the one remaining case, the cause of a mass desertion was obscure, perhaps the result of insulting behavior on the part of a regular officer: see Abner Barrows, diary excerpt, 23 July 1758, quoted in Williams's orderly book.

> For if we stay within the camp,
> And on our wages spend,
> We shall have nothing for to take
> When our campaign will end.

The next day supplies arrived, grumbling ceased, and Harris commemorated the event with a dozen more couplets.[56] That he had taken the time to turn his complaint into verse, however, and that he obviously had not felt uneasy about advocating desertion imply that he thought little of subordination and duty once the provisions ran out. Similarly, the candor of diarists in recording their participation in mutinies and desertions and the very frequency and openness of such rebellions indicate that loyalty mattered less to provincial soldiers than equity, whenever they concluded that they were being abused.[57] Such considerations justified resistance and protest of a sort that was, by military definition, irresponsible.

Beyond their consistency in cause, the mass desertions and mutinies show a strikingly consistent pattern of action, a protocol of protest governing the behavior of the rebels and the responses of their commanders. Two cases—one a mutiny, the other a mass desertion—exemplify provincial patterns of resistance.

Private Gibson Clough, who served at Louisbourg in 1759 and 1760, recorded the mutiny of Colonel Jonathan Bagley's regiment at what the troops understood was the end of their eight-month tour of duty. A month before their enlistments expired, Bagley's soldiers began to worry that they would not be allowed to go home as promised.

> [30 September 1759.] Cold weather. [We] hear a great talk of things uncertain and thus time spends away and so we spend our days. . . . Cold weather is coming on apace, which will make us look round about us and put [on] our winter clothing, and we shall stand in need of good liquors for to keep our spirits on cold winter's days. And we, being here within stone walls, are not likely to get liquors or clothes at this time of the year; and although we be Englishmen born, we are debarred Englishmen's liberty. Therefore we now see what it is to be under martial law and to be with the regulars, who are but little better than slaves to their officers. And when I get out of their [power] I shall take care of how I get in again.

At the end of October, the provincials' worries were realized.

56. Obadiah Harris, 20–22 Aug. 1758. For the rest of Harris's poetic effort, see above, chap. 2.

57. Rufus Putnam, *Memoirs*, 16; Obadiah Harris, 1 July 1758; John Woods, 27 Oct.–4 Nov. 1759; Gibson Clough, 31 Oct.–3 Nov. 1759; Robert Webster, 13 Nov. 1759.

31 [October]. And so now our time has come to an end according to enlistment, but we are not yet got home nor are like to.

November 1. The regiment was ordered out for to hear what the colonel had to say to them as our time was out and we all swore that we would do no more duty here. So it was a day of much confusion with the regiment.

In effect, on 1 November the soldiers of Bagley's regiment determined to go on strike. Since their term of service had expired, they felt no further responsibility to perform their duties. They may indeed have reasoned that to serve without a new agreement might prevent them from controlling their terms of service altogether. At any rate, the regiment went on strike as a unit, and as a unit accepted the consequences.

2nd [November]. The regiment was turned out for duty and we all stood to it that we would not do any duty at all, for which we was all sent to the guardhouse prisoners; but myself and three men were released because we belonged to the king's works [Clough had recently been detailed to the engineers who were refurbishing the fortifications]. And there was a letter read to the regiment which came from the governor and Council [of Massachusetts], which informed us that we were to stay here till the first of December or till we have news from General Amherst, which I hope will be very soon for our redemption from this garrison.

There were obvious problems with imprisoning a whole regiment, amounting to a quarter of the complement of the fortress, and the command soon decided to compromise by releasing some of the men to return to Massachusetts. This, in combination with a carefully orchestrated show of force, was enough to break the strike:

3rd [November]. The regiment was turned out for to hear their doom for denying their duty and for sending a round robin [petition] to the colonel desiring him to get us sent home according to enlistment, which they say was mutiny. But it was all forgave by the general [Brigadier General Edward Whitemore, military governor of Louisbourg], and a detachment of 140 embarked on board of the ship *Oliver*, a transport bound to Boston. And the three regular regiments was drawn up on the grand parade; so was our regiment, all but the prisoners. And they were brought up by four files of men and place[d] in the center and the general made a speech to them. The Articles of War was read to us and the letter that come from Boston, and then the colonel made a speech to us and told us that we was to stay one month more at least, and more if wanted.

On 5 December, a brig and two schooners arrived from Boston, carrying word that the regiment would be required to stay all winter. Bagley thereupon promised the remaining troops that he would take their cause to the General Court. Three weeks later, he and another officer left for Boston. This plunged Clough into gloom: "And now the major takes command of the regiment here, according to orders, and we are like to be here all winter, and God help us." [58]

Clough's experiences typify mutinous resistance among provincial soldiers. The similar response of desertion was an option not readily available to the troops of an isolated garrison on the outermost tip of Cape Breton Island. The constraints of isolation, however, did not apply in the case of Private Luke Knowlton, a twenty-one-year-old Shrewsbury man serving in Colonel Abijah Willard's regiment at Ticonderoga in 1759. Like Clough, he had enlisted to serve until 1 November and did not intend to remain long beyond that date.

On 28 October, Knowlton mentioned that Colonel Willard had assembled the regiment to read them the orders that had arrived from General Amherst and from the Massachusetts General Court, keeping them in service past 1 November. "The men in general seem to decline it," he noted, and said no more until four days later:

November the 1st, 1759. This day fair weather and we are preparing for a march. And some officers for threatening to lead off their men are confined and our captain [Aaron Fay] for one. And this morning there was a petition drawed up by the men and signed by near two hundred of our men, and sent to our colonel for a dismission. And he immediately sent it to the general [Jeffery Amherst].

November 2. This morning fair weather. We was drawed up by about six o'clock and our colonel read to us the letter which the general sent as a return to our petition; which is not to have us presume to go home before we have a regular discharge, though he confesses our time is expired. But the men went off from the parade in great haste, and in less than an hour there was two hundred of us on the parade with our packs swung in order to march, and Lieutenant [Thomas?] French who was confined yesterday at the head of us. And before we had got half a mile our officers came after us with orders to fire upon us if we would not return, but did not, though we refused to obey them and still kept on our march. Sun about half an hour high we was overtaken by Captain [Francis?] Peabody and two

58. Gibson Clough, 22 Dec. 1759. Bagley did not return until 13 June 1760, two weeks ahead of the replacement troops for his regiment. In the meantime, on 1 Apr., Clough and his remaining comrades had all enlisted—not entirely willingly—for the 1760 campaign.

subaltern officers with a letter from the colonel which says that if . . . we will return to our duty again, he will do his endeavor that there shall not be a man of us punished. But there was but very few returned with him.

After two generally hungry weeks of marching, mostly off the main roads to dodge redcoat patrols, the party of deserters reached central Massachusetts. Knowlton stayed with the group until 17 November, then "travelled to Shrewsbury, home to my father's house, and found my honored parents well" the following day.

These rebellions resembled other troop disorders in several important ways. In the first place, there was nothing secretive about the actions of the discontented soldiers, and they made no attempt to conceal their identities. Unlike the classic desertion—an individual soldier slipping away from an encampment under the cover of darkness or ducking out of the line of march—the provincial desertions occurred openly, often after some notice had been given.[59] Furthermore, they were always corporate, involving from a score of men to several hundred.[60] Nor did provincial mutinies resemble the classic mutiny in regard to the participants' disposition toward authority. Rather than seeking to overthrow or kill their commanders, the rebellious troops treated them either with respect or with simple indifference. In so doing, the mutineers were in effect informing their commanding officer that they no longer acknowledged his authority and would not do so until he had made a proposal that they as a group found acceptable. Their actions also bespoke a sharp limitation in their goals: instead of permanently rejecting the leadership of their commanding officers, they did so only until the grievance had been rectified or until they were forced by superior strength to submit.[61] The nonviolent character of the mutinies likewise demonstrates their limited aims. Although the soldiers retained their arms, there is no mention of any use or threatened use of them.

Mutinies were sometimes led by junior officers, which fact indicates a

59. See also Elisha Hawley, 1 Sept. 1755; Seth Pomeroy, 1 Sept. 1755; Nathaniel Dwight, 11, 20 Nov. 1755; Lemuel Lyon, 22 July 1758; Caleb Rea, 22 July 1758; William Henshaw, 30 Oct.–1 Nov. 1759; Putnam, *Memoirs*, 16–17.

60. See also Elisha Hawley, 1 Sept. 1755; Seth Pomeroy, 1 Sept. 1755; Nathaniel Dwight, 11, 20 Nov. 1755; Lemuel Lyon, 22 July 1758; Caleb Rea, 22 July 1758; William Henshaw, 30 Oct.–1 Nov. 1759; Putnam, *Memoirs*, 17; Abner Barrows, 23 July 1758, in Williams's orderly book.

61. See also Elisha Hawley, 1 Sept. 1755; Seth Pomeroy, 1 Sept. 1755; Nathaniel Dwight, 11, 20 Nov. 1755; Caleb Rea, 22 July 1758; Samuel Morris, 1 Nov. 1759; Enoch Poor, 14 June, 17 Oct. 1759; John Thomas, 5 July 1755; Samuel Greenleaf, 2 Nov. 1756; Robert Webster, 13 Nov. 1759.

degree of identification between company officers and enlisted men entirely consistent with enlistment agreements, but wholly incomprehensible in the British professional army.[62] In a larger sense, the actions of mutineers and deserters reflect an achieved consensus not dissimilar to that of a small town meeting. Clough and his fellow mutineers "all swore" that they "would do no more duty," and "all stood to it that [they] would not do any duty at all" when threatened with the stockade. According to another participant in the episode Luke Knowlton described, the deserters "all agreed to go off" together.[63] Similarly, Private Enoch Poor of Newbury noted in June 1760 that everyone in the three provincial companies stationed at Fort Frederick, Nova Scotia, "was of one mind [and] that was not to work without pay" for extra duties not covered in their enlistment understanding.[64] Instances in which whole units, like Clough's regiment, submitted to imprisonment after being given the opportunity to reconsider their conduct suggests that the solidarity of the mutineers could be sustained under considerable stress.[65]

The discontented provincials acted in symbolic, even theatrical, ways. Participants in mass desertions often marched off with "clubbed arms"— that is, with their muskets on their shoulders, grasping them by the barrels rather than the buttstocks. In contemporary drilling conventions, this inverted posture signaled the completion of duty.[66] Furthermore, the fact that the men carried off packs and arms that were usually crown property indicated an additional measure of defiance, a signal that the rebels intended to appropriate their own compensation.

Commanders reacted to troop rebellions in similarly consistent ways. When they received notice that a mutiny or mass desertion was imminent, most tried first to reason with their men; some offered to represent their case to the next higher commander. A few gave in; others tried to suppress the disorder by force. In response to such theatrical gestures of defiance, commanders sometimes resorted to symbolic countertheater, to give point to their power—perhaps by surrounding mutinous troops with regulars, bayonets fixed, and beating the prisoners' march; perhaps by seizing and

62. Putnam, *Memoirs*, 16–21; Luke Knowlton, 1, 2 Nov. 1759; John Woods, 2 Nov. 1759; Enoch Poor, 17 Oct. 1759.

63. John Woods, 2 Nov. 1759.

64. Enoch Poor, 14 June 1760; see also Samuel Morris, 1 Nov. 1759.

65. See also Samuel Morris, 1 Nov. 1759.

66. Seth Pomeroy, 1 Sept. 1755; Samuel Chandler, 22 Nov. 1755; Caleb Rea, 22 July 1758. I am grateful to Gregory J. W. Urwin for suggesting the exact meaning of the clubbed muskets to me. See Humphrey Bland, *A Treatise of Military Discipline* 6th ed. (London, 1746 [orig. publ. London, 1727]), 8–9, 16–17, 27–28, 160–161, for contemporary instructions on the practice.

summarily punishing a ringleader, if one could be identified and caught. In the great majority of cases commanders did manage to retain control of the situation, and the rebellious soldiers had to decide whether they would accept the conditions offered or continue to resist. Generally they elected to accept the commander's offer. The most frequent outcome was some form of accommodation. In only one instance was a troop rebellion crushed by force (and that without bloodshed). Every other incident either ended peacefully, with some degree of success for the rebels, or circumstances changed in such a way as to eliminate the grievance.[67]

New England provincials for the most part lacked a military ethos recognizable to officers like the earl of Loudoun, who identified loyalty, subordination, discipline, and regularity as the primary martial virtues. When defining their relationship to military and civil authority, provincials tended to regard themselves as employees of their provinces, contracted workers whose labor consisted of bearing arms against the French and Indians. Accordingly, they conducted themselves as civilians would when confronted with the expiration of a work contract or when faced with an unacceptable alteration in the terms of their employment. As Rufus Putnam and his fellow soldiers explained when they announced their intention to depart following the termination of enlistment, "He is a good soldier that serves his time out; and that [since] the province had nothing to do with us, neither would we tarry any longer."[68] No redcoat could ever have agreed.

IV

The behavior of the provincial officers in opposing Loudoun in 1756, the suspicions of the Massachusetts Council and the reservations of the House of Representatives, and the behavior of provincial troops in their various mutinies and desertions throughout the war indicate that contractual ideals were deeply held and broadly shared among inhabitants of the Bay Colony, at every social level. Contractual relations had been much more central to their daily experience than either royal authority or highly deferential social relationships. The cultural context of a covenanted society

67. Diarists other than Clough and Woods who give a complete account of this sequence are Nathaniel Dwight, 11, 20 Nov. 1755; James Hill, 14, 16 Nov. 1755; Samuel Merriman, 23 Oct. 1759, with Samuel Morris, 1 Nov. 1759 (an account that parallels that of Woods, above); William Henshaw, 29 Oct.–1 Nov. 1759; and Enoch Poor, 14 June, 17 Oct. 1759. For a description of the one mutiny crushed by force, see Samuel Morris, 1 Nov. 1759. For the instance of seizure and summary punishment of ringleaders, see William Henshaw, 1 Nov. 1759.

68. Putnam, *Memoirs*, 17.

and the demands of the provincial economy made contracts a part of every-day life and talk, while notions of royal sovereignty and of a naturally superior, titled elite remained for the vast majority of the colonists rather distant and abstract. The longstanding practice of fighting wars against the French without direct aid from the mother country had generated assumptions of autonomy at all levels of New England society that complemented this homegrown contractualism. New Englanders, accustomed to having their own governments raise, direct, supply, and pay the provincials, automatically identified the colonial assemblies as the agencies responsible for defense. For the soldier, the locus of authority was his annually negotiated contract of enlistment. That, not the king's say-so, specified the service he would render and the care and compensation he would receive in return.

The Seven Years' War transformed the scale of colonial military conflict and introduced the immediate participation and command of professional British soldiers. But no matter how hard they tried, redcoat officers could not prevent provincial soldiers from acting on ingrained notions about the contractual nature of military service. The result was twofold. On one hand, regular officers concluded that New Englanders (and by extension, all Americans) lacked the character to make good soldiers. Ultimately, their belittling of Americans' martial virtue would lead to an officer's famous boast in 1774 that he could take a thousand grenadiers to America "and geld all the males, partly by force and partly by a little coaxing." [69] On the other hand, the war put under arms a large proportion of the New Englanders eligible to serve and directly exposed them to imperial authority, even as it graphically illustrated the divergences between British and colonial ways of thinking. Just as the regulars drew conclusions from the war about Americans, so New Englanders drew their own conclusions about the British. The war was an education for both sides, and the lessons that New England soldiers learned reinforced their cultural heritage and their sense of themselves as a distinct people.

69. Benjamin Franklin to William Strahan, 19 Aug. 1784, quoted in Charles Royster, *A Revolutionary People at War: The Continental Army and American Character, 1775–1783* (Chapel Hill, N.C., 1979), 10.

Chapter 7 ❖ "Victory Undoubtedly Comes from the Lord"
Providentialism and the New Englanders' Understanding of Warfare

Among all the common soldiers of the eighteenth century, New England provincials were unique in leaving a detailed record of their everyday existence. Even more remarkably, provincials sometimes went beyond merely chronicling daily happenings to comment on the events' larger meanings.[1] Thus we have the rare opportunity to glimpse the soldiers' experience from their own broadest perspective, a chance to explore the ordinary colonists' understanding of war itself. Theirs was a profoundly religious conception, already rather old-fashioned in the mid-eighteenth century. Like their distinctive understanding of military service, the provincials' view of war served to raise a barrier between them and their British allies.

I

About two-thirds of the soldiers whose diaries survive were content simply to set down the mundane details of camp life; the other third, in varying degrees, commented reflectively. Whether they wrote purely reportorial accounts or ruminated on larger meanings, soldiers found the same occurrences worthy of note. In particular they paid attention to accidents, unusual natural phenomena, news from elsewhere in the war, encounters with the enemy, the weather, the presence or absence of disease in the army, and sudden death of all sorts. Soldiers who went on to comment on the significance of such events and natural conditions agreed quite closely on what they signified. Almost invariably they discerned in them the Lord interposing his hand in worldly affairs to effect his eternal design of salvation. The highly coherent, Christian conception of reality implicit in this can be identified as the providential world view. In formal terms, providentialism is the belief that God guides all events, intervening in the natural world and in human life to make his will manifest to men. Such inter-

---

1. See Appendix B; starred entries indicate the journals of soldiers who included reflective passages in their accounts of service.

ventions take the form of "ordinary" or "common providences," such as accidents or changes in the weather, and "special" or "remarkable providences," which are rarer and more spectacular—monstrous births, earthquakes, famines, and so on. Simple as it is to define, providentialism had complicated consequences for those who saw reality through its lens. The workings of the providential understanding of the world are best illustrated by example, beginning with a soldier whose campaign journal exemplifies provincial diary-keeping at its most unreflective. Indeed, if we had to judge the author by this document alone, we could only conclude that he was a man who gave no thought whatever to the larger meanings of events. What makes his case singularly valuable as an example of providential thinking, however, is that he was also maintaining a second journal, and that one was explicitly meditative.

Private Seth Metcalf, a twenty-two-year-old farmer from Rutland, Massachusetts, seldom made entries longer than a score of words in the diary he kept at Fort Edward during his service in 1757. Wholly unlike this spare and matter-of-fact record was the book of annual meditations he maintained from 1755 until 1767, and again from 1795 to 1807. Metcalf composed the following entry early in January 1758, with reference to his previous year's service experience:

> April 25, 1757, I set out to go into a campaign. And I was taken sick the first day of August and at the same time the enemy laid siege at Fort William Henry, within 17 miles. At the time I was under trouble, but God delivered us out of the hand of the enemy. And blessed be his holy name that he hath been so gracious and merciful to me as to return me to my friends the third day of January following. O may I never forget the goodness of God to me, an unworthy sinner.[2]

Metcalf's service diary gave no hint that he had been "under trouble" and mentioned his illness only indirectly. The terse entries in his military journal indicated nothing of the religious sensibility evident in his belief that the Almighty was responsible for delivering the New Englanders from the "hand of the enemy." For Metcalf, the meaning of his 1757 campaign was straightforward. Its events illustrated God's mercy to the army and, in returning him home safely, to himself. Moreover, he was mindful of the moral message these providences conveyed: his duty was to acknowledge the goodness of the Lord, which came to him freely, without any merit or worthiness on his part.

Metcalf's other entries in the annual journal indicate that he saw many kinds of occurrences as evidence of God's dealings with man—and par-

2. Seth Metcalf (1755 journal), entry dated 25 Apr. 1757 (probably composed in Jan. 1758).

ticularly with Seth Metcalf. His briefest entries were made at the ends of years that carried unambiguous or favorable messages, like 1759 and 1760.

> Upon consideration of the year 1759: This year hath been remarkable for successes against our enemies in the reduction of Quebec, Ticonderoga, and Crown Point, for which I would desire to give glory to God for his unmerited goodness.

> The year 1760: It hath pleased almighty God to give into our hands the rest of our enemy's country of Canada. Oh, may I never forget his goodness!

With a highly consistent orthodoxy, Metcalf did not congratulate New England or any human actor for the outcome of the war. He was too thorough a Calvinist to suppose that the Lord rewarded his servants for their merit, much less to imagine that anything could have been accomplished by human effort alone, without divine interposition. The providences of these victorious years carried only one message: since God in his unsearchable goodness had seen fit to reward rather than punish his people, it was their duty to render him praise and thanks for it.

Other years carried more complicated meanings, which Metcalf explained at much greater length. His account of 1762, for example, consisted of remarks on "the following instances of divine providence": a cold winter and a late spring; a summer of drought, "which threatens with cleanness of teeth in this land"; and the fall of Newfoundland to French invaders, even as "we were ready to say we [were] in no danger." Metcalf saw in these developments the "frowns" of the Lord upon a New England that had begun to grow self-satisfied. God had begun to smile again later in the year, however, when it became clear that despite the drought there would be sufficient food and when the news arrived that Newfoundland had been recaptured and Havana conquered as well. Metcalf concluded that "these and the like providences" ought to "excite me to put my entire dependence upon God and choose him for my portion and live to his glory."[3]

The year 1765 was of such formidable complexity that Metcalf needed hundreds of words to map out its meanings. It began with a cold, violent winter ("a frown of God's providence") and proceeded to a late spring and a dry summer—bad weather that produced a surprisingly good crop ("for which I would desire to bless and magnify his holy name"). A freakish blizzard in October contradicted this favoring sign as a providential judg-

---

3. *Ibid.*, 1762 entry. ("Cleanness of teeth" echoes Amos 4:6, a passage dealing with famine.)

ment. This storm, "as well as common providences," Metcalf thought, should "awaken me to a holy life and conversation. May it cause me to see my dependence upon God who can command even the wind and storm to destroy me." The political events of the year—the Stamp Act and the rioting it provoked—brought even heavier tidings from the Lord, especially when Metcalf realized that the winter was beginning to look like another bad one.

> The winter [is] very hard, the snow lying steady from the beginning of December. Considering what hath passed over this land this year, it shows that God is angry with us of this land, and is now smiting us with his rod, especially by the hand of our rulers. Oh, that I might see the rod and who hath appointed it! May God grant that these things awaken me to seek first the kingdom of God, and trust him for the addition of all other needful things.[4]

The pattern in the journal is clear: with a rigor that would have done credit to a Puritan cleric, Metcalf took the events of each year as his text and fashioned upon them an annual sermon to himself. The highly conventionalized message of each year's sermon shows a mind accustomed to casting events into the providential framework that, for Metcalf, undergirded all reality. Temporal events were the means by which God conducted his colloquy with New England and with each Christian, and always the message was the same: the Lord sends blessing and chastisement upon those whom he loves, to reform them, to purge them of their pride, to turn them to himself. Discerning God's hand in the world—being able to "see the rod" in affliction and to know "who hath appointed it"—was no easy task, nor was giving thanks, nor was depending solely upon the Lord. As Metcalf confessed when he resumed his journal in 1795, it was easy to set one's heart "on this vain world," to be "forgetful . . . of the providences of God." He had found it all too easy to be "unthankful for mercies," too easy to avoid making "a good improvement of the afflictive dispensations of providence."[5] Once he had learned to recognize the workings of God, Metcalf knew, he had all the more reason to prostrate himself before the Lord. His diary afforded one means of maintaining the self-critical frame of mind necessary to do so.

The case of Rufus Putnam underscores the seriousness with which believers approached these matters. When as an old man Putnam looked back on his service diaries in composing his *Memoirs*, he was disturbed to discover that he could not, in 1758, "find any acknowledgment to my divine benefactor and preserver; nor do I recollect that I had any serious

4. *Ibid.*, 1765 entry.
5. *Ibid.*, 30 Dec. 1795.

reflection on the subject." He found the same fault in his 1759 journals and chided himself, "Oh shame"; and he was clearly relieved to find that in 1760, at last, he "had not wholly omitted acknowledging dependence" upon the Lord.[6] Not to depend upon the Almighty was to commit the gravest of transgressions, the sin of pride. Seen in this light, the reflections of Metcalf and his comrades—for the meditations of the other diarists were strikingly similar to his—were not simply one-note moralizing, not mere reflexes of piety devoid of intellectual exertion. They were instead a kind of spiritual calisthenics, examples of the self-conscious application of the providential scheme to their own lives and to the world at large. As Metcalf's reflections suggest, providentialism encompassed all occurrences, but God signaled his purposes with special clarity in ungovernable, unpredictable events. Violent weather and great events of state were the ones to which Metcalf's attention was especially drawn. Other diarists found God's hand in earthquakes, disease, accidents, the outcome of battles, and a wide variety of other unpredictable, obviously significant occurrences. The causes of these lay outside the explanatory ambit of daily life, and they marked a kind of threshold for the providentialist, demanding his special reflection—"a good improvement."

Nothing triggered reflection more reliably among the provincials than a brush with death, or death itself (especially if it came accidentally or suddenly). The sequence of Joseph Nichols's reflections in 1758 illustrates this clearly. Early in the campaign, one of his acquaintances was badly hurt when a carelessly felled tree landed on him; Nichols recorded the accident, adding, "May such things as these be taken notice of." Two days later, a member of his company accidentally fired a musket into another soldier's pack, which stopped the ball before it could penetrate his body: "May this be a warning to us," observed the diarist. On 24 June another member of the company carelessly "presented his gun toward a number of Captain Moor's men," and it went off, killing a trooper. Nichols hoped that this "sudden and awful stroke of divine providence [might] be sanctified to all our regiment." When the first man in the battalion died from the "camp disease" in August, Nichols improved the event similarly: "May this stroke of divine providence and all other dispensations of that nature be sanctified to us for our spiritual good and for the glory of our God." When he heard of the death of a man in Framingham, his hometown, he exclaimed: "Oh, how certain death is! The time and place where a person will die is unknown to us—persons may go through many long campaigns and tedious marches and [be] exposed to imminent danger and yet live longer than hearty men who are in their business at home. Oh, how unex-

6. Rufus Putnam, *The Memoirs of Rufus Putnam* (Boston, 1903), 25, 31, 35.

pected death often comes! This should excite us to be ready and prepared."[7]

This pattern, of accident, illness, and death setting off reflections on the contingency of human life, was replicated in the journal of John Cleaveland, chaplain to the regiment in which Nichols served. In the execution of a regular soldier Cleaveland saw a divine warning against sin. In the death of his brother-in-law he perceived a lesson about "how frail we are and [how we ought] to give our hearts unto wisdom." In each unexpected death he heard a warning "to be always ready" for the great change.[8] Like those of Metcalf and Nichols, Cleaveland's reflections maintained with a stylized consistency that each dreadful event was intended to produce some good effect for the people of God. When a young townsman of Cleaveland's died, he hoped that "the Lord [would] sanctify this to his mother and friends for good, and sanctify all the deaths here to the soldiers."[9] Later, after visiting a sergeant who was dangerously ill with the throat distemper, Cleaveland prayed, "O Lord in wrath remember mercy to your army and remove from us mortal sickness, and sanctify thy righteous judgments."[10] In the chaplain's reflections, as in Nichols's, the operative term was *sanctify*. Cleaveland and Nichols, like all orthodox believers, hoped that the Lord would enable the sufferers and those who loved them to live holier, more God-pleasing ("sanctified") lives as a result of their afflictions. In good Calvinist style, such reflections also recognized that the believer had to rely upon God to bring about the salutary result.

Cleaveland often made such reflective petitions. A particularly illuminating one was occasioned by the departure of a raiding party of Rogers's Rangers: "Oh, that God would reform us, go forth with our scouts and so succeed them that our enemies may be humbled, so humbled as to submit to responsible living."[11] In its structure and the concerns expressed, this petition says a great deal about Cleaveland's perception of the world. He hoped for a successful raid, yet recognized that the moral reformation of the army was necessary for its success; unless the army became a fit instrument for God's purposes, he would not use it to accomplish them. In addi-

---

7. Joseph Nichols, 6 June 1758 (tree-felling injures man); 8 June 1758 (accidental but nonfatal shooting); 24 June 1758 (accidental shooting death); 9 Aug. 1758 (first death from camp disease); 3 Sept. 1758 (death of hometown acquaintance).

8. John Cleaveland, 25 July 1758 (execution); 10 Aug. 1758 (death of brother-in-law); 6 Sept. 1758.

9. *Ibid.*, 21 Sept. 1758. Cf. Cleaveland's reflection on the death of his sister, 15 Sept. 1758; the language is virtually identical. See also John Cleaveland to Mary Cleaveland, 22 Sept. 1758, John Cleaveland Papers, III, 173–175, Essex Institute, Salem, Mass. (hereafter cited as JCP); John Cleaveland to Mary Cleaveland, 26 Sept. 1758, JCP, III, 176–178.

10. John Cleaveland, 28 Sept. 1758.

11. John Cleaveland, 16 Aug. 1758.

tion to asking for reformation and divine favor for the soldiers, Cleaveland was also praying here for his enemies. This was unusual in his diary, and even more unusual in the others (although to do so was, of course, a Christlike act). Most significantly, the entry indicates that Cleaveland was aware of the war in a larger sense as a process which should bring good to pass for both God's people and their enemies. The war itself, in other words, was a providence of God, writ large. Like illness and death, the war too was a warning, a chastisement, an affliction to be sanctified for the reformation and salvation of the world.

To see the world providentially, as New Englanders did, meant to interpret reality in a binary way: to perceive not just an immediate cause, but an underlying *moral* cause to every occurrence. Thoughtful provincials were quite conscious of their binary vision and even wrote about it. When the Anglo-American forces lost the battle at Ticonderoga in 1758, for example, Caleb Rea cast about to explain the defeat. Eventually he decided that, at bottom, it was probably profanity that had been responsible.

> I can't but remark, and that with regret, the horrid cursing and swearing there is in the camp, more especially among the regulars. And as a moral cause I can't but charge our defeat on this sin, which so prevails even among the chief commanders. And those that were gasping for their last breath would commonly breathe out oaths and curses. But as for the politic cause I shall not at present give my opinion.[12]

The "politic cause," Rea finally decided, was that General Abercromby had betrayed the army's advantage and had been abetted in it by his sycophantic regular subordinates.[13] While Rea detested Abercromby, he was not prepared to believe that the commander's incompetence and cronyism alone were sufficient to explain the defeat. Because such a setback so clearly reflected divine disapproval, it required a spiritual as well as a temporal explanation.

Joseph Nichols, the company clerk who kept an unusually reflective and articulate diary in 1758, observed the distinction between temporal and eternal causes as scrupulously as Rea did. As with Rea, this trait did not prevent Nichols from being interested in worldly causes as well as spiritual ones. It did, however, introduce a note of caution into his speculations, for he feared becoming excessively worldly in his interests. Such, for instance, was the case in mid-July when Nichols complained about the inadequacies of provincial diet and worried over its effects on morale:

12. Caleb Rea, 10 July 1758.
13. Caleb Rea, 23, 31 Aug., 18 Oct. 1758.

The spirits of our men seem to fail. I doubt [i.e., "I fear"] we are losing our [*illeg.*] courage that in years past we had the credit of. It is a common saying that money makes the man to go; and I make no doubt if, in case our natures was refreshed with diet agreeable to what we are used to, our strength and courage would come to us like an armed man—I would be understood, in a natural cause.[14]

Nichols added the reservation, "in a natural cause," from concern that he was coming close to denying God's supernatural agency in restoring the spirits of the army. Mere food would change nothing, after all, unless the Lord vouchsafed his approval for their cause.

The meaning of this binary vision can best be understood by examining not just single events but those of several weeks, as seen through the eyes of a thoroughgoing providentialist. Joseph Nichols's diary, again, provides a clear example. The Anglo-American defeat at Ticonderoga on 8 July 1758 dominated Nichols's understanding of the campaign. He did not immediately reflect on its meaning. It was not until 11 July that he first attempted to assess the "astonishing disappointment we have met with." He initially concluded that "we must submit, for 'twas God's holy will and pleasure," but the next day he began to address the defeat at greater length.

Our people seems to be in a confused posture and our men are very much discouraged and beat out with their late hardship. 'Twas observed that in the late actions our men behaved bravely, not the least daunted when ordered to battle. But oh, our unhappiness and misfortune that we have sustained! May God of his infinite mercy and grace grant that our men may humble themselves before our Maker and repent of our sins, so that God would remember mercy and give success to our army; so that we may not return to our friends with shame as they have heretofore done. Observed our men refrain somewhat from profaneness and observe many reading in their books.

Thus Nichols's first reactions were dismay and the almost abject hope that this judgment upon the army might somehow be turned to good. He never questioned the divine authorship of the defeat and assumed that self-examination and repentance were necessary before the Lord would smile again upon the army. The subdued demeanor of Nichols's fellow soldiers in refraining from profanity and resorting to "their books" suggests that they, too, reacted reflectively and penitently. Nichols did not yet, however, venture to identify the sin that caused the loss.

14. Joseph Nichols, 17 July 1758.

The next weeks brought more setbacks. On 20 July a small provincial scouting party was ambushed and nearly wiped out near Halfway Brook. Nine days later, enemy raiders struck a supply train, again near Halfway Brook, "prodigiously and unhumanly butchered" the party of soldiers and civilians accompanying it, and made off with a regular payroll thought to amount to two thousand pounds sterling or more. About a week later a patrol of Rogers's Rangers at last managed to engage and bloody a party of enemy raiders that had been lurking in the forest near Wood Creek. This skirmish, though equivocal in result, was greeted as the first success the British had had since the debacle at Ticonderoga. It evidently boosted morale among the provincials at Lake George, who by this time were beginning to experience serious erosion of strength from disease.[15]

These were the developments on which Nichols commented on 25 August, after he had heard a rumor that the army would soon try again to capture Ticonderoga. His first reaction to the thought of another attack was doubt and puzzlement, since he knew that the army now had no more than two-thirds of its original strength. "But," he reflected, on second thought,

the battle is not to the strong nor the race to the swift, but victory undoubtedly comes from the Lord. It appeared to me when we went to Ticonderoga we boasted too much of our numbers, how we were able to drive Canada. As for Ticonderoga, that would be nothing in our hands. But alas! how was our designs blasted! Instead of driving Canada, we were not able to rout our enemies from their first stronghold, but retreated back from them who was much inferior in number, with the loss of my brave Lord Howe and a great number of brave officers and soldiers. Some affirm we had upwards of eighteen hundred killed, wounded, and missing. Then to make our case more deplorable, in a few days after we arrived from Ticonderoga we sustained two great losses by the enemy, who by waylaying our stores killed and took about one hundred persons and much spoil to our great [be]musement and discouragement. But it seems in the midst of our disappointment God had remembered mercy for us; in the late battle [i.e., Rogers's 8 August encounter with the French] we he had.[16]

Nichols was at last prepared to assess the cause of defeat. The boasting pride of the army before it set out against the French, its sinful confidence

15. Joseph Nichols, 11 July 1758 (initial reaction); 12 July 1758 (men grow pensive after defeat); 20, 29, 30 July 1758 (setbacks, ambushes); 8 Aug. 1758 (Rogers's defeat of French raiders).

16. Joseph Nichols, 25 Aug. 1758. ("We he had": we had God with us.)

in its own strength, had apparently occasioned God's displeasure. This led the Lord first to "blast" the English design and then to humiliate and further discomfit the army by allowing the enemy's raids to succeed. The possible return of divine favor, signaled by Rogers's success in his skirmish with the French at Wood Creek, gave cause for hope. God had "remembered mercy" to his erring people, perhaps because he had managed to quench their vanity. Thus Nichols found himself able to face the unpleasant prospect of a second attempt upon Ticonderoga, even with the army weakened by disease and battle losses. If God were with them again, there was nothing to fear: for "the battle is not to the strong . . . but victory undoubtedly comes from the Lord."

Just three days later, word arrived that the English forces under Amherst and Wolfe had succeeded in reducing Louisbourg, key to the Saint Lawrence River. The joyous news confirmed Nichols's impression of God's returning favor and sent him back to his diary:

> Oh, that God would enable us to sing of mercy in the midst of judgment, discouragement, and disappointment! Our people have been very much disheartened here at the lake occasioned by our great disappointment*. . . . Oh, that God would enable us to rejoice at our heart and return him sincere praise for such a great favor!
>
> *July 8th at Ticonderoga; when we expected to take their fortress with ease. But God who is wise ordered it otherwise and we returned with shame and as it were with astonishment.[17]

The shame of their defeat was still hard to bear, but now it was evident that God had kept faith with their cause, and had seen fit to reward the English (at Louisbourg) with a signal triumph. The pattern of the whole summer had now become clear. The Lord had given the English gall to drink instead of the wine of victory at Ticonderoga, a punishment they merited because of their vainglory. Lately, however, with the success of Rogers and particularly with the victory at Louisbourg, God had demonstrated his continuing love—*after* the chastening defeat, and *after* the soldiers' rededication (Nichols hoped) of heart, in an act of sovereign grace. Now it was incumbent upon the soldiers at Lake George to rejoice in the Lord, to return him "sincere praise for such a great favor," to remain humbly conscious of their dependence upon his power and mercy, and to bear patiently the burden of shame he had determined to make their portion.

What Nichols did with the events of the campaign, even as they occurred, was to assemble them in the form of a jeremiad, the venerable ser-

17. *Ibid.*, 28 Aug. 1758.

mon form most often used to explain God's dealings with New England. He did so incrementally, in reflections made over almost two months' time, steadily integrating new developments into the pattern. The conventions of New England preaching thus provided the structure for Nichols's serious thinking, even as they limited and constrained it. While elsewhere in his diary he complained bitterly of irregular diet, inadequate shelter, and the bad health that seemed to accompany them, he never pressed on to draw purely rationalistic conclusions from his observations, never blamed the army's leaders for bad management. Instead, he looked for the spiritual lesson in it all. Even though he clearly realized, for example, that the soldiers would perform better if they were fed better, he stopped short of naturalist pronouncements and fell back instead to incantatory appeals ("Oh, that God would enable us . . .") for supernatural aid. For Nichols, and indeed for the reflective provincials as a group, any kind of physical or administrative reform in the functioning of the army would have been pointless unless it followed spiritual reformation of the kind that God himself induced by chastening his childish and self-willed people. After all, it was axiomatic for Nichols, as for all orthodox believers, that they "must not trust in an arm of flesh. God may blast us a thousand ways." [18]

The providential conception of reality had important implications for the expectations of the provincial soldiers. If New Englanders truly believed that God would fight their battles for them, then the spiritual state of the army had to represent a vital concern. Without the Lord's approval, mere technical proficiency or numerical strength—let alone adeptness in field sanitation techniques or regularity in encampments—would avail nothing. Although the Christian soldier was obligated to learn and perform his duty to the best of his ability, he did not dare rely solely on the "arm of flesh." Above all, provincials knew they needed to be always ready to take humble, trusting advantage of whatever opportunities God saw fit to put in their way.

Whenever the tide of battle seemed to run in their favor, conscientious provincials were especially emphatic that it was not their doing, but that of the Lord, who fought in their behalf. Hence, in 1755 after the successful defense of the provincials' Lake George position against the French attackers, Seth Pomeroy repeatedly maintained that "had not the Lord been on our side we must all [have] been swallowed up." [19] Similarly, as the Brit-

18. John Cleaveland to Mary Cleaveland, 26 June 1758, JCP, III, 160–161.

19. Seth Pomeroy to Rachel Pomeroy, 11 Sept. 1755, in Louis Effingham de Forest, ed., *The Journals and Papers of Seth Pomeroy, Sometime General in the Colonial Service* (New Haven, Conn., 1926), 142; cf. Seth Pomeroy to Israel Williams, 9 Sept. 1755, *ibid.*, 138–139; and Seth Pomeroy, 13, 14 Sept. 1755. Following the battle, the provincial forces found

ish landed near Ticonderoga in 1758, John Cleaveland felt "much inclined to pour out desires to the God of Heaven that he would appear for us and intimidate the enemy." Later he thought it "wonderful how God appeared for us. For though the enemy had four battalions in the advanced guard . . . we were all safely landed. The French only fired off a few small arms, which did no harm, and then run off."[20]

The experience of the next two days showed how risky it could be to read a great deal into apparently favorable events. Victory, even more than defeat, had to be interpreted cautiously. The most striking example of such providentialist caution came from the pen of no less notable a military figure than Colonel Israel Williams of Hatfield, the preeminent militia commander in western Massachusetts. In August 1759 he wrote to an old subordinate, Captain John Burk, who was then commanding a company in Abijah Willard's regiment, on Amherst's expedition down Lake Champlain. Williams was writing in his official capacity to inform Burk that reinforcements were on their way to join him at Crown Point. The bulk of the letter, however, was an extended commentary on the news that had been reaching Hatfield of the astonishing ease with which the Anglo-American forces had taken Ticonderoga and Crown Point.

> We rejoice with you for your successes, . . . that the place of blood in times past is given into your hands with so little effusion of it; that your enemies are intimidated and flee before you. . . . In all these things the hand of Heaven is very visible. Our fears are disappointed and joy for our forces exults in every breast.
>
> . . . Yet we tremble for the event. But if it be for the glory of God's name, he will make your arms victorious, and with that view we ought principally to desire it. This may be the day of vengeance upon our enemies, . . . and they may not longer have it in their power to oppress, vex, and imbrue these [lands?] in innocent blood.

---

themselves badly in need of reinforcements. It is an index of Pomeroy's perspective that he requested aid from his militia superior, Colonel Israel Williams, in these terms:

> We design to make a stand here till we have a sufficient reinforcement. What number that must be I can't tell. . . . I judge *humanly speaking* our all depends on the success of this expedition; therefore I pray God would fire the breasts of his people with a true zeal and a noble, generous spirit to come to the help of the Lord against the mighty. I trust all those that value our holy religion and our liberties will spare nothing, even to the one-half of their estate. . . .
>
> I desire the prayers of God's people for us, that we may not turn our backs upon our enemies, but stand and make a victorious defense for ourselves and our country; crown us with victory to the glory of God and return us in safety. [Emphasis added]

20. John Cleaveland, 6 July 1758.

> The righteous governor of the world will certainly punish for the
> wrong done to his people, but when and in what way must be left to
> [his] infinite wisdom. The counsel of the Lord will stand. However,
> though we are unacquainted with the plan of the divine government,
> yet from events we are let into the knowledge of some of it, and from
> thence are to draw encouragement to do our duty and submit to the
> plan. . . . From what is past you have reason to hope for greater
> good things—not to place pride in your own [strength], but in him
> who emphatically styles himself the Lord of hosts. And may your
> eyes behold, and your heart rejoice in, victory and success, that we
> hope be yet granted to our forces in their several enterprises.[21]

Williams was obviously encouraged by events, but his providential world
view dictated both caution and a renewed reliance on the all-powerful, unpredictable God who would ultimately resolve the issue. In the end, he
knew, it was not the hosts of the Lord, but the Lord of hosts who achieved
the victory.

Given so restrained an approach to interpreting the war, it is hardly surprising that the most sustained use of this rhetoric of reliance upon God
would accompany the longest string of British successes. In 1760, when
Captain Samuel Jenks participated in the climactic expedition of the war
on the New York front, the march from Crown Point to Montreal, he
never ceased to remark the participation of the Almighty. Initially he had
prayed only that "God [would] grant that we may behave ourselves like
men and play the man for the city and people of our God, and let him do as
seemest him best."[22] But soon it became clear that the Lord was doing a
great deal in forwarding the Protestant cause. When on 30 August the
French fled their fort at Saint-Jean without a fight, Jenks marveled: "The
enemy are gone to Montreal. Thus Heaven apparently fights for us, and
therefore it is our duty to acknowledge it's the hand of divine providence,
and not done by any force of ours, or arm of flesh." The next day he
learned that the enemy had had sufficient supplies to resist a siege, which
made their flight seem all the more miraculous. "Had the enemy behaved
like men," he observed, "they could a-stood out a month longer, but it
plainly appears that they were intimidated and Heaven is against them."[23]

21. Israel Williams to John Burk, 13 Aug. 1759, John Burk Correspondence, American
Antiquarian Society, Worcester, Mass.

22. Samuel Jenks, 15 Aug. 1760. Cf. 2 Sam. 10:12, where Joab speaks to Abishai as they
prepare to do battle with the Syrians and Ammonites: "Be of good courage, and let us play
the men for our people, and for the cities of our God: and the Lord do that which seemeth
him good."

23. Samuel Jenks, 30 Aug. 1760 (French flee Fort Saint-Jean); 31 Aug. 1760 (the French
"intimidated").

Less than a week thereafter, with the three British armies, under Haviland, Amherst, and Murray, converging on Montreal in perfect synchronization (a fact that was itself considered providential),[24] the French abandoned another stronghold, Fort Chambly. Again there was no battle. "Oh, how apparently does divine providence interpose in our favor!" Jenks exclaimed, "although I believe if he [i.e., the chevalier de Lévis, the French commander] had come, it would have been to their own cost. God be praised, we are in a condition to receive them. Our men are animated and in high spirits, and fine lines [are] thrown up, and redoubts with cannon in front. And above all, I trust God [is] on our side; therefore we fear them not. Although an host encamp around us, we will not fear." Most amazing of all, and clear proof (if any more were needed) that the Almighty was directing the outcome, was the French surrender, which occurred without further resistance on 8 September: "I desire to bless God [that] we have all Canada under our command without any more blood shed."[25] To Jenks, the disarray and panic of the French retreat was unmistakably divine in origin, God's masterful intervention in the war effort. It was not British valor or tactical brilliance, but the Lord acting in his own time; to ascribe the victory to any but divine strength was blasphemy.

It was, of course, a matter of degree. Pure professionalism lies at one pole on the spectrum of attitudes toward warfare, pure providentialism at the other. It is unlikely that many British (or French, or German) regular officers in the mid-eighteenth century would have been willing to exclude the Almighty from their thinking about war altogether, unlikely that many would have cynically maintained that God sides only with the big battalions. The eighteenth century was still, after all, an age of belief. It is equally unlikely that the provincial officers of New England were wholly nonplussed by the professionalism of the British and were simply willing to trust the Lord of hosts to confound their enemies. The New Englanders were still human, after all, and prone (as they readily admitted) to trust in the arm of flesh. Nonetheless, there *was* a spectrum, on which regulars undeniably occupied the professional end, while provincials were disposed by their culture and social experiences to occupy the other.

Recognizing such divergences of belief does much to clarify provincial attitudes toward the regulars. If God sent defeat to punish wickedness, there was every reason for provincials to minimize the benefits of alliance with the redcoats. If victory was the gift of God to his people, they had

24. See, e.g., Samuel Niles, "A Summary Historical Narrative of the Wars in New England with the French and Indians in the Several Parts of the Country," Massachusetts Historical Society, *Collections*, 1st Ser., VI (1836), 154–279; 4th Ser., V (1861), 311–600.

25. Samuel Jenks, 5 Sept. 1760 (French abandon Fort Chambly); 8 Sept. 1760 (Canada capitulates; cf. Niles, "Narrative," Mass. Hist. Soc., *Colls.*, 4th Ser., V [1861], 571–573).

every reason to credit themselves (within the limits of a just humility) for contributing to the moral health of the army and thus making it an instrument fit to execute the divine purpose. Ultimately, such a perspective on the war might even enable a New Englander to maintain that the victory had been achieved as much in spite of the British as because of their participation. If such an assessment seems absurd in light of Britain's heavy contributions of men and money, it must be remembered that, to the eye trained upon providence, nothing could be more misleading than the obvious. After all, the battle is not to the strong, nor the race to the swift; but victory undoubtedly comes from the Lord.

II

The providential scheme was continually explicated to provincial soldiers by their army's many chaplains, each of whom was supposed to preach to his regiment twice on Sundays and to conduct daily prayers. Weather and the demands of duty prevented most chaplains from addressing their regiments weekly, but preaching was frequent nonetheless. The difference in regular and provincial attitudes toward the chaplaincy can be graphically illustrated by a survey of the clergy at Lake George in 1758. Of the fifteen chaplains present, fourteen were members of provincial battalions, which included in all somewhat less than six thousand men; only one, the Reverend John Ogilvie, served the regular regiments, which together numbered more than six thousand.[26] The provincial chaplains were often men of evangelical tendencies—"warm" preachers like John Cleaveland of Chebacco Parish, Ipswich, and Samuel Chandler of Gloucester—though they were by no means uniformly New Light in sympathy, as the participation of parsons like Daniel Shute of Hingham and Gad Hitchcock of Pembroke indicates. In general, provincial chaplains seem fairly to have represented country parsons throughout New England, without leaning unduly toward any particular persuasion. The only group that was definitely underrepresented was the ecclesiastical aristocracy of the province: the divines of Boston generally steered clear of the service, leaving room for younger and more obscure men (including ministerial candidates like Robert Treat

26. Franklin Bowditch Dexter, ed., *Biographical Sketches of the Graduates of Yale College with Annals of the College History*, 6 vols. (New York, 1885–1912), II, 174–177; Milton W. Hamilton, ed., "The Diary of the Reverend John Ogilvie, 1750–1759," Fort Ticonderoga Museum, *Bulletin*, X (1957–1962), 331–381; Stanley Pargellis, ed., *Military Affairs in North America, 1748–1765* (Hamden, Conn., 1969 [orig. publ. New York, 1936]), 283. (Ogilvie, Yale 1748, had been a missionary among the Indians before being recruited as a temporary regular chaplain.)

Paine of Taunton and William Crawford of Worcester) to care for the spiritual welfare of the troops.

A survey of the provincial sermons indicates that the chaplains used their weekly worship services "to declare . . . the counsel of God" in the typological terms of classic New England preaching.[27] Soldiers noted the texts of 134 sermons in their journals over the course of the war. If these accurately represent what the provincials heard on campaign, then military service not only gave the provincials experiences to ponder but also provided them with ample instruction in the providential meanings of the experiences. Chaplains preached rather more frequently from the Old Testament than the New—seventy-one times, in the known sermons, as opposed to sixty-three. In these addresses, chaplains often reminded the soldiers of God's covenantal relationship with the people of Israel—typologically speaking, that is, with the New English Israel, themselves.[28] Along with such explanations of God's special calling for his people went complementary discourses describing God's intervention on behalf of Israel in battle and celebrating the martial aspects of divinity.[29] The texts of these sermons show, in example after example, how God had used the ancient Israelites to destroy his enemies, how he had interposed in battle to deliver the wicked into the hands of his people. Thus when the Reverend Eli Forbes of Brookfield took up the story of Moses' fight with Amalek (Exod. 17:8–16) in July 1758, or that of David and Goliath (1 Sam. 17:45) a year later, he was doing more than recounting God's participation

27. John Cleaveland, 15 Oct. 1758. Cf. Acts 20:27.

28. The sermons, by text, date delivered, preacher, and theme, are listed in Appendix D. Each has been assigned a number for reference in the following discussion of sermon content.

29. Thematically, the sermons can be broadly grouped as follows by theme, subtheme, and sermon number (see Appendix D).

Covenant: 1, 2, 3, 4, 6, 7, 11, 12, 13, 14, 23, 25, 33, 34, 66, 67, 72, 107, 120, 121.

Conduct: prescribing norms: 5, 10, 20, 51, 70, 74, 75, 78, 79, 80, 85, 90, 100, 108, 111, 112, 113, 114, 124, 125; condemnation of wickedness: 55, 60, 106; the Law: 52, 54.

God fights for Israel: 8, 9, 15, 16, 17, 18, 19, 24, 38, 39, 43, 45, 56, 61, 64.

Judgment: chastisement: 21, 58, 62, 63, 65, 68, 69, 86, 87, 99, 101, 116, 122; the last times: 73, 84, 88, 118, 126, 129, 130, 131, 132, 135.

Attributes of God: power and strength: 27, 31, 49, 50; sovereignty: 28, 29, 57, 98; greatness: 30, 44; justice: 40, 46, 47; omniscience: 48; all-sufficiency: 96, 133; faithfulness: 32, 71, 104, 109, 110; mercy: 35, 36, 37, 41, 89; love: 42, 53, 77, 91, 103.

Faith: 59, 81, 94, 97, 115, 117, 119, 127, 128, 134.

Discipleship: 82, 92, 93.

Prayer: 105, 123.

Mortality: 22, 26.

Promises of reward: 76, 102.

The Sabbath: 83.

The chaplaincy: 95.

in battles on behalf of the biblical Israel.[30] He was promising the soldiers of New England that if they, too, took the field "in the name of the Lord of hosts, the God of the armies of Israel" against those who had set their faces against Israel's God, then Jehovah would surely come to their aid. In 1758, the army that had set off with Forbes's descriptions of Israel's victory before it suffered a stunning defeat; but such was the comprehensiveness of the providential interpretation that the chaplains immediately identified Biblical parallels to explain the loss. After the defeat John Cleaveland preached to his regiment first on the necessity of repentance, then on the fear of God and on his faithfulness to the people of his covenant. Finally, he expounded Josh. 7 : 1–13, exhorting them to search their hearts for the abominations that had caused the Lord to forsake them in battle—violations of divine ordinances like Achan's concealment of an "accursed thing," the secret sin that had caused Israel to lose the siege of the Canaanite city of Ai.[31]

Sermons like these were clearly oriented toward present circumstances, making what were called "improvements" of recent events. At least a quarter of the recorded sermons were so adapted.[32] The daily prayers, conducted at morning or evening parade, served the same purpose almost constantly. For example, on the day of an earthquake that "lasted ab[ou]t a minute," 18 November 1755, the Reverend Samuel Chandler's prayers centered on the event. In addition, he noted, "we sang Ps. 68 : 8 and 77 : 16, 18, and 99 : 1, 5."[33] Even without a formal homily, the improvement of the tremor should have been clear to anyone who sang the verses that Chandler lined out to them:

> The earth shook, the heavens also dropped at the presence of God: even Sinai itself was moved at the presence of God, the God of Israel.
> The waters saw thee, O God, the waters saw thee: they were afraid: the depths also were troubled.
> The voice of thy thunder was in the heaven; the lightnings lightened the world: the earth trembled and shook.
> The Lord reigneth; let the people tremble: he sitteth between the cherubims; let the earth be moved.
> Exalt ye the Lord our God, and worship at his footstool; for he is holy.

30. John Cleaveland, 2 July 1758; Constantine Hardy, 8 July 1759.
31. John Cleaveland (Luke 13:2–3, Ezek. 33:11), 23 July (Mal. 1:6), 13 Aug. (Gen. 28:15, Ps. 84:11), 20 Aug. 1758 (Josh. 7:1–13).
32. See Appendix D.
33. Samuel Chandler, 18 Nov. 1755.

The earthquake, in other words, had been the handiwork of the Lord. It reflected his power and majesty; it illustrated his sovereign rule and placed his people (indeed, the whole creation) in fear; it called forth the exaltations of the faithful in worship and praise. The psalm thus explained the cause of the event, adumbrated its meaning, and gave directions on the appropriate response. In this it paralleled, in a highly compressed form, the classic Puritan sermon pattern of text, doctrine, and application.

Not all sermons were specifically adapted to current events; they were sometimes suited in ways not obvious from the evidence in the fragmentary record of the soldiers' journals. Chaplains often preached general-purpose sermons on soldierly conduct, either prescribing norms—for which they drew mainly upon the New Testament—or (less frequently) thundering against wickedness, for which they resorted to the prophetic books of the Old Testament. More often than any other set of themes, chaplains preached on the attributes of the Deity, and their portrait of God had a strongly Calvinist cast. Drawing largely upon passages from the Psalms, these sermons emphasized God's power, sovereignty, greatness, justice, and omniscience. The rest of the sermons on God's nature, which dealt with his mercy, love, and faithfulness, drew more extensively upon New Testament sources, especially the epistles of Paul. New Testament-based sermons otherwise concerned faith, prayer, discipleship, and promises of eternal reward—and the Last Judgment.

God's judgment, both immediate (in the form of temporal afflictions) and final, was yet another major theme expounded in the military sermons. Like the Covenant, God's active advocacy of Israel, and the Lord's majestic attributes, themes of judgment were not unique to the military, but, rather, marked the chaplains' adaptation of traditional New England clerical concerns to military audiences. The war was a time of high millennial expectation, and the sermons on God's judgment reflected the larger chiliasm of the time and region.[34] The absence of sermons on the classic millennial texts, however, especially the Book of Daniel, and the fact that Revelation 20 was preached only once, suggest that the chaplains made their eschatological emphases less to arouse soldiers' expectations of an immediate end than to fix the war within the larger pattern of God's judging providences. In doing so, the chaplains would have given pattern and meaning to occurrences that were otherwise confusing and frightening and

34. See Nathan O. Hatch, *The Sacred Cause of Liberty: Republican Thought and the Millennium in Revolutionary New England* (New Haven, Conn., 1977), 1–54; James West Davidson, *The Logic of Millennial Thought: Eighteenth-Century New England* (New Haven, Conn., 1977), esp. 196–215; Sacvan Bercovitch, *The American Jeremiad* (Madison, Wis., 1978), 115–118; and Alan Heimert, *Religion and the American Mind from the Great Awakening to the Revolution* (Cambridge, Mass., 1966), 13–14, 84–86, 324, and *passim*.

lent a measure of certainty to lives that were uncertain in the extreme. However indeterminate the temporal events that soldiers experienced, they were assured that the final outcome was never in doubt. God was working out his eternally conceived design for the world, a progression that would ultimately end in the New Creation. So long as the soldiers of New England remained on God's side and did his will, their preachers told them, they might share in the kingdom to come.

The chaplains, in serving as interpreters of the war to the men who were fighting it, used the intellectual and religious materials at hand, language and concepts that were familiar to the New England provincials. The figure and presence of the parson himself were equally familiar, and soldiers had a definite conception of how their preachers should behave. At different times Lemuel Wood and Samuel Jenks served in regiments burdened with a poor chaplain—William Crawford of Worcester, a young man who had not yet made up his mind whether to follow the vocation of pastor or that of physician. Wood sensed a certain lack of commitment on Crawford's part; he was, furthermore, a brief and infrequent preacher, which fact incensed both soldiers. On 8 July 1759, when Wood heard him preach the first time, he noted that the sermon was "about ten minutes long"; he heard "a piece" of a sermon on 5 August and another, "about seventeen minutes" long a week later.[35] Jenks echoed these complaints against Crawford in 1760. The first time he heard one of his sermons, the diarist noted "he stood eight minutes by the watch," to the chagrin of the audience.[36] Jenks was twenty-eight years old, a commissioned officer and a reflective man who spent his spare time in writing and reading (Milton on at least one occasion); Wood was a seventeen-year-old private with a common-school education and no discernible reflective tendencies. But despite their differing backgrounds, Wood and Jenks agreed closely about the chaplaincy. Both men took preaching seriously and wanted to hear it in larger quantities than they got from Crawford; both disliked the chaplain's timidity. Furthermore, Crawford preached in a dry, rationalist style, which helped further to alienate his audiences.[37]

Infrequent preaching, timidity, and excessive rationalism were characteristics no one could have ascribed to the Reverend John Cleaveland, chaplain to Colonel Jonathan Bagley's regiment in 1758 and 1759. Far from complaining of his sermons or his pastoral style, witnesses applauded them.

35. Lemuel Wood, 8 July, 5, 12, 26 Aug., 2 Sept. 1759.

36. Samuel Jenks, 5 Oct., 21 Sept. 1760.

37. L. H. Butterfield, ed., *Diary and Autobiography of John Adams*, I: *Diary, 1755–1770* (Cambridge, Mass., 1961), 43–44 (entry for 22 Aug. 1756); see also William Crawford to John Adams, 13 Jan. 1760 in Robert J. Taylor, ed., *Papers of John Adams*, I: *September 1755–October 1773* (Cambridge, Mass., 1977), 38.

Cleaveland's rough-hewn preaching—spontaneous, straightforward, and from the heart—had been practiced as a New Light country pastor and was perfectly suited to the task of addressing, usually in the open air, crowds that sometimes numbered in the thousands.[38] Cleaveland saw the war as a great opportunity to reach men with the gospel, a concern intensified by his conviction that the army needed to be a God-pleasing body in order to be an effectual instrument in the hands of the Lord. Thus Cleaveland was especially encouraged by the attendance of regular soldiers at his sermons, since he regarded them as the least likely to be converts already and the least likely to have been exposed to "affecting" preaching.[39] When he arrived at Louisbourg in 1759, for example, Cleaveland received a letter from one of the redcoat privates there that he found so encouraging he copied it into a letter to his wife. The soldier wrote that Cleaveland's arrival had answered his prayers for a godly preacher at the wicked fortress. "This from a regular soldier," Cleaveland marveled, delighted to see a harbinger of the Holy Spirit among the British. "It is said," he added,

> there is a number among them seriously disposed and inclined. The Lord increase the number, and make me an instrument thereof. I need help from above to be wise and faithful. I desire you and the Christian friends to pray for me that I may be a fisher of men and may cast the net on the right side of the ship.[40]

Cleaveland was less pleased with the deportment of regular officers. He was flattered by the fortress's second in command, Lord Andrew Rollo, who complimented Cleaveland's sermons and advocated him over the hard-drinking, foul-mouthed Anglican priest who was the chaplain of the regular regiments. But Cleaveland was not deceived. He knew, he wrote his wife, that Rollo was not yet "a man of real and eminent piety and godliness"—although he hoped that Rollo might eventually become such a man.[41]

It is unlikely that Cleaveland ever held out such hopes for his command-

---

38. On Cleaveland's style, see Christopher M. Jedrey, *The World of John Cleaveland: Family and Community in Eighteenth-Century New England* (New York, 1979), 107–108. For satisfaction with his preaching see, e.g., Caleb Rea, 18 June, 15 Oct. 1758; Joseph Nichols, 23 July, 6 Aug., 23 Sept. 1758. Although Cleaveland never made specific estimates of the size of the crowds that heard him, he often spoke of large numbers in attendance (e.g., 18 June, 23 July, 13 Aug., 10 Sept., 15 Oct. 1758). Another preacher, Henry True of Hampstead, New Hampshire, recorded addressing crowds that numbered 2,000–3,000 (Henry True [1759], 11 July 1762).

39. See, e.g., John Cleaveland, 23, 30 July, 6, 13, 27 Aug., 1, 15 Oct. 1758.

40. John Cleaveland to Mary Cleaveland, 3 Aug. 1759, JCP, III, 191–193.

41. *Ibid.*, 22 Aug. 1759, 194–195.

ing officer of 1758, General James Abercromby. On 4 July 1758, just before the expedition had left the head of Lake George for Ticonderoga, Abercromby had invited the chaplains to his quarters. He entertained them civilly enough, Cleaveland noted, but in the course of his remarks he told a story that Cleaveland apparently found distasteful. He said that he hoped the chaplains "would teach the people their duty and to be courageous. [He] told us a story of a chaplain in Germany, where he was, that just before the action the chaplain told the soldiers that he had not time to say much and therefore all that he should say would be in these words: 'Be courageous, for no cowards would go to Heaven.'"[42]

Abercromby saw the chaplain's duty in a purely practical light, as a means of aiding the army by improving the soldiers' performance. Cleaveland, on the other hand, knew that the chaplain's role was much more important than that. He believed that chaplains were there to proclaim the counsel of God, to help the members of the army reconcile themselves to God's will. "The Lord follow the wars with his blessing," Cleaveland prayed, "and make me an instrument of convincing and converting sinners and edifying and comforting the small number of saints that appear amongst us here. Amen and Amen."[43] War offered opportunities to spread the kingdom of God even as it fulfilled his providential design. Cleaveland was too thorough a realist to suppose that there was much chance for a regular army full of hardened sinners to be fully converted. But the provincials were in the field, too, and among them, he hoped, God could find a "small number of saints," like the saving remnant in Israel, upon whom to rely.

Ministers thus had a twofold duty. They had to take advantage of whatever opportunities to propagate the gospel that God would send their way, even as they cared for and spiritually nurtured the army's crucial core of righteous men. The burden of the chaplaincy was the military equivalent of the civilian parson's responsibilities of evangelism, reformation, and pastoral care; yet at war there was more at stake than in civil life, and the temptations to wickedness were greater. For Cleaveland the success of the army in some sense rested on the efficacy of its chaplains. He or any other orthodox Calvinist would have stopped short of maintaining that any specific person or group of people could be crucial to the army's welfare. Still, this would in no way have decreased in his mind the importance of the *office* of the chaplain.

The pervasiveness of providential language in the soldiers' reflections, like the importance of the chaplain in the provincial army, cannot be taken

42. John Cleaveland, 4 July 1758.
43. John Cleaveland, 13 Aug. 1758.

to mean that provincial forces were overwhelmingly pious. After all, John Cleaveland asked for God's blessing upon "the *small* number of saints that appear amongst us here," and provincials complained of wickedness and vile language among their fellows, as well as among the redcoats.[44] Yet the same soldiers' writings offer evidence of considerable piety among the New England troops. Soldiers were known to hold their own prayer meetings in the absence of chaplains, for example; they attended divine service and public prayer in large numbers; they sought out their pastors for guidance and resorted to religious books for solace; they took notes on sermons and independently evaluated the quality of what they heard.[45] Most significantly, however, any attempt to assess the piety of the provincials invites the misinterpretation of their providential passages as *merely* religious.

What the provincials were doing in the reflective passages of their journals was describing their experience in the vocabulary of meaning and abstraction that was most accessible to them, a vocabulary inculcated by common-school educations and continually refreshed by the exhortations of their pastors. Whether the soldiers of New England were personally devout men matters less than the fact that, if they wanted to think seriously or abstractly about their experiences at all, the profound religiosity of New England's formal discourse offered them few alternatives to thinking in religious terms. This is not to say that other vocabularies of thought were wholly lacking: the lexicons of the law and of politics offered alternatives that would largely displace religious terminology within the next half-century. But legal expression and metaphor were entirely absent from the diaries, and examples of whiggish political vocabulary occurred on only two occasions in the diarists' reflections.[46] Either the soldiers were not

44. In fact there were comparatively few complaints specifically concerning provincial behavior; but see John Graham, 7, 18 Aug. 1756; John Cleaveland to Mary Cleaveland, 10 June 1758, JCP, III, 158–159; Joseph Nichols, 8 June 1758 (both this and the previous complaint seem to have been about bad behavior that was corrected shortly thereafter by provincial leaders); David Holdin, 5 May 1760; Nathaniel Dwight, 13 Nov. 1755; "A Good Advice from a Gentle Man to the Soldiers in Fort Cumberland, October 6, 1759," Boyd's orderly book (1759).

45. Prayer meetings: Stephen Cross, 4, 18 Apr. 1756; Seth Metcalf, 8 May 1757; Putnam, *Memoirs*, 11; Luke Gridley, 1 May 1757. Attendance at divine services: John Cleaveland, 18 June, 2, 23 July, 6, 13, 27 Aug., 3, 17 Sept., 1, 15 Oct. 1758. Seek out pastors: Samuel Chandler, 23 Oct. 1755; John Cleaveland, 5 Aug. 1758; John Cleaveland to Mary Cleaveland, 10 Aug. 1759, JCP, III, 193–194. Seek solace in religious books: Joseph Nichols, 12 July 1758; Samuel Jenks, 19 Oct. 1760. Evaluation of sermons: Lemuel Wood, 8 July, 5, 12 Aug. 1759; Caleb Rea, 23 July 1758, and *passim*; Samuel Jenks, 21 Sept. 1760, and *passim*; Nathaniel Dwight, 2 Nov. 1755, and *passim*.

46. Seth Pomeroy, 10 Oct. 1755; Gibson Clough, 30 Sept. 1759. Clough spoke of "slavery" and of being "debarred Englishmen's liberty" when he was compelled to serve past the end of his enlistment term. Pomeroy wrote of the "tyranny" of a fellow officer in such a way

fully aware of such alternative ways of expressing themselves, or they simply found the providential framework to be the one most satisfactory for interpreting their wartime experiences.

III

Soldiers' writings offer a multitude of clues to the comprehensive operation of the providential mentality. The most compelling, sustained example of a popular providentialist interpretation of wartime events, however, comes not from the soldiers' diaries, but from an anonymous ballad concerning the events of 1755. This remarkable poem of forty-seven couplets was transcribed "not later than 1796" in Worcester County, Massachusetts, apparently from a version that was then current.[47] It takes the form of an account rendered by one who speaks for survivors of 1755, recounting the occurrences of the year, describing their significance, and offering advice. It is possible that the author had firsthand experience in the provincial army, since the themes addressed in the ballad are identical to those found in soldiers' diaries. The ballad speaks of the importance to soldiers of pecuniary motives, of the providential meanings of victory and defeat, of the prominence of chaplains in provincial forces, of God's active intervention in battle, of the cosmic import of natural phenomena, and of the heavy toll of disease in the last months of a campaign. The narrator begins with a prologue:

> We that did live in 'fifty-five,
> That were preserved and kept alive,
> We may record what God has done
> Beneath the circuit of the sun.
>
> How he displayed his mighty power
> And passed before us in an hour,
> In various ways which he did take,
> By thunderstorms and the earthquake.

---

as to suggest that his personal understanding of the term could be extended to include something like "high-handedness." Both usages were in line with commonwealthman vocabulary, but were limited and much out of the ordinary. Clough reflected repeatedly in religious terms, as did Pomeroy; thus while both men were clearly acquainted with secular discourse, both preferred to rely on providential language to gauge the meaning of their experiences. (For a more complete discussion of this point, see Anderson, "War and the Bay Colony," II, 583–584.)

47. S. A. Green, "Note," Mass. Hist. Soc., *Procs.*, 2d Ser., IX (1894), 2; "Verses Relating to the Events of 1755," *ibid.*, 3–5.

Thus the narrator speaks as a witness not just of the events of 1755 but of God's own doings. The ballad proper begins by recognizing the chastising purpose of war and then describing the process of enlistment.

> First in the spring the wars begin,
> To punish men then for their sin;
> They beat their drums and so they cry,
> Who will unto the battle fly?
>
> They list amain with courage bold,
> Their armor bright and money told.
> The time comes on, they must not stay,
> But quit their friends and go away;
>
> While husbands parting with their dears,
> And mothers for their sons in tears,
> Not knowing but that they must die
> Or go into captivity.

Pecuniary considerations receive equal play here with the courage of the soldiers, and the general depiction of the recruits' departure stresses the recruits' family bonds. These are not rootless riffraff, but good New England family men: the loss of a soldier will mean not just the loss of an individual life but the bereavement of a wife or a mother.

The first events of the year are the New Englanders' successful actions against the French in Acadia: the taking of Forts Beauséjour and Gaspereau, followed by the expulsion of the neutral French civilians and the expropriation of their property.

> They first arrive at eastward shores,
> Where drums do beat and cannons roar;
> A hero spirit they retain,
> Which puts the Frenchmen to great pain.
>
> They take their forts and so possess
> Their pastures and their wilderness.
> The joyful news spreads o'er the land
> That we have gained the upper hand.

New England's rejoicing is short-lived, however, since news arrives almost simultaneously of Braddock's defeat at the Monongahela. The narrator introduces a millennialist characterization of the enemy, and it becomes clear that the war has eschatological significance.

> But then a cloud o'erspread the sky,
> For Braddock and his men did die;

They lost the day and so did fly,
And fell before the enemy.

Their foes rejoice and shout aloud,
And Antichrist grows very proud;
While we are mourning in distress
The widow and the fatherless.

In the summer a second provincial expedition leaves New England, intending this time to strike against the enemy at Lake Champlain. The great advantage they enjoy in this expedition is the presence of their dark-robed chaplains (figurally, the bearers of the ark of the covenant) who enjoin the Lord to forgive New England's sins and sustain its contribution to the holy cause.

The spring is gone and passed away,
And then comes on the summer's day,
While nature smileth with her charms
While we are claspèd in her arms.

But yet again there is a cry
To 'list and fight the enemy.
Another army is gone forth
To meet the heathen in the north.

Towards Crown Point they also go,
To meet the fury of the foe.
While they have teachers in the dark,
Christ's ministers to bear the Ark,

Which pray unto the God of heaven
That all their sins may be forgiven;
And we may hope for victory,
When we in faith to God do cry.

Summer ends. The year's third (and climactic) battle is finally joined at Lake George on 8 September 1755, beginning with the "Bloody Morning Scout," the provincial reconnaissance in force that first engages the French.

The summer now is passed away,
And then comes on a bloody day;
They go to meet and so do spy
The faces of the enemy.

A furious fight comes on amain
And many valiant men are slain;

> Of all the battles now the third
> Was fought with garments rolled in blood.

God responds to the prayers of his people, intervenes in favor of New England, and throws the French into confusion. The Lord gives the provincials victory—and loot.

> A frightful noise and hideous yell,
> As though it came from the jaws of Hell;
> The smoke did as a cloud arise,
> While Christian prayers did pierce the skies.
>
> And God did hear when they did call
> And Antichrist received a fall.
> Oh, may she bleed and also die,
> That Christ may gain the victory!
>
> They quit the field with shameful flight,
> As though they saw it dark as night.
> Our men did plunder on the place,
> And smiles returnèd to their face.

Despite this mighty favoring providence, after the victory the army falls into sinful ways and provokes the Lord to wrath. He punishes them, not by the hand of their enemy, but by sickness. As mortality levels rise late in the campaign, camp diseases reach epidemic levels among the troops at Fort William Henry:

> But yet our God, provoked by sin,
> Did cause the plague to enter in;
> And those that 'scaped the enemy
> Did fall by sickness and did die.

God sent a further warning early in the morning of 18 November: an earthquake to shake New England into a sensibility of its offenses and to precipitate his people's repentance. Even as New Englanders ponder this sign, however, they are made to understand how great their peril and how tolerant the Lord has heretofore been. Word arrives that on 1 November Lisbon was devastated by an immensely more powerful earthquake.

> While we was sleeping on our beds,
> The Lord did shake our drowsy heads,
> Saying, Awake, ye sleepy fools,
> Lest ye are drownèd in the pools;
>
> Yea, rise and call upon your God,
> Lest he sends forth his dreadful rod.

The trembling earth doth testify
He is displeased and angery.

Hear the sad noise from Lisbon town,
Which shook and fell unto the ground;
And multitudes there buried were
In the dark regions of despair.

The message of 1755 is unmistakable. The Lord has foreborne much but will not stay his righteous hand forever. New England must repent and submit to God's holy will, or he will destroy it, root and branch.

And now, O land, New England land,
Amazèd be, and trembling stand,
Because the Judge stands at the door;
Forsake your sins, repent therefore.

These are the hints which I have made
In 'fifty-five it shall be said.

This ballad demonstrates the durable vitality of popular providential understandings of the war and its significance, at least within Massachusetts. Its redaction at the end of the eighteenth century suggests that the song enjoyed some currency through the Revolutionary period. The song proffers stern advice, based on lessons learned by those who remember the events of the war. The lessons are as timeless as they are powerful: God shapes temporal events to his own ends and judges sinners for their iniquity; the course of wisdom is repentance and reliance upon his mercy. Yet by the time the ballad was finally written down, the outcome of the war was known, too: the destruction of the French papist threat in all of North America. The song would thus have carried a second, equally significant message for anyone who sang or heard it after about 1761 or 1762. New England *did* repent, and the Lord *did* use his people to accomplish the glorious end he had intended all along.

For the provincials as for those who listened to the ballad of 1755, the war functioned as a striking confirmation of the exceptionalist traditions of New England culture. Unlike World War I, which blasted into irrelevance the values and vocabulary of the world that existed before August 1914, the Seven Years' War reinforced and intensified the New England provincials' received understanding of their world. The death and suffering that every soldier witnessed brought him face to face with God's judgment, even as the final victory demonstrated God's continuing favor for the people of his covenant. Campaigning created a common set of experiences for the young men of Massachusetts, most of whom were far from their birthplace for the first time in their lives. Military service for them meant experiencing a new and wider kind of community, composed of men from every part of New England, united in a common cause against their region's historic enemies. Military service also exposed most of them to the British for the first time in their lives. They encountered enlisted men who were undeniably different from themselves and who were treated with shocking brutality by their aristocratic officers—members of a social class that had no real counterpart in the Bay Colony. The war gave the provincials a sense, at a crucial point in their lives, of their identity as a distinct people. It provided a shared set of reference points, a unifying groundwork of experience that knit their generation more closely together than any other in New England since the Great Migration. The war in effect offered a brief, advanced education for its soldiers, an education made memorable by the conditions under which it occurred. The war's lessons touched powerfully on elements of New England culture that ranged from its formal Calvinist providentialism to its everyday emphasis on the centrality of contracts to social relations.

But as well as they learned their lessons, the soldiers did not go home intent on revolution. Far from it: they expected only to begin making their way in what should have been a newly peaceful and prosperous colony, safe under the protection of the world's mightiest empire. When the government of Great Britain began to behave with unwonted harshness toward its American subjects, however, countrymen in every town of Massachusetts found themselves drawn toward agreement on the significance of events. As spokesmen for political (and later military) resistance began to make themselves heard in Boston, the veterans in the countryside could scarcely ignore the similarities between what they were hearing and what they themselves had witnessed during the last war. Public criticism of the British, couched in the terms of republican rhetoric, found a ready confirmation in the veterans' personal experiences. The provincials who matured in the 1770s were not ideologues, bent on making a revolution; nor were they driven to revolutionary action by the operation of inexorable economic forces. They were merely men who found themselves agreeing that they and their way of life were being threatened by other men: not by the abstract forces of corruption and power, but by flesh-and-blood men, whom they personally knew to be capable of behaving in disturbing, threatening ways. As the great imperial crisis gathered momentum through the late 1760s and the 1770s, the collective military experience of Massachusetts' veterans thus promoted the widespread agreement that was necessary to transform their province, in an astonishingly short time, from the British Empire's most enthusiastic advocate into its most intractable opponent.

Appendix A ❖ Tables
Massachusetts Provincial Forces during
the Seven Years' War

Unless otherwise noted, these tables are based on the analyzed descriptive lists of July and August 1756 and the condition rolls of 11 and 12 October 1756, in "Muster Rolls, 1755–1756," Vol. XCIV of the Massachusetts Archives, at the State House, Boston.

Table 1
Wages and Bounties of Private Soldiers (in Lawful Money)

Year	Duration of Campaign	Monthly Wage £ s. d.	Bounty		Total Income	
			Minimum £ s. d.	Maximum £ s. d.	Minimum £ s. d.	Maximum £ s. d.
1754	3 mos.	1 6 0	2 0 0		5 18 0	
1755	8 mos.	1 6 8	2 18 0	4 14 0	13 10 10	15 6 8
1756	8 mos.	1 12 0	2 8 0ᵃ	5 14 0	15 4 0	18 4 0
1757	8 mos.	1 16 0	4 2 7ᵇ		18 10 7	
1758	8 mos.	1 16 0	14 12 0ᵃ		29 0 0	
1759	8 mos.	1 16 0	6 12 0ᵃ	14 12 0	21 0 0	29 0 0
1760	8 mos.	1 16 0	12 0 0ᵃ	26 12 0ᶜ	27 0 0	41 16 0ᵈ
1761	8 mos.	1 16 0	9 0 0ᵇ		23 8 0	36 0 0ᵈ
1762	8 mos.	1 16 6	9 0 0	19 12 0ᶜ	23 12 0	41 10 0ᵈ

Sources: *The Acts and Resolves, Public and Private, of the Province of the Massachusetts-Bay,* XV (Boston, 1908), 144–145; 1755: XV, 299–300, 304, 311–312, 347; 1756: XV, 442, 454–455; 1757: XV, 669, 671, 686–687; 1758: XVI (1909), 160–161; 1759: XVI, 307–309, 348–349; 1760: XVI, 460–461, 567; 1761: XVI, 721–723; 1762: XVII (1910), 10, 177–178, 201.

ᵃIncludes blanket, approximate value 12s.
ᵇIncludes clothing, approximate value £2 6s. 7d. (in 1756) and £3 14s. 8d. (in 1761).
ᶜBased on reenlistment bonus for men currently serving.
ᵈAnnual wage and bounty compensation for men currently serving.

Table 2

Regiments of 1756, with Unit Strengths

Regimental Commander	No. of Companies	Strength
Col. Jonathan Bagley	10	599
Col. Joseph Dwight	10	548
Col. Richard Gridley	9[a]	503
Col. Ichabod Plaisted	9	485
Col. Timothy Ruggles	9	458
Col. Joseph Thacher	9	432
Total	56	3,025[b]

[a] Includes the artillery train as one company.

[b] Total does not include 22 replacements who had not yet been assigned as of 11 and 12 Oct. 1756.

Table 3

Rank Composition, 1756

Rank	No.	Rank	No.
Enlisted men		Commissioned officers	
Centinel	2,288	Ensign	63
Corporal	219	Lieutenant	71
Sergeant	174	Captain	47
Clerk	56	Major[b]	1
Drummer	44	Lieutenant colonel[b]	1
Gunner	18	Colonel[b]	1
Bombardier	20	Adjutant[b]	1
Matross	39	Quartermaster[b]	1
Sergeant major[a]	1	Volunteer[c]	1
Drum major[a]	1		
Total (enlisted men)	2,860	Total (commissioned officers)	187

[a] Ranks without official sanction in the provincial establishment in 1756, apparently informal recognitions of precedence within a single regiment.

[b] Present on the lists by virtue of a clerk's special zeal, since there was no order for these to be included in the tally.

[c] A gentleman accompanying the army without formal rank, who was accorded the status of an officer and could be promoted to ensign if a vacancy occurred.

Table 4

Careers of Captains Serving in 1756

	Terms Served									Overall No. of Men
	1	2	3	4	5	6	7	8	9	
	No. of Men									
Captains in 1756	8	15	10	6	3	2	0	0	1	45
Continuity of Service										
Uninterrupted, more than one term		9	4	0	0	0			1	14
Interrupted by one or more years		6	6	6	3	2			0	23
Commanding officers served under										
1	8	1	1	0	0	0			0	10
2	0	9	7	2	1	1			0	20
3 or more	0	0	1	1	1	0			1	4
Unknown	0	5	1	3	1	1			0	11
Rank										
Same in all terms	8	13	3	3	1	1			0	29
Increased	0	2	2	2	2	1			0	9
Decreased or fluctuated	0	0	5	1	0	0			1	7

Source: Nancy S. Voye, ed., *Massachusetts Officers in the French and Indian Wars, 1748–1763* (Boston, 1975).

Note: Mean number of terms served by the 45 captains of 1756 was 2.8; median number was 2.0; mode was 2.0. For the captains serving in 1756, the year 1756 was the final term of service for 22; 1757, for 1; 1758, for 8; 1760, for 6; 1761, for 1; 1762, for 6; 1763, for 1.

Table 5
Careers of Field Officers

	Terms Served									Total in Rank	Avg. Service in Yrs.		
	1	2	3	4	5	6	7	8	9		Mean	Median	Mode
Rank	No. of Men												
Major	2	7	3	3	1	0	1	0	0	17	2.9	2	2
Lieutenant colonel	10	4	1	0	2	0	1	0	0	18	2.1	1	1
Colonel	12	11	2	3	2	1	1	0	1	33	2.5	2	1
Overall	24	22	6	6	5	1	3	0	1	68	2.5	2	1

Source: Nancy S. Voye, *Massachusetts Officers in the French and Indian Wars, 1748–1763* (Boston, 1975).
Note: All field officers who held only militia appointments are excluded.

Table 6
Promotions of Field Officers, by Average Length of Service and Rank

	Final Rank			
Initial Rank	Major	Lieutenant Colonel	Colonel	General Officer
Ensign	7 terms (1)			
Lieutenant	3.5 terms (2)			
Captain	3.3 terms (6)	5.7 terms (3)	8 terms (2)	
Major	1.9 terms (8)	2.3 terms (3)	4.3 terms (3)	
Lieutenant colonel		1.2 terms (12)	2.8 terms (5)	6 terms (1)
Colonel			1.7 terms (23)	4 terms (2)

Source: Nancy S. Voye, *Massachusetts Officers in the French and Indian Wars, 1748–1763* (Boston, 1975).
Note: Figures in parentheses are the total number of officers in each category.

Table 7
Number of Promotions of Field Officers, by
Length of Service

Number of Promotions	Number of Officers	Mean Length of Service
0	43	1.6 yrs.
1	16	3.0 yrs.
2	9	4.3 yrs.
3	3	7.7 yrs.

Source: Nancy S. Voye, *Massachusetts Officers in the French and Indian Wars, 1748–1763* (Boston, 1975).

Table 8
Conditions of Service, 1756

Condition of Service	No. of Men	% of Total
Voluntary	2,190	87.9
Impressed	54	2.2
Hired	247	9.9
Total	2,491	100.0

Table 9

Profile of Provincial Soldiers, 1756

Trait	Volunteer	Impressed	Hired
Age			
N	1,816[a]	53	238
Mean yrs.	25.6	27.4	28.7
Median yrs.	23	24	25
Rank			
N	2,190	54	247
Centinel	71.9%	81.5%	85.8%
Noncommissioned officer	15.7%	18.5%	10.1%
Officer	8.4%	0.0%	0.0%
Other	4.0%	0.0%	4.1%
Dwelling place			
N	2,190	54	247
Birthplace	49.9%	48.1%	38.9%
Native province	29.1%	38.9%	29.9%
Outside native province	21.0%	13.0%	31.2%
Occupation			
N	1,802[a]	50	236
Laboring	35.5%	46.0%	52.0%
Farming	17.9%	22.0%	6.0%
Artisanal	40.7%	26.0%	36.0%
Maritime	3.7%	4.0%	6.0%
Nonmanual	2.2%	2.0%	0.0%
Skill level			
N	2,190	54	247
Less skilled	32.2%	49.0%	57.4%
More skilled	30.6%	20.6%	25.9%
Unknown or not applicable	37.2%	30.4%	16.7%
Physical condition at close of campaign			
N	2,190	54	247
Present and fit	53.5%	31.5%	48.2%
Sick	22.7%	33.3%	26.3%
Dead	5.7%	3.7%	9.7%
MIA, POW	0.8%	1.9%	1.6%
AWOL	4.2%	1.9%	6.1%
On leave	4.7%	9.3%	4.5%
Dropped from roll	8.4%	18.5%	3.7%

[a]Excludes officers.

Table 10
Age Distribution of Provincial Troops, 1756

Age Group	N	%	Cumulative %
14–19	591	24.7	24.7
20–24	758	31.7	56.4
25–29	395	16.5	72.9
30–34	208	8.7	81.6
35–39	158	6.6	88.2
40–44	117	4.9	93.1
45–49	87	3.6	96.7
50–54	48	2.0	98.7
55 +	29	1.2	99.9

Note: Deviations in percentage totals from 100.0 are a function of rounding.

Table 11
Residence at Enlistment by Colony, 1756

	N	%
Massachusetts	2,410	93.8
New Hampshire	106	4.1
Connecticut	34	1.3
Rhode Island	16	0.6
New York and Nova Scotia	2	0.1
Total	2,568	99.9

Table 12
Residence at Enlistment by Massachusetts County, 1756

	N	%
Essex	496	20.6
Suffolk	488	20.2
Worcester	337	14.0
Middlesex	280	11.6
Plymouth	270	11.2
Hampshire	206	8.5
Bristol	173	7.2
York	124	5.1
Barnstable	36	1.5
Total	2,410	99.9

Table 13
Birthplace by Province or Region, 1756

	N	%
Massachusetts	2,013	82.4
New Hampshire	83	3.4
Connecticut	72	3.0
Rhode Island	28	1.2
Other, North America	22	0.9
Colonies outside North America	12	0.5
Great Britain	193	7.9
Continental Europe	19	0.8
Total	2,442	100.1

Table 14
Birthplace of Massachusetts Natives, by County, 1756

	N	%
Essex	515	25.6
Suffolk	370	18.4
Middlesex	330	16.4
Plymouth	224	11.1
Worcester	173	8.6
Bristol	152	7.6
Hampshire	94	4.7
York	94	4.7
Barnstable	60	3.0
Nantucket	1	0.05
Total	2,013	100.15

Table 15
Birthplace of Nonnatives of Massachusetts, 1756

	N	%
Great Britain		
England, Wales	57	13.3
Scotland	10	2.3
Ireland	120	28.0
Channel Islands	6	1.4
Total (Great Britain)	193	45.0
Continental Europe		
France	6	1.4
Germany	6	1.4
Portugal	2	0.5
Spain	1	0.2
Switzerland	2	0.5
Holland	1	0.2
Total (Continental Europe)	19	4.4
Other colonies		
New England	183	42.7
Other, North America	22	5.1
Outside North America	12	2.8
Total (other colonies)	217	50.6
Total	429	100.0

Table 16
Persistence in Region of Birth of Massachusetts Natives, by Occupation, 1756

	Persistence until Enlistment							
	Artisans		Laborers		Farmers		All Occupations	
	N	%	N	%	N	%	N	%
Original Bay Colony counties	467	55.5	269	55.0	210	41.0	1,207	56.8
Old Colony counties	138	53.6	214	69.2	37	48.6	433	63.4
Western counties	50	36.0	42	54.8	142	66.2	267	59.9
York County	30	43.3	29	59.2	3	100.0	85	58.8
Overall Massachusetts	685	53.1	554	60.7	392	51.3	1,992	58.7

Table 17
Levels of Movement Prior to Enlistment, by Cohort, 1756

Cohort	N	Remained in Birthplace	Moved within Native County	Left Native County	Left Native Province or Country
14–19	591	55.7%	15.6%	15.1%	13.7%
20–24	758	52.8	15.8	13.9	17.5
25–29	395	44.1	15.9	19.2	20.8
30–34	208	47.6	16.8	12.0	23.6
35–39	158	32.3	18.4	24.7	24.7
40–44	117	41.9	16.2	15.4	26.5
45–49	87	33.3	21.8	14.9	29.9
50–54	48	27.1	12.5	12.5	47.9
55 +	29	24.1	3.4	34.5	37.9
Overall	2,391	48.1	16.1	15.9	19.9

Table 18

Levels of Movement Prior to Enlistment, by Average Age, 1756

	Remained in Birthplace	Moved within Native County	Left Native County	Left Native Province or Country, Overall	Emigrated from Britain
N	1,151	384	381	475	171
Mean age	24.8	26.4	27.3	28.9	29.8
Median age	22	23	24	25	27
Modal age	18	20	18	21	24

Table 19

Occupational Distribution, Massachusetts Natives and British Immigrants, 1756

Occupational Group	Massachusetts Natives		British Immigrants	
	N	%	N	%
Farmer	392	19.7	16	9.4
Laborer	554	27.8	44	25.7
Artisan	685	34.4	56	32.7
Seafarer	41	2.1	17	9.9
Nonmanual worker	21	1.1	11	6.4
Unknown	299	15.0	27	15.8
Total	1,992	100.1	171	99.9

Table 20

Occupational Distribution among Artisans, by Trade, Massachusetts Natives and British Immigrants, 1756

Trade	Massachusetts Natives		British Immigrants	
	N	%	N	%
Woodworking	220	32.1	11	19.6
Leatherworking	175	25.5	7	12.5
Metalworking	97	14.2	8	14.3
Maritime	68	9.9	0	0.0
Cloth working	67	9.8	12	21.4
Other manufacturing	20	2.9	7	12.5
Nonwood-based housing	19	2.8	3	5.4
Consumer goods	14	2.0	3	5.4
Food-processing	5	0.7	5	8.9
Total	685	99.9	56	100.0

Table 21
Occupational Distribution, by Rank, 1756

Rank	N	Farmers	Laborers	Artisans	Sea-farers	Non-manual Workers	Un-known
Centinel	1,734	19.3%	35.8%	33.4%	3.6%	1.2%	6.7%
Corporal	201	20.9	24.4	43.8	4.5	0.5	6.0
Sergeant	159	23.9	11.9	50.9	3.1	1.9	8.2
Ensign	40	27.5	2.5	40.0	0.0	2.5	27.5
Lieutenant	51	15.7	2.0	27.5	0.0	9.8	45.1
Captain	29	24.1	0.0	24.1	0.0	10.3	41.3
Clerk	53	18.9	9.4	50.9	5.7	9.4	5.7
Drummer	42	19.0	33.3	35.7	2.4	4.8	4.8
Overall	2,309	19.8	30.8	35.8	3.5	1.8	8.3

Note: The program that generated these figures, BREAKDOWN, requires a continuous variable, in this case age, as the criterion variable. Consequently, these percentages are for men of known age only, and not for the entire army. The net effect is the exclusion of 82 cases, or approximately 3.4% of the possible cases.

Table 22
Average Age of Principal Ranks, 1756

Rank	N	Averages		
		Mean	Median	Mode
Centinel	1,734	25.8	22	18
Noncommissioned officers				
Corporal	201	26.2	24	22
Sergeant	159	29.8	26	25
Overall	360	27.8	25	22
Commissioned officers				
Ensign	40	28.1	26	22
Lieutenant	51	31.6	30	26
Captain	29	35.2	32	32
Overall	120	32.8	30	26
Overall (all ranks)[a]	2,391	26.3	23	18

[a] Includes the ranks of clerk, drummer, gunner, bombardier, matross, adjutant, quartermaster, major, lieutenant colonel, and colonel.

Table 23
Mean Age of Various Ranks, by Occupation, 1756

		Mean Age					
Rank	N	Farm-ers	Labor-ers	Arti-sans	Sea-farers	Non-manual Workers	Un-known
Centinel	1,734	26.5	25.8	24.9	27.0	24.6	25.8
Corporal	201	26.1	26.5	26.5	26.3	25.0	29.7
Sergeant	159	31.6	29.7	29.0	28.4	33.7	29.3
Ensign	40	31.0	37.0	26.3		—	27.2
Lieutenant	51	34.8	40.0	28.2		32.5	32.3
Captain	29	37.1		33.4		43.0	34.5

Table 24
Levels of Movement at Enlistment, by Rank, 1756

Rank	N	Remained in Birthplace	Moved within Native County	Left Native County	Left Native Province
Centinel	1,619	46.6%	15.2%	16.7%	21.6%
Noncommissioned officers	335	46.9	20.6	17.0	15.5
Commissioned officers	70	48.6	25.7	17.1	8.6
Overall	2,024	46.7	16.5	16.7	20.1

Table 25
Residential Composition of Regiments, 1756

	Regiments (Regimental Strength[a] and Residence of Commander in Italics)					
Residences of Soldiers	Bagley's, *481, Amesbury*	Dwight's, *377, Brookfield*	Gridley's, *355, Boston*	Plaisted's, *388, Salem*	Ruggles's, *384, Hardwick*	Thacher's, *312, Yarmouth*
Suffolk	19.3%	2.4%	47.0%	2.8%	13.3%	19.6%
Middlesex	26.2	9.5	10.4	9.8	8.6	9.3
Essex	36.6	1.6	0.6	63.4	0.0	1.0
Plymouth	0.0	6.4	10.4	0.0	0.5	57.4
Bristol	0.4	11.1	18.0	0.0	12.5	1.9
Barnstable	0.0	0.0	0.0	0.0	0.0	9.6
Worcester	10.8	3.7	9.6	0.3	60.2	0.0
Hampshire	0.6	37.4	0.3	0.6	3.4	0.0
York	0.6	14.6	0.3	16.2	0.0	0.0
New Hampshire	5.2	4.8	1.4	7.0	1.6	0.0
Connecticut	0.0	6.6	0.8	0.0	0.0	1.3
Rhode Island	0.2	1.9	1.1	0.0	0.0	0.0
Total	99.9	100.0	99.9	100.1	100.1	100.1

Sources: Descriptive lists, in "Muster Rolls, 1755–1756," Vol. XCIV of the Massachusetts Archives, at the State House, Boston; Nancy S. Voye, ed., *Massachusetts Officers in the French and Indian Wars, 1748–1763* (Boston, 1975), for commanders' residences.

[a] Less replacements; men with known residences only.

Table 26
Overall Physical Condition of Troops, 1756

	Original Troops		Replacements		Overall	
Condition	N	%	N	%	N	%
Present and fit	1,365	50.9	299	81.7	1,664	54.6
Sick or wounded	606	22.6	44	12.0	650	21.3
Dead	154	5.7	2	0.5	156	5.1
MIA, POW	24	0.9	0	0.0	24	0.8
AWOL	122	4.6	13	3.6	135	4.4
Accounted absences	132	4.9	8	2.2	140	4.6
Dropped from rolls	278	10.4	0	0.0	278	9.1
Total	2,681	100.0	366	100.0	3,047	99.9

Note: Data as of 11, 12 October.

Table 27
Physical Condition of Troops, by Rank, 1756

Ranks	N	Present, Fit	Sick, Wounded	Dead	MIA, POW	AWOL	Ac-counted Absences	Dropped from Rolls
Officers	174	67.2%	13.2%	2.9%	0.6%	0.0%	4.0%	12.1%
Noncommissioned officers	388	60.3	24.7	4.1	0.5	0.0	4.4	5.9
Centinels	1,936	48.6	24.2	6.7	1.1	6.1	5.4	7.9

Note: Data as of 11, 12 October.

Table 28
Crude Death Rate, by Rank, 1756

Rank	N	Death Rate / 1000
Officers		
Captain	47	85.1
Lieutenant	70	0.0
Ensign	57	17.5
Overall (officers)	174	28.7
Noncommissioned officers		
Sergeant	172	40.7
Corporal	216	41.7
Overall (noncommissioned officers)	388	41.2
Centinel	1,936	61.7

Table 29
Physical Condition of Troops, by Age Cohort, 1756

Age Group	N	Present and Fit	Sick or Wounded	Dead	MIA, POW	AWOL	Ac-counted Absences	Dropped from Rolls
14–19	590	60.5%	21.5%	3.7%	2.0%	0.8%	3.1%	8.3%
20–24	753	55.1	21.4	6.5	0.9	3.1	4.6	8.4
25–29	394	56.3	20.6	4.1	0.5	5.8	5.1	7.6
30–34	208	43.3	23.1	6.2	0.5	5.8	7.7	13.5
35–39	155	41.3	28.4	4.5	0.0	6.5	7.1	12.3
40–44	116	37.1	30.2	6.9	0.9	5.2	6.9	12.9
45–49	87	21.8	40.2	16.1	0.0	2.3	9.2	10.3
50–54	47	27.7	36.2	14.9	0.0	12.8	2.1	6.4
55 +	29	17.2	34.5	27.6	0.0	6.9	10.3	3.5

Note: Data as of 11, 12 October.

Table 30
Crude Death Rate, by Age Cohort, 1756

Cohort	N	Death Rate / 1000
14–29		
14–19	590	37.0
20–24	753	65.0
25–29	394	40.6
Overall (14–29)	1,737	50.1
30–44		
30–34	208	62.5
35–39	155	45.2
40–44	116	69.0
Overall (30–44)	479	58.5
45–68		
45–49	87	160.9
50–54	47	148.9
55–68	29	275.9
Overall (45–68)	163	177.9

Table 31

Composition of General Courts-Martial in Amherst's Expeditionary Force, 1759

Date Convened	Type of Court-Martial	President	Membership	
			Regulars	Provincials
23 May	Line	Regular	7	5
10 June	Line	Regular	7	5
15 June	Line	Provincial	6	6
23 June	Line	Provincial	?	?
5 July	Line	Provincial	7	5
12 July	Regular	Regular	12	0
16 July	Line	Provincial	6	6
19 July	Regular	Regular	12	0
28 July	Line	Regular	12	0
7 August	Line	Provincial	7	5
13 August	Line	Provincial	5	4
11 September	Regular	Regular	12	0
13 September	Line	Provincial	6	6
3 October	Regular	Regular	12	0
30 October	Regular	Regular	12	0
31 October	Line	Provincial	6	6

Source: Wilson's orderly book (1759).

Appendix B ❖ Diaries and Orderly Books

The following list contains the soldiers' diaries and orderly books cited in the text. The entries are arranged in chronological order, by year of composition. (Diaries which run for more than one campaign are listed under the first year they cover.) Within each year, diaries and orderly books are arranged alphabetically. The right-hand column consists of a full citation for each entry; the left-hand column lists the short titles used in the footnotes to identify the journal or orderly book. A footnote citing a diary entry as "Seth Pomeroy, 1 Sept. 1755" thus would refer the reader first to the diaries for 1755, then (alphabetically) to the sixth entry in the left-hand column for that year. Opposite it is the full citation: Louis Effingham de Forest's edition of *The Journal and Papers of Seth Pomeroy, Sometime General in the Colonial Service* (New Haven, Conn., 1926), in which the 1755 diary is reprinted beginning on page 100.

About two-thirds of the journals below are straightforward accounts of daily life without further comment or embellishment; the ones that contain reflective passages have been identified with asterisks in the left column.

1754

John Barber	"Journal of Capt. Eleazer Melvin's Company, Shirley's Expedition, 1754. . . ." *New England Historical and Genealogical Register*, XXVII (1873), 281–286.

1755

*Samuel Chandler	"Extracts from the Diary of Rev. Samuel Chandler. . . ." *New England Historical and Genealogical Register*, XVII (1863), 346–354. MS at the American Antiquarian Society, Worcester, Mass.
*Nathaniel Dwight	"The Journal of Capt. Nathaniel Dwight of Belchertown, Mass., During the Crown

	Point Expedition, 1755." *New York Genea-logical and Biographical Record*, XXXIII (1902), 3–10, 65–70.
Elisha Hawley	James Russell Trumbull. *History of North-ampton*, II, 254–259. Northampton, Mass., 1902.
James Hill	Edna V. Moffett, ed. "The Diary of a Private on the First Expedition to Crown Point." *New England Quarterly*, V (1932), 602–618.
*Seth Metcalf (journal)	William S. Piper, ed. *Diary and Journal (1755–1807) of Seth Metcalf.* Boston, 1939. Journal of annual entries, 1755–1767, 1795–1807.
*Seth Pomeroy	Louis Effingham de Forest, ed. *The Journal and Papers of Seth Pomeroy, Sometime General in the Colonial Service*, 100–150. New Haven, Conn., 1926.
John Thomas	J. T. B., ed. "Diary of John Thomas." Nova Scotia Historical Society, *Collections*, I (1878), 119–140.
Abijah Willard	J. C. Webster, ed. "Journal of Abijah Willard of Lancaster, Mass." New Brunswick Historical Society, *Collections*, XIII (n.d.), 1–75.
John Winslow	"Journal of Colonel John Winslow, of the Provincial Troops, . . . 1755." Nova Scotia Historical Society, *Collections*, III (1882–1883), 71–196; IV (1884), 113–246.

1756

Anonymous (a commissary)	Soldier's diary, 1756, 1760 [misidentified as 1758 and 1760]. MS. French and Indian War Collection. American Antiquarian Society, Worcester, Mass.
*Stephen Cross	Sarah E. Mulliken, ed. "Journal of Stephen Cross, of Newburyport. . . ." Essex Institute, *Historical Collections*, LXXV (1939), 334–357; LXXVI (1940), 14–42.

*John Graham	"Original Documents." *Magazine of American History*, VIII (1882), 206–213.
*Samuel Greenleaf	Samuel Greenleaf Accounts, 1746–1776; Diary, 1756. MS Greenleaf. Massachusetts Historical Society, Boston.
Isaac Wyman	Diary of Isaac Wyman, in Arthur L. Perry, *Origins in Williamstown* (New York, 1896), 277–282.

1757

Jonathan French	Jonathan French Journal, 1757. MS. 74. William L. Clements Library, Ann Arbor, Mich.
Joseph Frye	"A Journal of the Attack of Fort William Henry by the French on the third day of August 1757 and the surrender on the 9th of the same month." MS copy. Parkman Papers, XLII, 137–153. Massachusetts Historical Society, Boston.
Luke Gridley	F. M., ed. *Luke Gridley's Diary of 1757 While in Service in the French and Indian War.* Hartford, Conn., 1906.
Lyman's orderly book	Worthington C. Ford, ed. *General Orders of 1757: Issued by the Earl of Loudoun and Phineas Lyman in the Campaign Against the French.* New York, 1899.
Seth Metcalf	William S. Piper, ed. *Diary and Journal (1755–1807) of Seth Metcalf.* Boston, 1939. Diary, 1757.

1758

| Anonymous (a centinel) | "The Anonymous Journal. . . ." Fort Ticonderoga Museum, *Bulletin*, XII (1968), 291–297. |
| Benjamin Bass | "Account of the Capture of Fort Frontenac, by the Attachment Under the Command of Col. Bradstreet." *New York History*, XVI (1935), 449–452. |

John Bradstreet	An Impartial Account of Lieut. Col. Bradstreet's Expedition to Fort Frontenac (Seventeen Fifty-Eight). Toronto, 1940.
Asa Burr	Asa Burr Journal, 1758. MS. French and Indian War Collection. American Antiquarian Society, Worcester, Mass.
*John Cleaveland	"Journal of Rev. John Cleaveland, June 14, 1758–October 25, 1758." Fort Ticonderoga Museum, Bulletin, X (1959), 192–233. MS at Fort Ticonderoga Museum, Ticonderoga, N.Y.
Moses Dorr	"A Journal of an Expedition Against Canaday By Moses Dorr Ensin of Capt Parkers Company Roxbury May 25th 1758." New York History, XVI (1935), 452–464.
Asa Foster	"Diary of Capt. Asa Foster of Andover. . . ." New England Historical and Genealogical Register, LIV (1900), 183–188.
*Archelaus Fuller	"Journal of Col. Archelaus Fuller of Middleton. . . ." Essex Institute, Historical Collections, XLVI (1910), 209–220. (Fuller was, however, a lieutenant in 1758, not a colonel.)
*Obadiah Harris	MS. HM 591. Henry E. Huntington Library, San Marino, Calif.
*James Henderson	James Henderson Journal, 1758, 1759. MS. New England Historic and Genealogical Society Library, Boston.
Joseph Holt	Frederic Kidder, ed. "Journals of Joseph Holt, of Wilton, N.H., in the Canada Expedition of 1758." New England Historical and Genealogical Register, X (1856), 307–311.
Nathaniel Knap	"The Diary of Nathaniel Knap of Newbury." Society of Colonial Wars in the Commonwealth of Massachusetts, Publications, II (1895), 1–42.
Henry Lyon	William H. Hill, ed. "Lyon's Journal." In Hill, Addenda: Old Fort Edward Before 1800. Campaigns of 1756–58–60 (Fort Edward, New York, 1956), 23–29.

Lemuel Lyon	"Military Journal for 1758." Abraham Tomlinson, ed. *The Military Journals of Two Private Soldiers, 1758–1775 . . .* , 11–45. Poughkeepsie, N.Y., 1855.
Moneypenney's orderly book	"The Moneypenney Orderly Book." Fort Ticonderoga Museum, *Bulletin*, XII (1966–1970), 328–357, 434–461.
*Samuel Morris	MS. 153. William L. Clements Library, Ann Arbor, Mich.
*Joseph Nichols	MS. HM 89. Henry E. Huntington Library, San Marino, Calif.
John Noyes	"Journal of John Noyes of Newbury. . . ." Essex Institute, *Historical Collections*, XLV (1909), 73–77.
*Caleb Rea	F[abius] M[aximus] Ray, ed. *The Journal of Dr. Caleb Rea. . . .* Salem, Mass., 1881.
Amos Richardson	"Amos Richardson's Journal, 1758." Fort Ticonderoga Museum, *Bulletin*, XII (1968), 267–291.
Joseph Shaw	Diary, 1758, 1759. In Joseph Shaw Accountbook and Miscellaneous Papers. MS. Massachusetts Historical Society, Boston.
*Daniel Shute	"A Journal of the Rev. Daniel Shute, D.D., Chaplain in the Expedition to Canada." Essex Institute, *Historical Collections*, XII (1874), 132–151.
William Sweat	Paul O. Blanchette, ed. "Captain William Sweat's Personal Diary of the Expedition Against Ticonderoga, May 2–November 7, 1758." Essex Institute, *Historical Collections*, XCIII (1957), 36–57. (Sweat was a private, not a captain, in 1758.)
Williams's orderly book	"The Expedition to Fort Craven, Oneida Great Carrying Place and Frontenac." *Colonial Wars*, I (1914), 178–215. Includes fragment of the diary of Abner Barrows, 1758 (p. 214).

1759

Bangs's orderly book	"Nathaniel Bangs's Orderly Book Began April 11th 1759 Castle William New En-

	gland." MS. Massachusetts Historical Society, Boston.
Boyd's orderly book	"John Boyd his Orderly Book—1759." MS. New England Historic and Genealogical Society Library, Boston.
John Burrell	"Diary of Sergeant John Burrell, 1759–1760." *New England Historical and Genealogical Register*, LIX (1905), 352–354.
*Gibson Clough	"Extracts from Gibson Clough's Journal." Essex Institute, *Historical Collections*, III (1861), 99–106, 195–201. MS at Essex Institute, Salem, Mass.
Constantine Hardy	Charles A. Flagg, ed. "Extracts from the Journal of Constantine Hardy. . . ." *New England Historical and Genealogical Register*, LX (1906), 236–238. MS at American Antiquarian Society, Worcester, Mass.
Hawks's orderly book (1759)	Hugh Hastings, ed. *Orderly Book and Journal*, 1–62. Syracuse, N.Y., 1901.
William Henshaw	Ellery Bicknell Crane, ed. "William Henshaw's Journal for the Campaign in the Year 1759." Worcester Society of Antiquity, *Proceedings*, XXV (1912), 43–64. MS at American Antiquarian Society, Worcester, Mass.
Henshaw's orderly book	"William Henshaw's Orderly & Journal Book. . . ." American Antiquarian Society, *Transactions*, IX (1909), 183–254.
Jonathan Holman	Jonathan Holman Journal, 1759–1775. MS. French and Indian War Collection. American Antiquarian Society, Worcester, Mass.
Luke Knowlton	Luke Knowlton Diary, 1759. MS. French and Indian War Collection. American Antiquarian Society, Worcester, Mass.
Samuel Merriman	George Sheldon. *A History of Deerfield*, I, 661–665. Deerfield, Mass., 1895.
Timothy Nichols	"Timothy Nichols His Book." MS. Massachusetts Historical Society, Boston.
Josiah Peary	"The Orderly Book of Sergeant Josiah Perry." *New England Historical and Genea-*

logical Register, LIV (1900), 70–76, 164–167. Peary was in fact a corporal, and this journal was not merely an orderly book.

Enoch Poor · MS. HM 610. Henry E. Huntington Library, San Marino, Calif.

Cornelius Stowell · Cornelius Stowell Journal and Orderly Book, 1759. MS. French and Indian War Collection. American Antiquarian Society, Worcester, Mass.

*Henry True · Henry True, ed. *Journal and Letters of Rev. Henry True, of Hampstead, New Hampshire.* . . . Marion, Ohio, 1900.

Samuel Ward · "Old French War." Diary and account book, 1759, 1760. MS. Massachusetts Historical Society, Boston.

Robert Webster · "Robert Webster's Journal." Fort Ticonderoga Museum, *Bulletin*, II (1931), 121–153.

Wilson's orderly book · J. Watts dePeyster, ed. *Commissary Wilson's Orderly Book.* Albany, N.Y., 1857.

Lemuel Wood · Sidney Perley, ed. "Diaries Kept by Lemuel Wood, of Boxford. . . ." Essex Institute, *Historical Collections*, XIX (1882), 61–74, 143–152, 183–192; XX (1883), 156–160, 198–208, 289–296; XXI (1884), 63–68.

John Woods · Alice Lee Clark, ed. "John Woods, His Book. . . ." *Genealogical Magazine*, I (1906), 307–312, 339–342. MS at American Antiquarian Society, Worcester, Mass.

1760

Anonymous (a centinel) · MS diary, Louisbourg, 1760. French and Indian War Collection. American Antiquarian Society, Worcester, Mass.

*John Frost · "The Diary of John Frost, Jun'r, Eliot. . . ." Eliot, Maine, 1899.

Hawks's orderly book (1760) · Hugh Hastings, ed. *Orderly Book and Journal*, 62–92. Syracuse, N.Y., 1901.

David Holdin

"Journal of Sergeant Holden." Massachusetts Historical Society, *Proceedings*, XXIV (1889), 387–409.

*Samuel Jenks

"Samuel Jenks, His Journall of the Campaign in 1760." Massachusetts Historical Society, *Proceedings*, 2d Ser., V (1890), 352–391.

*Thomas Moody

P. M. Woodwell, ed. *Diary of Thomas Moody: Campaign of 1760 in the French & Indian War*. South Berwick, Maine, 1976.

*Jonathan Procter

"Diary Kept at Louisbourg, 1759–1760, by Jonathan Procter of Danvers." Essex Institute, *Historical Collections*, LXX (1934), 31–57.

Appendix C ❖ Provincial Troop Disorders, 1755–1759

In chronological order, the "troop disorders"—mutinies and mass desertions—described in provincial writings were as follows.

5 July 1755: A riotous disturbance occurred among about a battalion (at least five hundred) New Englanders at Fort Cumberland, Nova Scotia, over a shortage in the rum ration. "Several were committed to guard for words tending to mutiny," and four ringleaders were punished by regimental court-martial two days later. (John Thomas, 5, 7 July 1755.)

1 September 1755: Thirty to fifty men attempted to desert from the Massachusetts provincial camp at Lake George because they were denied an overdue rum issue. They marched four or five miles from camp with clubbed muskets before being overtaken and persuaded to return. (Elisha Hawley, 1 Sept. 1755; Seth Pomeroy, 1 Sept. 1755.)

10 November 1755: Five to seven hundred Connecticut provincials made known their intention to leave Lake George since their enlistments had expired nine days earlier. They agreed to remain a few days longer when promised by their commander, Phineas Lyman, that they would be promptly dismissed. On 20 November they decided to desert; they were overtaken on the way out of camp and dissuaded—with difficulty—by Lyman's personal appeal. (Nathaniel Dwight, 11 Nov. 1755, and after.)

11 November 1755: Thirty New York troops deserted from the camp at Lake George with guns and packs; they were convinced that their enlistments had expired. (Nathaniel Dwight, 11 Nov. 1755.)

16–17 November 1755: A company of carpenters at work on fortifications at Fort William Henry ceased work in protest over short rations. An additional allowance was made, and they returned to work. (James Hill, 14–17 Nov. 1755.)

22 November 1755: An unspecified number of men clubbed arms and marched away from the camp at Lake George with guns and packs; they returned, apparently as a body. (Samuel Chandler, 22 Nov. 1755.)

About 26 September 1756: A mixed body of about 150 provincials at Fort Edward deserted on the basis of the rumor that, having accepted an issue of rations from the king's stores, they were now liable for service during the king's pleasure. They were overtaken, reassured, and returned to service. (Phineas Lyman to Loudoun, 6 Oct. 1756, Loudoun Papers, LO 2855, Henry E. Huntington Library, San Marino, Calif.)

2 November 1756: The carpenters at work on Fort William Henry (two hundred men?) ceased work and made "a great noise about their pay." Promises were made concerning payment, and on the next day "the most of the carpenters went to work again." (Samuel Greenleaf, 2, 3 Nov. 1756.)

3 February 1758: The members of Captain Ebenezer Learned's company of Massachusetts provincials (about seventy men) deserted from Stillwater, New York, under the leadership of their commander, following the expiration of their enlistments. They escaped successfully to Massachusetts. (Rufus Putnam, *The Memoirs of Rufus Putnam* [Boston, 1903], 16–21.)

1 July 1758: Soldiers detailed to work with civilian carpenters refused to obey orders unless they received additional pay; they required a written assurance from their commanding officer before "part" of them returned to work. (Obadiah Harris, 1 July 1758.)

22 July 1758: The light infantry provincial battalion commanded by Colonel Oliver Partridge deserted from Fort William Henry with clubbed muskets in protest over short rations. They returned after receiving their full allowance. (Lemuel Lyon, 22 July 1758; Caleb Rea, 22 July 1758.)

23 July 1758: Sixty Massachusetts provincials from Colonel Thomas Doty's regiment clubbed firelocks and marched off from Halfway Brook after some sort of affront by a regular officer, Captain Charles Cruikshanks. They were recaptured, and their leaders were bound over for court-martial; "about 50 or so . . . were released by making good promises for the future etc." (Abner Barrows's diary, 23 July 1758 entry, reprinted with Williams's orderly book.)

14 June 1759: The three provincial companies garrisoning Fort Frederick, Nova Scotia (now New Brunswick), refused to perform fatigue duty without additional pay. The provincial commander acquiesced in their demands, and the troops returned to work on the basis of his promises of reimbursement. (Enoch Poor, 14 June 1759.)

17 October 1759: A woodcutting party under two lieutenants at Fort Frederick, probably amounting to about fifty men, refused to work without additional pay. Colonel Joseph Frye, commanding the fort, gave personal assurances, and the party returned to woodcutting. (Enoch Poor, 17 Oct. 1759.)

1 November 1759: New Jersey's provincial regiment refused to work beyond their term of enlistment at Crown Point. They were surrounded by regular troops and acquiesced, with the exception of five holdouts who were imprisoned. Similar disorders, which apparently did not have to be suppressed by force, occurred among the regiments of Massachusetts, New Hampshire, and New York on the same day. (Samuel Morris [1758], 1 Nov. 1759.)

1 November 1759: A group of Massachusetts provincials, numbering about two hundred, deserted the command of Colonel Abijah Willard at Ticonderoga, following the expiration of their enlistments. (John Woods, 27 Oct.–1 Nov. 1759; Luke Knowlton, 28 Oct.–18 Nov. 1759; Cornelius Stowell, 1 Nov. 1759.)

1 November 1759: A score of New Jersey troops attempted to desert from Fort Edward after the expiration of their terms of enlistment; they were recaptured and returned. (William Henshaw, 29 Oct.–1 Nov. 1759.)

1–3 November 1759: The Massachusetts provincial regiment of Colonel Jonathan Bagley, garrisoning the fortress of Louisbourg, refused to perform duty when their enlistment terms ended. Accommodation was achieved by a combination of negotiation and coercion. (Gibson Clough, 30 Sept., 1–3 Nov. 1759; also Jonathan Procter [1760], 2, 3 Nov. 1759.)

13 November 1759: From a mixed force of Connecticut and New Hampshire troops at work constructing a road from Crown Point to Township No. 4 in New Hampshire, 250 provincials refused to work when their meat ration was curtailed. Meat was issued in the afternoon of the same day, and work was resumed. (Robert Webster, 11–13 Nov. 1759.)

Appendix D ❖ Provincial Sermons, 1755–1762

Sermons preached to the provincials during the war were as follows. In all, the Old Testament provided sixty-seven texts for seventy-one sermons; the New Testament, fifty-eight texts for sixty-three sermons. Themes were determined by examining the scriptural passage in context, taking into account whatever notes the soldiers who recorded it made on the doctrine or applications. Where there was doubt about the implications of a text and no indication from a witness on the nature of the sermon, I consulted the standard Puritan exegetical work, Matthew Poole's *Commentary on the Holy Bible* (3 vols. [London, 1962 (orig. publ. 1683–1685)]). Sermons that were adapted to the occasion are indicated by asterisks. These instances were determined by diary notations of soldiers who commented on the appropriateness of a sermon to the circumstances and by comparison of the theme to recent events. Sermons are numbered down the left-hand column to facilitate subsequent reference.

No.	Text	Preacher, Date	Theme	Source
1.	Gen. 15:1	Chandler 12 Oct. 1755	Covenant: God chooses Abram	Chandler
2.	Gen. 28:20–21	Shute 18 June 1758	Covenant renewed: God chooses Jacob	Shute
3.	Gen. 28:15	J. Cleaveland 13 Aug. 1758	Covenant renewed: God chooses Jacob	J. Cleaveland
4.	Gen. 28:12	J. Cleaveland 17 Sept. 1758	Covenant renewed: God chooses Jacob	J. Cleaveland
5.	Gen. 4:7	E. Cleaveland 8 Oct. 1758	Righteousness averts wrath	Morris
6.	Exod. 19:5	Williams 5 Oct. 1755	Covenant: God keeps faith with the obedient	Dwight
*7.	Exod. 32:10	? 11 Sept. 1757	Covenant: God's wrath against unfaithful Israel	Metcalf
*8.	Exod. 17:8–16	Forbes 2 July 1758	God fights for Israel	J. Cleaveland
*9.	Exod. 23:20–21	Shute 2 July 1758	God fights for Israel	Shute

No.	Text	Preacher, Date	Theme	Source
*10.	Deut. 23:9	J. Cleaveland 18 June 1758	Soldierly conduct: importance of good behavior on expedition	J. Cleaveland
11.	Deut. 32:29	Pomeroy 25 June 1758	Covenant, judgment: Israel must remember God's dealings	Shute
12.	Deut. 29:4	E. Cleaveland 3 Sept. 1758	Covenant: God's actions remind Israel of relationship	Rea
*13.	Josh. 24:15	Graham 8 Aug. 1756	Covenant: Israel must choose whether to serve or forsake the Lord	Graham
*14.	Josh. 7:1–13	J. Cleaveland 20 Aug. 1758	Covenant: God causes Joshua to seek out the accursed thing in Israel's midst	J. Cleaveland
15.	Judg. 5:9	J. Cleaveland 11 June 1758	God blesses the willing warriors of Israel (Deborah)	J. Cleaveland
16.	Judg. 5:2	Pomeroy 21 Oct. 1759	God blesses the willing warriors of Israel (Deborah)	Morris (1758)
17.	Judg. 20:25–28	Morrell 2 July 1758	Covenant: God fights for Israel	Richardson
*18.	1 Sam. 14:6	Crawford 15 July 1759	God fights for Israel (Jonathan vs. Philistines)	Knowlton
*19.	1 Sam. 17:45	Forbes 8 July 1759	God fights for Israel (David and Goliath)	Hardy
*20.	2 Sam. 10:12	? 8 July 1759	Courage in the Lord	Webster
21.	2 Kings 4:26	Forbes 17 Sept. 1758	Faith in affliction	Harris
22.	1 Chron. 1:1	Paine 26 Oct. 1755	Mortality (all men must die)	Chandler
*23.	1 Chron. 16:31	Shute 27 Aug. 1758	Covenant: God is faithful, therefore greatly to be praised	Shute
*24.	2 Chron. 5:20	? 29 July 1759	God fights for Israel when Israel trusts in God	Wood, Holman, Knowlton

No.	Text	Preacher, Date	Theme	Source
*25.	2 Chron. 14:11	Norton 2 Nov. 1755	Covenant: God delivers his people in danger and war	Dwight
26.	Job	Dunbar 2 Nov. 1755	Mortality	Chandler
27.	Job 36:5	Chandler 9 Nov. 1755	God's power	Chandler
28.	Ps. 103:19	Chandler 19 Oct. 1755	God's sovereignty	Chandler
29.	Ps. 103:19	? 19 Nov. 1758	God's sovereignty	Knap
30.	Ps. 145:3	Chandler 16 Nov. 1755	God's greatness	Chandler, Dwight
*31.	Pss. 66:8; 77: 16–18; 99:1, 5	Chandler 18 Nov. 1755	Earthquake reflects God's power, sovereignty	Chandler
32.	Ps. 84:12	Graham 27 June 1756	God strengthens and preserves the faithful	Graham
*33.	Ps. 78:37	Graham 7 June 1756	Wickedness violates the covenant	Graham
34.	Ps. 119:43	Jones 28 Apr. 1757	Covenant: the necessity of respecting God's laws	Metcalf
35.	Ps. 16:2	? 11 Sept. 1757	God's mercy in the preservation of his people	Metcalf
36.	Ps. 16:2	? 11 Sept. 1757	God's mercy in the preservation of his people	Metcalf
37.	Ps. 16:2	? 9 Oct. 1757	God's mercy in the preservation of his people	Metcalf
38.	Ps. 68:30	? 11 June 1758	God fights for Israel	Richardson
*39.	Ps. 112:7–8	E. Cleaveland 18 June 1758	God fights for his people	Morris
*40.	Ps. 37:7	Morrell 16 July 1758	Trust in the Lord; God will avenge evil	Richardson
*41.	Ps. 107	E. Cleaveland 25 July 1758	God's mercy, deliverance	Morris
42.	Ps. 23	J. Cleaveland 30 July 1758	God's preserving love	Rea, J. Cleaveland

No.	Text	Preacher, Date	Theme	Source
43.	Ps. 83:14–15	Ingersoll 30 July 1758	A cursing psalm: God's wrath called down on his enemies	L. Lyon
44.	Ps. 113:5	Ogilvie 8 Aug. 1758	God's greatness	Morris
45.	Ps. 84:11	J. Cleaveland 13 Aug. 1758	God strengthens and shields his faithful people	J. Cleaveland
46.	Ps. 11:6	J. Cleaveland 17 Sept. 1758	God's justice: a trial for the righteous, punishment for the wicked	J. Cleaveland
47.	Ps. 76:7	Hitchcock 17 Sept. 1758	God's wrath against the wicked	Shute
48.	Ps. 139:23–24	Hitchcock 17 Sept. 1758	God's omniscience	Shute
*49.	Ps. 91:2	? 15 July 1759	God's protection and strength	Morris (1758)
50.	Ps. 144:1	Crawford 5 Aug. 1759	God's strength; divine approval of war	Wood, Knowlton
51.	Ps. 39:1	Leavenworth 5 Aug. 1759	Beware of profanity and all sins of speech	Wood, Knowlton
52.	Ps. 119:15	Pomeroy 16 Sept. 1759	Blessedness of God's law	Morris (1758)
53.	Ps. 63:3	? 5 Oct. 1759	God's lovingkindness	Jenks (1760)
54.	Prov. 3:16–18	Morrell 17 Sept. 1758	Excellence of knowing God's will	Richardson
*55.	Isa. 8:19	Graham 15 Aug. 1756	Israel's wickedness, need of reformation	Graham
*56.	Isa. 16:9	Pomeroy 16 July 1758	God promises vengeance against Israel's enemies	L. Lyon
57.	Isa. 66:1, 2	Beckett 6 Aug. 1758	God's mercy and sovereignty	Morris
*58.	Isa. 1:5	Forbes 10 Sept. 1758	Suffering comes of revolt against God; repent and be comforted	Harris
59.	Isa. 55:6	J. Cleaveland 1 Oct. 1758	The search for faith must not be delayed	J. Cleaveland
*60.	Jer. 23:10	Shute 16 July 1758	The evils of profanity	Shute

No.	Text	Preacher, Date	Theme	Source
*61.	Jer. 48:10	Forbes 15 July 1759	God curses Israel's enemy, sanctions shedding blood	Hardy, Merriman
62.	Jer. 6:16	True 22 Aug. 1762	God will punish transgressors of his way	True (1759)
63.	Ezek. 33:5	Chandler 9 Nov. 1755	Deliverance from judgment, battle	Chandler
64.	Ezek. 25:12–17	Woodbridge 18 June 1758	God fights for Israel	Richardson
*65.	Ezek. 33:11	J. Cleaveland 16 July 1758	Judgment and the necessity of repentance	J. Cleaveland
66.	Ezek. 37:26	Pomeroy 24 Sept. 1758	Covenant: God promises peace and blessing	L. Lyon
67.	Ezek. 36:37	Pomeroy 8 Oct. 1758	Covenant: God promises peace and blessing	L. Lyon
*68.	Amos 4:12	Eals 16 July 1758	God's judgment and the necessity of repentance	L. Lyon
69.	Amos 4:12	J. Cleaveland 15 Oct. 1758	God's judgment and the necessity of repentance	Sweat, Morris
*70.	Micah 6:6, 7	? 23 July 1758	God-pleasing conduct: how one ought to approach God	L. Lyon
71.	Nah. 1:7	Little 25 June 1758	God is faithful to his people in the day of judgment	Shute
72.	Mal. 1:6	J. Cleaveland 23 July 1758	Covenant: God's paternal relation to his adopted people	Rea, J. Cleaveland
73.	Matt. 24:30–31	Chandler 26 Oct. 1755	The last times	Chandler
*74.	Matt. 3:8	J. Cleaveland 18 July 1758	Soldierly conduct: repentance is necessary in wartime	Rea, J. Cleaveland
75.	Matt. 17:13–14	Shute 23 July 1758	Necessity of righteousness (the strait gate)	Shute
76.	Matt. 19:28	Emerson 6 Aug. 1758	Jesus promises glory to his followers	Morris
77.	Matt. 7:12	Shute 8 Oct. 1758	God's goodness and love	Nichols

No.	Text	Preacher, Date	Theme	Source
78.	Matt. 5:44	Forbes 24 June 1759	Love your enemies	Hardy
79.	Matt. 5:2, 3	Crawford 8 July 1759	Humility	Wood, Holman
80.	Matt. 5:8	Forbes 23 Sept. 1759	Purity and the pursuit of holiness	Hardy
81.	Mark 16:16	Graham 11 July 1756	Belief leads to eternal life; unbelief, to damnation	Graham
82.	Mark 10:21	J. Cleaveland 27 Aug. 1758	Discipleship: the necessity of total commitment to Christ	J. Cleaveland
83.	Mark 2:26–27	Forbes 30 Sept. 1759	The Sabbath; Jesus' dominion	Morris (1758)
84.	Luke 19:41–42	? 25 Sept. 1757	The coming judgment	Metcalf
85.	Luke 3:14	J. Cleaveland 11 June 1758	Soldierly obedience	J. Cleaveland
*86.	Luke 16:19–22	Morrell 16 July 1758	God raises up the afflicted	Richardson
*87.	Luke 13:2–3	J. Cleaveland 16 July 1758	The nature of God's judgment and the necessity of repentance	J. Cleaveland
88.	Luke 21:36	? 13 Aug. 1758	Preparedness for the judgment day	Richardson
*89.	Luke 7:41–43	J. Cleaveland 27 Aug. 1758	God's great forgiveness demands great thanksgiving	J. Cleaveland
90.	John 5:39	Eals 16 July 1758	Search the Scriptures	Morris
91.	John 3:16	? 23 July 1758	God's surpassing love	L. Lyon
92.	Acts 24:25	? 2 Oct. 1757	Immediacy of judgment; belief cannot be put off	Metcalf
93.	Acts 24:25	? 3 Sept. 1758	Immediacy of judgment; belief cannot be put off	L. Lyon
94.	Acts 10:12	Forbes 30 July 1758	Faith transcends outward observance of the law	Harris
95.	Acts 20:27	J. Cleaveland 15 Oct. 1758	The role of the pastor as he who declares the counsel of God to the faithful	J. Cleaveland

No.	Text	Preacher, Date	Theme	Source
96.	Rom. 11:36	E. Cleaveland 30 Sept. 1759	The all-sufficiency of God	Morris (1758)
97.	Rom. 3:31	E. Cleaveland 6 Aug. 1758	Faith completes the law	Morris
98.	Rom. 9:18	? 17 June 1759	God's sovereignty	Woods
99.	Rom. 2:3, 4	Pomeroy 19 Sept. 1759	God's judgment	Webster, Morris (1758)
100.	2 Cor. 4:18	Morrell 24 Sept. 1758	Regard eternal, not temporal things	Sweat
101.	2 Cor. 5:11	? 3 Dec. 1758	Judgment: the terror of God	Knap
102.	2 Cor. 1:12	Forbes 16 Sept. 1759	The joy of Christian living	Webster, Morris (1758)
103.	Eph. 5:2	Chandler 16 Nov. 1755	Salvation as the gift of Christ; love	Chandler, Dwight
*104.	Eph. 6:13	E. Cleaveland 25 June 1758	God preserves the faithful (the whole armor of God)	Morris
*105.	Eph. 6:18	J. Cleaveland 2 July 1758	Prayer and God's preservation (the whole armor)	Rea, J. Cleaveland
106.	Eph. 5:14	J. Cleaveland 3 Sept. 1758	Exhortation to refrain from sin, and escape death	J. Cleaveland
107.	Eph. 2:12	Cleaveland 1 Oct. 1758	Covenant: extended by faith in Christ	J. Cleaveland
108.	Eph. 5:15–16	Crawford 12 Aug. 1759	The necessity of virtuous conduct; the coming judgment	Wood, Holman, Knowlton
109.	Phil. 1:6	Cleaveland 4 June 1758	God's faithfulness to his people	Rea, J. Cleaveland
110.	Phil. 1:6	Cleaveland 10 Aug. 1758	God's faithfulness to his people	Rea, J. Cleaveland
111.	Phil. 4:8	Cleaveland 30 July 1758	Virtuous conduct	Rea, J. Cleaveland
112.	Phil. 1:10	Cleaveland 6 Aug. 1758	Perseverance in virtue until the end	Rea, J. Cleaveland
113.	Phil. 2:15–16	J. Cleaveland 10 Sept. 1758	Virtuous conduct: the lives of the saints as examples	J. Cleaveland

No.	Text	Preacher, Date	Theme	Source
114.	Phil. 1:27	J. Cleaveland 15 Oct. 1758	Exhortation to be faithful and confident to the end	J. Cleaveland
115.	Col. 1:23	Shute 16 July 1758	Faith brings eternal life	Shute
116.	Col. 3:3	Emerson 6 Aug. 1758	Judgment will surely come	Morris
117.	Col. 3:11	J. Cleaveland 3 Sept. 1758	Faith in Christ brings renewal of life and unity	J. Cleaveland
118.	1 Thes. 1:10	J. Cleaveland 24 Sept. 1758	The last things: watchfulness	J. Cleaveland
119.	2 Tim. 2:8–10	? 9 Sept. 1759	Endurance in faith	Holman
120.	Heb. 8:10	Eals 25 July 1758	Covenant: the nature of God's relationship with his chosen	Morris
121.	Heb. 8:10	Eals 27 Sept. 1758	Covenant: the nature of God's relationship with his chosen	Morris
122.	Heb. 2:3, 4	? 27 Oct. 1759	The duty of obedience, the certainty of judgment	Morris (1758)
123.	James 5:16	Eals 2 July 1758	The efficacy of prayer	L. Lyon
124.	James 5:12	? 10 Sept. 1758	Swear not	L. Lyon
125.	James 5:12	Pomeroy 17 Sept. 1758	Swear not	L. Lyon
126.	2 Pet. 3:10–12	? 8 Oct. 1758	The last things: the day of judgment	Morris
127.	1 John 5:12	J. Cleaveland 6 Aug. 1758	Salvation by faith (he that hath the Son hath life)	Nichols, J. Cleaveland
128.	1 John 5:12	J. Cleaveland 8 Oct. 1758	Salvation by faith (he that hath the Son hath life)	Nichols, J. Cleaveland
129.	Jude 6	J. Cleaveland 24 Sept. 1758	The last things: God will punish those who depart from his paths	J. Cleaveland
130.	Rev. 1:7	Crawford 9 Sept. 1759	The last things; Christ is coming in power	Holman
131.	Rev. 12:11	Chandler 2 Nov. 1755	The last things: the battle against Satan	Chandler

No.	Text	Preacher, Date	Theme	Source
*132.	Rev. 2:6	? 16 July 1758	God will favor even the erring believer who opposes the enemies of the Lord	Sweat
133.	Rev. 3:18	J. Cleaveland 10 Sept. 1758	God is all-sufficient for the needs of sinners	J. Cleaveland
134.	Rev. 3:20	True 9 Sept. 1759	Christ's invitation to faith	True
135.	Rev. 20:14	True 22 Aug. 1762	The last things: the day of judgment	True (1759)

Index